Chinese Texts
and
Philosophical
Contexts

Angus C. Graham

Critics and Their Critics

VOLUME I

Chinese Texts and Philosophical Contexts

ESSAYS DEDICATED TO ANGUS C. GRAHAM

EDITED BY

Henry Rosemont, Jr.

OPEN 🕸 COURT

La Salle, Illinois

Critics and Their Critics

OPEN COURT and the above logo are registered in the U.S.
Patent and Trademark Office.

© 1991 by Open Court Publishing Company

First printing 1991

Printed and bound in the United States of America.

Library of Congress Cataloging-in-Publication Data

Chinese texts and philosophical contexts: essays dedicated to Angus
    C. Graham/edited by Henry Rosemont, Jr.
        p.   cm.
    Includes bibliographical references and index.
    ISBN 0-8126-9121-0.—ISBN 0-8126-9122-9 (pbk.)
    1. Philosophy. Chinese. 2. Chinese language—Grammar.
I. Graham. A. C. (Angus Charles) II. Rosemont, Henry, 1934-
B5231.C5139   1990
181'.11—dc20   90-41104
                                                                      CIP

CONTENTS

CONTENTS

CONTRIBUTORS

ROGER T. AMES studied at the Chinese University of Hong Kong, National Taiwan University, the University of British Columbia, Tokyo University of Education, and received his Ph.D. from the School of Oriental and African Studies of the University of London in 1978. He has published many articles and reviews in Chinese and in English, is the author of *The Art of Rulership*, and co-author (with David Hall) of *Thinking Through Confucius*. He is Professor of Philosophy at the University of Hawaii, and in 1988 succeeded Eliot Deutsch as the Editor of *Philosophy East and West*.

LEO S. CHANG wrote all of the calligraphy in this volume. He has an A.B. from Catholic University and a Ph.D. from Georgetown. His articles and reviews have appeared in *Philosophy East & West*, and he is the author, with Wang Hsiao-po, of *The Philosophical Foundations of Han Fei's Political Theory*. He is Professor of Political Science at Regis College in Massachusetts.

HERBERT FINGARETTE is Professor of Philosophy Emeritus at the University of California at Santa Barbara. He studied at U.C.L.A., receiving a B.A. in 1947, and Ph.D. in 1949. He has been a Fellow of the American Council of Learned Societies, the National Endowment for the Humanities, and the Center for Advanced Studies in the Behavioral Sciences at Stanford. In 1976 he was elected President of the Pacific Division of the American Philosophical Association. Among his books are *The Self in Transformation, On Responsibility, Self-Deception, Confucius—The Secular as Sacred*, and, most recently, *Heavy Drinking*.

CHAD HANSEN earned his B.A. from the University of Utah in 1966, and Ph.D. from the University of Michigan in 1972, and was a Mellon Fellow at Stanford University in 1977. His articles have appeared in *Philosophy East and West*, the *Journal of Chinese Philosophy, Journal of Asian Studies*, and the *Journal of the University of Hong Kong Philosophy Society*, and in 1983 he published *Logic and Language in Ancient China*. He has held visiting appointments at the University of Michigan, U.C.L.A., the University of Hong Kong, and the University of Hawaii, and is currently Professor of Philosophy at the University of Vermont.

CHRISTOPH HARBSMEIER studied at Oxford and the University of Oslo, where he is now Senior Lecturer in Chinese at the East Asian Institute. He contributed the section on the Chinese language for Joseph Needham's *Science and Civilization in China* project, and is the author of *Aspects of Classical Chinese Syntax.*

D. C. LAU is best known for his translation of *Lao Tzu: Tao Te Ching,* which has sold over a half-million copies. He has also translated the *Analects* and the *Mencius,* all of which were published in the Penguin Classics series. From 1970 to 1978 he taught at S.O.A.S., and then moved to the Chinese University of Hong Kong, where he is Professor of Chinese Language and Literature. Both the Chinese University of Hong Kong and Hong Kong University have awarded him honorary degrees.

JOHN S. MAJOR studied at Haverford (B.A., 1964) and at Harvard (M.A., 1965, Ph.D., 1973). He has held fellowships from the A.C.L.S., N.D.E.A., Woodrow Wilson Foundation, and Clare Hall, Cambridge. From 1971 to 1984 he was a member of the History faculty at Dartmouth College, publishing articles and reviews in *Early China, T'oung Pao, Philosophy East and West, Chinese Science, History of Religions, Journal of the Royal Asiatic Society,* the *Harvard Journal of Asiatic Studies,* and the *Journal of the American Oriental Society.* Currently Senior Editor of the Book-of-the-Month Club, his *Land and People of China* will be published this year.

DAVID SHEPARD NIVISON was educated at Harvard (B.A., 1946, M.A., 1948, Ph.D., 1953), and spent his teaching career at Stanford, where he is currently Professor of Philosophy Emeritus. He also held concurrent appointments in the departments of Religious Studies, and East Asian Languages, and was the first Evans-Wentz Distinguished Professor of Oriental Studies. He has held Guggenheim, Ford, Harvard-Yenching and Fulbright fellowships and in 1978 was President of the Pacific Division of the American Philosophical Association. In addition to numerous articles, he has written *The Life and Thought of Chang Hsueh-ch'eng,* and co-edited (with Arthur Wright), *Confucianism in Action.*

EDWIN G. PULLEYBLANK is Professor of Chinese at the University of British Columbia. He holds degrees from the University of Alberta (B.A., 1942), the School of Oriental and African Studies of the University of London (Ph.D., 1951), and Cambridge (M.A., 1953). He has taught at S.O.A.S., and from 1953 to 1966 was Professor of Chinese at Cambridge. His articles have appeared in such journals as *Asia Major, Journal of the Royal Asiatic Society,* the

Journal of Chinese Linguistics, and *Monumenta Serica*; he is the author of *The Background of the Rebellion of An Lushan*, and *Chinese History and World History*.

HENRY ROSEMONT, JR. studied at the Universities of Illinois (A.B., 1962), and Washington (Ph.D., 1967) and did post-doctoral work at M.I.T. and S.O.A.S. He served as Book Review Editor of *Philosophy East and West* from 1972 to 1988, President of the Society for Asian and Comparative Philosophy, 1976–78, and was Visiting Fulbright Professor of Philosophy and Linguistics at Fudan University in Shanghai, 1982–84. Professor of Philosophy at St. Mary's College of Maryland, his publications include a translation (with D. J. Cook) of Leibniz's *Discourse on the Natural Theology of the Chinese*, and articles in such journals as *Monumenta Serica*, *Journal of the History of Ideas*, and *Synthese*.

HAROLD D. ROTH is Assistant Professor of Religious Studies at Brown University. He holds degrees from Princeton (A.B., 1970), McMaster (M.A., 1974), and the University of Toronto (M.A., 1975, Ph.D., 1981), and he has been the recipient of post-doctoral fellowships from the Mellon Foundation, Social Sciences and Humanities Research Council of Canada, and the Japanese Ministry of Education. His articles and reviews have been published in *Philosophy East and West*, *Journal of Chinese Philosophy*, and the *Journal of the Royal Asiatic Society*. His book, *The Textual History of the Huai-Nan Tzu*, will be published this year.

A BRIEF INTRODUCTION

Some of the essays in this volume are concentrated discussions of specific problems in early Chinese syntax, semantics, etymology, and paleography (particularly the contributions of Lau, Pulleyblank, and Harbsmeier). Other essays range rather broadly over the broad areas of aesthetics, ethics, religion, and epistemology (especially the essays by Hansen, Fingarette, and Rosemont). And still other contributions are admixtures, treating here with an etymological and there with an epistemological issue, and/or with problems of translation, interpretation, or the dating of Chinese texts (the essays by Major, Roth, Nivison, and Ames).

The polygenous nature of this volume is intentional, for it is perfectly in keeping with the polymathic nature of the person to whom it is dedicated: Angus Graham has written at length and in detail on early Chinese grammar and philology; he has translated Chinese poetry, and published poetry of his own; he has translated and interpreted many Chinese philosophical texts—from the Daoism of the *Zhuang Zi* and the *Lieh Zi* to the Mohists and the Neo-Confucians—and he has published philosophical texts of his own. On all of these subjects, and others, Graham has had important things to say, amply evidenced by the numerous citations to his writings in sinological scholarship over the past thirty years.

What binds all of these essays together, then, is that while they are all individually conceived and executed scholarly works that stand in their own right, they all bear directly on, and have in part been inspired by the scholarship of Angus Graham. Indeed, they were written with the understanding that he would be invited to write a commentary on each of them, which he has done, to the delight of all.

As a consequence, this book can be read not only for the several and varied individual contributions the essays make to the fields of linguistics, sinology, religion, and philosophy, it can and should also be read as a series of dialogues between Angus and some of his many colleagues, students, and friends. To readers altogether unfamiliar with him and his work a longer introduction would probably not be helpful; read on. To his many colleagues, students, and friends a longer introduction is not necessary; read on.

Biographical Note

Angus Charles Graham was born in Penarth, Wales, in July 1919, the elder of two sons of Charles Harold and Mabelle Graham. His father was originally in the coal business, but left Wales for Malaya (now Malaysia) in 1925, where he was a rubber planter until he succumbed to malaria in 1928.

Angus attended Ellesmere College in Shropshire from 1932 to 1937, after which he read Theology at Corpus Christi College, Oxford, graduating in 1940, (but ceased to be a believer shortly afterwards). He then joined the Royal Air Force, was put on a Japanese course in 1944–45, and served thereafter as a Japanese interpreter in Malaya and Thailand, concluding his service with the rank of Flying Officer.

In 1946 he enrolled in the School of Oriental and African Studies at the University of London, with which he remained affiliated throughout his academic career. Fortunately for sinology—but much less so for the field of Japanese Studies—the three-year course then required for a degree at S.O.A.S. was not reduced for former military students of Japanese (even though he had studied it there), so he read Chinese, graduating with a B.A. Honours First in 1949. The following year he was appointed Lecturer in Classical Chinese, and in 1953 was awarded the Ph.D. for his dissertation on the Cheng brothers, later published under the title *Two Chinese Philosophers*.

Angus married Der Pao Chang in 1955, and a daughter, Dawn, was born to them in 1964. Der Pao Graham is owner and manager of an import-export firm, and Dawn, following in her father's footsteps, read Chinese at S.O.A.S. They currently reside in Nottinghamshire.

Although London would always be his home, Graham has nevertheless led a fairly peripatetic academic life, holding visiting fellowships or professorships at Hong Kong University (1954–55), Yale (1966–67), the University of Michigan (1970), the Society of Humanities at Cornell (1972–73), the Institute of East Asian Philosophies at Singapore (1984–86), Tsing Hua University of Taiwan (1987), Brown (1988), and the University of Hawaii (1989 and 1990).

Angus became Professor of Classical Chinese at S.O.A.S. in 1971, the position he held until his retirement thirteen years later, at which time he was made Professor Emeritus. In 1981 he was accorded the high honor of being elected a Fellow of the British Academy.

The bibliography of Graham's writings at the close of this volume was complete at the time it was prepared for the press. An exception is the lack of citations of book reviews, especially from the *Times Literary Supplement*, to which he has been a frequent contributor.

Acknowledgements

The genesis of this volume was a conversation at the 1987 Association of Asian Studies meetings between Roger Ames, Chad Hansen, Christoph Harbsmeier and myself. All of us were highly positive about the idea of a book devoted to the writings of Angus Graham, and quickly became committed to its realization, my own enthusiasm waning only slightly when the first three voted unanimously to have the fourth assume the overall supervision of putting it together.

But the deed is now done, with pleasure and pride at the result. The bulk of the credit must go in the first instance to the other contributors who, in addition to writing excellent works of scholarship, have been cooperative (always) and prompt (usually) in helping to complete the book. I must stress the cooperative nature of the effort, because stylistically it may appear that anarchy reigns in these essays. Readers will encounter the term for China's primal 'matter/energy' translite- rated here as *qi*, and there as *ch'i*; see 'ritual' written as both 禮 and 礼; and learn that while some Taoists disparaged honor, other Daoists disparaged honour. Appreciating the virtue of uniformity for scholarly as well as stylistic reasons, I nevertheless did not impose it on the authors, whose many and original contributions to their fields over the years have earned them the right to their own orthographies, and to defend their uses thereof. A more important reason for wielding a blue pencil sparingly is that scholars of a sinological bent have long been notorious for their eccentricities, a venerable tradition I cherish, especially as it has been so steadfastly maintained throughout the life of the person to whom this book is dedicated.

And at least partially because of his eccentricities, it has been a delight, as always, to work with Angus. Much of the substance of this volume resides in the considered and detailed commentary he undertook to write on each of the other essays, for which all readers of his prior work must be grateful (including the present contributors, despite the accuracy of Angus's autobiographical observation that in composing his text, "I have very probably managed to bite all of the hands that have fed me"). He also assisted my efforts greatly by providing many materials necessary for writing his biography and compiling his bibliography.

The candid frontispiece photograph of Angus was taken by David Lattimore at a seminar in Graham's honor organized by Hal Roth at Brown University in April, 1988. The difficult but important work of compiling a useful index was entrusted to Constance and Samantha Rosemont, who, although sinologically skilled, normally display only indifference to arcane matters of ancient Chinese philology; which in the present case was happily offset by their affection for Angus.

For the physical appearance of the book the Editor can claim no credit whatsoever. The beauty of the Chinese graphs which grace these pages came from the hand of Professor Leo S. Chang, for whose patience and time as well as aesthetic talent I am deeply grateful. To the design and production staffs at Open Court go thanks for assembling a handsome book.

I am also indebted to Open Court's Editorial Director David Ramsay Steele for advice and encouragement, and even more indebted to my Editor Kerri Mommer, whose combination of warmth, wit, and efficiency has made working with her altogether pleasurable.

Bouquets to all of the above; any brickbats should be aimed at the undersigned.

HENRY ROSEMONT, JR.

SPRING RIDGE, MARYLAND
AUGUST, 1990

Transcription Conversion Table

Pinyin	Wade-Giles
b	p
c	ts', tz'
ch	ch'
d	t
g	k
ian	ien
j	ch
k	k'
ong	ung
p	p'
q	ch'
r	j
si	szu
t	t'
x	hs
yu	u
you	yu
yu	yü
z	ts, tz
zh	ch
-i (zhi)	-ih (chih)
zi	tzu

PART
ONE

GRAMMATICAL
AND
PHILOLOGICAL
ISSUES

On the Expression Zai You 在宥

D. C. Lau

I

Chapter 11 (*Zai you* 在宥) of the *Zhuang zi* 莊子 opens with the passage:[1]

聞在宥天下,不聞治天下也。在之也者,恐天下
之淫其性也;宥之也者恐天下之遷其德也。
天下不淫其性,不遷其德, 有治天下者哉!

The expression *zai you* is very puzzling, and different commentators have suggested different explanations.

Guo Xiang's 郭象 comment is:[2]

宥使自在則治, 治之則亂也。

Guo does not gloss *you* and takes *zai* as meaning *zi zai* 自在. He shows, however, that he is aware of the fact that *zai* is used transitively by adding the causative *shi* 使, but the comment as a whole is not particularly helpful.

In the *Wen xuan* 文選 there is a poem by Xie Lingyun 謝靈運 entitled *Jiuri cong Songgong ximatai ji song Kongling shi* 九日從宋公戲馬臺集送孔令詩 in which appears the line:

在宥天下理.

Li Shan's 李善 commentary cites the *Zhuang zi* passage together with Sima Biao's 司馬彪 comment:[3]

在, 察也。宥, 寬也。

Both *cha* 察 and *kuan* 寬 are common glosses, but they throw little light on the passage.

Ma Qichang 馬其昶 in his *Zhuang zi gu* 莊子故 comments as follows:[4]

案《說文》:"在,存也。"吳先生 [i.e. 吳汝綸] 謂:"宥與囿同。"

Ma takes *zai* as meaning *cun* 存 and quotes with approval Wu Rulun's view that *you* 宥 is the same as *you* 囿. Qian Mu 錢穆 in his *Zhuang zi zuanjian* 莊子纂箋 , after quoting Ma's comment, goes on to quote the comments of Lü Huiqing 呂惠卿:[5]

在者, 存之而不亡, 任自然而不益。宥者放之而不縱, 如囿之宥物.

If Qian intends Ma's comment to be taken as based on Lü, then *cun* is to be taken as the opposite of *wang* 亡 , and *you* 宥 to be taken to mean 'given freedom that is not unbridled'.

Professor Graham has written on this expression in his "How much of *Chuang-tzu* did Chuang-tzŭ write?", and I quote him in full:[6]

The Primitivist's philosophy is as distinctive as his vivid, idiosyncratic, combative manner of writing. It starts from the concepts of *hsing* (性), the specific "nature" of a man, or a crane, or a duck, in accordance with which it is generated and lives out its term, and of *te* (德), the "power" specific to it, its capacity to "achieve" *te* (得), which is to hit spontaneously on the course which is the Way. The difference is explained at the start of *Webbed toes*: webbed toes or a sixth finger grow out of a man's *hsing* but are extraneous to his *te* (they grow naturally but add nothing to the body's powers); on the other hand a wart or a wen is extraneous even to his *hsing*. Unfortunately in civilized society the simple living out of man's term and the simple exercise of eyesight, hearing, and the other capacities of his *te*, are complicated by additions as superfluous as a sixth finger, such as visual adornments, music, moral rules, and logical disputation. The effect is to over-stimulate natural inclinations (淫其性 "indulge his nature to excess") and divert capacities to the wrong objects (遷其德 "displace his powers").

The Primitivist looks back to a tribal Utopia in which men lived as spontaneously as the animals, there was no distinction of gentleman and knave, and leaders had names followed by *shi* (氏) implying that their position was that of head of a clan or family. Ever since the Yellow Emperor the original, spontaneous harmony has progressively deteriorated, hastened first by the invention of moral rules, later by disputation to settle disagreements over moral rules. The two great bugbears of the Primitivist are the moralism of the schools of Confucius and Mo-tzǔ and the disputation of the schools of Mo-tzǔ and Yang Chu.

The Primitivist's concerns are exclusively social and political, and he hardly mentions the pursuit of the Way as a personal and mystical quest. In the present degenerate times, "if a gentleman has no choice but to preside over the empire" (故君子不得已而臨蒞天下 chapter 11/13) he should refrain from governing but take care to "keep in place and within bounds" (*zai you* 在宥), allow the people to act according to their nature and power but deny them opportunities to over-indulge and be diverted to the wrong objects. The obscure term *zai you* seems to be taken from *Equalizing things* in the 'Inner' Chapters, where there is a phrase which in one text cited in the *Shiwen* (釋文) reads 左宥, surely *zai you* with one accidentally deleted stroke; the standard text reads 左右 'left and right', unintelligible in the context:

chapter 2/55–57

請言其畛，有在有宥，有倫（=論）有義（=議）有分有辯，有競有爭。此之謂八德。六合之外，聖人存（=莊）而不論，六合之內，聖人論而不議，春秋經世，先王之志，聖人議而不辯。

"Let me speak of the marking of its boundaries. One may recognize as there and enclose by a line, sort out and assess, divide up and argue over alternatives, compete over and fight over; these I call the Eight *Te*.

What is outside the cosmos the sage recognizes as there but does not sort out, what is inside the cosmos the sage sorts out but does not assess, the successive ages of the annals and the records of the former kings the sage assesses but does not argue over."

There are then eight degrees of aptitude, the least of which are the capacities for competing and fighting; the sage with the highest *te* has the capacity simply to put things in their places and enclose them with a boundary.

Professor Graham, in this discussion of the Primitivist position, suggests that there is a link between the *zai you* 在宥 of chapter 11 and the *you zuo you you* 有左有右 of chapter 2 on the authority of the *Jingdian shiwen* 經典釋文 by Lu Deming 陸德明, but the textual question is a shade more complicated than it appears on the surface. In the *Shiwen* on the *Zhuang zi*, under the entry 有左有右 is the note:[7]

崔本作"有",在宥也.
Cui's version reads 有, in other words 在宥.

There is obviously something wrong with the *Shiwen* text as it stands. Hence Lu Wenchao 盧文弨 in his *Jingdian shiwen kaozheng* 經典釋文考證 comments,[8]

舊作崔本作有   譌. 案下云在宥也,
則當作宥明甚. 今改正.

The traditional text reads 崔本作有, which is erroneous. As it goes on to say 在宥也, it is obvious it should have read 宥. This has been emended accordingly.

Lu is surely right in his suggestion.[9] If Lu is to be followed, Professor Graham is also justified in suggesting the further emendation of 左 to 在, making Cui's text 有在有宥. But there is a further complication. In chapter 2 (*Chu zhen* 俶真) of the *Huainan zi* we find[10]

於是在上位者左右而使之, 毋淫其性;
鎮撫而有之, 毋遷其德.

As chapter 2 of the *Huainan zi* is essentially an exposition of the philosophy of Zhuang Zi and is peppered with quotes and echoes from the *Zhuang zi*, this cannot but be an echo of the opening words of chapter 11 of the *Zhuang zi*. It would seem that in the *Zhuang zi* text the editors of the *Huainan zi* read 左右 in place of 在宥. This complicates matters: on the one hand, the present text of chapter 11 reads 在宥, but an alternative text, according to the *Huainan zi*, reads 左右. On the other hand, the present text of chapter 2 of the *Zhuang zi* reads 有左有右, but an alternative text, according to the *Shiwen*, seems to have read 有在有宥. Now there are three possibilities: (1) chapter 11 has a reading different from chapter 2 and the two are unconnected; (2) both chapters should read 左右; (3) both chapters should read 在宥. Only if we opt for the last alternative is there a connection between the expression 在宥 in chapter 11 and the passage concerning boundaries in chapter 2. The snag is that even if we choose to see a connection, not much light is thrown by the chapter 2 passage on the expression. Even if *zai you* means, as Professor Graham suggests, 'recognise as there and enclose by a line', what does it really mean to say, as is said in chapter 11, *zai you tianxia* 在宥天下? It looks as if we have to search elsewhere for connections which may throw light on the expression.

II

There is one passage in the *Zhuang zi* that has a bearing on the expression *zai you* which it is easy to overlook. In chapter 28 (*Rang wang* 讓王) we find[11]

堯以天下讓許由, 許由不受. 又讓於子州支父,
子州支父曰: 以我為天子, 猶之可也. 雖然,
我適有幽憂之病, 方且治之, 未暇治天下也.
夫天下至重也, 而不以害其生. 又況他物乎!
唯无以天下為者, 可以託天下也.

This passage is also to be found in chapter 2 (*Gui sheng* 貴 生) in book 2 of the *Lüshi chunqiu*. The text is practically identical, but what concerns us is that the *Lüshi chunqiu* text reads[12]

未 暇 在 天 下 也。

This occurrence of *zai tianxia* has hardly attracted any attention, perhaps because Gao You 高 誘, in his comment[13]

未 暇 在 於 治 天 下,

by repeating *zai* and, at the same time, inserting *zhi* 治 , seems to hint that this text should be taken in the sense of *zhi tianxia* as in chapter 28 of the *Zhuang zi*. It is true, *zai* 在 and *zhi* 治 are close in their archaic pronunciations, being K.943i *dz'əg* and K.976z *d'i̯əg* respectively, and it is quite possible one of the two is a phonetic corruption of the other. But the question is: Is *zai* a corruption of *zhi*? Or is *zhi* a corruption of *zai*? The fact that *zai you tianxia* occurs independently in chapter 11 of the *Zhuang zi* argues against *zai* being a corruption of *zhi*. If the reading of the *Lüshi chunqiu* is, indeed, correct, it will be worth our while pursuing our inquiries a bit further in this direction. There is, however, a preliminary question we should attempt to answer. Of the two texts, which is prior? Is it the *Zhuang zi*? Or is it the *Lüshi chunqiu*? It is fortunate for us, that it is possible to give an answer to the question. Practically everything in the text of chapter 28 of the *Zhuang zi* is paralleled elsewhere, mainly in the *Lüshi chunqiu*. The whole chapter can be divided into 17 sections. They are here listed with the parallels in the *Lüshi chunqiu*.

	Zhuang zi: *Rang wang*	Parallel in the *Lüshi chunqiu*
1a	堯 以 天 下 讓 許 由 許 由 不 受. 又 讓 於 子 州 支 父, --- 可 以 託 天 下 也.	*Gui sheng* 貴 生 (2.3b)

(*Zhuang zi* [1], 28/1–3)

1b 舜讓天下於子州
支伯.⋯此有道者
之所以異乎俗
耆也.(3–5)

2 舜以天下讓善卷
⋯莫知其處.(5–7)

3 舜以天下讓其友　　　*Li su* 離俗 (19.1b)
石戶之農⋯⋯
終身不反也.(7–9)

4 大王亶父居邠　　　*Shen wei* 審為 (21.6b–7a)
⋯豈不惑哉.(9–15)

5 越人三世弒其君,　　*Gui sheng* (2.3b–4a)
⋯⋯此固越人之所
欲得為君也.(15–18)

6 韓魏相與爭侵地.　　*Shen wei* (21.7a–7b)
⋯⋯子華子可謂知
輕重矣.(18–23)

7 魯君聞顏闔得道　　　*Gui sheng* (2.4a–5a)
之人也.夫生者豈
特隨侯之重哉!
(23–31)

8 子列子窮,容貌有　　*Guan shi* 觀世.(16.5b–6a)
飢色.⋯⋯其卒,民果
作難而殺子陽.
(31–35)

9 楚昭王失國屠羊
說走而從於昭王.
⋯⋯遂不受也.(36–44)

10 原憲居魯,環堵
之室.⋯憲不忍
為也.(44–49)

11 曾子居衛,縕袍
无表,⋯致道者忘
心矣.(49–51)

12 孔子謂顏回曰：
"回，來！家貧居卑，
胡不仕乎？"……是丘
之得也．(51–55)

13 中山公子牟謂瞻　　　　　　*Shen wei* (21.7b–8a)
子曰：……可謂有其
意矣．(55–59)

14 孔子窮於陳蔡　　　　　　　*Shen ren* 慎人 (14.17a–18b)
之間，……故許由娛
於潁陽而共伯得
乎共首．(59–68)

15 舜以天下讓其友　　　　　　*Li su* (19.1b)
北人无擇，……因自
投清泠之淵．(68–70)

16 湯將伐桀，因卞隨　　　　　*Li su* (19.1b–2b)
而謀，……乃負石而
自沈於廬水．(70–73)

17 昔周之興，有士二　　　　　*Cheng lian* 誠廉 (12.6b–7b)
人，處於孤竹，曰伯
夷叔齊。……此二
士之節也．(73–87)

As twelve out of the seventeen sections have parallels in the *Lüshi chunqiu*, one of the two texts is likely to be derivative. There are various indications that chapter 28 of the *Zhuang zi* has taken these passages from the *Lüshi chunqiu*. (1) Sections 1, 5, 7 all come from the *Gui sheng*; sections 3, 15, 16 all come from the *Li su*; and sections 4, 6, 13 all come from the *Shen wei* chapter of the *Lüshi chunqiu*. As grouped together in the *Lüshi chunqiu*, these sections show a greater coherence, particularly in the case of the *Li su*, than in the *Zhuang zi*. Section 15 which is a story about Shun is continuous with section 3, another story about Shun, in the *Li su* whereas in the *Zhuang zi* it is detached from sections 2 and 3 which are also stories about Shun. (2) Zhan zi 瞻子 figures in section 13, and this is the only time he appears in the whole of the *Zhuang zi*, whereas he appears again as 詹子 or 詹何 in chapter 8 (*Zhi yi* 執一) in book 17[14] and chapter 2 (*Chong yan* 重言) in book 18[15] in the *Lüshi chunqiu*. (3) The central character in section 8 is Lie zi 列子. He is referred to as Zi Lie zi 子列子. Now in the *Zhuang zi*, he is referred to as Lie zi in chapters 1 (*Xiaoyao you* 逍遙遊), 7 (*Ying diwang* 應帝王), 18 (*Zhi le* 至樂) and 32 (*Lie yukou* 列禦寇). Besides chapter 28, he is only referred to once as Zi Lie zi in chapter 19 (*Da sheng* 達生), but he appears only as Zi Lie zi in the *Lüshi chunqiu*. These indications are not conclusive singly, but together they form an argument in favour of the priority of the *Lüshi chunqiu* text. If that is the case, perhaps we should look for clues as to the meaning of *zai tianxia* and *zai you tianxia* in the *Lüshi chunqiu*.

III

The basic meaning of *zai* 在 is 'to be at or in some place', for example[16]

子在齊聞韶。

The Master, while in Qi, heard the shao.

It came in due course, however, to mean 'to lie in', for example[17]

得在時不在爭：治在道不在聖。

Success lies in being opportune and not in contention; order lies in the Way not in the sage.

In this meaning, *zai* is often used in connection with a substantive indicating the mind or the focus of the mind. The following is a well-known example.[18]

心不在焉,視而不見,聽而不聞,食而不知其味。

When the mind is not in it, one may look without seeing, listen without hearing and eat without being aware of the taste.

Apart from *xin* 心, *zhi* 志 and *yi* 意 also occur.[19]

伯牙鼓琴,鍾子期聽之。方鼓琴而志在太山。

Bo ya was playing on the *qin* with Zhong ziqi listening on. While he was playing on the *qin*, he was intent upon the Tai Shan.

Again,[20]

夫疾呼不過聞百步。志之所在,(蹻)諭于十里.

A sharp call can, at most, be heard a hundred paces away, but what the mind is intent upon will be comprehended a thousand miles away.

The following is an example using *yi* 意 :[21]

觀射者遺其藝;觀書者忘其愛,意有所在,則忘其所守。[22]

One who is watching archery forgets his own craft; one who is reading a book, forgets what he is partial to. Where there is something upon which the mind is intent, one forgets what one should be watching over.

Sometimes, *zai* is used on its own without explicit reference to the mind.[23]

拘圄圉者以日為脩;當死市者以日為短.
日之脩短有度也.有所在而短,有所在而脩也.

One who is in prison finds the day long. One who is due for execution finds the day short. The day has its fixed measure, but attention focused on one thing makes it short, while attention focused on another makes it long.

Let us turn to *you* 宥 . The basic meaning of *you* is *kuan* 寬 and *she* 赦, i.e., to be tolerant, to forgive, but *you* was often used as a loan for other characters. It is used for *you* 侑, 'to assist', 'to urge someone to drink',[24] for *you* 右 'right',[25] and for *you* 祐 'to help, to bless'.[26] We saw that the *you* 右 in *zuo you* 左右 had a variant 宥 . This can be viewed as a case of a loan character. But this basic meaning of 'to assist' does not seem to be relevant to the expression *zai you tianxia* 在宥天下 . We also noted a suggestion by Wu Rulun that *you* 宥 was the same as *you*

囿. This suggestion is worth following up. Wu, as quoted by Ma Qichang, does not elaborate. This omission we shall attempt to make good. In chapter 33 (*Tian xia*) of the *Zhuang zi* is the following:[27]

接萬物以別宥為始.

Cheng Xuanying 成玄英 in his sub-commentary says:[28]

宥,區域也.

Although he does not say so explicitly, Cheng is, in fact, taking *you* 宥 as *you* 囿.

This point is made explicit by Ma Xulun 馬敘倫, who comments,

宥借為囿。
You 宥 is a loan for *you* 囿。

He, then, goes on to cite from the *Shi zi* 尸子,

料子貴別囿.
Liao zi valued *bie you*.

He further cites at length the stories from chapter 7 (*Qu you* 去宥) in book 16 of the *Lüshi chunqiu* and the passage cited ends with the remark,

故凡人必別宥,然後知.別宥則能全其天矣.
Hence a man must *bie you* before he can have knowledge. If he can *bie you*, he will be able to preserve what pertains to heaven in himself.

Ma adds a final explanation of his own,[29]

囿為有所蔽,別囿謂解蔽也.
You is to be blinkered. By *bie you* is meant *jie bi*.

Ma's remark shows great acumen. If *jie bi* can best be translated as 'to remove blinkers', *bie you* can, perhaps, be rendered 'to detach oneself from one's confinement'.[30]

What is important to us is that *bie you* 別 宥 as a term is found both in chapter 33 of the *Chuang zi* and *Qu you* chapter of the *Lüshi chunqiu*. This confirms the hunch that the clue to the meaning of the expression *zai you* 在 宥 is to be found in the *Lüshi chunqiu*.

From the *Zai you* 在 宥 chapter Ma Xulun quotes two stories. One is about the man who, having advised a neighbour to cut down a tree because it was harmful, went on to ask to be given the wood and met with displeasure. The other is about a man who went to a goldsmith's and grabbed a bar of gold in broad daylight. The *Lüshi chunqiu's* comment in the one case was:[31]

此 有 所 宥 也.

This was because there is that by which the man was confined.

and in the other,[32]

此 真 大 有 所 宥 也.

This was truly because there was that by which the man was greatly confined.

We can see that as the title suggests, the *Qu you* 去 宥 chapter deals with 'the ridding of one's confinement', and in this sense there is not much difference between the expressions *qu you* 去 宥 and *bie you* 別 宥.

Now the third chapter in book 13 has the title *Qu you* 去 尤 which can only be looked upon as a variant of *qu you* 去 宥, both *you* 尤 and *you* 宥 being used as loans for *you* 囿. It, too, deals with the problem of *you*. What, then, is the relation between the two chapters? The present *Lüshi chunqiu* consists of three parts, the twelve *ji* 紀, the eight *lan* 覽 and the six *lun* 論. The part comprising the eight *lan* is from book 13 to book 20. There is one feature in this part which is worth noting. There is a formula which is found in all the chapters in book 13, the opening book of the eight *lan*, viz., *jie zai hu* 解 在 乎. This refers to illustrative stories located elsewhere in the eight *lan*. There is an instance of this in the *Qu you* 去 尤,[33]

解 在 乎 齊 人 之 欲 得 金 也.

The explanation is in the story of the man from Qi who wanted to get possession of gold.

This story, we have seen, is in the chapter *Qu you* 去 宥 in book 16. Thus there is an intrinsic link between chapter 3 *Qu you* 去 尤 in book 13 and chapter 7 *Qu you* 去 宥 in book 16. The opening passage of the *Qu you* 去 尤, runs as following:[34]

世 之 聽 者 多 有 所 尤. 多 有 所 尤 則 聽 必 悖 矣.
所 以 尤 者 多 故 其 要 心 因 人 所 喜, 與 因 人 所 惡.
東 面 望 者 不 見 西 墻 南 鄉 視 者 不 覩 北 方.
意 有 所 在 也.

People in the world who listen with their ears in order to distinguish the true from the false, very often suffer from being confined. This being the case, they end up with what is the opposite to what is the case in their listening. The reasons for being confined are many, but essentially they come from one's likes and dislikes. One who looks eastwards does not see the west wall, and one who looks southwards does not see the north. This is because there is that on which his mind is intent.

In this passage we find the phrase 意 有 所 在 也, a phrase we met with in a passage quoted from the *Huainan zi* above. Here we find *zai* 在 not only used in the sense of focusing the mind on something but also used to explain why the mind is 'confined' in the sense of 'blinkered'.

We have at last tracked down the expression *zai you*. What does it mean, then, to say *zai you tianxia* 在 宥 天 下? It means getting the Empire to focus its mind on something so as to prevent it from noticing other things. Chapter 49 of the *Lao zi* says,[35]

聖 人 在 天 下, 歙 歙 為 天 下 渾 其 心.
百 姓 皆 注 其 耳 目. 聖 人 皆 孩 之.

The sage in his attempt to distract the attention of the empire seeks urgently to muddle its mind. The people all have something on which to direct the flow of their ears and eyes, and the sage treats them all like children.

The idea is that the sage treats the empire as he would treat children. He provides it with some toy to distract its mind rather than imposing order upon it through coercion.

As it turns out to be the case, *zai you tianxia* as a political theory derives ultimately from the *Lao zi* rather than the *Qiwu lun*, as has been suggested by Professor Graham, and this goes to confirm what one has suspected all along that much in the 'Outer' Chapters of the *Zhuang zi* was written as an exposition of the teachings of Lao zi rather than those of Zhuang zi.

NOTES

1. *Zhuang zi* (2), 364.
2. Ibid.
3. *Wen xuan*, 20.23b–24a.
4. 3.10a.
5. *Zhuang zi* (6), 79. Lü's comment is indirectly taken from Jiao Hong's 焦 竑 *Zhuang zi yi* 莊 子 翼; 3.20a–20b.
6. Graham, 303–305.
7. Lu Deming, 26.8b.
8. Lu Wenchao, 2a–2b.
9. In fact there are cases of *you* 宥 used as a loan character for *you* 右 and *you* 祐. See nn. [24]–[26].
10. *Huainan zi*, 2.3a.
11. *Zhuang zi* (2), 965.
12. *Lüshi chunqiu*, 2.3b.
13. Ibid.
14. Ibid., 17.19a.
15. Ibid., 21.7b.
16. *Lunyu*, (VII.14) 96.
17. *Huainan zi*, 1.8a.
18. *Daxue*, (7) 8.
19. *Lüshi chunqiu*, 14.4b.
20. *Huainan zi*, 9.2b.

21. *Huainan zi*, 17.4b.

22. It is possible that *yi* 意 is a taboo substitute for *zhi* 志, the name of Emperor Huan 桓 of the Eastern Han.

23. Ibid., 16.4a.

24. See Duan, VIIB. 11a.

25. 宥 坐 之 器 in chapter 28 of the *Xun zi* (20.1a) appears as 右 坐 之 器 in the *Shuo yuan* 説 苑 10/4 (10.3b).

26. In 神 若 宥 之,傳 此 無 疆 (*Han shu*, 1055), 宥 is used for 祐.

27. *Zhuang zi* (2), 1082.

28. Ibid., 1083.

29. *Zhuang zi* (5), 33. 10a–10b.

30. Different schools of thought often used different terms for more or less the same thing. What the Yin Wen school called *bie you* 別 宥, the school of Xun zi called *jie bi* 解 蔽 (see *Xun zi*, 15.1a–19a).

31. *Lüshi chunqiu*, 16.18a.

32. Ibid., 16.18b.

33. Ibid., 13.7a.

34. Ibid., 13.6a.

35. *Lao zi*, Part II, 6a–6b.

REFERENCES

1. *Daxue* 大 學, *Sishu zhangju jizhu* 四 書 章 句 集 注 (*Xinbian zhuzi jicheng* 新 編 諸 子 集 成 ed.), Zhonghua shuju 中 華 書 局, Peking, 1983.

2. Duan Yucai 段 玉 裁, *Shuowen jiezi zhu* 説 文 解 字 注, (Jingyunlou 經 韻 樓 ed.), 1815.

3. Graham, A. C., *Studies in Chinese Philosophy and Philosophical Literature*, Singapore, 1986.

4. *Han shu*, Zhonghua shuju, Peking, 1962.

5. *Huainan zi* (*Sibu congkan* 四 部 叢 刊 ed.).

6. Karlgren, Bernhard, *Grammata Serica Recensa*, Stockholm, 1957.

7. *Lao zi: daodejing* (*Sibu congkan* ed.).

8. Lu Deming, *Jingdian shiwen* (*Tongzhitang jingjie* 通 志 堂 經 解 ed.), 1680.

9. Lu Wenchao, *Jingdian shiwen kaozheng* (*Baojingtang congshu* 抱經堂 叢書 ed.), 1791.
10. *Lüshi chunqiu* (*Sibu congkan* ed.).
11. *Lunyu* (*Sishu zhangju jizhu* ed.).
12. *Shuo yuan* (*Sibu congkan* ed.).
13. *Wen xuan*, Hu reprint, 1869.
14. *Xun zi* (*Sibu congkan* ed.).
15. *Zhuang zi* (1) *A Concordance to Chuang Tzǔ*, Harvard, 1956.
16. *Zhuang zi* (2) Guo Qingfan, *Zhuang zi jishi* 莊子集釋 (*Xinbian zhuzi jicheng* ed.), Peking, 1982.
17. *Zhuang zi* (3) Jiao Hong, *Zhuang zi yi*, Jinling, 1588.
18. *Zhuang zi* (4) Ma Qichang, *Zhuang zi gu* 莊子故 (*Jixu Caotang Congshu* 集虛草堂叢書 ed.), 1905.
19. *Zhuang zi* (5) Ma Xulun, *Zhuang zi yizheng* 莊子義證, Commercial Press, Shanghai, 1930.
20. *Zhuang zi* (6) Qian Mu, *Zhuang zi zuanjian* 莊子纂箋, Hong Kong, 1951.

Some Notes on Morphology and Syntax in Classical Chinese

Edwin G. Pulleyblank

In his article, "*Yún* 云 and *yuē* 曰 as verbs and particles," (1983), Angus Graham takes up a number of themes which have exercised him throughout his career, on some of which he and I have clashed in the past. It is fitting that I should take this occasion to acknowledge the fine contribution that he has made there. In the first place, he has elucidated the various uses of *yún* 云 as a verb of 'saying', demonstrating very clearly that, as one had long suspected, it can often be regarded as in some sense equivalent to the non-occurring *yuē* 曰 + *zhī* 之 'say it', paralleling *yān* 焉 = *yú* 於 + *zhī* 之, *yuán* 爰 = *yú* 于 + *zhī* 之 [1] and *rán* 然 = *rú* 如 + *zhī* 之. He has also made a very good case for regarding the *Shijing* particles *yún* 云 and *yuē* 曰 (to be distinguished from the homophonous verbs of 'saying') as members of a set of aspect particles which also includes preverbal *yú* 于. What I should like to do in this paper in honour of his seventieth birthday is to add a few footnotes to that article.

1. Verbs and Copulas

The verbs or quasi-verbs mentioned above, which exclude the object pronoun *zhī* 之 and instead have derivatives in *-n* which serve an equivalent function, have a number of other points in common. In the first place, in the *Shijing*, *yú* 于 '(go) to; to, at' and *rú* 如 'like' are followed by interrogative pronouns when these occur as complements—于 何 'to what, where?', 如 何 'like what, how?'. In this respect they contrast with normal transitive verbs which, in pre-Classical as well as Classical Chinese, are preceded by their interrogative pronoun objects—*hé yǒu* 何 有 'has what? there is what?' *hé yǐ* 何 以 'by means of what?'—and resemble the copula of noun predication, *wéi* 維, and the deictic pronouns *yī* 伊 and *sī* 斯 used as copulas—維 何 (伊 何, 斯 何) 'is what?'[2] Though *yú hé* 於 何 'in what?' does not happen to occur in the *Shijing*, it is found elsewhere, for example, in *Mozi* and *Xunzi*, and *何 於 certainly must be impossible in any form of Chinese.[3] In the case of *yuē* 曰, *何 曰 is as non-occurring as *何 於, but the reverse order 曰 何 can only mean '. . . says, "What?"', as a direct quotation. To express the meaning 'what does he/it say?' one has *yún hé* 云 何, which, though rarely, does occur in this meaning.

1. 子 張 曰. 子 夏 云 何
Zizhang said, "What does Zixia say?" (*Lunyu* 19/3)

2. 其 名 云 何.
"What should its name be?" (*Guanzi* 56 "Huan Gong Wen", p. 302)

In texts later than the *Shijing*, from the *Lunyu* and *Zuozhuan* onwards, *rú* 如 'like' mostly conforms to the word order of a normal transitive verb in its word order with interrogative pronouns. That is, *hérú* 何 如 replaces *rúhé* 如 何 in the meaning 'is like what?' *Rúhé* does survive, however, to a limited degree in the *Zuozhuan*. I find five examples of *rúhé*, as opposed to twenty-three of *hérú*, with no discernible difference of meaning. The *Guoyu* shows similar proportions, with three examples of *rúhé* as opposed to ten of *hérú*. *Lunyu* has only *hérú* (nineteen examples). *Mozi* prefers *héruò* 何 若 (eight examples) to *hérú* (one example), but has no examples of *rúhé*.

It is rather surprising to find that in *Mengzi*, although *hérú* predominates (fourteen examples), there are five examples of *rúhé*. In one case *rúhé* seems clearly to be abbreviated from *rú zhī hé* 如 之 何 "what is one to do about it", the double object construction which is only superficially an exception to the rule that *hé* does not follow its verb as object.

3. 曹交問曰.人皆可以為堯舜有諸...如何則可.

Jiao of Cao asked [Mencius], "Is it so that all men can become Yaos and Shuns? . . . . What must one do for this to be possible?" (*Mengzi* 6B/2)

Compare 如之何則可 in *Mengzi* 1A/5, 1B/14, 1B/15 and 1B/12. This explanation might also apply to the following example.

4. 敢問國君欲養君子.如何斯可謂養矣

I venture to ask how, when a ruler of a state wishes to support a superior man, he must do it so that it can (properly) be called support. (*Mengzi* 5B/7)

In another case the phrase *rúhé* is not an independent predicate but forms a descriptive complement after the main verb.

5. 憂之如何

What way is he anxious about it? (*Mengzi* 4B/28)

In the remaining cases (*Mengzi* 5A/4 and 5A/5), however, *rúhé* seems to mean simply 'is like what?' and it is difficult to see how it differs from *hé rú*.

In other texts for which we have concordances *hérú* predominates, with occasional examples of *héruò* and sporadic survivals of *rúhé*. Thus, in *Zhuangzi* one finds nine cases of *hé rú*, one of *hé ruò* and one of *rú hé*. In *Xunzi* and *Han Feizi* *rúhé* is not found, while *hé rú* is quite common. There are three instances of *xīrú* 奚如 in *Han Feizi*.

The change in the syntax of *rú* 如 'like' from that of a copula in the pre-Classical language to that of a transitive verb in the Classical language is probably associated in some way with the change in the normal pattern of noun predication from *wéi* 維 + NOUN to NOUN + *yě* 也. It should be noted that with the emergence of the new pattern of noun predication, a new way of expressing resemblance through noun predication as opposed to verbal predication also appeared, namely the construction with *yóu* 猶, as in 夫 兵 猶 火 也 "weapons are like fire" (*Zuozhuan* Yin 4/4). This construction is not found in the pre-Classical language, where *yóu* is found in a number of meanings, but not as a modifier of noun predicates, changing them from equations to similes. Though *yóu* is sometimes called a verb when it means 'like' (cf. Yang Shuda, *Ciquan*, p. 380), this is clearly not correct, at least in the full sense, since it cannot be negated, cannot take aspect particles and normally requires final *yě* to form an independent predicate. In spite of this, it resembles *rú* in being used as a means of adding a descriptive complement to another predicate, in which case final *yě* is omitted.

6. 民 歸 之 由 水 之 就 下

The people would turn to him like water going downward (*Mengzi* 1A/6, where 由 is used for the homophonous 猶)

7. 見 者 驚 猶 鬼 神

Those who saw it were astonished as if [seeing the work of] ghosts and spirits. (*Zhuangzi* 19/55)

Note that, like locative complements introduced by *yú* 於, descriptive complements introduced by *rú* 如 or *yóu* 猶 regularly *follow* the main verb, differing in this respect from transitive prepositional (coverbal) phrases introduced by such words as *yǐ* 以 'take; by means of, with', *yóu* 由 'follow; from', etc. The latter more commonly precede the main verb, but may also follow it.

While *rú* 如 and *yóu* 猶 as ways of making comparisons seem to occupy a shifting and ambiguous middle ground between nominal and verbal predication, *sì* 似 'resemble' behaves like an ordinary transitive verb. There are two examples of *sì zhī* 似 之 in the *Shijing*.

Locative complements introduced by *yú* 於 and descriptive complements introduced by *rú* 如 have in common not only their placement after the verb but also that they are both transformationally related to constructions in which a noun used adverbially in front of the verb replaces the prepositional phrase after the verb, e.g.

8. 舜勤民事而野死

"Shun was diligent in the people's business yet he died in the wilderness." (*Guoyu* 4:166). 野死 is equivalent to 死於野.

9. 豕人立而啼

"The pig stood up like a man and cried." (*Zuozhuan* Duke Zhuang 8/5) 人立 is equivalent to 立如人.

The reason why these transformations are possible is no doubt because the nouns in such phrases bear case relationships to the main verb and this probably also has a bearing on the fact that they have special rules of anaphora. Note that *zhī* 之 is case marked in Classical Chinese, serving as a generalized object pronoun but never as subject or possessive. The omission of *zhī* 之 after *yǐ* 以, the mark of instrumental case, is another example of special rules for anaphora for what in other languages would be oblique cases of nouns, though the rule for the placement of the instrumental case is different from that for the locative and descriptive cases. That one is dealing with an organized system of cases also seems to be implied by the fact that the locative case relationship marked by *yú* 於 can also be expressed simply by word order, with the preposition (coverb) omitted.

The interrogative pronoun *hé* 何 is also case-marked, in that it cannot normally occur as the subject of a verb[4] and has to be interpreted either as the object or the adverbial modifier of a verb which it precedes. It is not excluded as the complement of a copula in the pre-Classical language, just as it can occur as a noun predicate—*hé yě* 何也 "is what?"—in the Classical language; but it is evidently not governed by the copula in the same way as the object of a verb.

This difference in syntactical behaviour suggests that it is, strictly speaking, inappropriate to refer to the anaphoric forms in *-n* as equivalent to the incorporation of zhī 之. It has recently been suggested, rather plausibly at first glance, by Jerry Norman that yān 焉 and rán 然 were formed by the fusion of yú 於 and rú 如 respectively with "a third person pronoun or demonstrative beginning with *n" in some dialect of Old Chinese which had such a form (Norman 1988:86). In support of this possibility he notes, on the one hand, the post-Classical use of ěr 爾 EMC† ɲiă? as a demonstrative and, on the other hand, the Modern Mandarin pronoun nà 那 'that'. He also cites the sentence:

10. 君 子 哉 若 人
(*Lunyu* 5/3)

as evidence for the use of ruò 若 EMC ɲiak as a demonstrative adjective, 'this', even in the Classical period. His translation of the sentence as "This man is truly a gentleman" is not accurate, however. *Ruò* is, indeed, used here attributively but the phrase ruò rén must be rendered, with Legge and Waley, as "such a man".

Norman's suggestion of a non-standard dialect pronoun, equivalent to standard Chinese zhī 之, as the source for the forms in *-n is thus unsatisfactory both because such a pronoun is completely unattested and because the proposal does not take into account the other syntactical peculiarities of the words in question. Changing the perspective a little, one might conceivably look for a morpheme *n as the source of a fusion equation in the extensive word family to which ruò 若 'like; such; thus, etc.' and ěr 爾 'thus, so' belong, and which also contains rú 如 'like', ér 而 EMC ɲi < *nəɣ 'so, then', nǎi 乃 EMC nəj? < *nəɣ? 'then', etc. 'Said so' would often be as good a rendering for yún 云 as 'said it' and rán 然 can often be translated as 'thus' or 'so', rather than 'like it'—the analogy with English is less good for yān 焉 'in it, to it, there'. Even this, however, does not provide a very satisfactory solution. In other generally recognized fusion equations in Classical and Modern

---

†The abbreviation EMC stands for Early Middle Chinese as reconstructed forms in my book *Middle Chinese*, 1984 (Vancouver: University of British Columbia Press). Earlier forms are marked by an asterisk.

Chinese both parts are attested words, not roots. It seems to me likely that we are dealing here with ancient processes of suffixation rather than the fusion of independent morphemes. The meaning of the suffixes probably had nothing to do with anaphora as such and the anaphoric usage only developed secondarily. This seems especially clear in the case of *yún* 云, which contrasts with *yuē* 曰, ending in *-t, but for which there is no attested verb 'to say' ending in a vowel to which a reduced pronoun in *n- could have been attached. It should be remembered also that, although *yún* 云 often occurs without a following object in contexts that require the meaning 'said it' or 'said so', it can also occur with an explicit complement. Thus, it occurs as an alternative to *yuē* 曰 introducing a direct quotation, particularly one from a book as opposed to speech and, as we have seen, it must be used in place of *yuē* in the expression *yún hé* 云 何. There seems to be no clear warrant for the assumption that the anaphoric meaning is primary and the other uses are merely the result of blurring.

Let us now look at some other examples of *-n and *-t as suffixes.

2. *Yú* 于, *Yún* 云 and *Yuē* 曰 as Preverbal Aspect Particles

The identification of *yún* and *yuē* as aspect particles in the *Shijing* is one of the solid contributions of Graham's article. From a study of the contexts in which they occur he concludes that they are used as preverbal particles indicating respectively 'prospective' and 'actualising' aspect. In this way they form a three term set with *yú*, which Chou Fakao (1962:248–51) has shown to be a mark of inceptive or continuative aspect.

It is clear that *yú* 于 EMC wuǎ < *wàǎ in this sense is etymologically the same word as the preposition *yú* 于, meaning 'to, in, at, etc.' Both are from the same root meaning 'go' and are cognate to *wǎng* 往 EMC wuaŋʔ < *wàŋʔ 'go' (Pulleyblank 1986). The obvious phonetic similarity of *yú* to *yún* EMC wun < *wǝn and *yuē* 曰 EMC wuat < *wǝt creates a strong initial presumption that these, too, are derivatives of the same root meaning 'go'.[5]

Graham excludes this possibility, but on what I believe are insufficient grounds. He notes that Kennedy has identified *yuán* 爰 as the anaphoric derivative in -*n* of *yú* 于. This is correct but I would argue that both *yúan* 爰 < *wàn and *yún* 云 < *wən are derivatives of the root 'go' found in *yú* 于, differing from one another in their main vowels, respectively *a and *ə, or rather *a and zero, since I believe [ə] in Chinese is best analyzed, not as an underlying vowel, but as epenthetically inserted between consonants by rules of syllabification. As I have shown elsewhere, alternation between these two vowels, or better, the infixation of the vowel /a/, was an important derivational process in proto-Chinese and Sino-Tibetan, associated with a broad semantic contrast that can be called extrovert/introvert (Pulleyblank 1965, 1973, 1986, 1987). The fact that the suffix *-n had an anaphoric function in the case of *yúan* 爰, but not in the case of the aspect particle *yún* 云 is not relevant. *Yúan* 爰 *wàn = *wà + n was associated with *yú* 于 *waǎ in its use as a locative preposition and had the vowel *-a- found in the latter. *Yún* 云 *wən = *w + n came from the same root 'go' but in its extrovert form, without the vowel *-a-, and was associated with *yú* 于 *waǎ in its use as an aspect particle. We could be dealing with two different suffixes which just happened to be homophonous. However, I suspect that *-n the anaphoric function of the suffix in *yān* 焉 'in it, there', *rán* 然 'like it, thus, so', and *yún* 云 'say it, say so' represents a secondary, specialized development of the same *-n found in the aspectual particle *yún* 云.

Graham, who did not accept the possibility that the aspect marker *yún* 云 was a derivative of the same root as *yú* 于 'go', speculated, following Serruys, on a possible derivation of *yún* 云 from a homophonous full word meaning to 'revolve'. Though it is true, as he says, that there are many words of similar phonetic shape that have the general meaning of 'turn' or 'revolve'[6], and may even be ultimately related to the root *w-/*wa- 'go', it is not necessary to look so far afield. The same applies to the aspect particle *yuē*, which Graham does not seek to derive from a homophonous 'full' word. In this case he does recognize a suffix *-t and suggests that it may be the same *-t found in the negative particles *fú* 弗 EMC put < *pət, *wù* 勿 EMC mut < *mət, and *mò* 末 EMC mat < *mát, with its variant *miè* 蔑 EMC mɛt[7], and also in the question particle *hé* 曷 EMC ɣat < *gát. This is a highly interesting suggestion to which I shall return below. Meanwhile let us look at the more general question of the suffixes *-n and *-t in Sino-Tibetan and proto-Chinese.

3. The Suffixes *-n and *-t in Sino-Tibetan

The presence of *-n and *-t as formative suffixes in Tibeto-Burman has long been recognized (Wolfenden 1936, 1937), though Benedict, states that their "original function . . . cannot be delimited from the available material (1972:99 ff.)." Nevertheless, some general tendencies seem to be discernible. In the first place *-t, represented in Written Tibetan as *-d*, plays a part in Tibetan verbal inflection. Both as a regular final consonant added to vowel final roots and in the form of *da-drag*, the silent *-d* that is added as a second consonant to *-l*, *-r*, and *-n* but left unwritten after the archaic stage in the writing system, *-d* is associated with the so-called Present form of the verb, as in *byed-pa* 'to make', PERF. *byas*, FUT. *bya*, IMVE. *byos* (Coblin 1976). Benedict attributes a "causative or directive" function to it in some instances, for example, *ḥgyed-pa* 'to divide (trs.)', PERF. *bgyes*, FUT. *bkye*, as opposed to *ḥgye-ba*, PERF. *gyes*, 'to be divided' and *ḥbyed-pa* 'to open (trs.)', PERF. and IMVE. *phye*, *phyed*, *phyes*, FUT. *dbye*, as opposed to *ḥbye-ba* 'to open (intrs.)', but since *-d* is mostly confined to the Present form in these words, it is not certain that transitivity is its sole or primary meaning. We obviously need a much more sophisticated analysis of Tibetan verbal morphology before we can sort out the semantic effects of the various prefixes and suffixes that are involved, not to mention the vowel ablaut.

Benedict also points out that *-d* is found in nouns derived from verbs, as in *ŋud-mo* 'a sob' from *ŋu-ba* 'weep', *lud-pa* 'phlegm' from *lu-ba* 'cough, throw up phlegm', *drod* 'heat' from *dro-ba* 'to be warm', *blud-pa*, *blus-pa* 'ransom' from *blu-ba* 'to ransom', *ltad-mo* 'sight, spectacle' from *lta-ba* 'to look'.

As for the suffix *-n* in Tibetan, Benedict finds that it is frequently adjectival, though, like *-d* it can also occur in nouns derived from verbs. Among the examples he cites are *dron-mo* 'warm' from *dro-ba* 'to be warm', *rdzun* 'falsehood' from *rdzu-ba* 'deceive', *zan* (also *zas*) 'food' from *za-ba* 'eat', *gtsin* 'urine' from *gtsi-ba* 'urinate'. Compare also *rkun-ma* 'theft; thief' from *rku-ba* 'steal'.

From our present point of view examples in word families in which derivatives in *-n* and *-d* both occur, such as *dron* 'warm' and *drod* 'heat', are especially interesting. Compare also *rgyun* 'a continual flowing, the flow, current stream' and *rgyud* 'string, cord; connection, relation, reference', *rgyud-pa*, PERF. *brgyud* or *brgyus*, FUT. *brgyu*, IMVE. *rgyud* 'fasten or file on a string; pass through, traverse', which must all be related to *rgyu-ba* 'go, walk, move, wander, range' and *rgyu-ma* 'entrails', *rgyu-skar* 'lunar mansions, the constellations through which the moon passes in her revolutions through the heavens'. Very generally, one might suggest that, where there is a contrast, *-d* is associated more with punctual actions and concrete nouns, while *-n* is associated with states and abstract nouns.

Closely related doublets with and without final *-t are also found among full words as well as particles in Old Chinese. Note the following:

hū 呼 'shout', EMC xɔ < *xáǎ: *hè* 喝 'shout', EMC xat < *xát

jǔ 舉 'lift', EMC kɨǎʔ < *kàǎʔ: *jiē* 揭 'lift' EMC kiat, kɨat < *kàt

qù 去 'leave, go away from' EMC kʰɨǎʰ < *kʰàǎ-s, also EMC kʰɨǎʔ < *kʰàǎʔ 'get rid of', *qū* 祛 'dispel, exorcise' EMC kʰɨǎ < *kʰàǎ: *qiè* 揭 EMC kʰiat, kʰɨat < *kʰàt 'go away'

The forms here reconstructed in *-aǎ (*-o or *-io according to Karlgren) end in *-ag according to Dong Tonghe and F. K. Li and I have myself in the past reconstructed final *-ɦ (1962) or *-ɣ (1977–78). The question of a final consonantal closure in the Old Chinese *yú* 魚 category and the corresponding 'inner' *zhī* 之 category (Karlgren *-əg) is, however, a difficult problem on which I shall write more extensively elsewhere. Generally speaking Tibeto-Burman cognates have open *-a and words from the *yú* 魚 category are normally used to transcribe foreign open syllables in -a in the Han period. The solution to the problem undoubtedly involves the close phonological relation between the pharyngeal glide [ǎ], which I regard as the non-syllabic form of the vowel [a] and the velar glide [ɨ], which, on the one hand, is the non-syllabic form of the high back or central unrounded vowel [ɨ], and, on the other hand, is the frictionless, continuant, form of the voiced velar fricative [ɣ]. For many speakers it replaces smooth vocalic onset as the 'zero' initial of Mandarin before non-high vowels.[8]

To illustrate the probability that in the forms in *-t listed above the suffix is added directly to an underlying open *-a and that the final *-ă or *-ɣ of the unsuffixed forms is an automatic surface feature required for syllabification note the following case where the same word is written with alternative graphs, the phonetics of which belong, respectively, in the *-aă and *-at rhyme categories.

> è 關 EMC ʔat < *ʔát 'obstruct' (phonetic yú 於 EMC ʔɨă < *ʔàă): è 過
> EMC ʔat < *ʔát 'obstruct' (phonetic hé 曷 EMC ɣat < *gát)

Generally speaking *xiesheng* graphs fall within the same Old Chinese rhyme categories, which is no doubt why Karlgren did not accept the phonetic role of yú 於 in this case, but no other explanation of the graph seems possible. Our emended reconstruction of yú with the vowel *a and no final consonant (apart form the -ă glide which can be regarded as an automatic extension of the vowel) makes it easier to see the phonetic similarity with *ʔát than it was for Karlgren, who reconstructed the vowel of yú as *-o.

Clear examples of suffixed *-n added to open *-aă among content words as well as grammatical particles in Old Chinese are:

> yǔ 語, EMC ŋɨăʔ < *ʔàăʔ, 'speak', yán 言 , EMC ŋɨan < *ŋàn, 'say; word'
>
> tú 徒, EMC dɔ < *dáă, 'bare, naked; empty; vainly; merely, only', tǎn 袒, EMC danʔ < *dánʔ, 'to bare, strip to the waist', dàn 但, EMC danʔ < *dánʔ, 'only; but'. Tú 徒, EMC dɔ < *dáă, 'on foot' and tǎn 坦, EMC danʔ < *dánʔ, 'level, smooth; open, candid' may be different semantic extensions of the same root.[9]

Because of the additional phonological problems involved, I shall not enter into a full discussion of other examples of *-t and *-n where the unsuffixed form does not end in open *-aă. In some cases, however, the semantic connection is very simple and clear, for example:

zhī 知, EMC triă < *tràj, 'know'; *zhé* 哲, EMC triat < *tràt (*trjàt ?), 'wide'

    tōu 偷, EMC tʰəw < *łáw 'steal; careless, reckless'; *tuō* 脱, EMC tʰwat < *łwát and EMC dwat < *ăłwát, 'take off, take away; slip off, escape' (the intransitive meanings were probably associated with the reading with voiced intial). To the same word family belong *yú* 愉, EMC juă < *ăłàw, 'pleasant, enjoy; negligent', *yú* 俞, EMC juă < *ăłàw, 'satisfied, at ease; yes, agree', *yù* 喻 諭, EMC juăʰ < *łàw-s 'understand; instruct, explain', *yuè* 悦, EMC jwiat < *ăłwàt, 'pleased', *shuō* 説, EMC çwiat < *łwàt 'explain' and several other words.

    zài 在, EMC dzəjʔ < *-əɣʔ, 'be at a place, be present', *cún* 存, EMC dzwən < *-ẃən, 'exist, survive'. The source of the labialization in *cún* is a problem which I shall not discuss here.

    yī 依, EMC ʔɨj < ʔəl, 'lean on, depend on', *yǐ* 倚, EMC ʔiăʔ < *ʔàl, 'lean on, rely on; leaning to one side', later used for 'chair', *ē* 阿, EMC ʔaă < ʔál, 'slope, river bank', *yīn* 因, EMC ʔjin < *ʔ(j)əɲ < *ʔlən (?). 'rest on; rely on; continue; following; because of; because of that, therefore'. Though 因 does not occur as a rhyme in the *Shijing*, the homophonous *xiesheng* derivatives 駰 and 姻 do occur and show clearly that it should belong in the *-əɲ group (Karlgren *-en), rather than the *-ən group. Nevertheless, it is phonetic in *ēn* 恩, EMC ʔən, which also does not occur as a rhyme but which can only come from the *-ən group. I assume that the original final *-n was palatalized under the influence of a palatal element in the initial, which also shows up in the postinitial glide in Middle Chinese ʔjin. This could be derived from a medial *-l- which, in turn, would come from *ʔəl + n > *ʔlən. For the present the details of this development must be somewhat speculative but, in any case, the four words gathered here must certainly be cognate.

    The fact that *yīn* 因, without any following *zhī* 之, is often used with a backward reference, meaning 'following from that, because of that', might suggest that the suffix -n had the same kind of anaphoric meaning here as in *yān* 焉 and *rán* 然, but, unlike the latter pair, *yīn* can also occur with noun objects or with *zhī*. Other transitive verbs used as prepositions show the same capacity for the omission of an expected *zhī*. This is especially true of *yǐ* 以 'take, use; by means of, with', which is almost never found with *zhī*, but it is also quite common in the case of *yǔ* 與 'accompanying, with' and *wèi* 為 'for, for the sake of'.

From this brief and preliminary exploration it is clear that we have good reason to assume that Old Chinese, as well as Tibeto-Burman, had the suffixes *-t and *-n as formative elements.

4. *Yān* 焉

George Kennedy's demonstration (1940, 1953) that, as a postverbal particle, *yān* can, generally speaking, be equated in meaning (though not in form) to **yú zhī* 於 之 was a solid achievement that has received wide acceptance. Nevertheless he never claimed it was the whole story. Chinse grammars and reference works, while recognizing the anaphoric function, continue to treat *yān* as also a final particle of 'mood' (*yǔqì cí* 語 氣 詞). This is not just a matter of conservatism and inertia. There are facts about its syntactical behaviour that cannot be explained in a simple and straightforward way by treating it as combining a preposition and an object pronoun. Thus it is striking that it is never followed by the final perfective particle *yǐ* 矣 or by *yě* 也. There is no such restriction on *zhī* 之, nor on *yú* 於 followed by other pronouns. Compare, for instance, 不 能 進 於 是 矣 (*Mengzi* 1A/7). This suggests that there is something inherently aspectual about it in its role as a final particle.

Another peculiarity that it does not share with *yú* 於+ demonstrative pronouns is its use in preverbal position as a question particle. Kennedy, who made out a convincing case that the difference in pronunciation between the question particle and the postverbal particle (EMC ʔian versus ian in my reconstruction) was a sandhi phenomenon, due to the loss of initial glottal stop when the word became enclitic (see also Pulleyblank 1986), pointed to Mandarin *nǎ* 哪 'what?' versus *nà* 那 'that' as a parallel, but at least in this case there is a difference in tone, while in the case of *yān* 焉 the only apparent difference is the position in the sentence—sometimes not even that, since *yān* is occasionally used in preverbal position, not as a question particle but as a conjunction, equivalent to *yú shì* 於 是 'thereupon'. Presumably there may have been a difference in intonation to distinguish this from the meaning 'where?' or 'how?' but, even if we assume that this was so, it still leaves an unexplained divergence between the behaviour of *yān* and regular pronominal words.

What this may indicate, as I have already suggested above, is that *yān* was, in origin, not a fusion of *yú* 於 + a pronominal element, but a derivative of *yú* 於 + the same suffix *-n found in the aspect particle *yún* 云 and elsewhere in the lexicon. Its anaphoric meaning presumably came about in the same way that other coverbs—*yǐ* 以 , *yǔ* 與 , *wèi* 為 , *yīn* 因 —used without an explicit object were interpreted as anaphoric: the meaning required an object and this was supplied by reference back to to an appropriate noun in the previous discourse. There was, of course, the difference that, unlike *yin* or *yún*, which could be used either with an explicit object or anaphorically, *yú* 於 and *yān* 焉 were specialized in these respective functions.

A further question is why, in the case of *yān* 焉 , *yīn* 因 , and *yún* 云 , it was the *-n forms which acquired anaphoric meaning. My ideas on this are not sufficiently clear at present to make it useful to offer any suggestions.

5. The *-t Negatives

The question on which Graham and I have most seriously disagreed over the years is the interpretation of the negatives *fú* 弗 , EMC put, and *wù* 勿 , EMC mut. The controversy up to the time of Graham's 1983 article may be summarized as follows:

(1) Ding Shengshu (1935) argued that in very many cases in texts of the Classical period *fú* 弗 was functionally equivalent to *bù* 不 + the object pronoun *zhī* 之 . The same conclusion had already been anticipated by von der Gabelentz (1881). Ding attributed the failure of the formula to work for the *Shujing* to textual corruption.

(2) Boodberg (1937) went a step farther and suggested that 弗 was a phonetic fusion of *bù zhī* 不之.

(3) Lü Shu-xiang (1941) showed that there was a similar relationship between the negatives *wù* 勿 and *wú* 毋. He recognized, however, that the formulae *fú* 弗 = *bù zhī* 不 之 and *wù* 勿 = *wú zhī* 毋 之 were not valid for the pre-Classical language of the early inscriptions and that in consequence Ding's explanation for its failure in the *Shujing* was unacceptable. He hypothesized that *fú* 弗 and *wù* 勿 had originally differed from *bù* 不 and *wú* 毋 in relative strength and had only later become associated with the incorporation of the object pronoun, probably as a result of the loss of final *-g in *bù* and *wú*. He further showed that in post-Han times both *bù* and *wú* were replaced by forms in *-t, presumably descended from *fú* 弗 and *wù* 勿, and suggested that this was also an argument in favour of the view that the *-t forms had been stronger.

(4) Graham (1952) independently made a case for regarding *wù* 勿 as a fusion of *wú zhī* 毋 之.

(5) Huang Jingxin (1958) made an extensive study of *fú* and *bù* in pre-Han texts and concluded that neither Ding Shengshu's formula equating *fú* functionally to *bù zhī* nor Boodberg's fusion hypothesis could be sustained.

(6) Dobson (1959) rejected the fusion hypothesis and interpreted both *fú* and *wù* as more emphatic than *bù* and *wú*.

(7) Graham (1959, 1961) abandoned the hypothesis of phonetic fusion for both *fú* and *wù* but continued to claim as a "rule of thumb" that in texts of the classical period they were nearly always followed by a transitive verb with a resumptive object, which was usually omitted but might actually be present in the form of *zhī*, or another personal pronoun after the verb. This formulation allowed him to regard as conforming to the rule cases in which *zhī*, or another personal pronoun

with an antecedent earlier in the discourse is found after a verb negated by *fú* or *wù*. Cases in which *fú* or *wù* negate intransitive verbs were considered to be too few to need to be taken into account.

(8) In my own paper (1978) I accepted Huang Jingxin's conclusion that one could not distinguish *fú* from *bù* on the basis of the kind of verbs they negated and attempted to develop criteria for validating the alternative hypothesis proposed by Lü Shuxiang that the distinction was one of strength. I drew attention to a common pattern in which *fú*, often followed by an intransitive verb or a transitive verb with the object pronoun *zhī*, occurred in association with the final particle *yǐ* 矣 and I also noted that there was another negative particle ending in *-t, *miè* 末 EMC mɛt or *mò* 蔑 EMC mat (see footnote 7), which showed very similar syntactical behaviour but could not possibly be interpreted as incorporating a pronoun object. I assumed that this bore the same relationship to *wú* 無 EMC muǎ < *màǎ 'not have' as the other *-t negatives bore to *bù* 不 'not' and *wú* 毋 'do not' and I hypothesized that there was a derivational process in Old Chinese for creating emphatic negatives by adding a suffix *-t.

(9) Graham (1983) rejected, as he had done in the past, the explanation of *fú* 弗 and *wù* 勿 as emphatic but he seized on the pattern which I had noticed in which these negatives are associated with the final particle *yǐ* 矣 . He concluded, and I must admit that it now seems obvious to me too, that their meaning in such passages must be aspectual rather than emphatic. He associated the 'prospect-closing' function of the negatives in *-t in such cases with the 'actualizing' aspect which he saw as the function of the affirmative *-t particle *yuē* 曰. He hypothesized that this was a survival of pre-Classical usage into the classical period, but that outside this formula the new function of marking transitive verbs as having a resumptive object had supplanted the pre-Classical, aspectual meaning.

Let me say candidly that, since writing my 1978 paper and even before reading Graham's 1983 paper, in spite of the doubts I had previously expressed, I had become convinced that in at least some

Warring States texts *fú* and *wù* had the function of incorporating the object pronoun *zhī* 之. One thing that forced me to reconsider my earlier opinion was an examination of the Ma Wang Dui *Laozi* texts, which restore many cases of *fú* that have been replaced by *bù* in the transmitted text because of a Han taboo. It became very clear that, as I put it in an unpublished paper prepared for a workshop on the Ma Wang Dui manuscripts held at Berkeley in 1979, "*Fú* is not found in front of adjectives, intransitive verbs or transitive verbs with objects expressed, while *bù* is not found in cases where context leads one to expect the presence of the object pronoun *zhī*. There are one or two doubtful cases but in general the rule works *in both directions*."

Another thing that wore down my resistance to the fusion hypothesis was the experience of reading year after year with successive classes of beginning students a familiar passage in the first book of Mencius, in which the only explanation for the use of *wú* 無 in the first sentence and *wù* 勿 in the second that makes sense is that the latter incorporates *zhī* 之, with the antecedent *bǎi mǔ zhī tián* 百畝之田, as the indirect object of the verb *duó* 奪 'take away, deprive.'

11. 雞豚狗彘之畜. 無失其時. 七十者可以食肉矣.
百畝之田. 勿奪其時. 數口之家可以無飢矣.

(*Mengzi* 1A/4) "Let the domestic animals—fowls, pigs, dogs and swine—not lose their breeding seasons and the seventy-year olds may eat meat. Do not deprive the hundred *mu* fields of their proper seasons [of agricultural work], and households of several mouths may be without hunger."

Explaining the residue of examples which did not fit the formula remained a difficulty and, for me, this applied not only to the cases in which *fú* 弗 and *wù* 勿 appeared with intransitive verbs but also the cases in which they appeared with transitive verbs followed by a pronoun object. It has always seemed to me that, as Lü Shuxiang suggested, even if the particles in question did not originate as fusions, the only reasonable explanation for their association with an anaphoric function was that they were felt to be fusions of *bùzhī* 不之 and *wúzhī* 毋之 at the relevant period. Graham's compromise "rule of thumb", which abandoned the fusion hypothesis for the two words in question and merely claimed that "classical *fu* nearly always marks the verb as having a resumptive object, generally implicit but occasionally supplied" (1983:64), has never seemed to me to be the sort of rule one should expect to find in a natural language.

The contribution of Graham's 1983 article has been to offer a convincing alternative to the hypothesis of relative strength as a way of accounting for pre-Classical *fú* 弗 and *wù* 勿 which circumscribes the contexts in which survivals of the pre-Classical usage can be expected and accounts not only for most of the cases in which *fú* and *wù* appear with intransitive verbs but also those in which they appear with transitive verbs with an explicit pronoun object.

As far as the pre-Classical language itself is concerned, Graham merely sketched his hypothesis that *fú* and *wù* functioned as aspect markers. Quite a lot has, however, been written on the subject of the negative particles in the oracle bone language by two specialists in that area, Paul Serruys and Kenichi Takashima. Without going exhaustively into what they have said on the subject one can sum up their most recent conclusions as follows. According to Serruys *bù* 不 and *wú* 毋 are "used with verbs in stative, intransitive, passive functions," while *fú* 弗 and *wù* 勿 are "used for active, transitive, causative roles." (1981:342) In his latest work on the subject Takashima (1988) finds the intransitive/transitive opposition unsatisfactory and proposes instead the opposition stative/non-stative. In the sense in which he uses them the terms 'stative' and 'non-stative' can each be applied to both transitive and intransitive verbs. At one point he remarks "The exact meaning of this 'stativity' can, I think, be expressed in English as 'be + vb-ing,' not so much in its progressive aspect but as in its eventive or happening aspect." (p. 125) While he does not explicitly set up the *bù* 不 /*fú* 弗, *wú* 毋 /*wù* 勿 opposition as one of aspect in Chinese, this seems to be what is implied. The suggestion one would like to make is that, judging by later usage, one should regard *bù* 不 and *wú* 毋 as the unmarked terms and define the opposition as, perhaps, non-punctual versus punctual or aoristic or as stative versus change of state. Whether such a reformulation, which seems to fit very well with the general meaning that we have postulated for the suffix *-t in Sino-Tibetan as well as for the survivals of the pre-Classical use of the *-t negatives in classical times, will work satisfactorily in the pre-Classical language must be left for future investigation.

While it seems quite possible to derive the anaphoric functions of the particles in *-n that were discussed above from their aspectual function, the same does not, it seems to me, apply to *fú* and *wù* . In the case of *yān* 焉 regarded as a derivative of *yú* 於 and *yún* 云 regarded as a verb 'to say' the absence of an explicit object where one was implied by the context could be sufficient to set up a usage in which these particles themselves were implicitly anaphoric. In the case of the negative particles there would be no reason for such an implication to become attached more to *fú* and *wù* than to *bù* and *wú*, and indeed, as Huang Jingxin and others have stressed, *bù* at least was often used where anaphora was implied. If, therefore, we accept that *fú* and *wù* each stand for two separate negative particles, (a) a pre-Classical aspectual particle, and (b) a new particle that arose only at a later stage of the language which marks the presence of an incorporated pronoun object, one can scarcely avoid the conclusion that the latter must have arisen through phonetic fusion of 不 之 and 毋 之 respectively.

Karlgren's Old Chinese reconstructions, *pĭug and *tiəg, for *bù* 不 and *zhī* 之, and even F. K. Li's *pjəg and *tjəg, seem to put certain obstacles in the way but these are of little consequence, as I already showed in my 1978 article. It is now widely accepted that the palatal affricates, tç, etc. of Middle Chinese were derived from Old Chinese dentals, not from a separate category of palatal stops as Karlgren supposed, so that we can reconstruct the initial of 之 as *t, corresponding exactly to the final consonant of 弗 and 勿 . His reconstruction would also require us to suppose that final *-g was lost from both syllables in the fusion but this is probably a mirage. My own reconstruction has a weak fricative *-ɣ rather than a stop. Tibeto-Burman cognates to words in this category often end in open vowels. I suspect that the negative 不 , which was normally enclitic, consisted etymologically simply of the consonant *p. When pronounced as a separate, fully accented, syllable, it was provided with a *shwa* vowel and a final glottal stop, *pəʔ, giving the Early Middle Chinese pronunciation puwʔ, Pekingese *fǒu*, now written with a separate character 否 , but originally simply 不 . Note that the consonant *p alone is relevant in other fusions containing 不 such as *hé*, 盍 EMC ɣap, = 何 不 (better 胡 不 ?) 'why not', and *pǒ* 叵 EMC pʰaʔ, = *bù kě* 不 可 'not possible'. Similarly *zhī* 之 probably consisted of the root *t, supplied with a *shwa* vowel and a final glide to conform to the rules of syllabification. In its colloquial pronunciation, it has given rise to the modern genitival particle *de* which probably differs little from the way the word was pronounced in Old Chinese. The combination *p + *t would have been syllabified as *pət, from which, assuming what I call Type B prosody symbolized by a grave accent *pə̀t, one derives EMC put by regular rule.

Very much the same applies to *wù* 勿 , EMC mut, considered as a fusion of *wú* 毋 , EMC muă, 'do not' + *zhī* 之 . Though *wú* 毋 had become homophonous with *wú* 無, EMC muă, 'not have' at an early period, the graph, which is merely a variant form of *mǔ* 母 EMC məwʔ 'mother' clearly indicates that it must originally have belonged in the *zhī* rhyme category, leading to the reconstruction *mə̀ɣ. Again we can hypothesize that the root was *m, which when fused with a following *t would give rise to *mə̀t > EMC mut.

The fact that uncontracted forms *bùzhī* 不 之 and *wúzhī* 毋 之 are not found has been raised as an objection to the fusion hypothesis but this could be accounted for if we suppose that object pronouns placed between the negative and the verb were always unaccented clitics, so that *pə̀-t(ə) and *mə̀-t(ə) would have automatically contracted to *pə̀t and *mə̀t.

The fact that throughout the classical period *bù* 不 , as well as *fú* 弗 , can occur in front of a transitive verb where the sense requires the object *zhī* 之 but *zhī* is not found remains unexplained. This needs to be considered as part of the larger question of when overt anaphoric reference is obligatory in Classical Chinese, when it is optional, and when it is regularly omitted and how these rules change over time. Thus it is well known that Classical Chinese has no third person subject pronoun corresponding to modern *tā* 他 . Omission of the object pronoun is less regular but it is also found in affirmative, as well as negative, sentences. For example, *zhī* 之 is quite often omitted after *shǐ* 使 'cause, make'. Whether my impression is correct that this is more common in the *Zuozhuan* than in later Warring States texts needs to be investigated in detail, however. The surprising discovery that the Ma Wang Dui texts of *Laozi* nearly always restore *fú* where the sense requires the object pronoun *zhī* after *bù* in the current text suggests that there was a diachronic trend towards making anaphoric reference obligatory after the negative also.

A further problem that remains unresolved is why the *-t forms of the negatives eventually lost their anaphoric meaning and replaced the corresponding unmarked forms as the ordinary negatives in post-Han Chinese. Lü Shuxiang's suggestion that it has something to do with the obsolescence of the rule for placing object pronouns between the negative particle and the verb is very plausible but it is difficult to avoid the implication that *fú* and *wú* were somehow still felt to be stronger negatives, perhaps simply because they were phonologically more marked. Was there also, perhaps, influence from a dialect in which the pre-Classical usage survived more prominently than it did in the literary language of the Warring States period? At present I do not see any way of investigating these questions.

REFERENCES

Where possible, classical texts are cited according to the Harvard-Yenching Index Series. Guanzi *and* Han Feizi *are cited in the edition of the* Zhuzi Jicheng, *Beijing: Zhonghua shju, 1954. The* Guoyu *is cited in the edition of the Shanghai guji chubanshe, 1978.*

Benedict, Paul K., 1972. *Sino-Tibetan: a conspectus.* Cambridge: Cambridge University Press.

Bodman, Nicholas C., 1980 'Proto-Chinese and Sino-Tibetan: data towards establishing the nature of the relationship', in Frans van Coetsem and Linda Waugh, eds., *Contributions to Historical Linguistics*, 34–199. Leiden: Brill.

Boodberg, Peter A., 1937. 'Some proleptical remarks on the evolution of Archaic Chinese', *Harvard Journal of Asiatic Studies* 2:329–372.

Chen Mengjia 陳夢家, 1956. *Yinxu buci zongshu.* Beijing: Kexue chubanshe.

Chou Fa-kao 周法高, 1962. *Zhongguo gudai yufa, Gouci bian* (A

historical grammar of Ancient Chinese, Part II: Morphology). Taipei: Academia Sinica.

Coblin, W. South, 1976. 'Notes on Tibetan verbal morphology', *T'oung Pao* 62:45–70.

Ding Shengshu 丁聲樹, 1935. 'Shì fǒudìng cí fú bù', in *Qingzhu Cai yuanpei xiansheng liushiwu sui lunwenji*. Vol. 2, 967–996.

Dobson, W. A. C. H., 1959. *Late Archaic Chinese*. Toronto: Toronto University Press.

Dong Tonghe 董同龢, 1948. 'Shànggǔ yīnyùn biǎogǎo', *Bulletin of the Institute of History and Philology, Academia Sinica* 18:1–249.

Gabelentz, Georg von der, 1881. *Chinesische Grammatik*. Leipzig.

Graham, Angus, 1952. 'A probable fusion word: 叚 *wuh* = 毋 *wu*/之 *jy*', *Bulletin of the School of Oriental and African Studies* 14:139–148.

————, 1959. 'Observations on a new Classical Chinese grammar', *Bulletin of the School of Oriental and African Studies* 22:556–571.

————, 1961. 'The date and composition of *Liehtzyy*', *Asia Major* 8:138–198.

————, 1983. '*Yún* 云 and *yuē* 曰 as verbs and particles', *Acta Orientalia Havniensia* 44:33–71.

Huang Jingxin 黃景欣, 1958. 'Qìn Hàn yǐqián gǔ Hànyǔ zhōng de fǒudìngcí 'fú' 'bù' yánjiǔ', *Yuyan yanjiu* 3:1–23.

Karlgren, Bernhard, 1957. *Grammata Serica Recensa*. Reprinted from the *Bulletin of the Museum of Far Eastern Antiquities* 29.

Kennedy, George A., 1940. 'A study of the particle *Yen*', *Journal of the American Oriental Society* 60:1–22, 193–207.

————, 1953. 'Another note on *Yen*', *Harvard Journal of Asiatic Studies*, 16:226–236.

Li, Fang-kuei 李方桂, 1971. 'Shanggu yin yanjiu', *Qinghua Xuehbao* n.s. 9:1–61.

Lü Shuxiang 呂叔湘, 1941. 'Lùn 'wú' yǔ 'wù', in *Hanyu yufa lunwenji* 1954. Beijing: Kexue chubanshe, 12–35.

Norman, Jerry, 1988. *Chinese*. Cambridge: Cambridge University Press.

Pulleyblank, Edwin G., 1960. 'Studies in Early Chinese Grammar, Part I', *Asia Major* 8:36–67.

————, 1962. 'The consonantal system of Old Chinese', *Asia Major* 9:58–144, 206–265.

————, 1965. 'Close/open ablaut in Sino-Tibetan', in G. B. Milner and E. J. A. Henderson, eds., *Indo-Pacific Linguistic Studies* (= *Lingua* 14) 230–240.

_____, 1973. 'Some new hypotheses concerning word families in Chinese', *Journal of Chinese Linguistics* 1:111–125.

_____, 1977–78. 'The final consonants of Old Chinese', *Monumenta Serica* 33:180–206.

_____, 1978. 'Emphatic negatives in Classical Chinese', in David T. Roy and Tsuen-hsuin, eds., *Ancient China: studies in early civilization.* Hong Kong: The Chinese University Press, 115–136.

_____, 1979. 'Linguistic notes on the Laozi manuscripts', unpublished paper prepared for a workshop on the Ma Wang Dui manuscripts held at the University of California, Berkeley.

_____, 1986. 'The locative particles yü 于, yü 於, and hu' 乎, *Journal of the American Oriental Society* 106:1–12.

_____, 1986b. 'Ablaut and initial voicing in Old Chinese morphology: *a as an infix and prefix', Paper for the 2nd International Conference on Sinology, Taipei, December 1986.

Serruys, Paul L-M., 1981. 'Towards a grammar of the language of the Shang bone inscriptions', *Zhongyang yanjiuyuan guoji hanxue hui lunwenji, Yuyan wenzi zu* (Taipei: Academia Sinica), 313–364.

Shima Kunio 島 邦 男 , 1971. *Inkyo bokuji s﹒rui*, rev. ed., Tokyo: Kyfiko Shoin.

Takashima, Kenichi, 1988. 'Morphology of the negatives in oracle-bone inscriptions', *Computational Analyses of Asian and African Languages* 30:113–133.

Wolfenden, Stuart N., 1936. 'On certain alternations between dental finals in Tibetan and Chinese', *Journal of the Royal Asiatic Society*, 401–416.

_____, 1937. 'Concerning the variation of final consonants in the word families of Tibetan, Kachin and Chinese', *Journal of the Royal Asiatic Society*, 625–655.

Yang Shuda 楊 樹 達 , 1954. *Ciquan*. Beijing: Zhonghua shuju.

NOTES

1. *Yú zhī* 于 之 is found on the oracle bones and there is at least one example in a bronze inscription (Chen Mengjia 1956:97–8). On the oracle bones *zhī* 之 is also found after *yuē* 曰 and after the copula *wéi* 隹 (=惟 ,維),

neither of which occurs in the *Shujing* or *Shijing* (Shima 1971:64–5). It may be that at that stage of the language, *zhī* was a fully accented, independent demonstrative pronoun and that by the time of the first literary texts it had become cliticized and replaced by *shí* 時 in its earlier free function.

2. Even in Classical Chinese interrogative pronouns follow the verb *wéi* 為 when it is used as a copula 'to be' rather than as a transitive verb 'to make'. I have not found an example of *hé* 何 used in this way but note the following examples with *shuí* 誰, which, like *hé* 何, regularly precedes a verb of which it is the object. (a) 沮 曰, 夫 執 輿 者 為 誰。子 路 曰, 為 孔 丘。(*Lunyu* 18/6) [Chang]ju said, "Who is the one holding the reins in the carriage?" Zilu said, "It is Kong Qiu." (b) 桀 溺 曰, 子 為 誰。曰, 為 仲 由。Jieni said, "Who are you, sir?" He replied, "I am Zhongyou." (*Lunyu* 18/6)

3. The Classical interrogative binome *wūhū* 惡 乎, EMC ʔɔɣɔ < ʔáɣá 'where? how?', has commonly been glossed as *yú hé* 於 何, EMC ʔiǎ ɣa < *ʔà ɣál, at least since Zheng Xuan's commentary to the 'Tan Gong' section of the *Liji* (cited by Yang Shuda, *Ciquan* p. 399). Yang Shuda thought that it was made up of the interrogative pronoun *wū* 惡 + the preposition (or rather, in this case, postposition) 乎 'in, at', but *wū* 惡 (sometimes written 烏) as an interrogative seems to be simply an abbreviation of the two character phrase. The phrase itself is probably based on a phonetic fusion of *yú* 於, EMC ʔɔ < *ʔà, and the pronominal root found in *hé*, perhaps in the form *hú* 胡, EMC ɣɔ < *gá 'why, how'. Note that the graph 於 has an alternative reading *wū*, EMC ʔɔ < *ʔá, as an exclamation and appears to be originally merely a variant of 烏 'crow'. With a change in prosody on the first syllable and intervocalic lenition of the initial of the second syllable in close juncture *ʔà gá would give ʔáɣá. The use of the graph 惡, which, in its full-word meanings, was read *ʔák 'bad' and *ʔáks > *áx (?) 'to hate', was probably for the sake of spelling the shared intervocalic -ɣ- on the end of the first syllable as well as on the beginning of the second. There are a number of other phonological issues which this fusion question raises that I will not go into here.

4. On the special use of the combination *hé shí* 何 實 as subject of a verb in *Zuozhuan* and *Guoyu* see Pulleyblank 1960:44–45

5. This is a common Sino-Tibetan root, recognized by Benedict in *yú* 于 but not in *wǎng* 往, and reconstructed by him as *s-wa 'be in motion, go, come' (where *s- is the causative prefix). It is found in such words as Newari *wa* 'come', Kachin *wa* 'be in motion', Chepang *hwa* 'walk, move', Burmese *waŋ* 'enter, go or come in', *swàŋ* 'put into', *swà* 'go', Kuki *wa, verbal affix used with verbs of motion (Benedict 1972: 105, 167; see also Bodman 1980).

6. Cf. Pulleyblank 1973:121.

7. The source of the fronting of the vowel in EMC mɛt, which belongs in the Old Chinese *-at rhyme, compare wà 襪 EMC muat < *màt, is not clear. It may be that this reading properly belongs to the full word miè 'destroy', written with the same graph and that, in this sense it had a prefix *s-mát which caused the fronting of the vowel. In this case the reading miè for the negative particle may have been borrowed from the full word 'destroy' after the particle became obsolete and the two graphs 末 and 蔑 as negative particles may simply be alternative ways of writing the same word *mát. Note that, if *mát is derived from wú 無 EMC muă < *màă + -t, there is a change in prosody from grave ˋ to acute ´. This is also found in mò 莫 EMC mak < *mák 'no one, nothing' which must also be derived from 無 EMC muă < *màă 'not have, there is no'. The existence of such alternations, also found in such cases as the synonymous question particles an 安 'how? where?', EMC ʔan < *án, and yān 焉 'how? where?', EMC ʔian < *ʔàn, is one of the types of evidence that supports my hypothesis that this distinction between what I call Type A and Type B syllables is prosodic in origin and does not reflect an infixed post-initial *j glide as implied by Karlgren's reconstruction.

8. One possibility is that *-ɣ (or *-ɨ) is the final of the 'inner' zhī 之 category, with [ə] as the rhyme vowel, and *-ă the final of the 'outer' yú 魚 category, with [a] as the rhyme vowel. Or one may even have to consider the possibility that *-ɣ and zero or *-ă were both found in the yú and zhī categories as phonemically contrasting endings with partially different reflexes in Middle Chinese, which were nevertheless phonetically close enough to be allowed to rhyme with one another in Old Chinese poetry. Though this is a highly unorthodox suggestion, it would provide a way of accounting for (a) the contrasting Grade I and III finals that developed out of the zhī category after labial initials, e.g. mǔ 母 EMC məwʔ < *mə́ʔ(?), but měi 每 EMC məjʔ < *mə́ɣʔ; fǒu 否 EMC puwʔ < *pə́ʔ and EMC pʰi < *pʰə́ɣʔ, and (b) the Grade III finals of the má 麻 rhyme after palatal initials, e.g. zhě 者 EMC tɕiaʔ < *táɣʔ, contrasting with zhū 諸 EMC tɕiă < *tăă. I shall not discuss this highly unorthodox idea further here, however.

9. The Mandarin readings tǎn for EMC danʔ, already found in the Zhongyuan yin yun, are irregular.

PROBLEMS OF TRANSLATION AND INTERPRETATION

The Mass Noun Hypothesis and the Part-Whole Analysis of the White Horse Dialogue

3

Christoph Harbsmeier

The logician W. V. O. Quine, in perhaps the most famous part of his most widely-read book *Word and Object*, maintains that in some ways we may attribute to others different and mutually contradictory structures of thought without risking ever being refuted by any evidence from their speech. Quine takes the hypothetical "native" word *gavagai* 'rabbit', and shows that without risk of being refuted one can attribute to a people a notion not of an enduring entity but only of rabbity time-slices. Another alternative is to attribute to the native a notion not of a rabbit as such but only of all and sundry undetached rabbit parts. He then continues:

> A further alternative likewise compatible with the same old stimulus meaning (of the word *gavagai*) is to take "gavagai" as a singular term naming the fusion, in Goodman's sense, of all rabbits: that single though discontinuous portion of the spatiotemporal world that consists of rabbits. Thus even the distinction between general and singular terms is independent of stimulus meaning.[1]

Chad Hansen attributes what Quine reconstructs as the notion of a spatiotemporal fusion to the ancient Chinese with the difference that Gongsun Long talks not of a rabbit but a horse:

> Then the question, "Of what is *ma* 馬 "horse" the name?" has a natural answer: the mereological set of horses. "Horse-stuff" is thus an object (substance or thing-kind) scattered in space-time. . . . As a result,

Chinese theories of language tend to treat adjectives as terms denoting mass substantives; for example, red is the stuff that covers apples and the sky at sunset.[2]

The thought of a mereological set consisting of apples and skies at sunset scattered through space and time is, since the great mathematician Stanislaw Lesniewski developed his very abstract and complex theory of mereology (thus introducing the term "mereological set" which Hansen employs), and since Einstein has been able to establish a relationship between space and time, perhaps a formally and physically feasible construct. However, I find nothing whatever in all of traditional Chinese literature that even remotely suggests that the ancient Chinese ever thought of anything like mereology, or of apples and evening skies as one object scattered through time and space.

Angus Graham has in the past taken a most enthusiastic view of the mass noun hypothesis:

Chad Hansen in his *Language and logic in ancient China* has opened the first radically new approach to the "White Horse". It is an application of his hypothesis that Classical Chinese nouns function like the mass nouns rather than the count nouns of Indo-European languages.[3]
We start from one of Hansen's crucial insights, that thinking with mass nouns is in terms of whole and part of which what for us class and member are only one variety.[4]

Graham explicitly takes the mass noun hypothesis as his starting-point for a new interpretation of the White Horse dialogue. But for all his enthusiasm Graham wisely avoids the attribution of the notion of a mereological set to the ancient Chinese when he writes:

But if he (i.e. Gongsun Long) is thinking of horse as a mass with discontinuous parts similar in shape, and of white as a mass of discontinuous patches of colour, then for him a white horse is indeed a part of the former mass combined with a part of the latter.[5]

Let us call Graham's interpretation the part-whole interpretation of the White Horse dialogue. In view of his reticence about the concepts of a 'mereological set' and 'object' we might perhaps try to avoid attributing to Gongsun Long such notions as that of single objects scattered through space and time and still save the essence of the part-whole interpretation for which Graham argues so eloquently. Perhaps we can take the much simpler line that Gongsun Long treated terms like *bai* 白 'white' and *ma* 'horse' as mass terms **without** thereby anachronistically envisaging an object consisting of all white patches or horsey stuff past, present, and future scattered through space and time forming one single object.

The Mass Noun Hypothesis

We know that 'information' is a count noun in French, German, Danish, Norwegian, Russian, and many other languages, but not in English. What most languages refer to by count nouns, may in some language be referred to by noncount nouns. One can imagine a language structured in such a way that it treats physical objects as the English rather than the French 'information' treats information. If Classical Chinese were such a language then we should read the Classical Chinese *yi ren* 一 人 ONE MAN as 'one of mankind' or *san ma* 三马 THREE HORSE as 'three of horse-kind' even when there is no measure word (like *pi* 'horse-like item of') between *san* and *ma*. One would thus treat *ren* and *ma* as mass nouns of the same order as *shi* 食 'food' and *shui* 水 'water'.[6] Let us call such a hypothesis about Classical Chinese nouns the mass noun hypothesis. This hypothesis has, needless to say, no essential link whatsoever with mereology.

Graham claims that *ma* should be interpreted as a mass term. He does not inquire whether *ma* 'horse' behaves syntactically differently from other common nouns like *shui* 'water' or like *sheng* 牲 'domestic animal', not to speak of proper nouns like *Zhongni* 仲 尼 and pronouns like *ci* 此 'this item'. Among the common nouns the possible grammatical distinction between count nouns, generic nouns, and mass nouns in Classical Chinese certainly needs careful attention before we are entitled to decide whether *ma* is a mass noun or not. Let us try to identify provisionally some of the diagnostic syntactic environments that might bring out into the open any grammatical distinction that might exist between count nouns, generic nouns, and mass nouns.

Count Nouns

It turns out that count nouns may not only be quantified by *duo* 多 'much/many' and *shao* 少 'little/few' but also by *shu* 数 'a number of', *ge* 各 'each', *jian* 兼 'each of the objects', *mei* 每 'every'. Mass nouns are never quantified by *shu, ge, jian,* or *mei* and when they are counted by ordinary numbers, the semantics of counting is entirely different (e.g. 'three **kinds of** wine', as we shall see below).

If we study the scope of quantifiers like *ge, jian, mei,* and *shu* we can make an extensive list of count nouns in Classical Chinese. Let us take *shu* 'a number of' which is frequent with measure phrases. Measure phrases are count nouns. We have *shu ri* 数日 'a number of days',[7] *shu yue* 数月 'a number of months',[8] *shu nian* 数年 'a number of years'[9] or *shu ren* 数仞 'a number of ren-lengths',[10] *shu chi* 数尺 'a number of feet'.[11] However we also have the common *shu hang* 数行 'a number of rows (of tears)',[12] *shu ren* 数人 'a number of people',[12] *bu guo shu ren* 不过数人 'no more than a few people',[13] *ci shu zi* 此数字 'these several words',[14] *zhi shu wu* 之数物 'these several things',[15] *zhi shu ti* 这数体 'these several limbs',[16] *shu gui shen* 数鬼神 'the several ghosts and spirits',[17] *shu bai ren* 数百人 'several hundreds of people',[18] *ci shu jie* 此数节 'these several accomplishments',[19] *shi shu guo* 是数国 'these several states',[20] *shi shu ju* 是数俱 'these several tools',[21] *shu kou zhi chia* 数口之家 'a home of a number of persons',[22] *shu shi* 数世 'a number of generations'.[23]

Huan 患 'disaster' turns out to be a count noun because we have *ci shu huan* 此数患 'these several disasters', but we do also have *qi huan* 七患 'seven kinds of disastrous behaviour'[24]. *Huan* is used both generically, and as a count noun.

Some nouns are used both as mass nouns and as count nouns. Thus we have *shu jin* 数金 'a number of units of money'[25] in spite of the fact that *jin* is also often used as a mass noun meaning 'metal'. This is simply a case of lexical ambiguity.

None of the nouns that can be counted by *shu* can also be counted with itemizing classifiers. *Che* 车 'cart' is sometimes used as a classifier indicating a container-measure: 'a cart-load'. As a count noun meaning 'cart' it can in turn be counted with *shu: de che shu sheng* 得车数乘

GET CART A-NUMBER-OF ITEMS 'get a number of carts'.[26] The measure *sheng* is frequent and always comes after (not before) *che*.[27] We can also count them like ordinary count nouns with an itemizing classifier: *ge che san bai liang* 革 车 三 百 两 WAR-CHARIOTS THREE HUNDRED VEHICU-LAR-ITEMS 'three hundred war chariots',[28] not: *san bai liang ge che* 三 白 两 革 车 . One might at first sight suspect that the complexity of the phrase may be a motive for the choice of this construction. But we regularly have *che yi sheng* 车 一 乘 VEHICLE ONE VEHICULAR-ITEM 'one chariot',[29] *yi che shi sheng zhi Qin* 以 车 十 乘 之 秦 WITH VEHICLE TEN VEHICULAR-ITEM GO-TO QIN 'go to Qin with ten chariots'.[30]

Some count nouns are naturally counted in pairs, for example *ge lü wu liang* 葛 履 五 两 FIVE PAIR GE-SHOE 'five pairs of dolichos shoes'.[31] Others are counted in fours: *xi ma qian si* 系 马 千 驷 TIE HORSE 1000 QUADRUPLETS 'one thousand teams of four horses'.[32]

With count nouns like *ma* we find a construction like *ma san pi* 马 三 匹 HORSE THREE ITEMS 'three horses'[33] but never *san pi ma* 三 匹 马 THREE ITEM HORSE. We have *qi wan pi* 骑 万 匹 CAVALRY-MAN TEN-THOUSAND ITEM 'ten thousand cavalrymen'[34] but never TEN-THOUSAND ITEM CAVALRYMAN. We have *ge zhong er si* 歌 钟 二 肆 MUSICAL BELL TWO SET-ITEM 'two sets of musical bells',[35] but never TWO SET-ITEM MUSICAL-BELL.[36] We have common constructions like *you ma qian si* 有 马 千 驷 HAVE HORSE 1000 QUADRUPLETS 'have one thousand teams of four horses each',[37] *you ma er shi sheng* 有 马 二 十 乘 HAVE HORSE TWICE TEN CARRIAGE(-TEAM) 'had twenty carriage-teams of horses'.[38] When count nouns are counted by itemizing (or set-identifying) classifiers, the number phrase always comes after the main noun. I have found dozens of examples of this, and not a single one where the itemizing classifier comes before the main noun.

Container classifiers like *bei* 杯 'cup', on the other hand, can freely occur in front of the main noun, as in *yi bei shui* 一 杯 水 ONE CUP WATER 'one cup of water', as we shall see below.

The count noun *ren* 'man, person, individual' may serve as an itemizing classifier, as when 'Shun had five ministers' is expressed by Confucius as *Shun you chen wu ren* 舜 有 臣 五 人 SHUN HAD MINISTER THREE INDIVIDUAL.[39] (Compare *you ma yi pi* 有 马 一 匹 HAVE HORSE ONE PIECE 'he had one horse'.[40]) Cases of this sort where *ren* may be construed as an itemizing classifier for humans are very common, and the number phrase always comes after the main noun, e.g. *yong shi yi ren* 勇 士 一 人 VALIANT KNIGHT ONE INDIVIDUAL 'one courageous knight',[41] *mei qie er shi ren* 美 妾 二 十 人 BEAUTIFUL CONCUBINE TWENTY INDIVIDUAL 'twenty beautiful concubines',[42] *you qie er ren* 有 妾 二 人 HAVE CONCUBINE TWO INDIVIDUAL 'he had two concubines',[43] *you zi san ren* 有 子 三 人 HAVE SON THREE INDIVIDUAL 'have three sons'.[44] We also have slightly more complex structures like this: *cong li wu bai ren yi shang* 从 吏 五 百 人 以 上 ATTENDANT OFFICIAL FIVE HUNDRED ABOVE 'more than five hundred attendant officials'.[45] In the newly discovered law texts of the third century B.C.E. we read *nü zi yi ren dang nan zi yi ren* 女 子 一 人 当 男 子 一 人 WOMAN ONE PERSON CORRESPOND-TO MAN ONE PERSON 'one woman is reckoned as equivalent to one man'.[46] (Note the suffix *zi* 子 here, which would seem to be limited to count nouns as it spreads in the language.) The point about *ren* 'man' being used as a classifier is particularly useful in our context, since it is so common and **always** comes **after** the noun counted.

Not all count nouns are countable by classifiers: for example the noun *ren* 'man, individual' itself is very often counted, but never with a classifier, and neither is *sheng* 乘 'carriage', *bu* 步 'pace' or any of the nouns obviously referring to measures, quantities or units of any kind. We have the count noun *yan* 言 'word, sentence'[47] which is never counted with a classifier, versus the more general *yu* 语 'talk', which is rarely, if at all, counted. There is ample scope for further subcategorisation of Classical Chinese count nouns. For our present purposes the present rough first orientation must suffice.

Generic Nouns

Consider the following pairs of Classical Chinese words:

1. *niao* 鸟 (count noun) 'bird' versus *chu* 畜 (generic noun) 'domestic animal'

2. *wang* 王 (count noun) 'king' versus *sheng* 牲 (generic noun) 'domestic animal'

3. ren 人 (count noun) 'man' versus *min* 民 (generic noun) 'common people'[48]

Unlike count nouns, generic nouns are never modified by *shu* 数 'a number of'. Like count nouns, but unlike mass nouns, generic nouns can be modified by *qun* 群 'the whole flock/crowd/lot of', *zhu* 诸 'the various', *zhong* 众 'all the many', *wan* 万 'the ten thousand, i.e. all the various', *bai* 'the one hundred, i.e. all the' and so on. We have *zhong min* 众 民 'the many people',[49] *shu min* 庶 民 'the numerous people',[50] and *wan min* 万 民 'the ten thousand people (never: ten thousand common individuals)',[51] *zhao min* 兆 民 'the innumerable people'.[52] Generic nouns are never counted with classifiers in the manner of mass nouns with container classifiers (*yi bei shui* 'one cup of water')[53] or in the manner of count nouns with itemizing classifiers (*ma san pi* 'three horses').[54] They thus constitute a proper subcategory of nouns in their own right.

The semantics of counting is different in generic nouns and in count nouns. *Ci liu ren zhe* 此 六 人 者 means 'these six individuals (or people)',[55] whereas a little further on in the same text *ci liu min zhe* 此 六 民 者 means 'these six kinds of people'.[56] *Wu min* 五 民, again, are 'five kinds of people'[57] and certainly not five individuals of lower rank. *Si min* 四 民 are explained as 'the four categories of people'.[58] *Yi min* 一 民 is mostly a verb-object phrase meaning 'unify the people'. When *yi min* is nominal it means 'one population' or 'the whole population'.[59] This is what the phrase means in Jia Yi, *Xin Shu*.[60] The standard expression for 'one commoner' is not *yi min* but *yi fu* 一 夫.[61]

Yi ren, on the other hand, means 'one person'.[62] *Ren* 'individuals' are very often counted, and as far as I can see they are never counted generically as so-and-so many 'kinds of persons'. On the other hand I seem to be unable to find *min* 'commoner' ever counted as such, except by unspecific numbers such as *wan* 'the ten thousand'.[63]

Consider this passage from *Zuo zhuan*:

One looks after the six kinds of domestic animals (*liu chu* 六 畜) (**not**: 'six beasts'), the five kinds of hunting animals (*wu sheng* 五 牲) (**not**: 'five hunting beasts'), the three sacrificial animals (*san xi* 三 牺)

(**not**: 'three individual sacrificial beasts') in order to maintain the five kinds of taste (*wu wei* 五 味) (**not**: 'five individual dishes').

One looks after the nine kinds official patterns (*jiu wen* 九 文)[64] (**not**: 'nine individual badges'), the six colourings (*liu cai* 六 采) (**not**: 'six individual patches of colour'), the six kinds of red and white insignia *liu zhang* 六 章 (**not**: 'six individual insignia') in order to maintain the (proper use of) the five colours (*wu se* 五 色) (**not**: 'five individual patches of colour').

One looks after the nine kinds of songs (*jiu ge* 九 哥), the eight airs (*ba feng* 八 风), the seven tonalities (*qi yin* 七 音) and the six kinds of pitch-pipes (*liu lu* 六 律) in order to maintain the five kinds of musical sounds (*wu sheng* 五 声).[65]

Liu wang must mean 'six kings', and *liu ma* will normally mean 'six horses', whereas *wu sheng* must mean '(the) five kinds of domestic animals' and *liu chu* must mean 'six kinds of domestic animals'.[66] The *liu zhi* 六 志 are, according to the oldest commentary, 'the six passions', love, hate, joy, anger, grief and pleasure.[67] They are **not** 'six individual fits of passion.'

Zheng Xuan (127–200 C.E.) defines *jiu Yi* 九 夷 of *Lunyu* 9.14 not as nine individual barbarians but as *dong fang zhi I, you jiu zhong* 东 方 之 夷 有 九 种 'the I-barbarians of the East of which there are nine kinds'. Similarly *wu Di* 五 狄 has to mean 'the five **kinds of** Di barbarians', just as *si Yi* 四 夷 in *Mengzi* 1A7 are 'the four **kinds of** I barbarians', since *di* 'Di barbarian' and *Yi* 'Yi barbarian' are generic nouns.

As for the state of the Nine (kinds of) Yi-barbarians (*jiu Yi zhi guo*)[68] they were positioned outside the Eastern Gate. . . . As for the states of the Eight (kinds of) Man-barbarians (*ba Man zhi guo*) they were positioned outside the Southern Gate. . . . As for the states of the Six (kinds of) Rong-barbarians (*liu Rong zhi guo*) they were oppositioned outside the Western Gate. . . . As for the states of the Five (kinds of) Di-barbarians (*wu Di zhi guo*), they were positioned outside the Northern Gates.[69]

Ren 'man', *min* 'common people', as well as *Di*, all refer to humans. But these words refer to humans in radically different ways. *Min* and *Di* are generic nouns which are counted only generically, not by individuals.

Ren is an ordinary count noun. The distinction between count nouns and generic nouns in Classical Chinese deserves to be studied in more detail.

For example, we need to investigate whether *wan wu* really are, as I suspect, 'the ten thousand kinds of things', or whether we were right all the time taking it to mean 'the ten thousand individual things'. For example *er wu* in the *Zuo zhuan* seems to mean 'two kinds of things',[70] and the crucial question is whether *wu* are ever counted as in *(ci) wu wu* 此 五 物 '(these) five individual things'. My intuition is that one would use *zhe* 者 instead of *wu* in those instances. But this intuition has to be tested against the facts.

Mass Nouns

Compare the following pairs:

1. *dan* 箪 (count noun) 'basket' versus *rou* 肉 (mass noun) 'meat'
2. *shu* 树 (count noun) 'tree' versus *xin* 薪 (mass noun) 'firewood'
3. *fu* 斧 (count noun) 'axe' versus *tie* 铁 (mass noun) 'iron'

With mass nouns like *shui* we regularly find container classifiers which are designations of containers: *yi bei shui* ONE CUP WATER 'one cup of water',[71] *yi piao yin* 一 瓢 饮 ONE LADLE DRINK 'one ladleful of drink',[72] *yi hu jiu* 一 壶 酒 ONE POT WINE 'one pot of wine',[73] *yi dan shi* 一 箪 食 ONE BASKET FOOD 'one basketful of food',[74] *yi qie jin* 一 箧 锦 ONE BOX BROCADE 'one box of brocade',[75] *yi che xin* 一 车 薪 ONE CART FIREWOOD 'one cart-load of firewood'.[76] We also find other measuring but not itemizing classifiers: *yi gu tie* 一 鼓 铁 ONE KU-MEASURE OF IRON 'one *ku* of iron',[77] *san zhong shi shu xin* 三 钟 十 束 薪 THREE BELL TEN BUNDLE FIREWOOD 'three bells and ten bundle of firewood',[78] *yi bing gan* 一 秉 秆 ONE HANDFUL STRAW 'one handful of straw'.[79]

We have passages like this:

> He takes one plate of meat (*yi dou rou* 一 豆 肉]) and feeds the knights with the rest.[80]

If you taste one piece of meat (*yi luan rou* 一 脔 肉)) you know the taste of the whole pot and the flavour of the whole tripod.[81]

Shu Guyang took a beaker of wine (*yi shang jiu* 一 觞 酒) and offered it up.[82]

There may be no explicit number in this sort of construction:

If you leave goblets of wine and platters of meat (*zhi jiu dou rou* 卮 酒 豆 肉) in the inner court . . .[83]

Some mass nouns frequently occur with fixed numbers, the most well-known being *wu gu* 五 穀 'five **kinds of** grain'. *Yi gu* 一 穀 means 'one kind of (**not**: kernel of) grain'.[84] *San jiu* 三 酒 means 'three kinds (**not**: bottles or measures) of wine',[85] *si yin* 四 饮 means 'four kinds of drinkables' (**not**: 'four individual portions of drink',[86] *wu rou* 五 肉 'the five kinds (**not**: portions) of flesh',[87] *wu du* 五 毒 means 'five kinds (**not**: doses) of poison',[88] *wu qi* 五 气 'the five kinds (**not**: portions) of ether',[89] *liu qi* 六 气 are 'the six kinds (**not**: portions) of ether.[90]

It is perfectly true that *qi* 气 illustrates very well the usefulness of the mass noun analysis. But this is because *qi*, in sharp and clear contrast to the count noun *ma* 马 is not a count noun. The exact classification of *qi* remains a problem to be investigated.

We conclude that there is a reasonably clear grammatical distinction in Classical Chinese between count nouns, generic nouns, and mass nouns. One may also try to define a fourth category of abstract nouns. It remains entirely unclear in what sense *ma* 'horse' can be classified as a mass noun (like *shi* 'food'), although in point of fact I have come upon a single isolated and late instance where *ma* is indeed used generically.[91]

The Problem of the Plural

In English, as in many other languages, the opposition mass noun versus count noun affects the semantics of the plural. 'Horse', unlike 'tea', is a count noun in English. 'Horses' refers to several **individual** horses. 'Teas' is much rarer and would refer to several **kinds of** tea. This difference is essential.

The post-Classical rise of Chinese plural morphemes (or suffixes) roughly coincides with the emergence of the pre-nominal itemizing classifiers like *pi* as in *san pi ma* THREE ITEM HORSE 'three horses'.[92]

> When Wang Zishen was a few years old, he was once watching his father's pupils (*zhu men sheng* 诸 门 生) play . . .
>
> The pupils (*men sheng bei* 门 生 辈), not showing any respect for him as a small child, said to him: . . .[93]
>
> "My little boys (i.e. his nephew, Hsüan, and his younger brother, Shi) have inflicted a crushing defeat on the invader (*xiao er bei da po zei* 小 儿 辈 打 破 贼)."[94]

Such use of plural suffixes seems uncomfortable for a mass noun analysis of the nouns so modified. For if *men sheng* 门 生 'student' is a mass noun meaning 'student-kind', its plural form (*men sheng pei* 门 生 辈) should presumably come to mean 'student-kinds', 'kinds of students'. Exactly similar observations apply to *xiao er* 小 儿 'little boy'.

Parts and Wholes

A part-whole interpretation of the notion *ma* 'horse' would seem to be doomed to failure because it either has to introduce an anachronistic mathematical construct (the concept of one spatio-temporally discontinuous object, the horsey mass), or because there is no whole and therefore no horsey part. For the notion of a part does not seem to make sense without that of a whole. It is of the essence of a part to be a part of a whole.

A comparison with English will bring out our point. Compare the mass noun *luggage* or the mass noun *tea*. When we use the mass noun *luggage*, we are not thereby explicitly or implicitly committed in any way to an ontology of some giant luggage-like mass-like whole consisting of all manner of luggage past, present, and future as proper parts.

If one asks "Please make me a cup of tea" (in Chinese or in English), one is not committed to an ontology of a discontinuous sea of tea scattered through space and time, of which one wishes to obtain a certain part. A cup of tea may properly only be called a part of that mass of tea which is in the tea pot, although logicians like Lesniewski would have us think of both the cup of tea and the pot of tea (as well as the teacups and the teapots) as a proper part of some very abstract object consisting of all manner of tea (or teacups and teapots) past, present, and future. On the other hand, when one is asking for a cup of tea, one is simply contemplating the **possibility** of some more tea being brought into existence for one's benefit. In no sense is one asking for something conceived as actually existing in an over-arching time-space universe. One imagines that this cup of tea may never come into existence, but one is presumably hoping that it will.

If we completely give up the notion of a horsey whole and of horsey parts, and if we simply cling to the central idea that the Chinese always thought of horses as a 'stuff-kind', (and presumably of vegetation rather than of plants, of offspring rather than of children), then such an account is directly refuted by the above preliminary survey of the neat grammatical contrasts between count nouns, generic nouns, and mass nouns which shows that the Chinese did make a reasonably clear overt grammatical difference between names of kinds of stuff, names of kinds of objects, and names of individual objects.

The objection that the distinction between mass nouns and other nouns is not always clear in Classical Chinese for all nouns, and that there are many ambiguous cases, carries no weight at all. It applies with equal force to languages like English where the division between count nouns and noncount nouns is recognized as grammatically basic. Compare the use of *analysis* in the following dialogue:

"Do you like this analysis?"
"No, I don't like analysis."[95]

The observation that the distinction between mass nouns, generic nouns, and count nouns may not be so clearly defined in pre-Classical Chinese or in post-Classical Chinese (the language before 600 B.C.E. or after 150 B.C.E.) goes to show that here as elsewhere the Chinese language underwent important changes in its history. It does not affect the present argument.

On the other hand nothing of what I have said directly affects the possibility of interpreting the construction *bai ma* as a whole consisting of one part 'white' and another part 'horse' which I take to be explicitly advocated by Gongsun Long. The aggregate of 'white' and 'horse' is taken by Gongsun Long not to be 'horse'. If we detach Graham's interpretation from the untenable mass noun hypothesis we can still attribute to Gongsun Long the view that the aggregate whole (*bai ma*) is not (identical with) its constituent part (*ma*).

The crucial point that then remains is that *bai* and *ma* constitute parts of very different types and that the relation between these is not a symmetrical relation. The historically plausible part-whole analysis of the White Horse Dialogue must be detached from the historically implausible and grammatically quite wrong-headed mass noun hypothesis.

In any case, however we are to understand the White Horse Dialogue, if Gongsun Long's aim was to construct a logically stimulating intellectual teaser, we can all cheerfully agree that he has succeeded.

NOTES

1. W. V. O. Quine, *Word and Object* (Cambridge, Mass.: MIT Press, 1969 [first ed. 1960]), p. 52.

2. Chad Hansen, *Language and Logic in Ancient China* (Ann Arbor: The University of Michigan Press, 1983), p. 35. Hansen does acknowledge his debt to Quine.

3. A. C. Graham, *Studies in Chinese Philosophy and Philosophical Literature*, (Singapore: Institute of East Asian Philosophies, 1986), p. 196.

4. A. C. Graham, *Studies . . .*, p. 199.

5. A. C. Graham, *Studies . . .*, p. 197.

6. I disregard the meaning 'river' for *shui*.

7. *Hanfeizi* (Peking: Zhonghuashuju, 1983), 30.49.2.

8. *Hanfeizi*, 32.57.12.

9. *Lunyu*, ed. D. C. Lau, *Confucius, The Analects* (Hong Kong: Chinese University Press, 1983), 7.17.

10. *Lunyu*, 19.23.

11. *Mengzi*, ed. D. C. Lau, *Mencius* (Hong Kong: Chinese University Press, 1984), 7B34.

12. *Mengzi*, 2B2. Cf. *Zuo zhuan* Duke Zhao 8, ed. J. Legge *The Chinese Classics* (Hong Kong: Hong Kong University Press, 1961), p. 621, line 5.

13. *Zuo zhuan*, Duke Ai 12, ed. Legge, p. 836, line 10.

14. *Zhuangzi* (ed. Harvard Yenching Institute Index Series), 8.21.

15. *Zhuangzi*, 23.14.

16. *Laozi jiaben juan hou gu yishu shiwen*, p. 19b, bamboo strip no. 318.

17. *Mozi* (ed. Harvard Yenching Institute Index Series), 31.58, 31.73, 31.60.

18. *Hanfeizi*, 30.39.5.

19. *Xunzi* (ed. Harvard Yenching Institute Index Series) 7.9, ed. Liang Qixiong (Taibei: Commercial Press, 1973), p. 69.

20. *Xunzi*, 15.36.

21. *Xunzi*, 16.67.

22. *Mengzi*, 1A3.

23. *Zuo zhuan*, Duke Xiang 31; Duke Xi 33, ed. Legge, p. 222, line 12 et passim.

24. *Zhuangzi*, 20.38 and *Mozi* 5.1.

25. *Zhuangzi*, 1.39.

26. *Zhuangzi*, 32.23, cf. B. Watson, *The Works of Chuang-tzu* (New York: Columbia University Press, 1968), p. 356, who translates: 'four or five carriages'. *Che* 'carts' are very frequently counted with the itemizer *cheng* throughout pre-Qin literature.

27. Cf., for example, *Liji*, *Tan Gong*, ed. S. Couvreur, *Li Ki* (Ho Kien Fou: Imprimerie de la Mission Catholique, 1913), vol. 1, p. 189, for three relevant examples within one very brief passage.

28. *Mengzi*, 7B4, cf. also 3B4 and 7B34.

29. *Zuo zhuan*, Duke Cheng 18.2, cf. S. Couvreur *La chronique de la principeauté de Lou* (Paris: Cathasia, 1951), vol. 2, p. 167. Cf. also *Shuihudi Qinmu zhujian* (Peking: Wenwuchubanshe, 1978), p. 58 et passim for examples of itemized counting with postposed number phrase.

30. *Lüshi chunqiu*, 12.5, ed. Chen Qiyou (Shanghai: Xuelin Publishing Company, 1983), p. 641.

31. *Shijing*, 101.2. B. Karlgren *The Book of Odes* (Stockholm: Museum of Far Eastern Antiquities, 1950), p. 65, misconstrues this as 'the dolichos shoes were five pairs', failing to notice the rules governing the position of individual counting phrases in Classical Chinese with which we are here concerned.

32. *Mengzi*, 5A7.

33. Cf. *Zuo zhuan*, Duke Zhuang 18 for the phrase *ma san pi*. Compare also Duke Xuan 2, ed. S. Couvreur, vol. 1, p. 565, for *wen ma bai si*, again with the postposition of the classifier.

34. *Zhanguoce*, no 393, ed. Zhu Zugeng, p. 1364. I find a similar construction in *Wuzi*, ch. 6, ed. Li Shuozhi and Wang Shijin, p. 104.

35. *Zuo zhuan*, Duke Xiang 11.10, cf. S. Couvreur, vol. 2, p. 274.

36. For details see Wang Li *Hanyu shigao* (3 vols., Peking: Zhonghuashuju, 1957), vol. 2, p. 240f, as well as J. S. Cikoski, *Word Classes in Classical Chinese* (Dissertation: Yale, 1971), p. 101f.

37. *Lunyu*, 16.12.

38. *Zuo zhuan*, Duke Xiang 22, cf. J. Legge, p. 493, line 18.

39. *Lunyu*, 8.20.

40. *Shuihudi Qinmu zhujian* (Peking: Wenwuchubanshe, 1978), p. 218.

41. *Zhuangzi*, 5.11.

42. *Hanfeizi*, 34.13.32.

43. *Hanfeizi*, 22.31.2.

44. *Hanfeizi*, 35.25.5, cf. 38.7.19.

45. *Weiliaozi*, 24, ed. Zhong Zhaohua (Henan: Zhongzhoushuhuashe, 1982), p. 77.

46. *Shuihudi Qinmu zhujian*, p. 75. There are several similar instances on the preceding page.

47. Cf. *Zhanguoce*, ed. Zhu Zugeng (Yangzhou: Jiangsu guji Publishing Company, 1985), p. 475 where *san yan* means 'three words'. Sima Qian speaks of the *Daodejing* consisting of *wu qian yan* 'five thousand characters' (*Shi Ji*, ch. 63, ed. Takigawa [Peking, Zhonghuashuju, 1967], p. 6, cf. also ibid, p. 16). *Yanzi chunqiu*, 6.16, ed. Wu Zeyu (Peking: Zhonghuashuju, 1982), p. 407, uses *san yen* to mean 'three sentences', similarly for *Hanshi waizhuan*, 2.9, ed. Xu Weiyu (Peking: Zhonghuashuju, 1980), p. 41.

48. Note that *min* is not a collective noun for a certain people: *fan min* 凡 民 (*Mengzi*, 7A10) means 'vulgar people', not 'a common people'.

49. *Mengzi*, 7A2.

50. *Mengzi*, 1A2 et passim.

51. *Guo Yu* (Taibei: World Book Company, 1961), p. 282, *Hanfeizi*, 8.4.22.

52. *Guo Yu*, p. 405.

53. This construction will be discussed below under the heading, "Mass Nouns".

54. The apparent counterexample *Zuo zhuan* Duke Min 2.7 (ed. Yang Bojun, p. 267, line 1) turns out to be spurious. Cf. also S. Couvreur, vol. 1, p. 221.

55. *Hanfeizi*, 44.2.7 and 44.4.2. We have *ci er ren* 此 二 人 'these two individuals' (*Hanfeizi* 12.5.4), *ci san ren* 'these three individuals' (*Hanfeizi*, 14.7.72).

56. *Hanfeizi*, 46.1.19 and ibid. 46.1.39.

57. *Shangjunshu*, ch. 6, ed. Gao Heng (Zhonghuashuju, 1974), p. 66.

58. *Guoyu*, p. 161, cf. also *Shujing*, ed. J. Legge, *Chinese Classics*, vol. 3, p. 530.

59. *Guanzi*, ed. Dai Wang, vol. 2, p. 98, line 3, and *Mengzi*, 2A1. Note that in *Mengzi yi min* is quantified by *mo bu* and can therefore not be taken to mean 'one humble person'. James Legge, *Chinese Classics*, p. 518, construes this grammatically correctly: "There was not one of all the people who was not his subject".

60. Ch. *Xiu zheng, shang*, ed. Qi Yuzhang (Taibei: Privately published, 1974), p. 1044, but in *Shuoyuan* 1.6, ed. Zhao Shanyi (Shanghai: Huadongshifandaxue chubanshe, 1985), p. 4, ed. Xiang Zonglu (Peking: Zhonghuashuju, 1987), p. 5, we have an early instance of *yi min* meaning 'a single commoner', followed by a strictly parallel *yi ren* 'one person'. It would be interesting to investigate whether and when this usage became current.

61. *Zuo zhuan*, Duke Xi, 15.5, ed. Yang Bojun (Peking: Zhonghuashuju, 1985), p. 355 et passim.

62. Cf. e.g. *Hanfeizi*, 8.7.30 and 15.1.23, 20.20.3. (It can also refer to the emperor.)

63. The case of *chen* (count noun) 'minister' versus *li* (generic noun) 'official' is especially interesting and puzzling. *Ci wu chen zhe* means 'these five ministers' (*Zhanguoce*, ed. Zhu Zugeng, p. 770), whereas *wu li* 五 吏 means 'five kinds of officials'. (*Zuo zhuan*, Duke Hsiang, 25) However, I have found one isolated instance where in fact *li* is used as a count noun. In *Lüshi chunqiu*, 18.8, we find two officials first mentioned as *li er ren* OFFICIALS TWO MEN, and then in the end we hear that *er li* 'the two officials' made a report. One needs to study whether *li* 吏 is really ambiguous between a generic noun and a count noun reading, or whether this instance is just a stray case motivated by the special context. In any case *wu chen* 五 臣 apparently never has that generic reading.

64. The dragon pattern, the mountain pattern, the flower and insect pattern, the fire pattern, and the tiger and monkey pattern, according to Yang Bojun.

65. *Zuo zhuan*, Duke Zhao, 25, ed. Yang Bojun, p. 1457, cf. S. Couvreur, vol. 3, p. 380f, J. Legge, p. 708.

66. *Hanfeizi*, 37.13.45. Cf. also *wu sheng* 'the five domestic animals' (*Hanfeizi* 31.13.39).

67. *Zuo zhuan*, Duke Zhao, 25, ed. Yang Bojun, p. 1458, cf. S. Couvreur, vol. 3, p. 382f.

68. Cf. *Hanfeizi*, 22.25.7.

69. *Liji*, ed. S. Couvreur, vol. 1, p. 725ff.

70. Duke Zhao, 25, ed. S. Couvreur, vol. 3, p. 381.

71. *Mengzi*, 6A18. Note that in *si shui* 'the four rivers' we have a different lexical meaning of *shui*.

72. *Lunyu*, 6.11.

73. *Guoyu* (Shanghai: Guji Publishing Company, 1978), p. 635. In the same context we also find *er hu jiu* 'two pots of wine'.

74. *Lunyu*, 6.11.

75. *Zuo zhuan*, Duke Zhao, 13, cf. S. Couvreur, vol. 3, p. 229.

76. *Mengzi*, 6A18. For further examples see J. S. Cikoski, *Classical Chinese Word Classes* (Dissertation: Yale, 1971), p. 101ff.

77. *Zuo zhuan*, Duke Zhao, 29 fu 5, cf. S. Couvreur, vol. 3, p. 456.

78. *Zhuangzi*, 4.85.

79. *Zuo zhuan*, Duke Zhao, 27.4.

80. *Hanfeizi*, 34.7.24, cf. W. K. Liao, vol. 2, p. 90.

81. *Lüshi chunqiu*, 15.8, ed. Chen Qiyou, p. 935.

82. *Hanfeizi*, 10.2.7.

83. *Hanfeizi*, 34.29.3, cf. W. K. Liao *Hanfeizi. Works from the Chinese* (London: Probsthain, 1937 and 1959), vol. 2, p. 113. Cf. also *Zuo zhuan* Duke Ai 7.4 *shu jin* 與 薪 'bundles of brocade', *Mengzi*, 1A7, *yu xin* 'a cartload's worth of firewood'. We note here an isolated instance in the grammatically very idiosyncratic *Gong Yang* commentary (ed. Harvard Yenching Institute Index Series) Duke Xi, 33: *pi ma zhi lun wu fan zhe* 匹 马 只 轮 无 返 者 'not a single horse or a single wheel returned'.

84. *Guanzi*, ed. Dai Wang, vol. 3, p. 91. Cf. also *Guliangzhuan*, Duke Xiang (ed. Harvard Yenching Institute Index Series), 24.13, where *gu* ☐ is counted by kinds.

85. *Zhouli*, ch. 2, ed. Lin Yin (Taibei: Commercial Press, 1974), p. 49.

86. *Zhouli*, ch. 2, p. 49.

87. *Guanzi*, ed. Dai Wang (Basic Sinological Series), vol. 2, p. 75, line 8.

88. *Zhouli*, ch. 2, ed. Lin Yin, p. 47.

89. *Zhouli*, ch. 2, ed. Lin Yin, p. 46.

90. *Zuo zhuan*, Duke Zhao, 1, defines these. Cf. also *Guoyu*, ed. World Book Company, p. 96, *Zhuangzi*, 1.21, 11.46, 11.47, *Guanzi*, ed. Dai Wang, vol. 2, p. 16.

91. *Zhouli*, ed. Lin Yin, p. 339.

92. If such classifiers had been obligatory or at least common in Classical Chinese, the interpretaion of Chinese count nouns as mass nouns might at least have had some initial plausibility.

93. *Shishuo xinyu*, 5.59, ed. Yang Yong (Hong Kong: Dazhongshuju, 1970), p. 259, cf. R. Mather, *A New Account of Tales of the World* (Minneapolis: University of Minnesota Press, 1976), p. 176.

94. *Shishuo xinyu*, 6.35, ed. Yang Yong, p. 286, cf. R. Mather, p. 192.

95. Cf. R. Quirk et al. *A Comprehensive Grammar of the English Language* (London: Longman, 1985), section 5.4, *Nouns with dual class membership*, p. 247.

Substance, Process, Phase: *Wuxing* 五 行 in the *Huainanzi*

John S. Major

Some years ago I proposed that the old standard translation for *wuxing*, 'five elements', be replaced by 'five phases'.[1] That suggestion has engendered a good deal of subsequent comment; the outcome to date is that many, but by no means all, scholars in the field of early Chinese studies have adopted the new terminology.

The most penetrating analysis of the terminology of fives in early Chinese thought has been that of Angus Graham, who quite rightly has pointed out that the translation 'five phases' is appropriate for texts from the early Han onwards, but not for those from an earlier period.[2] The cosmology of the *Zuozhuan* speaks of the *wucai*, 'five materials'. Zou Yan uses the phrase *wude*, 'five powers'. The confusing early usage of the phrase *wuxing* in Mencius refers to five modes of human conduct, not to the familiar list of wood, fire, etc. Only with the cosmology of the late third–early second century B.C.E., fully developed in the *Huainanzi*, does *wuxing* denote the 'five phases', and it is worth remembering as well that HNT continues to employ *wucai*, *wude*, and other categories of fives that were found in the earlier texts mentioned.

Here I should like to reiterate my principal objection to the term 'five elements', which was that (leaving aside all etymological questions about the original meaning of *elementum*, and so on) in the common parlance of modern times, 'elements' seems to connote 'ingredients', irreducible substances from which all other things are compounded. Nowhere, in my reading, have I found any hint that the early Chinese thought of wood, fire, earth, metal, and water in such terms. Even as *wucai*, the five are paradigmatic, not constituent, materials.

For us, elements are such that things can be made of them; sulphuric acid is made of the elements hydrogen, oxygen, and sulphur in the ratio H_2SO_4; nowhere is there a suggestion in early Chinese texts that coral, say, might be made of four parts earth, one part metal, and one part wood. Or again: there is no suggestion in early Chinese proto-science that, for example, the liver is made of wood, although it is correlated with the *xing* wood. It is made of flesh, though that flesh, by virtue of its function (and perhaps its location, but *not* its substance), interacts resonantly with all other things in the category wood. It remains flesh, and is not substantially different from the flesh of a kidney (which is correlated with water, but not made of water). So what is flesh made of? What is anything made of?

Although the *wuxing* are by no means equivalent to chemical elements, nevertheless my suggestion of the term 'phase' was rooted in modern chemistry. Phases, in chemical terms, are different states of the same substance: ice, water, and vapor are phases of H_2O; graphite and diamond are phases of carbon. Phase transformations take place under specific, and predictable, circumstances. Just so, the *wuxing* are different states of an underlying cosmological unity; phase transformations, as from wood to fire, take place under specific, and predictable, circumstances.

The observation that the earliest cosmological category of five in Chinese literature is *wucai*, 'five materials', raises a quite literally fundamental question for early Chinese cosmology: What is substance? What are things made of? An answer to this question emerges from a careful reading of the beginning of HNT 3, which Graham has called "the most developed cosmogony in early Chinese literature".[3] Quite simply, things—all things—are made of *qi*.

> When Heaven and Earth were yet unformed, all was ascending and flying, diving and delving. Thus it was called the Grand Inception. The Tao began in the nebulous void. The nebulous void produced spacetime; spacetime produced *qi*. *Qi* had a boundary [lit. a 'shoreline']. That which was pure and bright spread out to form Heaven; the heavy and turbid congealed to form Earth. It is easy for that which is pure

and subtle to coalesce, but difficult for the heavy and turbid to congeal. Therefore Heaven was completed first, and Earth established afterwards.[4]

Cosmogonically, it is interesting to note that *qi* itself is a product of the universe itself—spacetime—and that *qi* gives spacetime its physical reality. *Qi* has a 'shoreline', and for the first time in the evolution of the cosmos, a distinction can be made between 'there' and 'not there'. *Qi* itself differentiates into the ethereal and the mundane; all things in the sub-celestial world are made of 'heavy, turbid' *qi*. (Later, in the final stage of cosmogonic evolution, categories of things (*lei*) become differentiated out from the original *qi*; things within categories mutually interact. As a passage in HNT 4 puts it, 'All things are simulacra of their *qi*; all things respond to their own class'.[5]

It is customary, in discussions of early Chinese cosmology, to think of *qi* as an immaterial, or at least infinitely rarified, medium; the carrier of resonant action-at-a-distance among things in a category of being, say, or (in a translation often used by Nathan Sivin) the 'specific activity' of a substance. But HNT 3 is much more direct in its import: *Qi* can congeal to make things.[6] As the term is used in the *Huainanzi*'s cosmogony, *qi* must mean something like 'primordial matter'.

If substance is *qi*, what is the *process* by which undifferentiated turbid *qi* becomes the myriad things? And how does it happen that *qi* exists in five distinct phases, which undergo transformations in regular and predictable ways? Other passages in HNT 3 and 4 provide, with careful study, a fairly complete set of answers.

First, the author of HNT 3 explains that the differentiation of the phenomenal world is mediated through yin-yang and the four seasons:

> The conjoined essences of heaven and earth produced yin and yang.
> The supercessive essences of yin and yang caused the four seasons. The
> scattered essences of the four seasons created the myriad things.[7]

This, however, went on only in the subcelestial world, where *qi* was heavy and turbid, that is to say, substantial and impure. In the heavens, pure *qi* coalesced to form the heavenly bodies:

> The hot *qi* of accumulated yang produces fire; the sun is the essence of
> fiery *qi*. The cold *qi* of accumulated yin produces water; the moon is the

essence of watery *qi*. The overflow of the essences of the sun and moon made the stars and the planets. To heaven belong the sun, moon, stars, and planets; to earth belong waters and floods, dust and soil.[8]

The power of the four seasons to transform undifferentiated turbid *qi* into the myriad things may be supposed to operate in two ways. First, the seasons (themselves the product of yin and yang, as we are told) are emblematic of a quality shared by all creatures, that they contain yin and yang in different proportions. Each day of the year, throughout the four seasons, contains a different proportion of yin and yang, seen in concrete terms as the ratio of sunlight to darkness as the sun advances and recedes.[9] Second, the creation of each of the myriad things takes place over time (and the creation of the seasons transforms the universe from a timeless to a temporal world: spacetime). This is made clear in the famous alchemical passage at the end of HNT 4:

> The *qi* of balanced earth is received into the yellow heaven, which after 500 years engenders a yellow jade [realgar?]. This after 500 years engenders yellow quicksilver, which after 500 years engenders yellow metal [gold]. After 1000 years gold engenders the yellow dragon. The yellow dragon, going into hiding, engenders the yellow springs. When the dust from the yellow springs rises to become a yellow cloud, the beating together of yin and yang make thunder, their rising to a crescendo makes lightning. What has ascended then descends as a flow of water which collects in the yellow sea.[10]

And so on for the other four phases, following the general formula:
    The *qi* of X earth——Y years——> Z mineral——Y years——> Z
    quicksilver——Y years——> Z metal——1000 years——> Z
    dragon——> Z springs [etc.].
Where X is an attribute, Y is a number of years, and Z is a color.[11]

This passage refers, of course, specifically to the transformation of minerals and metals over time, but other passages in HNT 4 make it apparent that transformation through time is a common attribute of other types of matter as well.[12]

It will be immediately apparent from the passage just quoted that the transformation of matter over time occurs within the framework of the five phases. That is, if time (the four seasons, and by extension, any number of years—cycles of the four seasons) is responsible for the differentiation of turbid *qi* into the myriad things, that differentiation is structured by the fivefold phase division characteristic of all matter. The link between the four seasons, the five phases, and the fashioning of the world is made in another passage from HNT 3. It occurs near the beginning of the chapter, closely following the cosmogonic hymn that opens the chapter but separated from it by a few sections of technical description of the heavens. It is as follows:

What are the five planets?

The east is wood. Its god is Tai Hao. His assistant is Zhu Mang. He controls the compass and governs spring. His spirit is *sui xing* ['yearstar', the planet Jupiter]. His animal is the azure dragon. His note is *jue*. His days are *jia* and *yi*.

The south is fire. Its god is Yan Di. His assistant is Zhu Ming. He controls the level and governs summer. His spirit is *ying huo* [the planet Mars]. His animal is the vermilion bird. His note is *zhih*. His days are *bing* and *ding*.

The center is earth. Its god is Huang Di. His assistant is Hou Tu. He controls the (marking-) cord and regulates the four quarters. His spirit is *zhen xing* ['chronogram star', the planet Saturn]. His animal is the yellow dragon. His note is *gong*. His days are *wu* and *ji*.

The west is metal. Its god is Shao Hao. His assistant is Zhu Shou. He controls the T-square and governs autumn. His spirit is *tai bo* [the planet Venus]. His animal is the white tiger. His note is *shang*. His days are *geng* and *xin*.

The north is water. Its god is Zhuan Xu. His assistant is Xuan Ming. He controls the plumb-bob and governs winter. His spirit is *chen xing* [the planet Mercury]. His animal is the Dark Warrior. His note is *yu*. His days are *ren* and *gui*.[13]

The content of this passage may conveniently be displayed in tabular form (See table below.)

This passage is significant for the links that it posits amongst the five phases, the four seasons, and the cosmogonic process. Cosmogony is associated, morever, with the generation order of the five phases; the conquest order appears to have been the earliest to appear in philosophical speculations about orders of five, but for the author(s) of HNT, the generation order is more important.

What are the Five Planets?

East	South	Center	West	North
Wood	Fire	Earth	Metal	Water
Tai Hao	Yan Di	Huang Di	Shao Hao	Zhuan Xu
Zhu Mang	Zhu Ming	Hou Tu	Ju Shou	Xuan Ming
Compass	Level	Cord	T-square	Plumb-bob
Spring	Summer	*si fang*	Autumn	Winter
Jupiter	Mars	Saturn	Venus	Mercury
Azure	Vermilion	Yellow	White	Dark
Dragon	Bird	Dragon	Tiger	Warrior
Jue	Zhih	Gong	Shang	Yu
jia, yi	ping, ding	wu, ji	geng, xin	ren, gui

Two points deserve additional emphasis. First is that the planetary gods are depicted as fashioning deities; they all hold as emblems tools of the builder's trade. Yan Di's *heng* is often translated as 'balance-beam' or 'steelyard', but here it clearly is a level. Huang Di's cord is what we would call a chalk-line (used for setting out straight lines); East Asian carpenters employ a similar device in which a string is inked by being pulled through an ink-soaked pad held in a wooden bowl. Zhuan Xu's weight is not the weight of a steelyard, as is often thought, but rather the plumb-bob at the end of a plumb-line. The tools themselves set up a nice set of binary pairs: East–West/round–square; South–North/horizontal–vertical; the Center then functions to unify the four by being multi-directional, inscribing the crosslines that link the directional pairs.

This unifying function of the center is reiterated in the scheme that associates the directions with the seasons. The pairs of East–Spring/South–Summer/West–Autumn/North–Winter are familiar; here, however, the Center is correlated with *si-fang*, the Four Quarters, linking and unifying the others. The seasons are defined, astronomically, by the solsticial and equinoctial nodes on the ecliptic (or projected onto the celestial equator, or, in Chinese terms, located amongst the twenty-eight

Lunar Lodges) at NE, SE, SW, and NW. Lines linking those four points account for the 'squareness' of the earth within the great circle of heaven, the sides of the square thus lying in the four cardinal directions; the diagonals of the square pass through the center, which links and unifies the whole. The center thus is correlated not with any one season, but with all of them—with, more specifically, the celestial geometry that creates the seasons. There is, in other words, no cosmological incommensurability between the four of the seasons and the five of the phases. The later awkwardness of attempts to create an artificial fifth season of 'midsummer' to correspond to earth/center/yellow etc. satisfied the demands, not of cosmology, but of ritual and astrology—worship and prognostication correlated with earth had to occur sometime.[14]

In light of this, it is worth raising again the question of how wood, fire, earth, metal, and water came to be called *wuxing*. In the *Huainanzi*, it seems clear that the literal sense of the term is 'five movers' or 'five goings', that is, agents in perpetual cycles of transformation; this seems especially apt because the primary correlations of the *wuxing* are the five directions (east, south, center, west, and north), and the four seasons (plus the 'four quarters'). The *xing* are constantly moving from one directionally correlated phase to another, in a time sequence governed by the seasons.

Graham has said that the question "Why would wood or metal be called a *hsing*, 'going'" is "just another of the pseudo-problems in which a sinologist again and again finds himself trapped by later uses of words."[15] He is quite right that it is useless to wonder about the meaning of *wuxing* in pre-Han times, when up to and during the time of Zou Yan the relevant cosmological terms were, rather, *wucai* and *wude*. It is, however, not entirely idle to enquire into the reasons for the changes in terminology, and into the meaning of *wuxing* once it does become established as the preeminent term in the cosmology of fives.

As Graham points out, down to around 300 B.C.E., *wucai* means quite literally 'five materials'; wood, fire, earth, metal, and water presumably already had connotations of paradigmatic types of physical substance. For Zou Yan, *wude* referred not to the five as substances, but rather to their 'powers' or 'processes': the growing and regenerative quality of wood, the soaking and descending quality of water, and so on.[16] Coming down to the time of the *Huainanzi*, however, the emphasis shifts again to the *transformative* nature of the *wuxing*, which now are clearly phases of matter.

This is seen clearly in the attention paid by the *Huainanzi*'s author(s) to different cycles of fives, which are intended above all to predict the types of phase transformations that will take place under certain circumstances. In the *Huainanzi*'s cosmology, the attention that early writers focused on the conquest order of the five is subordinated to an attempt to understand a variety of orders—ways in which the primordial matter of *qi* evolves and is transformed into different things. Implicit in the following passage from HNT 4 is the assumption that if one can correctly assign phenomena to their correct order, their transformations can be understood and predicted.

Wood overcomes earth, earth overcomes water, water overcomes fire, fire overcomes metal, metal overcomes wood. Thus:

Grain is born in the spring and dies in the fall.

Legumes are born in the summer and die in the winter.

Wheat is born in the autumn and dies in the summer.

Herbs are born in the winter and die in midsummer.

When wood is in its prime, water is old, fire is born, metal is paralyzed, and earth is dead.

When fire is in its prime, wood is old, earth is born, water is paralyzed, and metal is dead.

When earth is in its prime, fire is old, metal is born, wood is paralyzed, and water is dead.

When metal is in its prime, earth is old, water is born, fire is paralyzed, and wood is dead.

When water is in its prime, metal is old, wood is born, earth is paralyzed, and fire is dead.

In music there are five notes, the chief of which is *gong*.

There are five colors, the chief of which is yellow.

There are five flavors, the chief of which is sweet.

For positioning there are five materials (*wucai*), the chief of which is earth.

That is why earth when refined produces wood, wood when refined produces fire, fire when refined produces clouds [metallic *qi*], clouds when refined produce water, and water when refined reverts to earth.

Sweet when refined produces sour, sour when refined produces acrid, acrid when refined produces bitter, bitter when refined produces salty, and salty when refined reverts to sweet.

Gong when changed produces *zhih*, *zhih* when changed produces *shang*, *shang* when changed produces *yu*, *yu* when changed produces *jue*, *jue* when changed produces *gong*.

Thus one uses water to pacify earth, earth to pacify fire, fire to transform metal, and metal to control wood; wood reverts to earth. The five phases regulate each other, and thus useful things are brought to completion.[17]

This section presents and describes six different orders of the five phases, which can be used to understand and predict various sorts of natural processes. The first is the familiar conquest order. The author demonstrates that natural phenomena do conform to this order by pointing to the germination and maturation of various crops. The reasoning is as follows: Grain = wood = spring; fall = metal. Metal overcomes wood, so grain sprouts in the spring and dies in the fall. And so on. The conquest order is thus applicable to cyclical phenomena, such as crops, where there is a strong implication of the extinction of the phase that is overcome. Crops germinate, mature, and die; in the next cycle one must begin again with new seeds. The applicability of this cycle to the rise and fall of dynasties was obvious to thinkers from Zou Yan onwards.

The next passage introduces the generation order, in the form of five parallel ten-character lines that create almost a mnemonic chant. The first character of each of those five lines gives the generation order in its familiar form, wood–fire–earth–metal–water, but each ten-character line forms a variant of the generation order, wood–water–fire–metal–earth, and so forth, under the headings prime–old–born–paralyzed–dead. This variant might be termed the 'life cycle' order of the phases. As Graham has pointed out, it unites the conquest and generation orders, because the phase that is in its prime generates the one that is born and conquers the one that is dead.[18]

In contrast to the conquest order, which implies the extinction of each phase at any point in the cycle and its rebirth at the same point in the next cycle (crops, dynasties), the generation order is applied to phenomena that can be described in terms of the waxing and waning of yin and yang. The generation order is thus, for example, applied to the seasons, and to their directional correlates (east–south–center–west–north).

The HNT 4 author next establishes, with four examples, that in any sequence of the five phases, the term that corresponds to earth/center is the 'chief'. Thus we have *wusheng*, 'five sounds', of which *gong* is the chief; *wuzhang*, 'five colors', of which yellow is the chief; *wubian*, 'five flavors', of which sweet is the chief; and *wucai*, 'five materials', of which earth is the chief. He then introduces three more variant phase orders, appropriate to alchemy, cooking, and music.

The alchemical order describes what happens when phases are 'refined'; the refining process produces physical changes in the substances involved. The order is earth–wood–fire–metal–water–earth. The processes appear to be approximately as follows: Earth produces wood (growth of plants out of the soil), wood produces fire (combustion), fire produces metal (clouds of metallic *qi*: smoke or vapor, perhaps especially that observed in the smelting of ores or the casting of metal), [metallic] clouds produce water (condensation or distillation), and water produces earth (precipitation of solids from a liquid). Significantly, the passage quoted earlier that describes the transformation over long periods of time of minerals from one into the other lists the five phases in precisely this 'alchemical' order.

The taste order given next is earth–wood–metal–fire–water–earth. This is a restatement of the conquest order, in the passive voice: 'is overcome by', rather than 'overcomes'. Again the alchemical term 'refined' is used, and the order is closely similar to the alchemical order just described (they differ only in that the placement of metal and fire is reversed). This order seems, however, essentially arbitrary; it would be far-fetched to see it in terms of a proto-chemistry of flavors. Perhaps the implication is that sweet goes by stages through progressively stronger tastes until it becomes its opposite, salty, which then reverts to sweet.

The next sequence given might be called the harmonic order, as it is applied explicitly to music. The order is earth–fire–metal–water–wood–earth. The usual order of the five notes is *gong–shang–jue–zhih–yu*, that is, earth–metal–wood–fire–water. That order produces a simple ascending pentatonic scale; the 'harmonic order' given here alters that to produce (leaving aside technical questions of the precise tonal values of the ancient Chinese pentatonic notes) a simple melody, approximately: fundamental——> up fifth——> down fourth——> up fifth——> down fourth——> up sixth; for example, c-g-d-a-e-c.

The final phase order given in the HNT 4 passage quoted above is unusual in that it is not strictly cyclical. Water 'pacifies' earth (irrigation), earth 'pacifies' fire (extinguishing), fire 'transforms' metal (smelting and casting), metal 'rules' wood (chopping and carving), wood 'reverts' to earth (decay; perhaps specifically composting and fertilizing). The order thus is water–earth–fire–metal–wood–earth; it is non-cyclical because earth follows water at the beginning, but follows wood at the end. Taken as individual pairs, however, all of these processes support the author's contention that "thus useful things are brought to completion".

What emerges from all of this, I think, is the remarkable complexity and sophistication of the cosmology of the *Huainanzi*. A cosmogony that explains the origin of the basic stuff of spacetime and its evolution into the myriad material forms of the sub-celestial world is elaborated into a full-fledged proto-science in which the phase transformations of various orders of the *wuxing* are used to explain, predict, and control the world around us.

NOTES

1. John S. Major, 'A Note on the Translation of Two Technical Terms in Chinese Science, *Wu hsing* and *hsiu*', *Early China* 2 (1976), 1–3.

2. A. C. Graham, *Yin-Yang and the Nature of Correlative Thinking*. Singapore: The Institute of East Asian Philosophies, Occasional Paper and Monograph Series No. 6 (1986).

3. Graham, *Yin-Yang and the Nature of Correlative Thinking*, p. 30.

4. HNT 3: lab. Here and elsewhere, citations of the *Huainanzi* are to the edition of Liu Shuya (Liu Wendian), *Huainan honglie jijie*, Shanghai: Commercial Press, 1926; reprinted, Taipei, 1969.

5. HNT 4:7b.

6. This idea is, of course, a commonplace of Neo-Confucian metaphysics; it seems surprising, however, in a text written some thirteen hundred years

earlier than the time of Zhu Xi. (We do not find in the earlier text, however, any parallel to Zhu Xi's 'Platonic' idea of *li*, an ideal form that provides a pattern for the substance of congealed *qi*.) Moreover, the roots of Neo-Confucian moral metaphysics can be seen in the HNT cosmology. Everything in the sub-celestial world is made of 'heavy, turbid' *qi*, just as the Neo-Confucians claimed; their quest for moral perfection involved the purification of one's *qi* through self-rectification and the 'investigation of things', in short, a quest for the purity of the celestial realm where (as HNT 3 tells us), everything is made of 'pure, rarified' *qi*.

7. HNT 3:1b.

8. HNT 3:1b.

9. HNT 3:12ab; see John S. Major, 'The Meaning of *Hsing-te*', in Charles Le Blanc and Susan Blader, eds., *Chinese Ideas About Nature and Society: Studies in Honour of Derk Bodde* (Hong Kong: University of Hong Kong Press, 1987).

10. HNT 4:17a–18b.

11. This formula was suggested to me by Nathan Sivin.

12. See, for example, HNT 4:16ab, where the five classes of animals (naked, hairy, feathered, scaly, armored) are seen as having evolved from archetypal ancestors via intermediate forms.

13. HNT 3:5b–6b. This text is identical to the opening passages of each of the five planetary sections of the Mawangdui text *Wuxingzhan*; it is thus dateable to the turn of the second century B.C.E.

14. Other solutions might have been adopted, but apparently never were: Earth/center could have been worshipped continually throughout the year, simultaneously with whatever phase was in season; or earth/center could have been worshipped exclusively on the equinoxes and solstices. Either might seemingly have provided a better reconciliation of cosmology and ritual, but both would have made life more difficult for astrologers—which is sufficient reason for them never to have been adopted. Both *Guanzi* 41 and HNT 3 also contain formulae for a year of five 72-day 'seasons' (with 'remainder days' at the end of each year). These would have satisfied the requirement for equal periods of rites for each of the five phases; nevertheless, they are wholly artificial in terms of the perceived natural year of four seasons, and they apparently never played an important ritual role.

15. Graham, *Yin-Yang and the Nature of Correlative Thinking*, p. 77.

16. Ibid.

17. HNT 4:11ab.

18. Graham, *Yin-Yang and the Nature of Correlative Thinking*, pp. 52–53.

Who Compiled the Chuang Tzu?

5

Harold Roth

I. Introduction

It has long been recognized that the *Chuang Tzu* is not a homogeneous text. As early as the seventh century scholars were expressing doubts about the integrity of the work,[1] and four centuries later, the famous poet and scholar Su Tung-po 蘇東坡 (1036–1101) concluded that chapters 28–31 could not have been written by the historical Chuang Chou, the man to whom the entire text had traditionally been ascribed.[2] In fact, the Southern Sung scholar Lo Mien-tao 羅勉道 (fl.ca. 1260) actually established a new twenty-six chapter edition of the *Chuang Tzu* in which he followed Su's conclusions by connecting chapters 27 and 32, and relegating chapters 28–31, and two more Lo himself doubted, 15 and 16, to a scrap bin at the end of his volumes where they remained without commentary.[3] However, despite these doubts about certain chapters many scholars have continued until quite recently to attempt to present the ideas in the text as if they contain a unified position.[4]

It is largely due to the research of Angus Graham, building on the earlier work of Kuan Feng, that we are now able to identify six basic strata and groups of authors in the three major sections of the extant thirty-three chapter recension of the *Chuang Tzu*, which consists of the *nei-p'ien* ('Inner' Chapters: 1–7), the *wai-p'ien* ('Outer' Chapters: 8–22), and the *tsa-p'ien* ('Mixed' Chapters: 23–33):[5]

1. Chapters 1–7: The writings of the man the Han historians call Chuang Chou, a contemporary of King Hui of Liang (370–319 B.C.E.) and King Hsuan of Ch'i (319–301 B.C.E.) This section contains all the major themes for which the *Chuang Tzu* has been renowned—the "free and easy wandering" of the sage grounded in the Tao, the relativity of all human experience, equanimity towards life and death, and so on. In addition, Graham has recovered fragments which he believes were originally included in this section from the 'Mixed' Chapters to which they may have been displaced when the text underwent a major revision at the hands of the commentator Kuo Hsiang (ca. 300 C.E.).

2. Chapters 8–11: Essays by an individual who was strongly influenced by the *Lao Tzu*. Kuan Feng omits the last section of chapter

11 (Harvard-Yenching Concordance lines 66–74), which he believes was displaced from the end of chapter 12. Graham, using much more detailed criteria, only includes the first part of chapter 11 (lines 1–28). He further sees the influence of the long lost School of the Tillers (*nung-chia* 農家) on these essays, which he believes were written by an anonymous author he refers to as the 'Primitivist'. Kuan dates these to the end of the Ch'in; Graham feels that they can be dated with some precision to about 205 B.C.E.

3. Chapters 12–16, 33: Kuan sees most of 12–14 (minus certain rather vaguely defined sections), and 15 and 16, which are individual integral essays, as written by early Han followers of the philosophers Sung Hsing 宋 鈃 and Yin Wen 尹 文, who were in attendance at the famous Chi-hsia Academy founded by King Hsuan of Ch'i, and who are included in the group of 'Huang-Lao' philosophers there.[6] He agrees with T'an Chieh-fu that chapter 33 (minus the final section on Hui Shih), the famous last essay in the book that presents a criticism and syncretic vision of six schools of thought, was written by Liu An, the King of Huai-nan (?180–122 B.C.E.). Graham includes the following sections of these chapters as the writings of a group of early Han eclectic Taoists he refers to as the 'Syncretists': 12/1–18, 13/1–45, 60–64, 14/1–5; also 11/66–74, and all of 15 and 33. He does not include 16 which he maintains is unlike any other section in the book.[7] The conclusions of both men point to one of the principal difficulties with chapters 12–14, that they include many sections that seem unrelated to the 'Syncretist' outlook. I will have more to say about them below.

4. Chapters 17–22: Material which often imitates the themes and style of the 'Inner' Chapters, which both scholars conclude represents the writings of later followers of Chuang Tzu. Kuan includes chapter 23 in this group.

5. Chapters 23–27, 32: A heterogeneous collection of fragments which probably originated in the other strata of the book. Graham finds some material here which belongs in the 'Inner' Chapters.

6. Chapters 28–31: These are the chapters which initially caused scholars to doubt the homogeneity of the entire work. They

represent a collection of materials from the 'Individualist' School of Yang Chu, which Graham dates to about 200 B.C.E. Kuan does not include 30 in this group, and maintains that it is the work of a philosopher named Chuang Hsing 莊 幸 that was erroneously added due to the similarity in name with Chuang Tzu.[8]

The text of the *Chuang Tzu* must therefore have been written and transmitted over about two centuries until it was compiled at some point during the first century of the Han. Because of the predominance of the traditional view of at least majority authorship by Chuang Tzu and the tendency to place him at the head of early Taoist philosophy along with the mysterious figure of Lao Tan, the reputed author of the *Lao Tzu*, the value of this text as a document for unravelling what I would like to call the 'hidden history' of early Taoist thought is just beginning to be appreciated. In this context the question of just who might have compiled the text, and when it might have been done gains added significance.

In recently completed research I have discovered what I believe is a significant textual and philosophical relationship between three essays in the supposedly 'Legalist' *Kuan Tzu*, a work associated with the state of Ch'i, whose composition, transmission, and compilation span roughly the same time period as the *Chuang Tzu*, and the supposedly 'Eclectic' *Huai-nan Tzu*, an early Han Taoist compendium of thought written under the sponsorship and direction of the above-mentioned Liu An and completed in 139 B.C.E..[9] The earliest of the *Kuan Tzu* essays, *Nei-yeh* 內 業 ('Inward Training') is a contemporary of the 'Inner' Chapters of *Chuang Tzu*, and presents the physiological basis of human psychology and self-cultivation grounded in a cosmology of the Tao. This text is unarguably the basis of the more sophisticated theories later developed in the *Huai-nan Tzu*, particularly in its seventh essay entitled *Ching-shen* 精 神 ('The Numinous Essence'). The next two essays from the *Kuan Tzu, Hsin-shu shang, hsia* 心 術 上 ， 下 ('The Techniques of the Mind', parts I and II) place these theories in the context of very Taoist-sounding advice to the ruler on how to govern effectively in keeping with the *Lao Tzu*'s principal prescription of *wu-wei* 無 為 ('Non-action'). These essays, probably completed early in the

Han, also contain very strong textual and philosophical parallels with the *Huai-nan Tzu*, and form a major part of its intellectual inheritance.

I have argued that these four works are part of the same lineage of thought, and that they very closely fit the description of the 'Taoist School' (*Tao-chia*) given by Ssu-ma T'an (d. 110 b.c.e.) in his important preface to the *Shih Chi*. It is this school that is alternately referred to by the Han historians as 'Huang-Lao'.[10] The existence of this school before the Han, and its association with the Chi-hsia Academy in Ch'i, are attested to in the *Shih Chi*, even if the attribution of texts to its philosophers and its relationship to Legalism are rather problematic.[11] Nonetheless it is this lineage of thought that first receives the label of 'Taoism', not the mystical philosophy of 'Lao-Chuang', which is virtually unknown as a distinct philosophical lineage in the Han. In fact the linking of the mystical aspects of *Lao Tzu* and *Chuang Tzu* into the category 'Lao-Chuang', which has so dominated the traditional under-standing of the early history of Taoist thought, seems instead to have been inaugurated by the Wei and Chin *hsuan-hsueh* ('Profound Learn-ing') literati.[12]

The fact that theories of the physiological basis of psychology and self-cultivation are an integral part of the Huang-Lao tradition and hence of early Taoist philosophy, and the fact that analogous theories are found later in Religious Taoism, indicates the possibility of a more tangible relationship between the two than can be discovered if one defines philosophical Taoism exclusively as Lao-Chuang.[13]

It is in the context of these theories on the nature of philosophical Taoism that the question of who compiled the *Chuang Tzu* is significant. If we are ultimately able to place this compiler in a philosophical lineage then we shall learn more about this lineage and be able to derive a more complete picture of early Taoism and its links to later forms.

There are several theories about who compiled the *Chuang Tzu* which will form the starting point for our inquiry. Kuan Feng maintains that the text was compiled by the scholars who assembled at the court of Liu An for a period of roughly three decades beginning in about 150 b.c.e.[14] He provides no justification for this conclusion, but one might infer that since he believes that the final chapter was written by Liu An that the text could not have been completed until then. Graham argues that the Syncretists were the compilers, and gives evidence that at least three of the three-word phrases that became titles in the 'Inner' Chapters can be found in the Syncretist parts of the text.[15] He also, I think, conclusively demonstrates that contrary to Kuan's opinions, the author of the last chapter shares the technical vocabulary of these other chapters and can be readily placed in the same lineage of thought, although stylistic differences indicate that it is likely that he did not write these others.[16] Therefore our search for the compiler of the *Chuang Tzu* resolves itself into the question of determining the identity of these Syncretists. We will also ask the related but distinct question of whether the author of any of the Syncretist chapters can be justifiably identified as the compiler, or if instead we must look elsewhere within a Syncretist tradition.

Kuan Feng's theory on the tradition of these chapters is that with the exception of chapter 33, they were written by the followers of Sung Hsing and Yin Wen, who are identified with Huang-Lao though in the *Shih Chi*. Graham does not further specify just who these 'eclectic Taoists' might have been, although at one point he does distinguish their outlook from the 'equally eclectic' *Huai-nan Tzu*.[17] An additional theory is provided by Benjamin Schwartz, who maintains that the Syncretists are actually members of the Huang-Lao school of Taoist thought.[18]

In the following study I will attempt to situate the Syncretist chapters in the lineage of Taoist philosophy of which the three *Kuan Tzu* essays and the *Huai-nan Tzu* form an integral part, a lineage which I believe can be labeled 'Huang-Lao'. I will do this by analysing the main elements of the philosophy of these chapters, and comparing them to the thought of the *Kuan Tzu* and *Huai-nan Tzu* material. I will end with a consideration of the question of whether the author of any of these chapters might have also been the compiler of the entire work, and speculate on a possible date for this compilation.

II. The Lineage of the Syncretists

In the Syncretist chapter 33 *T'ien hsia* ('Below in the Empire'), the author contrasts the comprehensive philosophy which he calls the *Tao-*

shu 道 術 ('Methods or Tradition of the Way') with the more limited *fang-shu* 方 術 ('Methods or Tradition of a Formula') represented by six groups of philosophers who only understood one aspect of this comprehensive Way. He includes in this group both Lao Tan and Chuang Chou, each of whom he admires for the profundity of their attainments in self-cultivation, but who were unable to derive much practical value from them. His own way is a blending of the best aspects of these and other early systems of thought, especially the Confucians and Legalists (most clearly explained in chapter 13), into a comprehensive system based in a cosmology of the Tao which is referred to as the *T'ien-ti chih tao* 天 地 之 道 , the Way of Heaven and Earth (HYC, 15/7–8; 33/84). This idea of a comprehensive Tao which embraces cosmology, psychology, and political thought is not exclusive to the Syncretist. It is found in two of the three *Kuan Tzu* essays mentioned above, as well as in the *Huai-nan Tzu* and in Ssu-ma T'an's description of the Taoist school, and is often given the same label.

The concept of *Tao-shu* is found in six places in the *Huai-nan Tzu*, and here it appears to be given a more specific meaning than it is by the Syncretists as those methods of self-cultivation conducive to creating the tranquility of mind needed to govern effectively.[19] For example we read that the Sage "inwardly cultivates the techniques of the Way and outwardly does not adorn himself with Benevolence and Rightness" (2/7b), and that he does not use these techniques to seek after fame but rather to cultivate his own person (*hsiu-shen* 修 身) so that he is able to follow the Way of Heaven (*T'ien-tao* 天 道 14/4b). Elsewhere we find the scholar T'ien Pien (a Huang-Lao teacher at Chi-hsia criticized in *Chuang Tzu* 33) teaching the King of Ch'i about the techniques of the Way and urging him to broaden his focus from the concerns of the state to the appreciation of the cosmological context in which his state exists, thus enabling him "to govern through not governing" (12/2b). It is this latter use of the idea of *Tao-shu* that approaches the Syncretist meaning of the term.

If the scope of the *Tao-shu* in the *Huai-nan Tzu* is somewhat more restricted than for the Syncretist, this is most certainly not the case in Ssu-ma T'an's description of Taoism. In fact T'an's description is so close to the spirit of the Syncretists' *Tao-shu* that one might justifiably suspect a Syncretist influence on his very choice of the term *Tao-chia* as a label for this system of thought. T'an says that methods (*shu*) of the Taoist school:

> . . . follow the general tendency of the Naturalists (Yin-yang chia), pick out the best of the Confucians and Mohists, and adopts the essentials of the Terminologists (Ming-chia) and Legalists . . .

IIA. Ssu-ma T'an's Essay on the Six Schools of Philosophy

Ssu-ma T'an's discussion of the six schools of thought presented in a colophon to the *Shih Chi* is important for a number of reasons. First, it parallels the Syncretist's examination of pre-Han thought in chapter 33 in that it examines the world of philosophy in the Han from a perspective based in a vision of the kind of comprehensive syncretic Taoism that informs these chapters in the *Chuang Tzu* and which finds some limited value in other schools of thought.[20] Second, it is one of the few sources whose date we can approximate with certainty, since we know that T'an died in 110 B.C.E. Finally, since T'an studied with a Huang-Lao teacher and clearly embraced the Taoist position as his own, we can conclude that his syncretic perspective and his description of the Taoist school are accurate reflections of the Huang-Lao tradition's self-understanding.[21] Let us examine what the tradition that first receives the name of Taoism looks like to Ssu-ma T'an:

> The Taoist school enables man's Numinous Essence (*ching-shen* 精神) to be concentrated and unified, enables him to move in unison with the Formless (*wu-hsing* 無形), and to provide adequately for the myriad things. As for its methods, it follows the general tendency of the Naturalists, picks out the best of the Confucians and Mohists, and adopts the essentials of the Terminologists and Legalists. It shifts with the times, changes in response to things, and in establishing customs and in practical applications it is nowhere unsuitable. The general drift of its teachings is simple and easy to hold onto; there is much achievement for little effort.[22]

In addition to the syncretism noted above, T'an touches on theories of government and psychology in this paragraph. Taoists provide adequately for all things (*tan-tsu wan-wu* 贍足萬物), and exhibit a flexibility in governing that enables them to respond to the transformations of things (*ying wu pien-hua* 應 物 變 化) and establish suitable customs and practical measures. This kind of flexibility is the main theme of chapter 11 of the *Huai-nan Tzu, Ch'i-su* 齊 俗 ('Placing Customs on a Par'), which applies Chuang Tzu's vision of the relativity of human experience from the perspective of the Tao in chapter 2 (*Ch'i-wu lun* 齊 物 論) to questions of social organization.[23] In addition T'an suggests techniques of self-cultivation that enable humans (in particular, the ruler) to preserve the essential energy (*ching*) of the Numen, which in the psychological theory of the *Kuan Tzu* essays and the *Huai-nan Tzu*, is the core of human consciousness, simultaneously the ground of the self and the source of metaphysical knowledge. These unexplained methods of self-cultivation (which are detailed in our earlier sources) also enable one's movements to harmonize with the Formless.

T'an proceeds to criticize the then prevalent Confucian theories of an active ruler for doing too much, and explains that it is better for him to rely on methods which relinquish strength, desire, and intellectual brilliance. The reason for this, he says, is that:

> When the Numen is overused it becomes depleted; when the body is overworked it becomes worn out. For the body and Numen to be restlessly active and to then wish to live as long as Heaven and Earth, is something that's never been heard of.[24]

A further description of Taoism is provided in a later passage:

> The Taoist school takes no action (*wu-wei*), but it also says that nothing is left undone. Its substance is easy to practice, but its words are difficult to understand. Its methods (*shu*) take Emptiness (*hsu* 虛) and Non-being (*wu* 無) as the root, and Adaptation (*yin* 因) and Compliance (*hsün-li* 循 理) as its practice. It has no set limits, no constant forms, and so is able to explore the genuine basis of things. (*neng chiu wu-chih-ch'ing* 能 究 物 之 情 . . . It blends with the Great Tao, obscure and mysterious (*hun-hun ming-ming* 混 混 冥 冥), and after illuminating the whole world it reverts to the Nameless (*fan wu-ming* 反 無 名).[25]

In this description we continue to see the blend of cosmological, psychological, and political elements established above. The basis for this philosophy is Lao-Tzu's concept of Non-action, which involves the two-fold practice of emptying the mind until one experiences Non-being, and then returning to the world and acting effortlessly through Adaptation and Compliance. This dual practice of stillness and action is characteristic of Huang-Lao philosophy. It is present in both the *Kuan Tzu* essays and the *Huai-nan Tzu*; and I would argue that it is also present in the Syncretist *Chuang Tzu* where it is given the now famous name of *nei-sheng wai-wang* 內 聖 外 王 ('inwardly a sage, outwardly a king').

This, then, is Taoism, as seen by the man who coined the term. Ssu-ma T'an's discussion contains a number of important technical terms and phrases which are found in the sources of Taoist thought I have already analysed, and which I hope to show are contained in the Syncretist writings as well. In addition it shows Huang-Lao to be a comprehensive system of thought which advocates a flexible government which draws its measures from the best of the other schools, which bases them in an understanding of universal principles, and which is headed by a Sage-ruler who has achieved the deepest levels of tranquility through techniques of self-cultivation.

IIB. *Three Taoistic Essays in the Kuan Tzu*

The three Taoistic essays in the *Kuan Tzu* are important early sources for the philosophical lineage which I believe can be called Huang-Lao, and they present the outlines of a system of thought that is most fully developed in the *Huai-nan Tzu*. Their dates and authorship have been intensely debated and the opinions generated have a direct relationship to the question of authorship of the Syncretist chapters of the *Chuang Tzu*. The prevailing opinion to this day in China is the one established forty years ago by Kuo Mo-jo, that they are the products of Sung Hsing and Yin Wen, two of the Chi-hsia Academy Huang-Lao scholars.[26] Because of the strong textual and philosophical parallels he sees between these texts and all but chapter 33 of the Syncretist *Chuang Tzu*, Kuan Feng concludes that they must have been written by the later followers of these men.[27]

This theory holds true if all three *Kuan Tzu* texts were written at roughtly the same time. However, a close reading of them shows that based on style and philosophical content, this cannot have been the case. *Nei-yeh* ('Inward Training') is written in rhymed verse, and because it mentions the same *hao-jan chih-ch'i* 浩 然 之 氣 'Floodlike Vital Energy' (16/3a9) as does Mencius (2A2), and shows no awareness of the Naturalist concepts of Yin and Yang and the Five Phases (*wu-hsing*), I agree with other scholars that it is clearly the earliest of the three, and can be dated to around 300 B.C.E.[28] *Hsin-shu shang* ('Techniques of the Mind', I) contains two distinct sections, the first third being a basic text, and the remainder a line-by-line commentary on it which for reasons I will present below, I believe was written in the early Han, contemporary or slightly later than the Syncretist *Chuang Tzu*. About two-thirds of the remaining essay, *Hsin-shu-hsia*, consists of passages that constitute about one-third of *Nei-yeh*, which are rear-ranged and rationalized in what I have concluded was a deliberate attempt to create a companion essay to *Hsin-shu shang* which elaborates on the application of the self-cultivation techniques of *Nei-yeh* to the enlightened government of the Taoist ruler.[29] These reasons under-score what Graham also concludes is the very dubious attribution of these essays by Kuo Mo-jo.[30]

Despite the fact that they cannot be products of Sung Hsing and Yin Wen, their influence on the *Huai-nan Tzu*, and the numerous concep-tual parallels they share with Ssu-ma T'an's descriptions, indicates their importance in the lineage of Huang-Lao philosophy. *Nei-yeh*, which Graham feels is " . . . possibly the oldest 'mystical' text in China",[31] presents theories on the nature and activities of the human mind and on the practice of several related methods of mental and physical self-discipline aimed at health, longevity, and self-transcendence, that are grounded in a cosmology of the Tao that shows striking parallels with the *Lao Tzu*. For example we read:

> The 'Tao' is what the mouth cannot speak of, the eyes cannot look at, and the ears cannot listen to. It is that by which we cultivate the mind (*hsiu-hsin* 修 心) and adjust the body. It is what a person loses and thereby dies, what a person gains and is thereby born. When undertakings lose it they fail; when they gain it they succeed.

> The Tao
> Never has a root or trunk,
> Leaves or flowers.

The myriad things are born by means of it
And by means of it develop.
We name it 'the Tao'. (16/2a2–4)

One of the main features that distinguishes this text from the *Lao Tzu* is its emphasis on the importance of the *ching* 精 ('Vital Essence'), which is conceived of as the mysterious aspect of the Tao which is responsible for the generation of life and the maintenance of vitality. It is defined as a concentrated form of *ch'i* ('Vital Energy'), and is closely linked with the concept of *te* 德, the potency which arises in an organism from the manifestation of the Tao within it.

The text speaks of the importance of settling the Tao within one's mind and generating and lodging the Vital Essence. This is accomplished by guiding the Vital Energy through a practice of regular breathing (16/1b10–2a4, and 3b6–7), so that the mind becomes tranquil (*ching* 靜) and stable (*ting* 定) (16/2a9–b1). It points out repeatedly that emotions, desires, and knowledge interfere with this process and can actually be detrimental to one's physical and psychological well-being (16/5a4–5a9; 2a9–b1). But if they can be cast aside through these practices then one can attain a level of experience associated with metaphysical knowledge and eventually self-transcendence:

By concentrating your Vital Energy like a Numen
The myriad things will all be contained within you.
Can you concentrate? Can you unify?
Can you know good and bad fortune
Without resorting to divination?
Can you stop? Can you halt?
Can you not seek it outwardly
But attain it inwardly?[32]
If you think, and think, and think further about this
But still cannot penetrate it,
The daemonic and numinous (*kuei-shen*) in you will penetrate it.
It is not due to the inherent power of the daemonic and
    numinous,
But rather to the utmost development of your Vital Essence.
(16/4a2–5)

Therefore, one concentrates the Vital Energy through controlled breathing. Or rather, since the concept of *ch'i* includes the breath, this really refers to breath-concentration. By concentrating the *ch'i* in this manner one attains the metaphysical knowledge of the future that is associated with the Numen. Throughout this text and others related to it the Numen is seen as the source of this kind of metaphysical knowledge. It is also worthy of note that the Numen itself is conceived of as a concentrated form of *ch'i*, or in other words, it is made of the Vital Essence, the most concentrated form of *ch'i*. Although the concepts of Numen and Vital Essence remain distinct in this text, the principal difference being that the Numen is associated with sentience while the Vital Essence is not, they later blend together in the *Huai-nan Tzu* into the concept of Numinous Essence (*ching-shen*), the manifestation of the Numen within the systems of Vital Energy which constitute a human being.[33] The important point here is that this text maintains that the psychological states of calmness and tranquility which allow one to stabilize the Numen are based on the physiological substrates associated with the Vital Essence, a concentrated form of the Vital Energy which pervades the cosmos. When, through controlled breathing, one chases away perception, thought, and emotions, one can return to the Way and the Power (*fan Tao-Te* 反 道 德,) (16/3b7). Elsewhere these practices are said to lead to longevity (16/4a11–b2), and to the ability to 'embrace unity' (*shou-i* 守 一), a concept that becomes important in later religious Taoist techniques of meditation.[34]

The above passage contains significant textual and philosophical parallels with two other sources in addition to the *Huai-nan Tzu*. The concept of concentrating and unifying (*chuan-i* 摶 一) the Vital Energy here is virtually identical to Ssu-ma T'an's 'concentrating and unifying the Numinous Essence' (*chuan i* 專 一). And the lines 3–8 in this passage from *Nei-yeh* are repeated almost verbatim in one of the 'Mixed' Chapters of the *Chuang Tzu* (23/34–5), in which Lao Tzu is explaining the meaning of the method of protecting one's vitality (*wei-sheng-chih-ching* 衛 生 之 經). Even if *Nei-yeh* and *Chuang Tzu* draw from a common source, the point remains that the compiler of the latter was aware of such techniques. It is not surprising therefore that related concepts should appear in the Syncretist material, as we shall see below.

The most significant difference between *Nei-yeh* and *Hsin-shu shang* is that whereas little or no attempt is made in the former to recommend these practices of self-cultivation to the ruler as ways to enable him to govern more effectively, the latter is devoted to precisely that. The theories of government are placed in the context of a cosmology of the Tao that parallels the *Lao Tzu*, and they center on an elaboration of the concept of *wu-wei* that is found therein. The elaboration involves a number of closely related ideas that are found in Ssu-ma T'an's description of the Taoists, such as *ying* 應 ('spontaneous response'), *yin* 因 ('adaptation'), *hsun-li* 循 理 ('compliance with Patterns'), and to the principle of assigning tasks which are suitable to the individual (*i* 宜). The prescriptions for self-cultivation in order to attain the state of mind needed to practice these principles center on *ching* ('stillness') and *hsü* ('emptiness'), relinquishing wisdom, desires, and preferences, and finally on cleaning out the mind in order to lodge the Numen and develop the Vital Essence. These close conceptual and textual parallels with both Ssu-ma T'an and the *Huai-nan Tzu* that are found most frequently in the explanatory section of this work make Rickett's conclusion of an early Han date even more probable.[35]

Because two-thirds of the text of *Hsin-hsu hsia* is a restatement of the theories and techniques of self-cultivation found in *Nei-yeh*, it provides little new information. Yet it does contain a linking passage that nicely sums up the unique blend of cosmology, psychology, and politics, which I believe is a hallmark of this lineage of thought. After a passage taken from *Nei-yeh* which discusses aligning the flow of Vital Energy in the body (*cheng-hsing* 正 形) by not allowing external things to disrupt the senses, and not allowing the senses to disrupt the mind, a practice called developing 'inward power', the text reads:

> Therefore, only after the awareness and Vital Energy are stabilized will the body be aligned.[36] The Vital Energy is what fills the body. The alignment [of the Vital Energy] is the standard pattern of its movement.[37] When what fills the body does not move according to a standard, the heart will not attain it [the power].[38] When the movement [of the Vital Energy] is not aligned [in the ruler], then the people will not submit. Therefore the Sage is like Heaven: selflessly (*wu-ssu*) 無 私 he covers; he is like Earth: selflessly he supports. Selfishness is what disrupts the world. (13/4b9–12)

IIC. *The Huai-nan Tzu*

The *Huai-nan Tzu* is unique among our sources: its date is relatively certain: 139 B.C.E.; we know who wrote it: Liu An and the eight retainers listed in Kao Yu's preface (ca. 212 C.E.); and it is a well-organized and coherent set of twenty essays, each with a specific topic, followed by a final essay (*Yao-lüeh* 要 略) which summarizes each of the others and explains the rationale for their inclusion and order of presentation in the text. In short, it is a compendium of knowledge about the nature of the cosmos and the human beings who live within it that was intended to give the enlightened ruler all that he needed to govern effectively. Continuing along the general outlines laid out in the *Lao Tzu* and the three *Kuan Tzu* essays, it embraces the interrelated themes of cosmology, psychology, and politics, and presents the most sophisticated and thoroughly syncretic discussion of them that is found in the entire tradition. Ssu-ma T'an's discussion of the Taoist school so closely parallels the basic philosophical stance and terminology of the *Huai-nan Tzu* that it could serve as a summary of the entire work. It would not be at all surprising if he had the *Huai-nan Tzu* in mind when he wrote this essay. I fully agree with K. C. Hsiao that it is the principal representative of Huang-Lao philosophy in the Han.[37]

The themes that are present in the three *Kuan Tzu* essays are elaborated in the *Huai-nan Tzu,* and there is solid textual as well as philosophical evidence that its authors were aware of the earlier material.[38] The physiological basis of psychology and self-cultivation found in *Nei-yeh* is explained in great detail in this work, particularly in its seventh essay, *Ching-shen* 精 神 ('The Numinous Essence'). As in the two parts of *Hsin-shu*, it is presented in the context of enabling the ruler to govern effectively in accord with Lao Tzu's principle of Non-action and with the related concepts of Spontaneous Response, Suitability, Adaptation, and Compliance with Natural Patterns, that are the hallmarks of Taoism for Ssu-ma T'an as well. Another of these hallmarks for T'an that is present in the *Huai-nan Tzu* is the utilization of certain aspects of the philosophy of other pre-Han schools of thought in a syncretic perspective which remains grounded in a cosmology that is thoroughly Taoist. It is undoubtedly this frequent use of material from other lineages of thought that resulted in the bibliographical classification of the *Huai-nan Tzu* as 'Eclectic' (*tsa-chia*). It is not that this syncretic perspective is new; it is fully consonant with that of the *Hsin-shu* essays and, I believe, with the Syncretist *Chuang Tzu*. It is just that this syncretism is so thoroughly absorbed by the authors that it appears almost natural. Roger Ames's excellent analysis of the ninth essay, *Chu-shu* ('The Art of Rulership'), shows how completely Legalist and Confucian concepts are absorbed into a Taoist perspective on government.[39]

The *Huai-nan Tzu* does not merely continue the established themes of the Taoist syncretic tradition, it innovates within that tradition as well. Three innovations are worthy of note. First is the incorporation of the Naturalist cosmology of Yin and Yang and the Five Phases of *Ch'i*, which is present in many of the essays.[40] Second is the development of the understanding of the nature and activities of the Numen, and of the mind in general, explained in terms of Naturalist philosophy.[41] Finally is the development of a Taoist theory of human nature, which the *Huai-nan Tzu* authors probably took over from the Primitivist *Chuang Tzu*, but which they present in a much more comprehensive fashion as the foundation of their theories of psychology, self-cultivation, and government.[42]

Despite this syncretism, it is clear that the two primary influences on the text of the *Huai-nan Tzu* are the *Lao Tzu* and the *Chuang Tzu*. Even though the *Huai-nan Tzu* advocates a philosophy of government whose syncretic use of certain aspects of Confucianism (in their own place of course) would have offended Lao Tzu, the general outlines on cosmology and government are the same: Tao and *wu-wei*. The differences in complexity and sophistication between the two texts, which could, following Schwartz, be characterized as 'primitivist' versus 'syncretist', are due to the vastly different social and political conditions at the times each was written. Certainly the *Huai-nan Tzu* authors regarded the *Lao Tzu* as canonical. It is quoted ten times more often than any other work, and an entire essay, *Tao-ying* 道 應 ('The Responses of the Tao'), is devoted to illustrating philosophical points from *Lao Tzu*.[43] The text of the *Chuang Tzu* is, most significantly, treated in a considerably different way. Although ideas, or sentences, or sometimes whole paragraphs from the *Chuang Tzu* are found in the *Huai-nan Tzu*, by one count, five times more frequently than is material from the *Lao Tzu*, only once in the entire work is the text actually quoted.[44] And quite often the *Chuang Tzu* material is presented in a different context, or interpreted differently.[45] This suggests a much less hallowed status for the *Chuang Tzu*: it is beloved, but it is not canonical. And, as we shall see, its text may not have even been fixed at this time.

IID. The Thought of the Syncretists in Context

The philosophy found in what Graham defines as the Syncretist chapters of the *Chuang Tzu* (11/66–74; 12/1–18; 13/1–45; 14/1–6; 15; 33) shares striking parallels in terminology and in general outlook with the three *Kuan Tzu* essays and the *Huai-nan Tzu*, and shows similarities as well with Ssu-ma T'an's description of Taoism. The Syncretist philosophy exhibits the three interlocking elements which form the basis of the thought detailed in these other sources: cosmology, psychology, and politics. I will analyse these parallels by first presenting a table of the shared terminology, and then proceed to a discussion of the main features of the Syncretists' philosophy in which I will identify similar material in these other sources.

IID1. Technical Terminology. In table 1, I compare the technical terms of the Syncretists with those found in *Hsin-shu shang* and *Huai-nan Tzu*. I have chosen to focus primarily on *Hsin-shu shang* because among the three *Kuan Tzu* essays it presents the most complete expression of the three aspects of Taoist thought I have identified. Those terms that are also found in Ssu-ma T'an's essay are indicated with an asterisk.

While there is a remarkable consistency in terminology among the three sources, there is a marked difference in frequency of occurrence (see table 1). This is due in part to the varying lengths of the sources: the *Huai-nan Tzu* is easily fifteen times longer than the Syncretist *Chuang Tzu*, which in turn is about twice as long as *Hsin-shu shang*. This must also be due in part to the terminology that was current at the time when each was written.

The most common terms to all are The Way of Heaven, Non-action, Stillness, and Emptiness, which is separated in the table because it is used in both cosmological (emptiness of the Tao or the Way of Heaven)

TABLE 1: The Technical Terminology of the Syncretists

Terms	Hsin-shu shang	Chuang Tzu	Huai-nan Tzu
1. COSMOLOGY			
Way of Heaven 天之道	13/3a2, 3b6	11/72(3), 73; 13/1b	10/1a; 12/5b; 14/14b; 15/2a; 20/2b
			20 times, especially chs. 3, 9, 15
Way of Heaven and Earth 天地之道		15/7–8; 33/84	3/12a; 7/2a; 20/6a
Non-action* 無為	13/1b12; 2a3, 12; 4a1,8	18 times, especially 13/5–10, 17–24	41 times, especially chs. 1, 9, 14
Formless* 無形	13/1b2; 3a5; 3b2	33/62; also 6/29 and 11 times in rest	31 times, especially chs. 1, 15
Pattern 理	13/2a10; 3a9–10; 4a10	15/11–12	24 times, especially chs. 9, 14
2. PSYCHOLOGY			
Stillness 靜	13/1a9; 2a3; 2b4, 7, 8; 3b6	17 times, esp. 13/1–17; 15/10–17; 33/49, 50, 57	33 times, especially chs. 1, 9, 14, 15
Cast off Wisdom and Precedent 去智與故	13/2a3;4a8; 2b11 (no precedent)	15/11; 13/36 is similar	1/5a, 9a; 6/7b; 7/10a (verbs different; object same)

Terms	Hsin-shu shang	Chuang Tzu	Huai-nan Tzu
Cast off Desires* 去欲	13/2b9–10; 3b7	12/5 (have no desires); 15/14 (implied)	2/4b; 14/2a, 7b, 10a; and throughout ch. 7
Techniques of the Mind 心術	Title; 2a12	13/26	1/15a; 7/11a; 14/2a; 21/4b
Vital Essence 精	13/2b7; 3a4	12/17; 15/20–21; 33/3, 54	23 times, especially chs. 2, 7, 8
Numinous* Essence 精神		13/4, 26; 15/18–19	Title of ch. 7; 34 times especially chs. 1, 7
Human Nature 性		only in Primitivist	90 times, especially chs. 1, 2, 7, 11
Longevity* 壽	*Nei-yeh*, 16/4b7	13/7; 15/7	4/5a, 7a; 7/3a, 11a; 10/3b

3. POLITICS

Terms	Hsin-shu shang	Chuang Tzu	Huai-nan Tzu
Nourishing the Myriads* 育萬物	13/1b2	13/22; 15/19; 33/5,7	5/17a; 9/7a; 10/4b; 12/16a, 22a; 15/3a
Spontaneous Response* 應	13/2a4, 6; 3b3, 9, 11; 4a9; 5a1, 2, 3	15/11	40 times, especially in chs. 1, 15
Adaptation* 因	13/2a3; 3a8; 3b10; 4a1, 9; 5a1	11/67, 71; 13/33 (*yin-jen*)	1/10b; 9/1a, 7a; 14/8a;

Terms	Hsin-shu shang	Chuang Tzu	Huai-nan Tzu
			15/8a, b; 20/3b, 4a; 21/2a
Compliance* 循	13/1a5	12/9; 15/11	1/7b; 7/4b; 9/1a, 3a; 10/7b; 11/6b; 14/2a, 3b, 4b; 19/3a
Suitability* 宜	13/3a8, 3b3	13/34	17 times, especially chs. 11, 13
Syncretism, especially Legalism, Confucianism*	13/1b5; 3a8–b1	13/27–41; 15/7; 33/2–6	In many chs., especially 9, 11, 13, 19
4. OTHER			
Emptiness* 虛	13/1a10, 1b2; 2b10; 2b12; 3b6; 4a5, 8, 11; 5a1, 3	13/1–17; 15/8,13,15	49 times, especially chs. 1, 2, 7

and psychological (emptiness of the mind) contexts in each of the sources. Interestingly, all four terms are found in the *Lao Tzu*, which is a strong indication of its influence. However, the syncretism that places Confucian and Legalist ideas under a Taoist umbrella which all three sources exhibit is certainly not found there. In addition to the syncretism in methods of government, the remaining political concepts are all found in Ssu-ma T'an, a fact which gives a strong indication that all the sources are part of the same lineage of thought.

The frequency of use of the terms must be related to the stage of development of the tradition. Based on this chart, the *Huai-nan Tzu* must be closest in time to Ssu-ma T'an, and, of course, we know it is. *Hsin-shu shang* would be next, followed by the Syncretist *Chuang Tzu*. The single occurrence of *ying* in *Chuang Tzu* 15 could indicate that it is the latest of these chapters, possibly a contemporary of *Hsin-shu shang*.

This impression is reinforced by the context: the phrase *kan-ying* 感應, is found in both the other sources, and thought to be a key term in Naturalist philosophy. Also chapter 15 contains more of these terms than any other chapter, although this may not be entirely fair since chapter 33 is largely devoted to discussing the philosophies of others. However it is significant that chapter 15 contains almost all the psychological terms. This is a strong indication of its links to the *Kuan Tzu* essays and the *Huai-nan Tzu*, and to its relatively late date.

IID2. The Way of Heaven; The Way of Heaven and Earth. Both Kuan Feng and Graham note that one of the unique characteristics of the Syncretist philosophy is the importance given to the Way of Heaven or the Way of Heaven and Earth.[46] It almost seems that in these phrases, and in the hierarchical list of governing measures in 13/32–41, that, as Graham says, the Way has assumed a secondary position.[47] In chapter 15, after the author criticizes the limited points of view of five groups of men who seem to include the Primitivists ('the hermits of mountains and valleys' who have 'finicky notions'), the Confucians ('the stay-at-home scholars' who expound 'Goodwill and Duty'), the Legalists ('The annexers of lands' who are 'interested only in governing'), Chuang Tzu himself ('The untroubled idler' who is 'interested only in Doing Nothing'), and the Esoteric Masters (*fang-shih* 方士) ('Grandfather P'eng's ripe old agers' who practice the 'guide-and-pull' exercises *tao-yin* 導引 to stimulate the flow of Vital Energy), the author continues:

> As for being lofty without having finicky notions, improving oneself without bothering about Goodwill and Duty, governing without caring about deeds and reputations, living untroubled not by riverside or seaside, living to a ripe old age without 'guide-and-pull', and forgetting them all and possessing them all, being serene and unconfined and having all these glories as the consequence, this is the Way of Heaven and Earth, the Power which is in the sage.[48] (15/7–8)

Here the Way of Heaven and Earth seems to refer to the syncretic philosophy of the author which takes the best from these limited points of view and blends them in the Power of the sage. The other use of this phrase at 33/84 is consonant with this interpretation.

In the *Huai-nan Tzu* the Way of Heaven and Earth pertains more to cosmology. It is the basis for determining the calendar (3/12a), and it is responsible for the macro-microcosmic parallels between universe and human beings and for their numinous aspects (7/2a–b). These two interpretations are not necessarily incompatible. One could maintain that the sagely Way is parallel to the cosmic Way. This is in fact the pattern in the Syncretist discussion of the Way of Heaven.

The Syncretist fragment at the end of chapter 11 (66–74) makes the distinction between the Way of Heaven and the Way of Man:

> ... To be exalted by Doing Nothing (*wu-wei*) is the Way of Heaven, to be tied by doing something is the Way of Man. The sovereign's is the Way of Heaven, the minister's is the Way of Man. That the Ways of Heaven and of Man are far apart is not to be overlooked.[49] (11/72–4)

Here *wu-wei* has both a cosmological aspect as the Way of Heaven, and a human aspect as it is manifested in the sovereign. These two aspects are continued in chapter 12:

> The Master said:
> 'The Way is the shelterer and sustainer of the myriad things. Vast, vast is its greatness. The gentleman has no choice but to scrape out everything in his heart for it.
> 'It is the doer of it by Doing Nothing that we call "Heaven", the teller of it by Doing Nothing that we call "Power". . . .[50] (12/6–8)

Heaven clearly accomplishes its tasks (for example, of completing the myriad things through its circuitings—13/1) by *wu-wei*. The sage who practices this form of selfless and effortless action is following the Way of Heaven. In a sense he is the microcosm to the macrocosm of Heaven.

This passage also points out an important distinction that some-times gets overlooked in these chapters. Despite the importance of Heaven, it has not actually replaced the Tao as ground of the cosmos. The two other passages which Graham refers to as the 'rhapsodies on the Way' affirm that the Tao still has this position (12/12–13; 13/60–62). I would argue that the significance of the Way of Heaven or the Way of Heaven and Earth is in its emphasis on the practical manifestation of the vast and profound Tao within the universe. Rather than a fundamental shift in cosmology, we have a shift in focus that seems perfectly in keeping with the overall practicality of the Syncretists.

This understanding of the Way of Heaven as the manifestation of the Tao within the cosmos is parallelled in both *Hsin-shu shang* and the *Huai-nan Tzu*. In the explanatory section of the former we read:

> The Way of Heaven is empty and formless. Empty, then it does not wear out. Formless, then there is nothing that it bumps against. Because there is nothing that it bumps against, it flows everywhere through the myriad things and does not change. The Power is the lodging of the Way . . . Non-action (*wu-wei*), this we call the 'Way'. To lodge it, this we call the 'Power'. Therefore there is no gap between the Way and the Power. (13/3a2–7)

In this passage, the Way of Heaven, although we cannot identify it as an object, is manifested throughout the phenomenal world. While we cannot objectify it, it can be 'lodged', or experienced. The *Huai-nan Tzu*, as well, talks of this intangible, yet palpable Way:

> The Vital Energy of Heaven is called *hun*魂; the Vital Energy of Earth is called *po*魄. If you return them to the Profound Chamber (*hsüan-fang* 玄 房), then each will rest in its abode. If you protect them and don't let them slip away, then above you will circulate freely with Vast Unity (*t'ai-i* 太 一). The Vital Essence of Vast Unity circulates freely in the Way of Heaven. The Way of Heaven is profound and silent. It is without contents, without guidelines. You cannot reach the limits of the Way of Heaven. It is deep and cannot be fathomed. Ascending, it transforms along with human beings, and knowledge cannot grasp it. (9/1b6–8)

This passage speaks of the mystical experience of merging with the Tao, here conceived of as *T'ai-i*. Yet even this most profound of experiences has a physiological basis, a Vital Essence, and it is this that flows freely within the Way of Heaven. Thus once again while this Way is mysterious and cannot be objectified, it can be experienced. The text proceeds to discuss the ideal reign of Shen Nung, a sage-ruler who was able to experience this profound Way and the benefits his subjects derived from it.

The *Huai-nan Tzu* puts more emphasis on the intangible qualities of the Way of Heaven than do the other two texts. Yet despite this it retains their emphasis on the experiential possibilities. The source for this concept of the Way of Heaven, the *Lao Tzu*, does this as well:

Without venturing outside
One can know the whole world
Without looking out a window
One can see the Way of Heaven.
The farther one goes
The less one knows.
Therefore the sage knows without doing
Sees without naming
Completes without acting. (chapter 47)

IID.3. *Nei-sheng wai-wang:* **The Harmony of the Psychological and the Political.**   Another of the central elements in the philosophy of the Syncretist *Chuang Tzu* that is recognized by Kuan, Graham, and others is the concept of being 'inwardly a sage, outwardly a king' (*nei-sheng wai-wang*) that is found in chapter 33 (33/14). Elsewhere in the 'Way of Heaven' chapter it is referred to as 'in stillness a sage, in motion a king' (*ching erh sheng, tung-erh wang* 静 而 聖 , 動 而 王) (13/10). It is parallelled in *Hsin-shu shang* by the concept of the 'Way of stillness and adaptation' (*ching-yin chih Tao* 静 因 之 道)(13/2a3–7), and through-out the *Huai-nan Tzu* in the idea that in order to govern effectively the ruler must cultivate the limits of his innate nature. This harmony between the psychological and the political is one of the hallmarks of this lineage of thought, even though it may not always be conceived of in precisely the same terms.

A classic statement of this position begins the 'Heaven and Earth' chapter of *Chuang Tzu*:

> The ruler finds his source in the Power and is full-formed by Heaven ... We say then that in profoundest antiquity ruling the empire was Doing Nothing; it was simply a matter of the Power which is from Heaven. . . .
>
> Hence it is said of those who of old were pastors of the empire that they desired nothing (*wu-yu*), yet the empire had enough; they did nothing, but the myriad things were transformed; they were still from the depths (*yuan-ching* 淵 静), but the Hundred clans were settled.[51] (12/2–6)

This passage maintains that the balance between inner cultivation and outer manifestation in the ruler is crucial to the flourishing of the empire. By being 'still from the depths' and 'desiring nothing', the ruler is able to be grounded in the Power and completed by Heaven. Through manifesting this profound inner experience through selfless and effortless action, he is able to govern effectively. In so doing he models himself after Heaven. These ideas are reiterated in 13/17–21, which also maintains the distinction seen in 11/72–74 between the role of the ruler and that of his ministers. The ruler is the one who must be self-cultivated according to these guidelines.

The action of the sage-king in the phenomenal world is spoken of in similar terms in the passage from *Hsin-shu hsia* examined above, in which the ruler is said to be like Heaven in that he selflessly covers; and like Earth in that he selflessly supports (13/4b11–12). It is parallelled in the opening section of *Hsin-shu shang* and its commentary (13/1a5–8, 2a7–11) in which the analogy is made between the non-acting position of the mind within the body, which through its emptiness of desires enables the senses to perceive accurately, and the empty and non-acting position of the ruler in the empire. "When the one above departs from his way," the passage concludes, "the ones below lose their activities."

The emphasis on the harmony between the inner realization of the ruler and his outward activity is found throughout the *Huai-nan Tzu*. For example:

> Therefore the sage inwardly cultivates the root (*hsiu ch'i-pen* 修 其 本) and outwardly does not adorn himself with the branches. He preserves his Numinous Essence and puts an end to wisdom and precedent (*chih-yu-ku* 智 與 故) . . . Therefore calmly (*mo-jan* 漠 然) he takes no action and there is nothing that is not done (*wu-wei erh wu pu-wei*). Tranquilly he does not govern, and there is nothing that is ungoverned. (1/8b12–9a2)

IID3.1. Stillness.   The discussion of the 'inner sageliness' of the ruler in the Syncretist *Chuang Tzu* centers on the development of stillness (*ching*), which is viewed as the common basis of both cosmos and psyche. In the long essay that begins the Way of Heaven chapter we read:

> Emptiness and stillness, calm and indifference (*t'ien-yen* 恬 惔), quiescence (*chi-mo* 寂 漠), Doing Nothing, are the even level of heaven and earth, the utmost reach of the Way and the Power; therefore

emperor, king or sage finds rest in them. At rest he empties, emptying
he is filled, and what fills him sorts itself out. Emptying he is still, in
stillness he is moved, and when he moves he succeeds. In stillness he
does nothing; and if he does nothing, those charged with affairs are
put to the test. If he does nothing he is serene; and in whoever is serene,
cares and misfortunes cannot settle, his years will be long.[52] (13/4–7)

This passage again shows the balance between the inward realization of
stillness attained through emptying the mind and the outward manifestation of Non-action. It is quoted in the 'Finicky Notions' essay, where
stillness, calm, and indifference (*t'ien-yen*) are associated with concepts
which find parallels in the three *Kuan Tzu* essays:

If he [the sage] is even and unstrained, calm and indifferent,

　　Cares and misfortunes cannot enter,
　　The deviant energies (*hsieh-ch'i* 邪 氣) cannot make inroads.

Therefore his Power is intact and his daemon (*shen*) is unimpaired.[53]
(15/8–10)

The association of states of stillness and tranquility with the Vital
Energy and Essence and the Numen are found throughout the *Kuan
Tzu* essays and the *Huai-nan Tzu*. For example, in *Hsin-shu shang*:

That which the sage directs is his Vital Essence. Relinquish desire
and the mind will be expansive. When it is expansive it will be still.
When it is still the Vital Essence is present. When the Vital Essence is
present one experiences solitude (*tu* 獨). In solitude there is clarity
(*ming* 明). With clarity comes the Numen. The Numen is the most
honored. Thus when the abode is not cleaned out, the honored one will
not dwell therein. (13/2b5–10)

In the *Huai-nan Tzu*, in the context of removing lusts and desires
through controlled breathing which leads to the proper flow of Vital
Energy within the entire organism, we read:

When the Numinous Essence is abundant and the flow of Vital En-
ergy is not dispersed then the organism functions according to
Pattern (*li* 理). When the organism functions according to Pattern [the
mind] is even. When it is even [the Numinous Essence] flows freely.
When [the Numinous Essence] flows freely [the mind] is numinous.
When it is numinous there is nothing that vision does not see, nothing

that listening does not hear, and nothing that action does not accomplish. For this reason cares and misfortunes cannot enter and the deviant Vital Energy cannot make inroads. (7/2b5–9)

There are certainly differences in the ways of conceiving of this process of achieving the stillness of mind necessary to govern effectively in the three passages. But it is important to note that in each this level of tranquility is given a physiological basis (Vital Energy or Essence, or Numinous Essence), and is associated with the Numen. In all our sources the emptying of the mind of knowledge, desires, and emotions is referred to as either lodging or nourishing the Numen. Other examples are found in *Nei-yeh* (16/2b9–12, 5a4), *Chuang Tzu* (15/14–16), and *Huai-nan Tzu* (i.e., 7/4b2–7, 20/8b11–9a1). The *Chuang Tzu* and second *Huai-nan Tzu* passages both refer to these methods as *yang-shen* 養 神 .

IID3.2. Stillness and motion. The harmony between inner realization and outer manifestation characaterized as *nei-sheng wai-wang* is directly related to stillness and motion in all of our sources. Not only do they all identify stillness with Yin and motion with Yang (*Chuang Tzu* 13/14, 15/10; *Hsin-shu shang* 13/2b3–4; *Huai-nan Tzu* 7/4b4–5), but they also conceive of the spontaneous response of the sage grounded in stillness in terms of the Naturalist idea of *kan-ying* (*Chuang Tzu* 15/11; *Hsin-shu shang* 13/4a5; *Huai-nan Tzu*, i.e., 7/5b1–2), and agree that he 'casts off wisdom (or knowledge) and precedent' (see above chart). An important statement of these ideas is found in the 'Finicky Notions' chapter of *Chuang Tzu*:

Hence it is said that the sage
In his life proceeds with Heaven
In his death transforms with other things
In stillness shares the Power in the Yin
In motion shares the surge of the Yang.

He will not to gain advantage make the first move
Will not to avoid trouble take the first step
Only when stirred will he respond,
Only when pressed will he move,
Only when it is inevitable will he rise up.

Rejecting knowledge and precedent
He takes his course from Heaven's pattern
    (*Hsun t'ien-chih-li* 循 天 之 理)[54] (15/10–12)

These ideas are parallelled in *Hsin-shu shang*:

> . . . Therefore the Superior Person is not enticed by likes, not pressed by dislikes. Calm and tranquil (*t'ien-yü* 恬 愉), he takes no action (*wu-wei*), and casts off wisdom and precedent (*ch'u chih yu ku* 去 智 與 故). His responses (*ying*) are not something pre-arranged. His movements are not something (deliberately) chosen. . . . (13/2a2–3)

> [*Commentary*] . . . When a person is pressed by dislikes then he loses what he likes. If he is enticed by likes then he forgets what he likes. This is not the Way. Therefore the text says "He is not enticed by likes, not pressed by dislikes". When one is not pressed by dislikes then dislikes do not lose their Pattern (*li*), and desires do not exceed what is genuinely needed. Therefore the text says "The Superior Person, calm and tranquil, takes no action and casts off wisdom and precedent". Thus it says that he is empty (*hsü* 虚) and pure (*so* 素).

> "His responses are not something pre-arranged. His movements are not something (deliberately) chosen." This says that he adapts (*yin* 因). Adaptation means that he abandons the self and takes other things as his models. Only when stirred will he respond (*kan erh-hou ying*). It is not something pre-arranged. To move according to Pattern is not something [deliberately] chosen. . . . (13/4a7–10)

In the *Huai-nan Tzu* we find similar descriptions:

> Therefore the Sage adapts to the times (*yin-shih*) and is thereby secure in his position. He matches his contemporaries and enjoys what he does. Sadness and joy are deviations from the Power. Pleasure and anger go beyond the Way. Likes and dislikes are the scorchings of the mind. Therefore it is said:

> > In his life proceeds with Heaven,
> > In his death transforms with other things.
> > In stillness he closes up with the Yin,
> > In motion he opens up with the Yang.

> > His Numinous Essence is placidly (*tan-jan* 澹 然) limitless
> > It is not dispersed amidst phenomena
> > And the entire world naturally submits. (7/4b2–5)

... The Perfect Person ... His form is like withered wood.
His mind is like dead ashes. He forgets his Five Orbs (*wu-tsang*
五臟—the systems of Vital Energy in the organism), and
loses his physical body.

He knows without studying.
He sees without looking.
He completes without acting.
He regulates without disputing.
When stirred he responds
When pressed he moves. . . . (7/5a12–b2)

All three texts exhibit close textual and conceptual parallels in describing the activity of the sage. They emphasize that he must attain stillness through relinquishing desires and preferences, and the *Huai-nan Tzu* even uses the famous simile of withered wood and dead ashes from the 'Inner' Chapters of the *Chuang Tzu* (2/2). They also maintain that when the sage is grounded in stillness that he will respond in a purely spontaneous fashion in accord with the natural guidelines of Heaven's patterns. This spontaneity is the basis of the ideas of Non-action, Adaptation, and Compliance, that are also mentioned by Ssu-ma T'an. The *Huai-nan Tzu*, as the most developed text among the three, provides the most sophisticated analysis of the physiological basis of the experience of stillness, conceiving of it as the preservation of the Numinous Essence, the most rarified form of the Vital Energy that actually constitutes the Numen. This represents an elaboration of similar ideas in the other sources that have been discussed above.

These passages again demonstrate the conceptual similarity among our sources, and show that the Syncretist *Chuang Tzu* is part of the same tradition as the other texts.

11D.4. The Political Philosophy of the Syncretists. The Syncretists' theories of government are concentrated in the long essay at the head of 'The Way of Heaven' (13/1–45) in which the author expounds the Ways of Heaven, the Emperor, and the Sage. In addition to the principles of Non-action, Adaptation, Spontaneous Response, and Compliance, discussed above, this philosophy contains three other significant aspects: nourishing the myriad things, deriving measures from the natural guidelines that constitute the Patterns of Heaven, and the use of ideas drawn from the political philosophy of the Confucians and Legalists within a Taoistic framework. All three aspects are included in Ssu-ma T'an's description of the Taoists.[55]

IID.4.1. Nourishing the myriad things. The idea of the sage's nourishing of the myriad things (*yü wan-wu* 育 萬 物) is found in several locations in the Syncretist *Chuang Tzu*, and is implied in the idea of being Pastor to the Empire (*ch'u T'ien-hsia* 畜 天 下) found at 12/5 and 13/17. It essentially means that the sage-ruler, through the profundity of his self-cultivation which connects him with the ground of Heaven and Earth, and through the appropriateness of his selfless actions which manifest this ground, is able to not only provide sufficiently for his people, but to also aid in assuring that the processes of Heaven and Earth function harmoniously. As 'Below in the Empire' says:

> Did not the men of old provide for everything? They were peers of the daemonic-and-illumined (*shen-ming* 神 明) and equals of heaven and earth, they fostered the myriad things and harmonised the empire, their bounty extended over the Hundred Clans.[56] (33/6–8)

Nourishing the myriad things is discussed once in the basic text of *Hsin-shu shang* as a characteristic of the Power (13/1b2), and the explanatory section makes it clear that the Power develops in the sage from the lodging of the Tao (13/3a2–8, quoted above in the section on the Way of Heaven). Hence the sage who is able to develop the Power will also possess this nurturing ability.

As the latest text among our sources, the *Huai-nan Tzu* develops this idea the furthest. It speaks in general terms of the ruler's ability to nourish. For example:

> The Way of the Ruler is round: it revolves without any starting points. He transforms and nourishes as if numinous. He is empty and vacant, he adapts (*yin*) and complies (*hsün*), and he always lays back and does not anticipate. (9/9a10–11)

It also discusses specific measures which embody this, such as 'making use of the masses' (*yung-chung* 用 衆) so that each will be able to develop his own inner nature, and 'benefitting the people' (*li-min*

利 民). These ideas are fully discussed by Roger Ames in his excellent analysis of the 'Art of Rulership' essay.[57]

IID.4.2. *Comprehending the Patterns of Heaven.* The idea of complying with Heaven's Patterns (*T'ien-li*) occurs only once in the Syncretist *Chuang Tzu* in the 'Finicky Notions' chapter quoted above (15/10–12). Here it refers to the guidelines which direct the spontaneous responses of the sage who cultivates stillness. However, it is clearly implied in the Syncretist notions that the hierarchical structure of government and society must be based on parallel structures in Heaven and Earth:

> The ruler comes first, the minister follows; the father comes first, the son follows . . . the senior comes first, the junior follows . . . Being exalted or lowly, first or last, belongs to the progressions of heaven and earth; therefore the sage takes his model from them. Being exalted if of heaven, lowly if of earth, are the stations of the daemonic-and-illumined; spring and summer first, autumn and winter last, is the sequence of the four seasons. . . . Heaven and earth are supremely daemonic yet have sequences of the exalted and the lowly, the first and the last, how much more the Way of Man! If you expound a Way without their sequences, it is not their Way. If you expound a Way which is not their Way, from what will you derive a Way?[58] (13/27–32)

This passage provides a clear example that the Way of Heaven and Earth advocated by the Syncretists has cosmological, social, and political dimensions. It is a way that embraces Confucian and Legalist concepts of social order and government, as is demonstrated in the continuation of this passage which will be quoted in the next section.

These dimensions are also discussed in the commentarial section of *Hsin-shu shang*:

> 'Rightness' (*i* 義) means that each rests in what is suitable (*i* 宜) to it. 'Ritual' is that which accords with the genuine feelings of human beings by going along with the Patterns of what is Right for them, and then creating limitations and embellishments. Therefore 'Ritual' means to have Patterns. Patterns are what clarify distinctions and thereby convey the meaning of Rightness. Therefore Ritual is derived Rightness; Rightness is derived from Patterns; and Patterns accord with the suitable.

Law is that by which uniformity is produced so people will have no
other choice than to do what is so. Thus execution and extermination,
prohibition, and punishment, are used to unify them [the people].
Therefore human affairs are supervised by Law; Law is derived from
authority (*ch'uan* 權), and authority from the Way. (13/3a8–b1)

This passage emphasizes that the key Confucian ideas of Rightness
and Ritual are grounded in the notion of Pattern. These natural
Patterns, which guide the spontaneous expression of human emotions,
are the basis for the Rituals which are the social forms through which
these emotions can be manifested. Rightness means what is suitable in a
given situation, and this is determined by the Patterns inherent in that
situation, especially the particular social relationship involved. Rightness determines the appropriate Ritual; both are based on Pattern. The
Patterns here are the natural guidelines through which human nature
is expresssed and the hierarchical guidelines of society which mould its
expression. The cosmological dimension of these Patterns is only
implicit here. This is however not the case in the next paragraph, in
which the cosmological basis of Law and authority is directly
proclaimed.

The value of understanding and complying with Heaven's Patterns
is well-understood by the authors of the *Huai-nan Tzu*. In fact, it is their
rationale for writing the book. In the twenty-first essay ('Summary of
the Essentials' *Yao-lüeh* 要 略), we read:

Therefore we wrote this book of twenty chapters so that the Patterns of
Heaven and Earth would be explored, the affairs of the human world
would be encountered, and the Way of Emperors and Kings (*Ti-wang
chih Tao* 帝 王 之 道) would be fully at one's disposal. (21/5b1–2)

The concern to comprehend the Patterns of the cosmos clearly led to
the writing of such essays as #3, *T'ien-wen* 天 文 ('The Patterns of
Heaven'), #4, *Ti-hsing* 地 形 ('The Forms of Earth'), and #5, *Shih-tse*
時 則) ('The Seasonal Ordinances'). The idea of complying with
Patterns is seen in this last essay in the idea that only certain types of
human activities are appropriate to a given season, and the specific idea
of *hsün-li* occurs in several locations, for example, 1/7b, 9/1a, 13a, and
14/4b. Finally, the idea that Pattern is the basis of Ritual and Rightness
found in *Hsin-shu-shang*, occurs as well in the *Huai-nan Tzu*:

'Rightness' is what complies with Patterns and practices what is suitable. 'Ritual' is what embodies genuine [emotions] and controls their expression. 'Rightness' is to be suitable. 'Ritual' is to embody. (11/6b11–7a1)

IID.4.3. Political syncretism.   The classic expression of the political syncretism of the Syncretist *Chuang Tzu* is found in the hierarchy of governing principles which constitute the 'Great Way' in chapter 13. This passage exhibits the blending of Confucian and Legalist ideas in a Taoist context which is a hallmark of these chapters:

> Therefore the men of old who made clear the Great Way
> first made Heaven clear
> and the Way and the Power were next:
> and when the Way and the Power were clear, Goodwill and Duty were
>   next:
> and when Goodwill and Duty were clear, portions and responsibilities
>   were next:
> and when portions and responsibilities were clear, title and
>   performance were next:
> and when title and performance were clear, putting the suitable man
>   in charge was next:
> and when putting the suitable man in charge was clear, inquiry and
>   inspection were next:
> and when inquiry and inspection were clear, judging right and wrong
>   were next:
> and when judging right and wrong was clear, reward and punishment
>   were next.[59] (13/32–36)

Hsin-shu shang only briefly deals with Confucian and Legalist social and governmental principles in the passage quoted in the previous section. It is a commentary on a passage in the basic text which provides a definition of terms and an indication of their relative value, which, while not as specific as the list in the *Chuang Tzu*, is consonant with it:

> That which is empty and formless we call the Tao. That which transforms and nourishes the myriad things we call the Power. That which is involved in the interactions between ruler and minister, father and son, and among all human beings, we call Rightness. That which determines the various levels of status, courtesy, and familiarity in

relationships we call Ritual. That which selects things both great and small for execution and extermination, for prohibition and punishment, according to a single standard (Tao), we call Law.[60] (13/1b2–5)

The political philosophy of the *Huai-nan Tzu* exhibits all the major elements that we have been discussing in the other sources, but presents them in a much more sophisticated synthesis than is found in these shorter and earlier works. Because of this there are no single passages that encapsulate the *Huai-nan Tzu*'s political thought that can be quoted. Instead I will provide a summary of the ninth essay, the 'Art of Rulership', in which this philosophy attains its fullest expression. For a more comprehensive treatment I refer the reader to Ames's excellent study of this essay on which the following summary is based.[61]

The political thought of the *Huai-nan Tzu* centers first and foremost on the person of the sage-ruler, who cultivates himself in solitude and who embodies the principle of Non-action. This ruler governs without concern for his own benefit, and must establish an administrative hierarchy based on clear differences between the responsibilities of ruler and officials which are found in the Legalist notion of *shih* 勢 ('political advantage'). However, unlike in Legalist thought, the relationship between ruler and officials is governed by what Ames calls "a reciprocity, a harmony in which each position responds to the other".[62] Furthermore, *shih* is not used as an instrument of the ruler's own power and self-maintenance, but as a "device for maintaining a desirable political organization conducive to universal personal realization".[63]

This selfless ruler follows a program of policies aimed at 'utilizing the people' (*yung-chung*—adapted from Confucianism and Mohism) in such a way that each is able to find work that is suitable to his own individual talents and abilities, and to thereby become more spontaneous and harmonious with his own inherent nature. An essential element of governmental policy is *fa*, 'Law', strongly altered from its Legalist service in reinforcing the power of the ruler to a notion of universal law applicable to the ruler himself.

There is also in this political philosophy what Ames calls "a sustained effort to subordinate the interests of the ruler to the welfare of the people".[64] This is embodied in the adaptation of the Confucian concept of 'benefitting the people' (*li-min*) found throughout the text. The contributions of Confucian thought in this essay can also be seen in the presence of ideas such as 'benevolence' (*jen* 仁) (e.g. 9/2b3–4, 22a12), 'uprightness' (*chih* 直) (e.g. 9/17b8), 'sincerity' (*ch'eng* 誠) (e.g. 9/23a6), and 'trustworthiness' (*hsin* 信) (e.g. 9/23a4).

Finally the essay calls on the ruler to comprehend and act in compliance with the Patterns of the cosmos in order for his policies to be fully effective. This emphasizes once again that the structure of society and government must reflect the structure of the cosmos which contains it.

The political philosophy of the *Huai-nan Tzu* thus exhibits not a mere synthesis of the earlier social and political ideas of other schools, but rather a thorough integration of them within a framework that remains fundamentally Taoist, that is, one which maintains a cosmology of the Tao and shows a concern for psychology and self-cultivation. It is fully in accord with the earlier sources, but is much more detailed.

IIE. Concluding Remarks

The clear terminological and conceptual parallels between the Syncretist *Chuang Tzu* and the four other sources studied above provide convincing evidence that they are not isolated texts, but are rather part of the same lineage of thought. The fact that there are also individual differences among them points to the fact that each had its own author, and each was written as a different point in time under unique circumstances. The early Han was a period when the Taoist political perspective was being seriously considered at the Imperial Court, and the challenge to the Taoists of the time was to create a system of government complex and specific enough to be practical, yet faithful to the founding vision of the *Lao Tzu*, written with a much simpler social and political unit in mind. These texts are, I believe, all the results of this effort. Because of the striking similarities between the philosophy in all these sources and Ssu-ma T'an's description of Taoism, I must conclude that they are all part of the philosophical lineage that the Han historians call Huang-Lao. I must therefore also agree with Schwartz, that the Syncretist chapters of the *Chuang Tzu* are an integral part of this lineage of thought.

Now that we have located the Syncretist chapters in a philosophical tradition, we must return to the question of who within this tradition might have compiled them.

III. Did a Syncretist Author Compile the *Chuang Tzu*?

By situating the Syncretist chapters of the *Chuang Tzu* within the Huang-Lao tradition we have taken a major step towards identifying the compiler of the entire text. The question remains, was it one of the authors of these documents, or was it someone else in this tradition?

The two opinions already mentioned on the compilation are those of Kuan Feng and Graham. Kuan states that the text was compiled by the retainers of Liu An, the second king of Huai-nan, the sponsor, editor, and partial author of the *Huai-nan Tzu*. He provides little evidence, however, to support his statement. Graham suspects that one of the Syncretist authors compiled the text and placed 'Below in the Empire' at the end " . . . to show the irresponsible genius of Chuang Tzu in proper perspective."[65] Additional evidence, he believes, is found in the presence of three phrases which became titles in the 'Inner' Chapters in the Syncretist writings. However, now that we have placed the philosophy of the Syncretist *Chuang Tzu* within the same lineage of thought as the *Huai-nan Tzu*, and we know that the authors were not isolated individuals, how does this change the analysis of this problem?

Although it is true that phrases from the titles of three of the 'Inner' Chapters (*Ch'i-wu*, *Ta-tsung*, and *Ti-wang*) occur in the Syncretist *Chuang Tzu*, phrases from six of the 'Inner' Chapters are also found in the *Huai-nan Tzu*. (See table 2.)

Using the same reasoning, one could conclude that the even more frequent occurrence of 'Inner' Chapter titles in the *Huai-nan Tzu* is an indication that the text was compiled by the authors of this later work. However, this is far from the only piece of evidence that points us in the direction of Huai-nan. Looking to others than the Syncretists helps to resolve the thorny problem of what I will call 'textual shuffling' in these chapters.

TABLE 2

Phrase	Huai-nan Tzu Location
1. *Hsiao-yao* 逍遙	1/15b; 19/8b; 21/6a
2. *Ch'i-wu* 齊物	occurs as *Ch'i-su*, title of chap. 11
3. *Yang-sheng* 養生	7/10b; 20/8b-9a; 21/5a
4. *Jen-chien* 人間	Title of chap. 18; 2/3b; 2/4a; 9/13b
5. *Te-ch'ung-fu* 德充符	no occurrences
6. *Ta-tsung* 大宗	1/11a; 2/9a, 9b
7. *Ti-wang* 帝王	10/6a; 18/17a; 19/2b; 21/2b, 5b

IIIA. 'Textual Shuffling' in the Syncretist Chuang Tzu

One of the principal contributions of Graham's new translation of the *Chuang Tzu* lies in his identification of several unique points of view in the book. This is especially valuable because there are some chapters (especially 11–14) in which more than one viewpoint is represented. Armed with this knowledge, we no longer have to try to rationalize the diverse sections of any of these chapters into one point of view. For example, in chapter 11 'Keep it in Place and in Bounds' (*Tsai-yu* 在宥), Graham has identified at least three viewpoints: Primitivist (1–28, 57–66), Immortalist (28–57) and Syncretist (66–74). However, as is often the case, increased knowledge raises new questions. The relevant one here is that if one of the Syncretist authors compiled the *Chuang Tzu*, why are diverse viewpoints present in chapters 11–14?

A possible answer to this question lies in the fact that the extant recension of the *Chuang Tzu* in thirty-three chapters established by the 'Profound Learning' scholar Kuo Hsiang (ca. 300 C.E.) is not the original recension of the text. The Bibliographical Monograph to the *Han-shu* written by Pan Ku (ca. 80 C.E.) lists a fifty-two chapter version, and most scholars agree that Pan Ku's work was largely based on the lost

Ch'i-lueh of Liu Hsiang (ca. 10 B.C.E.). In addition several of the third-century commentaries included in Lu Te-ming's 陸 德 明 *Ching-tien shih-wen* were based on this fifty-two chapter text: those of a certain 'Mr. Meng' 孟 氏, and the much more frequently cited one of Ssu-ma Piao 司 馬 彪.[66] Therefore it is likely that this fifty-two chapter version represents the original recension of the text.

Several scholars, including Ma Hsü-lun and Graham, suggest that when Kuo Hsiang revised the text he took sections he thought were valuable from the nineteen discarded chapters and placed them into the thirty-three chapters he retained.[67] Despite compiling the most complete collection of the lost *Chuang Tzu* fragments neither Ma nor Wang Shu-min could discover Kuo's rationale, nor any way of determining which fragments from the discarded material he had placed into the extant text.[68] However, Lu Te-ming's collection of earlier commentaries does give us one possible method. Whenever Lu Te-ming does not cite one of these early commentaries written before Kuo Hsiang for a particular section of text, and that section contains a different viewpoint than that of a prior section or the remainder of the chapter, we may suspect that that particular section was placed there by Kuo Hsiang and originated in the chapters he discarded. This method is not perfect: there is evidence that Lu sometimes omitted comments from earlier scholars, especially Ssu-ma Piao.[69] Also it assumes that Lu did not bother to look in others of the fifty-two chapters to find comments for these shuffled fragments. But it has been used before (for example, by Graham in identifying the Syncretist fragment at 11/66–74), and can give us a rough idea at least of which sections may have been shuffled into the extant text by Kuo Hsiang. Knowing this we can better determine if Kuo Hsiang is responsible for the divergent ideas in chapters 12–14.

In table 3 I have analysed the text of the most heterogeneous of the Syncretist chapters, 'Heaven and Earth' (#12), into its fifteen sections, and have provided the category into which Graham placed each of these sections. I have also indicated whether or not there are any comments from pre–Kuo Hsiang scholars for these sections included in Lu Te-ming's work, and have included brief comments on the topic of the section.

TABLE 3: 'Textual Shuffling' in Chuang Tzu 12

Section	Graham Category	Early Commentary	Comments
1–6	Syncretist	No	The Way of the ruler
6–12	Syncretist	Yes	'Rhapsody on the Way'
12–18	Syncretist	No	'Rhapsody on the Way'
18–20	Untranslated	Yes	Yellow Emperor
20–26	Untranslated	No	Yao and Hsü Yu
26–33	Immortality	Yes	Yao and the border guard
33–37	Utopia	No	Yao's rule
37–41	Rationalizing the Way	No	Great Beginning; Graham: broken off mutilated Autumn Floods dialogue
41–45	Confucius and Lao Tzu	Yes	Taoist self-cultivation
45–52	Untranslated	No	Government of sage
52–69	Stray Ideas	Yes	Methods of Mr. Hun-tun
69-77	Untranslated	Yes	Government of Sage
77–83	Utopia	Yes	When Supreme Power reigns
83–95	Primitivist-related	Yes	Criticism of hypocrisy
95–102	Primitivist	No	Five ways to lose one's nature; Graham: moved to Primitivist 8/26

Table 3 shows that despite a considerable degree of apparent heterogeneity in chapter 12, at the very least some of it must have been present in the version of this chapter included in the original fifty-two chapter recension, and that we cannot blame it all on Kuo Hsiang. This evidence represents a strong argument that the author of one of the Syncretist chapters could not have also compiled the entire book, for what could have been his rationale for including so much non-related material? It suggests instead that the compiler must have had a somewhat more liberal viewpoint, one that would have been willing to include, for example, stories about the Yellow Emperor (18–20) and Immortality (26–33) in a chapter whose overriding theme, it seems to me, is the government of the sage-king. However, we need not necessarily look outside the tradition of the Syncretists for the compiler. A later member of this tradition could easily have done this, someone who might have been rather more sympathetic to the Yellow Emperor and Immortality than an early Han Syncretist author. Given the presence of Esoteric Masters (*fang-shih*) at the court of Liu An, men who we know from the *Shih Chi* honored both that legendary ruler and that ultimate goal, I would suggest that we should look to Huai-nan to find our compiler. There is considerable evidence that if we did this, we would be looking in the right direction.

IIIB. The Chuang Tzu at Huai-nan

A significant part of the argument for placing the compiler of the *Chuang Tzu* at the court of Liu An has already been presented. The Syncretist chapters are part of the same philosophical lineage as the *Huai-nan Tzu*. There are about three hundred locations in the latter text which contain ideas, phrases, or entire paragraphs borrowed from the former, only one of which is attributed to Chuang Tzu. The ideological heterogeneity of chapters 11–14 indicates that an author of the Syncretist chapters is unlikely to have been the compiler. There are additional pieces of information which bolster the case.

To begin with, there can be no doubt that a version of the material contained in the extant *Chuang Tzu* was at the court of Liu An, and was influential in the writing of the *Huai-nan Tzu*. In addition to the many borrowings we can identify, Wang Shu-min has located eleven passages from the lost *Chuang Tzu* material that are presently in the *Huai-nan Tzu*, and he suspects there are many more.[70] The influence of the *Chuang Tzu* can be seen as well in the titles and topics of two of the essays in the *Huai-nan Tzu*: #11 *Ch'i-su* 齊 俗, in which the author applies the idea from the *Ch'i-wu lun* of the relativity of human experience to the subject of human customs, and #18 *Jen-chien* 人 間 .

However, the viewpoint of the authors of the *Huai-nan Tzu* is clearly different from that of the Inner Chapters of *Chuang Tzu*. They have the

Syncretists' concern for government that Chuang Tzu would have disdained. And when *Chuang Tzu* material is used it is often in a context that is alien to the man who wrote the 'Inner' Chapters. For example, see the Naturalist cosmogonic explanation of the famous infinite regress in the *Ch'i-wu lun* (2/49–52) at *Huai-nan Tzu* 2/1a, which is intended to demonstrate the futility of precisely the kind of reasoning used by the *Huai-nan Tzu* author. This suggests a strong influence from the *Chuang Tzu*, but not yet any clearly identifiable viewpoint associated with the text, most certainly not one determined primarily from the 'Inner' Chapters. This suggests to me a text in transition.

The name of Liu An is attached to two essays on the *Chuang Tzu* that were included in the original fifty-two chapter recension of the text. They are no longer extant, but a few lines from each of them have been preserved in the commentary on the *Wen-hsüan* 文選 written by Li Shan 李善 (d. 689), where they are accompanied by a comment from Ssu-ma Piao, thus indicating they were included in his edition of the text.[71] These fragments are as follows:

> From the 'Explanatory Colophon to the *Chuang Tzu*' (*Chuang Tzu Hou-chieh*):
>
> Keng Shih-tzu 庚市子 was a sage, a man without desires. There were men who were quarreling over valuables. Keng Shih-tzu divided some jade among them and they stopped quarreling.

This is attached to a line from the text which is now lost.

> From the 'Summary of the Essentials of *Chuang Tzu*' (*Chuang Tzu lüeh-yao*):
>
> The gentlemen of river and ocean, the hermits of mountain and valley (*shan-ku chih jen* 山谷之人) make light of the Empire, treat the myriad things as trifles, and traverse in solitude.

The two essays represented by these fragments must have been included in the three-chapter explanatory section (*chieh-shuo* 解說) of Ssu-ma Piao's edition.[72] They must have been included among the materials which "came from Huai-nan" which, in the colophon to the fragmentary Kozanji manuscript edition of the *Chuang Tzu*, Kuo Hsiang says he discarded.[73] They not only indicate an active interest in the *Chuang Tzu* by Liu An, but they also indicate that the text of the

Chuang Tzu must not have been fixed until it left Huai-nan. This is the only reason I can see for the inclusion of two of Liu An's essays in the original recension.

For all these reasons I think it likely that the text of the *Chuang Tzu* was compiled at the court of Liu An. However I do not think it is possible to identify the actual compiler.

Kuan Feng maintains the opinion that 'Below in the Empire' is actually the second of the lost *Chuang Tzu* essays of Liu An. Indeed, it does bear a striking resemblance to the title of the final essay of the *Huai-nan Tzu*, *Yao-lüeh*, which is likely to have been written by Liu. This seems to be the principal reason to identify him as the author. However there are a number of reasons why this is unlikely.

To begin with, the *Yao-lüeh* essay of the *Huai-nan Tzu* is a summary of each of the chapters of the text with a rationale for their inclusion and their order. This is certainly not the case for chapter 33 of *Chuang Tzu*. Second, it contains a discussion of the philosophy of Mo Tzu (21/7a) which is rather different from that found in 'Below in the Empire'. It is included in a section which explains the social and political conditions that led to the creation of certain philosophical texts and schools of thought, and does not criticize them from any superior standpoint. Third, the *Huai-nan Tzu* is written in regular parallel prose with rhymed verse interspersed; *Chuang Tzu* 33 is not. Finally, there is a distinct possibility that the fragment from Liu An's *Chuang Tzu lüeh-yao* quoted above can be linked to the opening section of 'Finicky Notions', in which the author criticizes the 'hermits of mountain and valley' (*shan-ku chih shih* 山 谷 之 士) (15/1). Liu An speaks of these hermits in the above fragment using virtually the same phrase. This fragment could have been part of a summary of this chapter similar to the summaries of the *Huai-nan Tzu* essays in *Yao-lüeh*. For these reasons it is highly unlikely that Liu An is the author of 'Below in the Empire'. His 'Explanatory Colophon' was probably a brief running commentary on the text appended to the end of it, as many early commentaries were; and his *Lüeh-yao* was probably a summary of the text similar to the final essay of the *Huai-nan Tzu*. It is a shame that Kuo Hsiang did not think these essays were worthy of transmission. Nonetheless their presence in the initial version of the *Chuang Tzu* provides further evidence for locating the compilation of the text at the court of Liu An.

IIIC. The Date of Compilation of the Chuang Tzu

Now that we have placed the compiling of the *Chuang Tzu* at the court of Liu An we have narrowed the possible date for this to between about 150 and 122 B.C.E., the years when Liu and his retainers were active. Is it possible to be even more precise? There are a few bits of evidence that could be construed to indicate that the text was compiled during the latter half of this period.

Wu Tse-yu mentions that in the 'Outer' Chapters all the occurrences of the character *heng* 恆 have been changed to *ch'ang* 常.[74] This was a taboo which began during the reign of Wen-ti (180–57 B.C.E.), and would hold for the next two reign periods of Ching-ti (157–40) and Wu-ti (140–87). The only two occurrences of *heng* in the 'Outer' Chapters are in locations for which there is no Ssu-ma Piao commentary recorded by Lu Te-ming (12/25 and 13/58). Hence they could be part of fragments inserted there by Kuo Hsiang.

There are occasional comments in some of the chapters which look like interpolations that could have been inserted by a Huang-Lao compiler. For example, Graham has noted two comments critical of the notion of 'abandoning affairs' at the beginning of the 'Fathoming Nature' chapter *Ta-sheng* 達生 (19/4,5) that come from a position of advocacy of involvement in the world that could be syncretist.[75] He also mentions four glosses in the Primitivist chapters which introduce an aphorism, three of which are taken from *Lao Tzu* (e.g. 11/28) PT.[76] This pattern of illustrating a saying from *Lao Tzu* with a story or a brief argument is found throughout the *Huai-nan Tzu*, especially in essay #12. Finally, there is a peculiar gloss at 33/9–10 which explains the utility of the Four Classics (*Shih, Shu, Li chi, Yueh*) and adds two others (*I*, and *Ch'un-ch'iu*). There was a revival of the study of the Six Classics under Han Wu-ti, and in the year 136 B.C.E. academic posts in the government bureaucracy were established for scholars who specialized in each of them.[77]

Finally, there is a brief comment about the Yellow Emperor's ascent to Heaven in the 'Inner' Chapters (6/33) that scholars have concluded is a late interpolation.[78] Yü Ying-shih maintains that this legend was originated by *fang-shih* during the reign of Wu-ti in their quest for political legitimacy. There were certainly *fang-shih* at the court of Liu An who could have inserted this idea into a text that was being compiled there.

There is one final piece to the puzzle: the frequent unattributed borrowings from the *Chuang Tzu* by the authors of the *Huai-nan Tzu*, and the totally random nature of these borrowings, suggests that they were not only thoroughly familiar with the *Chuang Tzu* materials, but that the text may have still been in flux while the *Huai-nan Tzu* was being written. This is also suggested by the fact that the Liu An essays were included in the original fifty-two chapter recension.

Based upon this admittedly circumstantial evidence, I would like to suggest the possibility that the *Chuang Tzu* was compiled at the court of Liu An after the *Huai-nan Tzu* was written, after the Six Classics were formally acknowledged with posts in the bureaucracy, and after the *fang-shih* began advocating their legend of the Yellow Emperor's ascent. This would approximate the date of compilation of the *Chuang Tzu* to about 130 B.C.E.

IV. Conclusions

I believe that the evidence presented in this study demonstrates that the authors of the Syncretist chapters of the *Chuang Tzu* were not isolated individuals, but were part of the lineage of thought that is called in the *Shih Chi* both the Taoist school and Huang-Lao. The Syncretist philosophy contains the three aspects that are characteristic of this philosophical lineage: a cosmology based on the Tao; a psychology whose theories are given a physiological basis in such concepts as the Vital Energy, Vital Essence, and the Numen, and which provides the theoretical basis for techniques of self-cultivation directed to the sage-ruler; and finally a political theory which begins with the Non-action of the self-cultivated ruler and which adopts elements from the political thought of other pre-Han schools, and which is based on an understanding of the Patterns of the cosmos of which human society is an integral part.

To be sure, there are certain differences in emphasis among the sources we have been considering which clearly indicate that none is from the same author or group of authors. But the striking conceptual and terminological parallels provide clear evidence that what we have here are different authors within the same philosophical lineage.

These conclusions enable us to begin to clarify the nature of Taoist philosophy and to begin to see it independent of the restrictions that have traditionally imposed on our understanding of it by the category of 'Lao-Chuang'. When we do so, we can begin to see, particularly in the element I have labeled as 'psychology', the possibilities of connections with parallel elements in the later Taoist religion. This would suggest that despite the fact that the origins of this religion remain obscure, that it does not represent the radical break with philosophical Taoism that many have suggested.

Our search for the compiler of the *Chuang Tzu* has enabled us to place its final chapters in a philosophical lineage, and also to trace its compilation to the court of Liu An, the King of Huai-nan. For the reasons presented above, I believe that the text of the *Chuang Tzu* was not fixed until after the completion of the *Huai-nan Tzu*. Further evidence, admittedly scanty, has enabled the approximation of the date of compilation to 130 B.C.E. So while we have not actually identified the actual compiler of the *Chuang Tzu*, we have been able to place him in a philosophical lineage, locate him in a specific place, and approximate when he completed his project. That may be as close to identifying him as it is possible to get.

NOTES

I would like to thank A. C. Graham, without whose pioneering scholarship, and generous help to a persistently obtuse younger scholar, this study would never have been attempted. I would also like to thank the students in my Han Taoism seminar at Brown University during the spring and autumn of 1988, whose perceptive and challenging questions enabled me to formulate many of the ideas in this study.

1. Lu Te-ming's (陸德明) *Chuang Tzu shih-wen* (莊子釋文) quotes an otherwise unidentified scholar named T'ang 唐 who questioned the

inconsistencies in chapter 28. All material from Lu is taken from his work as it is included in Kuo Ch'ing-f'an's 郭慶藩 *Chiao-cheng Chuang Tzu chi-shih* 校正莊子集釋. Taipei, 1974. This reference is at p. 989.

2. Wang Shu-min 王叔岷, *Chuang Tzu chiao-shih*. Shanghai, 1947, Preface.

3. Lo Mien-tao, *Nan-hua chen-ching hsun-pen* 南華真經循本. Tao Tsang edition, vols. 498–502.

4. For example, H. G. Creel, 'What is Taoism?', in *What is Taoism and Other Studies in Chinese Cultural History*. Chicago, 1970; and Huang Kung-wei 黃公偉, *Tao-chia che-hsüeh hsi-t'ung t'an-wei* 道家哲學系統探微, Taipei, 1981. Huang's book is a comprehensive study of Taoist thought including *Kuan Tzu*, and is an invaluable source for the later commentarial tradition of *Chuang Tzu*. However, he still attempts to present the *Chuang Tzu* as if the book contained the ideas of basically one man.

5. A. C. Graham, 'How Much of *Chuang Tzu* Did Chuang Tzu Write?', in *Studies in Chinese Philosophy and Philosophical Literature*. Singapore, 1986, pp. 283–321. Kuan Feng 關鋒 '*Chuang Tzu* wai tsa-p'ien ch'u-t'an', in *Chuang Tzu che-hsüeh t'ao-lun chi* 莊子哲學討論集. Peking, 1962, pp. 61–98.

6. Pan Ku's *Han-shu I-wen chih*, Hua-lien edition, Taipei, n.d., p. 38 mentions Sung Hsing as a Huang-Lao scholar. Yen Shih-ku's commentary on p. 33 quotes Liu Hsiang that both Sung Hsing and Yin Wen were at Chi-hsia. Kuo Mo-jo *Shih p'i-p'an shu* 十批判書 Peking, 1962, p. 154, lists them as Huang-Lao thinkers from Chi-hsia who formed one lineage of early Taoist philosophy. He further maintains that because Hsun Tzu did not understand the full range of Sung Hsing's ideas he thought he was a Mohist (pp. 162–63). Both men are criticized in the 'Below in the Empire' chapter of *Chuang Tzu* (*Chuang Tzu yin-te*, Harvard-Yenching Institute Sinological Series #33, 33/33–41. All references to the text are from the edition in this work). See A. C. Graham, *Disputers of the Tao* (LaSalle, Illinois: Open Court, 1989), pp. 95–100, for a detailed treatment of Sung Hsing.

7. 'Mending Nature' seems very close to the Primitivist perspective. It advocates a primal Utopia, and contains the only discussion of human nature outside the Primitivist documents. The principal reason it has not been classified as Primitivist is its advocacy of the Confucian moral virtues the Primitivist despises. This advocacy is contained in only two brief lines of text in which definitions of Benevolence, Rightness, Loyalty, Ritual, and Music, are linked to the Way and the Power (16/2–4). I would suggest the possibility that these lines are interpolations added by the Syncretist compiler to an essay in the

Primitivist mode written by a different author (because the style is so different). A. C. Graham, *Chuang Tzu: Textual Notes to a Partial Translation*. London, 1982, p. 45, cites Ma Hsu-lun on possible textual corruption here. The text makes sense without the forty-five characters beginning with 夫 德 and ending with 禮也.

8. Chuang Hsing was a late Warring States minister from Ch'u whose ideas are contained in a text entitled *Hsing-ch'en lun* 幸 臣 論. *Chung-wen ta-tz'u-tien* 31795.36

9. Harold D. Roth, 'Psychology and Self-Cultivation in Early Taoistic Thought'. *Harvard Journal of Asiatic Studies* 51.2, December, 1991.

10. The references to Huang-Lao teachings and masters scattered throughout the *Shih Chi* and *Han Shu* are summarized in K. C. Hsiao, *A History of Chinese Political Thought*, vol. 1 (translated by F. W. Mote). Princeton, 1979, pp. 552–56. See also Benjamin Schwartz, *The World of Thought in Ancient China*. Cambridge, 1985, pp. 237–54, for an excellent survey of Huang-Lao thought.

11. *Shih Chi*, ch. 74. Chung-hua edition, Peking, 1959, p. 2347, lists Shen Tao 慎 道 and T'ien Pien 田 駢 among the Huang-Lao thinkers at Chi-hsia. Both are criticized at *Chuang Tzu* 33/41–54. *Shih Chi*, ch. 80, p. 2436, gives a lineage of Huang-Lao masters, none of whom are the Huang-Lao scholars otherwise identified at Chi-hsia. There is as yet no scholarly consensus on the existence of any writings of any of these thinkers. Also *Shih Chi*, ch. 63, says that the thought of Han Fei-tzu and Shen Pu-hai was based in part on Huang-Lao. The relationship of pre-Han to Han Huang-Lao, and that (if any) of Huang-Lao to Legalism awaits further clarification, especially in light of the Huang-ti manuscripts discovered at Ma wang-tui. However, at this point I agree with Schwartz op. cit., p. 237, that Huang-Lao is much broader in scope than the fusion of Taoism and Legalism that many scholars now take it to be.

12. The term 'Lao-Chuang' seems to have first been used during the Wei and Chin Dynasties in the writings of, and about, the Profound Learning scholars such as Wang Pi, Ho Yen, Chi K'ang, and Kuo Hsiang. For details on this group see Ho Ch'i-min 何 啟 民 *Wei-Chin ssu-hsiang yu t'an-feng* 魏 晉 思 想 與 談 風. Taipei, 1967, pp. 103–15. See also Roth, op.cit., note 14.

13. The most complete discussion of Religious Taoist techniques of self-cultivation are found in two sources: Henri Maspero. 'Les Procèdes de Nourrir Le Principe Vitale Dans La Religion Taoiste Ancien', *Journal Asiatique*, 4–6, 1937, pp. 177–252; 7–9, pp. 353–430; translated by Frank Kierman in *Taoism and Chinese Religion*. Amherst, 1981, pp. 443–554.; and Joseph Needham, *Science and Civilization in Ancient China*, vol. 5, part 5. Cambridge, 1983.

These techniques involve the generation and manipulation of the Vital Energy (*ch'i*), the Vital Essence (*ching*), and the Numen (*shen*). These ideas are first developed in the three *Kuan Tzu* essays and the *Huai-nan Tzu*. For details see Roth, *op.cit.*

14. Kuan, op.cit., p. 61.

15. Graham, 'How Much', op.cit., p. 317.

16. Ibid., p. 316.

17. A. C. Graham, *Chuang Tzu: The Inner Chapters*. London, 1981, p. 257.

18. Schwartz, op.cit., p. 248.

19. *Huai-nan Tzu, Ssu-pu ts'ung-k'an* edition: 2/3b, 7b; 11/12b; 12/2a; 14/4b, 7a. All citations from this text and the *Kuan Tzu* are from the SPTK.

20. See the observations of Schwartz, op.cit., pp. 250ff.

21. Ssu-ma Ch'ien says that his father studied Taoist treatises with a man named Master Huang 黃子. The commentator Hsu Kuang identifies him as Huang Sheng 黃生, a Huang-Lao master. *Shih Chi*, ch. 130, p. 3288.

22. Ibid., p. 3289. For the rationale for translating *ching-shen* as 'Numinous Essence' (a shortened form of 'Numen as Vital Essence') see Roth, op.cit., note 19, and section on *ching-shen*.

23. Translated by Benjamin Wallacker in *Behavior, Culture, and Cosmos*. New Haven, 1962.

24. *Shih Chi*, ch. 130, p. 3289.

25. Ibid., p. 3292.

26. Kuo Mo-jo, 'Sung Hsing Yin Wen i-chu k'ao' 宋鈃尹文遺著考, in *Ch'ing-t'ung shih-tai* 清銅時代. Shanghai, 1951 (reprinted, Peking, 1957), pp. 245–71.

27. Kuan, op.cit., pp. 70–80.

28. See Kuo 'Sung Hsing', op.cit., and Allyn Rickett, *Kuan Tzu: A Repository of Early Chinese Thought*. Hong Kong, 1965, pp. 155–58. Graham, *Disputers of the Tao*, op.cit., p. 100 speaks of the *Nei-yeh* as a fourth-century B.C.E. work. A fourth text, *Pai-hsin* 白心 'The Purified Mind', is usually considered with these other three, but because of the virtual absence of any theories of self-cultivation in this work I see no compelling reason to do so.

29. Roth, op.cit.

30. Graham, 'How Much', op.cit., pp. 316–17.

31. Graham, *Disputers of the Tao*, op.cit., p. 100.

32. *Te* is absent from the SPTK edition but present in the Liu Chi edition.

33. See note 22.

34. Maspero (Kierman), op.cit., pp. 36, 282, 365, 368, 409, 419.

35. Rickett, op.cit., p. 156.

36. Textual notes: *Line 1*: I read 反 as 身 after Kuo Mo-jo *Kuan Tzu chi-chiao*. Peking, 1955, p. 652; *Line 3*: Reversing the order of 行 and 正, and reading 美 as 儀; after Kuo, p. 652; *Line 4*: Reading 美 as 儀; a similar-form corruption, based on context.

37. Hsiao (Mote), op.cit., pp. 570–73.

38. Roth, op.cit.

39. Roger T. Ames, *The Art of Rulership*, Hawaii, 1983.

40. For an excellent analysis of Naturalist philosophy in the *Huai-nan Tzu* see John Major, *Topography and Cosmology in Early Han Thought*. Unpublished doctoral dissertation, Harvard University, 1973.

41. See the analysis of the *Ching-shen* essay of the *Huai-nan Tzu* in Roth, op.cit.

42. Harold D. Roth, 'The Concept of Human Nature in the *Huai-nan Tzu*'. *Journal of Chinese Philosophy*, 12, 1985, pp. 1–22.

43. For a tabulation of the occurrences of textual borrowings in the *Huai-nan Tzu* see Charles LeBlanc, *The Idea of Resonance in Early Han Thought*. Hong Kong, 1985, p. 83. For an analysis of the use of *Chuang Tzu* material in the *Huai-nan Tzu* see Wang Shu-min, '*Huai-nan Tzu yu Chuang Tzu*' , in Ch'en Hsin-hsiung 陳新雄 and Yü Ta-ch'eng 于大成, *Huai-nan Tzu lun-wen chi*. Taipei, 1976, pp. 27–39.

44. *Huai-nan Tzu*, 12/15b8–9.

45. For example see the Naturalist cosmogonic interpretation in *Huai-nan Tzu* 2/1a of the famous infinite regress in *Chuang Tzu* 2/49–52.

46. Kuan, op.cit., pp. 71–73; Graham, 'How Much', op.cit., pp. 318–19.

47. Graham, loc.cit.,and *Chuang Tzu*, p. 257.

48. Graham, *Chuang Tzu*, p. 265.

49. Ibid., p. 268.

50. Ibid., p. 271.

51. Ibid., p. 269.

52. Ibid., p. 259.

53. Ibid., p. 265.

54. Loc.cit.

55. While Ssu-ma T'an does not actually use the term *li*, I interpret the sentence translated above in section IIA to refer to the discovery of the natural guidelines which govern the activity of all phenomena: '(The Taoist school) is therefore able to explore the genuine basis of things 故能究物之情.

56. Graham, *Chuang Tzu*, op.cit., p. 274.

57. Ames, op.cit., especially chapters 5 and 6.

58. Graham, *Chuang Tzu*, op.cit., p. 261.

59. Ibid., pp. 261–62.

60. Textual notes: *Line 1*: I read 無 as 而 after Wang Nien-sun (Kuo, *Kuan Tzu*, op.cit., p. 635); *Line 3*: I read 之 as 有 after Ting Shih-han (Kuo, p. 636); *Line 4*: I read 未 as 大 after Ting and Kuo (Kuo, p. 636).

61. Ames, op.cit.

62. Ibid., p. 149.

63. Loc.cit.

64. Ibid., p. 153.

65. Graham, 'How Much', op.cit., p. 317.

66. See Lu Te-ming's preface in Kuo Ch'ing-fan, op.cit., pp. 6–7.

67. Ma Hsü-lun *Chuang Tzu i-cheng*. Shanghai, 1930. Graham, 'How Much', op.cit., p. 302.

68. Wang Shu-min, *Chuang Tzu chiao-shih*. Wang collected 149 fragments of the lost *Chuang Tzu* material and Ma, 126.

69. Kuo Ch'ing-fan found fragments of the Ssu-ma Piao commentary that are not included in Lu Te-ming. For example, see pp. 386, 555, 1103, 1114.

70. Wang Shu-min, '*Huai-nan Tzu* yü *Chuang Tzu*', op.cit., pp. 39–40.

71. *Wen-hsüan chu* 文 選 注, SPTK edition, 26/24a; 31/29a; 60/16a.

72. See Lu Te-ming's preface in Kuo Ch'ing-fan, op.cit., p. 7.

73. The Kozanji manuscript edition containing seven chapters of the *Chuang Tzu* (23, 26–28, 30, 31, 33) contains the lost colophon of Kuo Hsiang previously only known in fragmentary form in Lu Te-ming. It is analysed in Wang Shu-min, 'Po Jih-pen Kao-shan-ssu chiu-ch'ao chüan-tzu pen *Chuang Tzu* ts'an chüan', reprinted in *Chu-tzu chiao-cheng*. Taipei, 1964, pp. 549–65.

74. Wu Tse-yü 吳 則 虞, '*Huai-nan Tzu* shu-lu', *Wen-shih* 文 史 2, 1963, p. 314.

75. Graham, *Chuang Tzu*, op.cit., pp. 181–2.

76. Ibid., p. 199.

77. Michael Loewe, *Chinese Ideas of Life and Death*. London, 1982, p. 182.

78. Yü Ying-shih, 'Life and Immortality in the Mind of Han China', *Harvard Journal of Asiatic Studies*, 25 (1965), p. 105.

Hsun Tzu and Chuang Tzu

6

David S. Nivison

[*Angus Graham's* Chuang Tzu: the Inner Chapters *I count as one of the most valuable books in my library, and I have used it in the following reflections, which are in part prompted by Graham's conjectures about the development of Chuang Tzu's thinking from its Yang Chu background (see especially pp. 117–118). But I take these conjectures just a notch farther, and my primary aim has been to understand Hsun Tzu better thereby.—D.S.N.*]

There are puzzling features of Hsun Tzu's philosophy, and one suspects that they are related. Hsun Tzu argued that language, understood as names for things, is artificial, having been invented and decreed by the sage-kings to satisfy human and administrative needs; yet he also thinks the language we have is right, and deplores the confusions of the sophists who treat names as merely conventional. He thought that the sage-kings likewise created 'rites and norms', i.e., the ordinary moral rules and standards of civilized society; and yet he also thinks that these rules and standards are universally binding on us and are not merely conventions. And when he tries to analyze the reasons an individual has for accepting the moral order (as, for example, in the latter part of the essay 'Rectifying Names'), he tries to show that a cool calculation will lead one from one's ordinary desires to acceptance of the moral 'Way' as the best means of optimizing satisfactions. Yet when he explains how one should 'cultivate oneself' (see the essay by that name) so as to make this acceptance effective, he portrays the cultivated gentleman as one who loves the 'Way' so that he is willing to die for it, as one who has trained himself to think, see, say, do only what is right, as one who has been transformed by this 'learning' so that it penetrates his entire being. And at times Hsun Tzu bursts out in paeans of praise of the 'rites' and the 'gentleman' as having a place in the cosmic order coequal with Heaven and Earth (for example, in 'A Discussion of Ritual' and in 'The Regulations of a King').

At a deeper level, to some Hsun Tzu has seemed to have two contrasting concepts of the mind: (1) There is the mind as fully engaged in the life of the self, as 'director', choosing which desires to satisfy and proceeding to suitable action—and so, in the 'cultivated' self, the mind so conceived is completely committed to the 'Way' of the gentleman. And (2), there is the mind as disengaged, as 'spectator' of the self, enabling one to be 'unattached' to one's own passions and actions, letting passions defuse themselves harmlessly without disturbing one's peace of mind or interfering with calm decision. Such a mind would be ultimately uncommitted.

The first of these concepts, one might argue, takes shape in Hsun Tzu's criticism of Mencius, who wrongly supposed that the self's natural movement is toward 'appropriate' (good) action, without the need of 'direction'. Here one may look at the way Hsun Tzu advises us to look at and manage ourselves in 'Human Nature Is Evil'. But perhaps one sees it also expressed in the many strongly hortatory passages and essays throughout the book, and especially in the 'paeans' I have referred to.

One might argue that the second is revealed in the cool, distanced analytical attitude that enables Hsun Tzu to counsel this kind of engagement. And one might even be tempted to say that the second Hsun Tzu comes to it by accepting Chuang Tzu's idea that for inner peace and steadiness we must be 'detached': One seems to see this concept of the mind most clearly in Hsun Tzu's essay 'Dispelling Obsession', in which there are obvious Taoist overtones. Thus the enlightened man's mind is like a still pan of water (compare the Taoist image of the mind as a mirror, *Chuang Tzu* 7), reflecting reality without distortion. It is able to be 'empty', in that while filled with stored past impressions it can be detached from these and so can accept and evaluate impartially a new impression. It is able to be 'unified', in that while constantly occupied with many things, it is able to single out and attend to the one thing that is its business. And it is able to be 'still', in that while always active, it is able to stand back from itself and see clearly the distinction between what it is really perceiving and what it is merely dreaming or imagining. In all of these ways the mind maintains its autonomy by distancing itself from and observing, at a higher level, the buzzing confusion of its own activity at a lower level.

Here I describe a Hsun Tzu that is readily found. It is now tempting to suggest that in taking this stance Hsun Tzu does follow Chuang Tzu, but rejects the Taoist assumption that to be the disengaged 'spectator' one must 'withdraw from the world': the mind is 'subtle' enough, Hsun Tzu thinks, to be able to be engaged in action and emotion yet be, as 'spectator', detached at the same time. The former ('mind as director') aspect of Hsun Tzu, oriented toward his critique of Mencius, is the obvious and 'exoteric' side of him; the latter ('mind as spectator') aspect, derived from Chuang Tzu, is the unrecognized but more basic 'esoteric' side. The real Hsun Tzu is 'unattached' even to the Confucian moral-ritual Way, seeing it ultimately as merely 'conventional', not 'universal'. Hsun Tzu's occasional rhapsodic paeans to the cosmic beauty of the order of 'Heaven', the order of the 'rites', and the role of the 'gentleman' belong to his 'exoteric' side, and have no logical place in his thinking, thus forcing us to recognize the 'esoteric' aspect as the real Hsun Tzu.

Against this picture, I shall argue that there is no need to suppose that Hsun Tzu's thought has both an 'exoteric' and an 'esoteric' aspect. This will require that I reexamine and criticize the picture of Chuang Tzu that was assumed here, and of the way Hsun Tzu responded to him.

In fact, the picture of Mencius is not quite right. We can read M 6A 15 as saying quite explicitly that our senses can move us toward inappropriate sensual gratification if the mind fails to perform its superintending function; to this extent, Mencius too has a concept of the mind as 'director'. But (M 2A 2, 6A 6, 7A 3, etc.) our mind does this ideally not by forcing the self but by 'seeking', bringing into focus and encouraging natural good-tending impulses, and giving them priority over the selfish ones; whereas for Hsun Tzu all our impulses are selfish, though some are such that the wise man will try to satisfy them and some not; and the ones we wisely satisfy are not the immediately compelling ones, so stern discipline is necessary. Hsun Tzu does, indeed, criticize the thought in Mencius 6 A 15: it is there that Mencius identifies 'obsession' (*pi*) as a psychic danger; but for Mencius this danger is only a danger that our senses will be 'obsessed' by beguiling objects, if the mind fails to perform its 'directing' job. Hsun Tzu's opening point in 'Dispelling Obsession' is that the really serious danger is that the directing mind will be obsessed by a beguiling but wrong idea.

The basic difficulty, I think, is that we have got Chuang Tzu wrong. This is easily done, since there is such a mad variety of ideas in the *Chuang Tzu*—a book that is obviously not by a single author, as we all agree (and as Graham has carefully shown, in 'How Much of *Chuang Tzu* Did Chuang Tzu Write?', *Journal of the American Academy of Religion*, Thematic Issue, Vol. XLVII, Three S [September 1979] 459–501). I grant that one does find in it the idea that detachment is the way to Taoist fulfillment, together sometimes with the idea that detachment requires withdrawal from the world; further, one can find this idea in the first seven chapters, that I and most others would accept as the 'basic' *Chuang Tzu*, whether or not actually the work of one person: consider, for example, the picture of the Taoist saint Lieh Tzu in chapter 7.

The trouble, however, is that the more characteristic idea in the earliest strata of the *Chuang Tzu* is precisely the idea that we have suggested was Hsun Tzu's 'esoteric' improvement on Chuang Tzu—that detachment is desirable, but that it does not require disengagement. In fact, Chuang Tzu goes farther than this: we are caught in the world as it is, and we cannot get out of it. Even a posture of withdrawal would itself be a form of engagement, and could be dangerous unless recognized as such.

Before I proceed, this claim calls for proof. Here I accept the suggestion of the late Henri Maspero ('Essai sur le Taoisme', IV Appendice 1, 'Les techniques d'immortalité et la vie mystique dans l'école Taoiste au temps de Tchouang-tseu' (pp. 201–218), pp. 215–216, in *Mélanges Posthumes sur les Religions et l'Histoire de la Chine* (Paris, 1950), vol. II *Le Taoisme*) that ancient Chinese philosophical Taoist mysticism, like other mysticisms, had a conception of a realisation that was the goal of a via mystica (though I think Maspero overlooks the great differences between the Taoist's 'mystic's path' and such 'paths' in Indian and Western systems; I am indebted to Lee Yearley for pointing this out to me). And I accept also a further suggestion of Maspero's, that we have in the *Chuang Tzu* an account that (whether true or not) is to be understood as Chuang Tzu's own entry upon such a 'path'. Entry upon the path, Maspero argues, is thought to require a 'conversion experience' that may be brought on by an experience of shock.

In Chuang Tzu's case, Maspero argues (p. 215), this experience is found in the semi-final section of chapter 20 ('the Mountain Tree'; not one of the earliest, but containing matter similar to the first seven chapters). Chuang Tzu is wandering in a private park (perhaps a sacred enclave containing a chestnut grove), and is intent on a bit of poaching, crossbow in hand. He sees a huge magpie, and takes aim—but just then notices that the bird, oblivious to the danger to itself, is about to snatch up a mantis, which in turn fails to see the bird because it is intent on making a meal of a cicada, blissfully relaxing in a spot of shade. (This is a tale, not biography: the magpie-mantis-cicada drama is a literary set-piece expressing the Yang Chu viewpoint; see *Shuo yuan** 9.4b–5a). Chuang Tzu the philosopher is fascinated: each of these creatures has forgotten its real interest—i.e., 'attached' to immediate gratification, is about to lose its life, which could have been preserved, we might suppose, only by 'withdrawal' from mindless pursuit of 'profit'. He shudders; 'Ah!—things do nothing but make trouble for each other—one creature calling down disaster on another!' He throws down his bow and runs—but is almost too late: the gamekeeper, spying him, is in hot pursuit. In a state of shock, Chuang Tzu stays home for three months. (Some texts have 'three days', but the point is the same. For this and the following, compare translations in Burton Watson, *The Complete Works of Chuang Tzu*, New York: Columbia University Press, 1968, p. 219; in Maspero, pp. 215–216; and in Graham, below.)

Graham, in his recent translation and study (*Chuang-tzu: The Seven Inner Chapters, and Other Writings from the Book Chuang-tzu*, London: George Allen & Unwin, 1981, pp. 117–118), also, like Maspero (and acknowledging a suggestion from my colleague Lee Yearley), recognizes this as a traumatic conversion experience. But Graham perhaps did not quite notice one important part of this experience. To fix it, I follow Graham himself: Graham argues that Chuang Tzu began as a follower of (or of the school of) the early fourth century B.C.E. recluse-philosopher Yang Chu, who taught that it is hopeless to take office seeking to reform the world, and dangerous to do so seeking fame or gain, and that the best personal course is to realize that self-preservation and equanimity can be attained only by an ascetic withdrawal from social life.

If this was Chuang Tzu's persuasion when he went wandering in the park of Tiao-ling, his experience had a double meaning for him. What he observed showed him that existence is a net of mutual trouble-making in which all creatures are caught, by their attachments; and his own experience of being rudely surprised by the game-keeper showed him that the philosopher's conceit that he can distance himself by simply observing is itself a mode of involvement; you are in the world at all times yourself, and you can't get out of it. His initial itch to shoot the bird was not what had trapped him; he had quite forgotten about that by the time he was surprised by the gamekeeper. It was his philosophy of withdrawal itself that caused him to be so fascinated by the three creatures he was watching, and to watch them so intently, that he forgot his own safety. That philosophy at that instant had 'self-destructed'. Withdrawal itself is an entanglement. "Staring at muddy water, I have been misled into taking it for a clear pool." (Following Maspero; Graham has "I have been looking at reflections in muddy water, have gone astray from the clear pool.")

Perhaps Chuang Tzu's own teacher had suggested the way out: "I have heard my master say, 'When you go among ordinary men, accept the ordinary ways'." (My translation, again following Maspero; Graham's "If it's the custom there, do as you're told," like Watson's, implies that Chuang Tzu's discomfort was due merely to his flouting park rules.) That is, withdrawal has to be an inner withdrawal, while one 'plays the game', engages in the ordinary activities that are normal in one's situation. Returning now to the 'Inner' Chapters, we find this idea explored again and again. Chapter 4 is especially rich: "Have no gate, no opening, but . . . live with what cannot be avoided. . . . Walk without touching the ground" (Watson p. 58; Graham has "leave off making footprints", p. 69). So Chuang Tzu has Confucius say to his disciple Yen Hui, bent on taking office in Wei, in the parody Chuang constructs in the opening section. (The parody is of Mencius, 2A 1–2; compare the "fast of the mind" with Kao Tzu's recipe for psychic steadiness, and notice the contrast between Taoist detachment and Confucian courage.)

Carried to its extreme, Chuang Tzu's attitude can even imply that one must recognize and accept as inevitable those basic social, political, and psychic commitments, such as loyalty to ruler and love for parents, that are prized by the Confucians. In this context, even fixation on one's own personal safety can be a form of entanglement that can threaten one's peace of mind and, paradoxically, can threaten personal safety itself (see section 2 of the same chapter, on the anxieties of the Duke of She). The real adept has attained a degree of detachment-in-engagement that is so subtle that he can actually concentrate with complete singleness of mind on the execution of the skill that is his in his role, without being in the least 'worn' by so doing; this is why the philosopher-cook, the Compleat Butcher in chapter 3, is said to teach us "how to care for life". (The story is allegorical: just as Yen Hui is to "walk without touching the ground", so Chuang Tzu's cook carves without letting his knife (sc. self) touch bone that would dull it.)

If I am right in all this, then we cannot say that Hsun Tzu took over Chuang Tzu's goal of detachment, but improved on Chuang Tzu by noticing that detachment does not require literal withdrawal from the world—for this is Chuang Tzu's own position. If the 'real' Hsun Tzu is not simply a Taoist rather than a Confucian moralist, he must be saying something else. What might it be?

Just as Chuang Tzu's Taoist cannot disengage from the world, but must at best be active yet unattached, so also he cannot step outside himself in a meditative withdrawal, to view the self as an other, an object of analysis that would reveal its structure and its 'true ruler' (chapter 2), for (we can fill in his thought) the adoption of such a stance is just another posture of the self: the 'I' is 'systematically elusive', and so (as Wang Yang-ming was to notice centuries later) any philosophically saving 'spectator'-like 'quiescence' must be concomitant with ongoing psychic and emotional 'activity'. Nor can he make the Tao, the 'Way' of everything, the object of his thought, for that attitude itself is part of what the 'Way' is the way of. The Way knows no boundaries. One can only empty the mind of its prejudices, Chuang Tzu hopes (chapter 4, part 1), and let higher daemonic energies enter (Graham, pp. 68–69). This inner freedom from 'attachment' is itself the tranquility that all men desire—for the Taoist.

For Hsun Tzu, tranquility is a common-sense good: the ease of mind that makes simple goods enjoyable, where riches and privileges would make one fret lest they be lost (chapter 22, 'The Correct Use of Names'). But Hsun Tzu makes this point only to make it obvious that the Tao—the Confucian Way of an ideal society, in which my desires are subjected to order—is the best way of life I can choose. There is no suggestion whatever here of a 'Way' that is beyond conception, or of an ataraxia as a supreme personal religious goal. It is true that Hsun Tzu values mental detachment, and one can point rightly to the 'Dispelling Obesession' chapter's analysis of the mind's capacity for 'emptiness', 'unity', and 'stillness', in Hsun Tzu's carefully defined senses, as explaining how the mind can concentrate on a problem without getting 'stuck' on it. I suspect that one would be right, also, in suggesting that Hsun Tzu is led to this matter by reflecting on Chuang Tzu's idea of detachment (indeed, Chuang's idea of detachment-in-engagement).

But this state of mind in Hsun Tzu is a means to clear thinking and correct judgment, not a religious goal, not an end in itself. Hsun Tzu is quite explicit in the 'Dispelling Obsession' chapter: "The mind must first understand the Way before it can approve it, and it must first approve it before it can abide by it and reject what is at variance with it" (Burton Watson, *Hsun Tzu: Basic Writings*, New York: Columbia University Press, 1963, p. 127). The mind can do this by being "empty, unified and still"—detached, if one wants the word, but in the sense Hsun Tzu proceeds to explain. Hsun Tzu's concept of 'obsession' comes from Mencius, as we noted; but Mencius speaks of 'obsession' as a danger that besets the physical senses only, and then only when the mind (*hsin*) fails to do its natural job of noticing the distinction between the 'higher' (*ta t'i*) and 'lower' (*hsiao t'i*) parts of the self. Hsun Tzu sees that the mind itself can be 'obsessed', so that it is drawn to pursue a wrong end, while thinking it to be right. The danger can be met only by cultivating the mind's capacity to keep itself in order as it is functioning: to be open to new impressions no matter how 'full' it is, to keep its contents clear and distinct no matter how diverse they are, and to maintain a sense of reality no matter how free the constant movement of thought and imagination. Hsun Tzu probably did notice Chuang Tzu's idea of mental balance (in chapter 2 of Chuang Tzu), and he may have been reflecting on it in the 'Obsession' chapter; but he obviously didn't accept it. For Chuang, for a mind to be partial to anything at all is for it to be unbalanced. For Hsun Tzu, balance is necessary if the mind is to make appropriate choices.

But Hsun Tzu's Confucianism really is something new; it is a Confucian vision that no philosopher could have conceived until after Chuang Tzu's Taoism had happened. And if I have to reject the idea that it is an ultimately 'unattached' Confucianism, in a supposed 'esoteric' aspect, ultimately seeing even basic Confucian norms as a kind of conventional 'game', I can nonetheless see why one is tempted to say this of Hsun Tzu. Hsun Tzu does have two quite different modes—the engaged, committed, almost poetic and passionate, and the cool, detached, objective, analytical; and he can shift from one to the other disconcertingly. Further, there is a distinct Taoist echo in him. Over and over, I think we can see Hsun Tzu's thought taking forms that we can understand only if we think of him as having first thought his way through Chuang Tzu.

Chuang Tzu in the second section of chapter 4 says, through the persona of Confucius himself, some startlingly Confucian things: "In the world there are two supreme commandments. . . . One of them is destiny, the other duty. A child's love of his parents is destined; it cannot be dispelled from the heart. A minister's service to his lord is duty; wherever he may go his lord is his lord" (Graham, p. 70). We can always suppose a Confucian interpolation in a book that all admit is textually out of control; but the trouble is that this is something, as I have already argued, that one can see a Chuang Tzu with his concept of detached engagement as being quite willing to say; and the text continues in just this way. If Chuang Tzu can go this far, could we perhaps say that Hsun

Tzu's Confucianism is the logical outcome of Chuang Tzu's Taoism, in some sense—even if not the sense we tried? Let us see.

'Detachment'—our word, not Chuang Tzu's—is misleading, in suggesting that we are 'attached' only to things we want or favor. But the mental attitude that prevents equanimity can as easily be toward something we fear. The paradigm is the fear of death. Many Taoists have thought that we can escape death, by a hermit-like life and by other means, and there are vestiges of this view even in the Chuang Tzu book; but the idea is not Chuang's. He took it for granted that we all die. Here, then, is something that we cannot remove ourselves from through a choice of life style. We can only escape 'attachment' to it, by an appropriate change of attitude.

By what change? The only answer Chuang Tzu gives is one that is similar to his approach to other attachments: we all have received attitudes toward everything—this is good, that bad, this to be hoped for, that to be feared; but these are merely prejudices. This is so, also, of death: we do not know what our state is to be after death, so we have no reason to fear it; we have to accept the thing, death, but the accepted attitude is silly. Chuang says this most memorably in chapter 2; there is much more in chapter 6, where we also find the thought, almost a Chuang Tzu trademark, that death, as part of the Process (tao) of all nature, is to be accepted as a marvellous transformation. "Therefore that I find it good to live is the very reason why I find it good to die" (chapter 6, Graham, p. 86).

Chuang could have gone farther, and the book hints at the possibility when talking of the attitude to be taken toward the death of another, in the anecdote about the death of Chuang Tzu's wife in chapter 18, part 2. Hui Tzu finds his friend beating on a tub and singing, and reproaches him. Chuang Tzu says, "When she first died, do you suppose that I was able not to feel the loss?" The hint is that it was perfectly natural to grieve; but the lesson drawn is that it was too common to be short-sighted about it, which the Taoist is not: Chuang reflected that his wife's death was part of the process that included her birth and her life; it would betray a lack of understanding of fate if he continued to grieve; "so I stopped" (Graham, p. 124).

The next step in the dialectic, which Chuang Tzu does not take, would have been to say, is it not fate also that I should grieve? Seeing this, I need not stop; but at least I should see what I am: bereaved husband, I grieve, naturally, perhaps inevitably; but becoming 'spectator' to myself as mourner, I can at a second level of myself maintain tranquility of mind; my grief need not interfere. While Chuang Tzu does not take this step vis-à-vis death and grieving, it is precisely the step he does take, in the persona of Confucius, in chapter 4, part 2: you are a man, says Confucius; therefore you have a ruler, and you have parents, and you cannot escape the obligation of loyalty to the one and love to the other; indeed the love is not just an obligation: "It cannot be dispelled from the heart" (Graham, p. 70). But if you can recognize this and accept it, you can still be at peace: ". . . in the service of one's own heart [there is] no higher degree of Power than, without joy or sorrow ever alternating before it, to know that these things could not be otherwise, and to be content with them as our destiny."

This is still the attitude of a Taoist. There is one more step in the dialectic that is possible, and if Chuang Tzu had taken it he would have thought his way to the Confucian Tao. Hsun Tzu took that step. Consider again grief, and consider with it the attitude Chuang does take toward death—lyrical acceptance of it as part of the marvellous process of nature. He might have applied this latter attitude to grief itself: grieving is not just "what I did at first like anybody else", until I realized I was being silly; on the contrary, grief is fitting, and it is beautiful. If one can see this, one can as easily see that the institutional forms for the expression of grief—not tub-thumping, but the decorous forms of mourning—are likewise fitting and beautiful; and the history of human culture, that gives us these forms, is to be recognized as an aspect of the tao-process just as much as the process of individual life and death. A Confucius with this point of view would have said, in chapter 4, not that inner peace can be maintained in spite of our involvement in loyalty and love, but that it is gained through those 'involvements', once we really understand them, seeing them as essential to a complete humanity.

The most obvious example of this viewpoint in Hsun Tzu is his treatment of ritual, grief, and mourning at the close of the long chapter 19, 'A Discussion of Rites'. "How full of grief it is, how reverent!" ". . . The sacrificial rites originate in the emotions of remembrance and longing, express the highest degree of loyalty, love, and reverence, and embody

what is finest in ritual conduct and formal bearing" (Watson, *Hsun Tzu*,
p. 110–11). One could quote and quote. It is no accident that earlier on in
this chapter we find one of the most eloquent of Hsun Tzu's rhapsodic
'paeans' to the rites as part of his whole vision of the world: "Through
rites Heaven and earth join in harmony, the sun and moon shine, the
four seasons proceed in order, the stars and constellations march, the
rivers flow, and all things flourish; men's likes and dislikes are regulated
and their joys and hates made appropriate" (Watson, p. 94). Hsun Tzu's
vision is more explicit in chapter 9, 'The Regulations of a King' (p. 44):
Heaven and earth are the beginning of life, rites and norms are the
beginning of order, and the gentleman is the beginning of rites and
norms (reading 'rites and norms' for Watson's 'ritual principles').

The vision is that the human world, centrally man's world of
institutions, ideals, and norms, is the flowering of what is most
fundamental in the entire world of nature, and is deserving of just that
savoring, admiration, and reverence that the Taoist accords to his tao,
the order of nature and all its manifestations; and like the Taoist, Hsun
Tzu focusses his attitude of wonder on both the whole of his world and
on its detail; but like the Taoist, he does not exclude social and religious
forms as being at best non-obstacles to realization; on the contrary they
are the very substance of it. Accordingly, realization can't be ataraxia;
reading Hsun Tzu's chapter 'On Music', one might almost say that it is
ordered passion. But—here, perhaps, one may see a Taoist tone—the
ordering, by way of 'rites' and 'music', is a systematic distancing, and is
liberating: our passions continue for a time, but no longer possess us.

The most interesting, and to us the most puzzling, aspect of this
vision is the way it leads one to see value and obligation as natural 'facts',
even, in Hsun Tzu, data for which one can give a ('detached'?)
naturalistic or historical account, without their in any way ceasing to be,
really, values, and obligations. The viewpoint is simply blind to the
'facts-values' dichotomy that is natural to most of us. Here, I think,
Hsun Tzu reveals a way of thinking that just seemed obvious to third
and second century B.C.E. China (and to much of later China too). The
text that follows is a paragraph from one of the *Yi Ching* appendices
(Hsu kua II):

There were Heaven and Earth, and after that there were the innumerable things. There were the innumerable things, and after that there were male and female. There were male and female, and after that there were husband and wife. There were husband and wife, and after that there were father and son. There were father and son, and after that there were ruler and subject. There were ruler and subject, and after that there was the distinction between high and low. There was the distinction between high and low, and after that rites and norms developed in turn.

The magical and religious assumptions that most readers of the Yi would have brought to this text were not Hsun Tzu's; and here Hsun Tzu and Chuang Tzu are alike: for neither of them is Heaven a divine being in the usual sense. For both, Heaven, nature, and all its works are the object of an ecstatic wonder, religious in tone: 'all', that is to say for each according to his point of view, and Hsun Tzu's was more inclusive than Chuang Tzu's. It was a view large enough for him to see human customs, 'rites', norms, as both products of human invention, and so 'conventional', and yet as 'universal'. They had to happen, come to be, in more or less the form they have, sooner or later; and the fact that we see they are man-made does not insulate them from our commitment to them: their 'artificiality' thus in no way renders them not really obligatory and normative.

Hsun Tzu's gentleman cannot, therefore, be seen as 'detached' from his Confucian commitments, so to speak 'playing' them as ultimately a kind of 'game'—the commitments being Hsun Tzu's 'exoteric' side, and the 'spectator' stance, the 'detachment', the 'game' perspective, being his 'esoteric' side. Like all of us, Hsun Tzu must have developed with time; and like most of us, he had his difficulties making completely consistent sense of his own position. But I cannot see that Hsun Tzu saw himself—or his ideal 'gentleman'—as having two faces, apparently completely committed, actually completely detached.

Perhaps, then, here at last is the solution to the puzzle Hsun Tzu struggles with in 'Human Nature Is Evil': How could the sage-kings, in the beginning of things, have created morality unless morality were already a part of their 'nature'? Hsun Tzu insists they did it through their superior creative intelligence; but (we keep wondering) wouldn't morality then have been, from their own point of view, merely a 'noble lie'? But no: through their superior intelligence they understood human nature and the inescapable human situation, and so also saw that the introduction of order was necessary (see opening paragraph to 'A Discussion of Rites'). So seeing, they formulated laws and norms, and then not only promulgated them to men, but also recognized them as binding on themselves—seeing their moral order as having the same sort of ordering authority over all human life as do the rising and setting of the sun. Through their intelligence they moralized themselves as well as us.

[*In working out this essay, I have derived much profit not only from Angus Graham's work, but also from reading and thinking about Professor Lee H. Yearley's article 'Hsun Tzu on the Mind', in* The Journal of Asian Studies *39.3 (May 1980) pp. 465–480. Using the 'mind as director'–'mind as spectator' concepts to describe Hsun Tzu is Yearley's experiment. I have, obviously, picked at both of my mentors; this, it seems, is my destiny.—D.S.N.*]

The Mencian Conception of *Ren xing* 人性: Does it Mean 'Human Nature'?

Roger T. Ames

In spite of the fact that *xing* 性—conventionally rendered 'nature'—is among the most heavily worked philosophic notions in the classical Confucian inventory, I am not persuaded that it is, as a consequence, one of the best understood. The project of this essay is to identify and articulate what I perceive to be a fundamental inadequacy in our current understanding of *xing*—particularly as it refers to the human being.

I want to suggest that the prevailing interpretations of *xing* have been inappropriately skewed in favor of what is continuous, general, and enduring about the human being at the expense of what is novel, particular, and creatively achieved. That is, the interpretative prejudice has stressed an ahistorical 'given' as opposed to what the human being makes of himself. In developing a more adequate interpretation of *xing*, it will be necessary to discover the appropriate distance between the familiar conception of human nature as a psychobiological starting point—an internalized, universal, and objectifiable notion of human being—and *xing* as an historically, culturally, and socially emergent definition of person. The general claim of this essay, then, is that for classical Confucianism, one's humanity is not decidedly precultural, but preeminently and distinctively a cultural construction. Said another way, *xing* does not have primarily a labelling or reference function, but rather requires explanation culturologically as something defined and enacted in community. I shall attempt to redress this interpretative problem by highlighting the existential, historical, and cultural aspects of *xing* which, for reasons I shall try to indicate, have been undervalued in our standard reading of this concept.

The classical and paradigmatic formulation of *xing* that came to be elaborated throughout the subsequent Chinese tradition belongs to Mencius. While my primary objective in this essay is to clarify the meaning of *xing* as it is used in the *Mencius*, my broader argument is that in stressing the reverence in a culture for traditional authority it is an easy matter to undervalue and even overlook the role of creativity. Much important work has been done to articulate this Mencian model of *xing* in the textual analyses of two contemporary philosophers, Angus Graham and the late Tang Junyi (T'ang Chün-i). I single out these scholars because the case that I want to make for understanding *xing* as an achievement concept, adumbrated in their recent works, is open to further development. I shall work from Graham's insights— particularly those found in his critique of his own earlier understand- ing of *xing*—and then attempt to elaborate and extend these insights in pursuit of an explanation that gives fuller value and emphasis to the more creative aspects of *xing*.[1]

We might begin this analysis by asking why the tendency has been to interpret *xing* broadly as, quoting Donald Munro, "a 'given' that exists from birth" that "cannot be altered through human action."[2] The most obvious reason for Western trained scholars, of course, is that *renxing* has been formularistically translated as 'human nature', and then, as is typically the case in translation, has come to be understood as what *we* generally mean in our tradition by 'human nature'—the genetically given.

Another less culturally specific reason for the currency of such a substantive understanding of *xing* is the traditionally conservative reading of classical Confucianism. This reading has, in its very nature, exaggerated the continuities in personal development to the extent that a proportionate explication of the discontinuous and creative aspects has not been forthcoming.[3]

A third factor that has been a source of some confusion in the commentary on *xing*, both traditional and modern, is conceptual equivocation. As Xu Fuguan (Hsü Fu-kuan) takes great pains to point out, different philosophers have meant *very* different things by this term.[4] While I am in obvious agreement with Xu Fuguan—a redefinition of conceptual content is the very business of philosophy—I hope that this discussion will demonstrate that Xu and others do not do justice to the *extreme* degree of difference concealed in the usages of *xing*, even among those thinkers most representative of classical Confucianism. I will argue that 'human nature' is a most inadequate rendering of *xing* in the *Mencius*, although it is at least more adequate a translation for *xing* as it is used in the *Analects* and in *Xunzi*. Somewhat paradoxically, I would further suggest that Xu Fuguan does not appreciate fully the degree of congruency shared by these same thinkers who articulate their models of cultivated personhood not through this or any single equivocal term, but through a complex of concepts.[5]

Another problem that limits our present understanding of *xing* in the *Mencius* is the failure on the part of many scholars to distinguish adequately between it and a second concept that has an intimate role in the cluster of concepts through which Mencius explicates the project of personal cultivation, 'heart-and-mind' (*xin* 心).[6] In fact, there is a decided tendency for scholars to conflate *xing* and *xin* without respecting their important differences. This confusion emerges because the *xing* as a creative act is rooted in the *xin* 'heart-and-mind', and human beings in general do have certain determinative propensities as a function of the *xin*. But it is precisely against these determinate propensities that we are able to observe the change, growth and refinement that constitute *xing*.[7]

As one example of this problem, Zhang Dainian suggests that "since the sage is also a man, the *xing* that the sage has is the *xing* that all people have."[8] Zhang would be closer to the mark were he to assert that the sage has the *xin* that all people have. In fact, Mencius describes the *xin* as an organ (*guan* 官) on a plane with the organs of sight and hearing.[9] But the assumption here is that *xing* like *xin* is a given potential shared by all, and that the sage is simply one who successfully actualizes it. In fact, the possibility of *xing* is not *xing* itself—*xing* is a creative act. Being a man does not make one a sage; being a sage makes one most fully a man.

We can make this same point by citing an analogy that Mencius develops most effectively. Observing that Ox Mountain has been denuded of its luxuriant forests by a combination of axes and grazing animals in spite of all of the climatic conditions that conduce to their growth, Mencius says:[10]

> People in seeing this denuded condition think that it never had any of these resources. But how can this be the *xing* of the mountain?

What is cast here as the *xing* of the mountain—not necessarily *all* mountains, but at least *this* mountain—is a 'culture' and 'character' that goes beyond its basic conditions. The forests which once covered the mountain are natural to it, not as an essential endowment, but as a refinement that takes place over its history. The trees are its cultivated beauty (*mei* 美). It is not surprising that Mencius in using *xing* to designate the mountain forests rather than the mountain itself seems to us to be giving a curious prominence to what we would perceive to be a relatively nonessential aspect of the mountain. But then for Mencius, *xing* refers to that which goes beyond the basic conditions.

Another possible source of concern about our current reading of *xing* is historical mediation. Our present interpretation has been filtered through prominent neo-Confucian thinkers whose understanding of *xing*, influenced as they were by an analogy with 'principle' (*li* 理), has a much stronger metaphysical import.[11]

Yet another source of distortion for *xing* that is probably more significant among those commentators familiar with Western conceptions of 'nature' is traceable to the willingness on the part of Western-trained philosophers to countenance a distinction between theory and praxis, and then to favor the theoretical side. In response to Graham's reflections on (and reticence to entertain) the "supposed vagueness of Chinese",[12] I would suggest that classical Chinese *does* tend to be more vague conceptually than our own language precisely because of its very real resistance to the separation between theory and practice. Chinese must pay a penalty for its insistence upon a fuller consideration of the rhetorical and 'poietic'[13] factors in determining what constitutes legitimate philosophical evidence. And, taking our present analysis of *xing* as an illustration, it is precisely this tendency to value abstract clarity at the expense of particular historical considerations that has prevented a more robust appreciation of it. To allow that Chinese is more vague or ambiguous, however, is not to say that it is more equivocal. In fact, the contrary is more likely to be true. The Taoists argue with some persuasive force that experience mediated conceptually introduces a very obvious source of equivocation.

In his recently republished essay, 'The Background of the Mencian Theory of Human Nature', Graham takes issue with the simple identification of the classical Chinese concept of *xing* with the familiar conception of 'nature' as something 'inborn and innate'—those qualities which a thing has to start with. Graham's first insight, then, is that the dynamic thrust of *xing* has not been adequately noticed. Working from Fu Sinian's researches,[14] Graham argues that *xing* is derived from, and is a refinement on, *sheng* 生, denoting the entire process of birth, growth and ultimate demise that constitutes the life of a living creature. As a corrective on his own earlier work, Graham argues that[15]

> early Chinese thinkers who discuss *xing* seldom seem to be thinking of fixed qualities going back to a thing's origin. . . . Mencius in particular seems never to be looking back towards birth, always forward to the maturation of a continuing growth.

In positing this revised interpretation of *xing*, Graham makes a more general point. He suggests that many of these early Chinese concepts such as *xing* are not well served by our nearest English equivalents because the more dynamic connotations of the original Chinese are often lost.

If we were going to speculate on why *xing* and other original Chinese terms tend generally to be more dynamic in meaning than our Western equivalents (which indeed seems to be the case), we might want to reflect on the implications of cosmogonic speculation, a signal feature of our own tradition that is made important in this analysis by its absence in classical Chinese cosmology. The notion of initial beginning, whether it pertains to the cosmos as a whole or to the creatures that populate it, must surely have a significant, if not determinative, influence over the way a culture comes to conceive of the nature and order of things.

Benjamin Schwartz, in his support for the conventional interpretation of *xing* as "a 'heavenly endowed' or 'heavenly ordained' tendency, directionality, or potentiality of growth in the individual", is encouraged by what he perceives to be a "striking resemblance" between *xing* and the Greek *phuo* 'to grow' and the Latin *nascor* 'to be born'.[16] But it is precisely the absence of cosmogonic beginning in the classical Chinese conception of creativity that renders just such a seeming resemblance deceptive.

It is significant that in the classical Greek vocabulary, *phusis* refers to both the sum of natural objects and events, and to some defining principle within each natural object. Hence we have both Nature broadly, and the 'nature' of particular things. Now, where something within a single-ordered *kosmos* is shaped and invested by an external creative *archē*, the most fully creative act lies in the creator's endowment of a given potential—the creature's subsequent actualization of that potential is only derivative. In a *kosmos* the totality of things is necessarily ordered, and hence is *in principle* explicable.

In the absence of cosmogonic beginning, on the other hand, the power of creativity and the responsibility for creative product reside more broadly in the phenomena themselves in their ongoing interactive processes of becoming. Phenomena are not marshalled (*kosmos*) like the Greek generals marshalling their troops for battle in Homer, but exist as interdependent yet self-disciplining *kosmoi*.[17]

Where a phenomenon is initiated by, and dependent upon, some externally derived or 'given' creative principle for the 'nature' of its existence, and, said another way, where it is other than self-generative (*zi ran* 自 然), the creative contribution of that phenomenon tends to be diminished. The existence of some antecedent and preassigned creative principle—be it Plato's abstract *eidos*, the Judeo-Christian deity, *phusis*, or *archē*—does in fact serve to account for natural and moral order. At the same time, such an explanation tends in some degree to delimit the dynamic possibilities of phenomena themselves in the natural world.

The difference between the 'nature' of a thing in a cosmogonic tradition and its *xing* in a non-cosmogonic cosmology is suggested by the kinds of questions that each culture's philosophers ask. Cosmogonic concern generates metaphysical questions, a search for essential principles: How did the cosmos begin? What are its first principles? What are the fundamental elements from out of which it was constructed? What is the origin of the existence and growth of natural phenomena?

Non-cosmogonic cosmology, on the other hand, will generate primarily historical and rhetorical questions: Who and what are our historical antecedents that have given us our present definition? What are their achievements that we can appropriate to enculturate ourselves? How can we further cultivate ourselves so as to contribute to the appropriated tradition as it is embodied in our contemporary exemplars? How can we turn this historical and cultural interdependence to maximum benefit? The thinker's role in the non-cosmogonic tradition, then, will not be as much to discover answers as to create a model of humanity that is persuasive, and that evokes emulation.

A related implication of this distinction between a cosmogonic and non-cosmogonic worldview is that in the absence of some overarching *archē* (or 'beginning') as an explanation of the creative process, and under conditions which are thus 'anarchic' in the philosophic sense of this term, although *xing* might indeed refer to 'kinds', genus and species as categories would be dependent upon generalizations made by analogy among *sui generis* phenomena. Difference is prior to identified similiarities. As we shall see, that is the case in Mencius, where what distinguishes a person from a human beast, for example, is not some inviolate natural endowment, but a tentative and always particular cultural refinement. Even Confucius, who insists that he cannot gather with the birds and beasts because he is, after all, a human being, still makes it abundantly clear that he will only associate with *some* human beings—only those who are refined and cultured.[18] The generalization 'human being' is graduated, including the masses (*min* 人), persons (*ren* 民) and authoritative persons (*ren* 仁).

For Graham, the dynamic force of *xing* is evident in the metaphors *Mencius* employs to characterize the concept: growing trees and animals, ripening grain, flowing water.[19] In extending the dynamic implications of *xing* to the human being, Graham is keen to correct his earlier understanding of human *xing* as 'that which one starts with', revising it instead to cover the career of a person's existence. In the human context, then, *xing* denotes the entire process of being a person. Strictly speaking, a person is not a sort of *being*, but first and foremost a *doing* or *making*, and only derivatively and retrospectively, something done. For this reason, at least in reference to the human being, I would question the wisdom of retaining the translation 'nature', not only because it invokes unwanted associations that more properly belong to a cosmogonic tradition and invites us willy-nilly to impose the presuppositions of alien models on *xing*, but also because this translation fails to capture the sense that *xing* is an ongoing poietic process. I am persuaded that a more satisfactory rendering for the Mencian *xing* needs to be found. For the human being at least, *xing* seems to come closer to 'character', 'personality' or 'constitution' than what we generally understand by 'nature'. To avoid begging the question of this analysis, however, I shall use the romanization *xing* rather than any English equivalent.[20]

A dynamic and more aesthetic interpretation of *xing* calls into question not only the conventional translation, but further the appropriateness of common terminologies frequently used to explain it: *xing* is not reducible to what is innate (L. *in* + *nasci*: 'to be born in') or a priori. Undoubtedly a contributing source of the tendency to reduce *xing* to what is given is the fact that, in the classical corpus, there are what seem to be numerous examples of *xing* being used as 'starting conditions' when referring to 'inanimate' things. But this again might be deceptive.

First, given the hylozoistic presuppositions that attend *qi* 氣 ('psychophysical stuff'), there is some question as to whether the animate/inanimate distinction that we can find in Xunzi has much currency in the earlier period. Certainly the application of *xing* 性, derived as it is from *sheng* 生 ('birth/life/growth'), to what we would consider to be inanimate phenomena suggests that *everything* in the classical Chinese world was considered to be 'alive' and even 'aware' in some degree. The absence of the animate/inanimate distinction generates an ambiguity. Certain things to which *xing* is applied—water and rocks, for example—are not over their respective careers marked by growth and cultivation, and hence, it makes little sense to speak of them in terms of starting conditions and mature state. The *xing* of such things remains relatively constant. However, the human being—that phenomenon among phenomena most given to cultivation and refinement—is a different case.

While the human *xing* might include certain conditions that define it at birth,[21] in its more important aspects it seems to refer to what is existentially achieved. In defining the human *xing*, the relatively constant and uninteresting tendencies which constrain the creative project of personal development are outweighed by the massive transformative process that occurs between the 'stirring' or 'germination' (*duan* 端) of the initial fundament and the full blown creative achievement. The distance between heart-and-mind (*xin*)—the locus of these 'stirrings'—and *xing* is like the distance between a palette of paint and a masterpiece. Would it not be a case of misplaced emphasis for one to reduce John Turner's *Sea Storm* to its initial fundament—a blank canvas and the range of oils deployed by this particular artist in its preparation?

Tang Junyi's extensive work on *ren xing* demonstrates great sensitivity to the existential coloring of the classical Chinese conception of the human being. For Tang Junyi, "in speaking of a thing's *xing*, what is important is not in saying what the *xing* of this entity is, but in what the direction of its existence is. It is only in that it has growth that it has *xing*."[22] And among things, the human being is a special case. The *xing* of man cannot be approached in the same way as the *xing* of other phenomena because man has an internal perspective on his own constitution which is not available to him in the investigation of other things. In reflecting on the relationships between experience and conceptualization, Tang Junyi asserts that[23]

> coming to know the human possibility is not like seeking to know the possibilities of other things which can, on the basis of inference and hypothesis, be known objectively. Rather it comes from the way in which a person realizes his internal ideal and what is realized in coming to know it. Once one already has an understanding of this human *xing*, he will of his own accord surely have the linguistic concepts through which to express it. Such linguistic conceptualization follows upon what is known of it and is formed continuously as the opportunity presents itself. It is not the case that we first have conceptualizations to which we then add conjectures, anticipations or presumptions.

Tang Junyi thus emphasizes the primacy of the realization of the human ideal over the conceptualization and articulation of it, giving full notice to the personal locus of that realization. He disassociates the conversation among classical Chinese philosophers over the meaning of *xing* from the contemporary science of psychology by asserting that in the latter case, there is a desire to treat the human being as an objective phenomenon. For Tang, it is the existential project that is the fundamental distinguishing characteristic of the classical Confucian conception of *xing*. In fact, it is precisely the indeterminate possibility for creative change that Tang identifies as the most salient feature of the human *xing*. He says that where *xing* in reference to some things might refer to fixed characteristics, properties, propensities or essences,[24]

> from the perspective of the embodied ideal that we have of man in relationship to his world, there is a real question as to whether or not man has a fixed nature. This is because the world and the ideal which man faces both entail limitless change.... The discussion of the human *xing* in Chinese thought has had as its one common feature the reference to this locus for boundless change in which it locates the special *xing* of man. This then is man's spiritual *xing* (靈 性) which differs from the fixity and lack of spirituality of the *xing* of other things.

What is 'innate' in the *xing* of persons is simply the propensity for growth, cultivation, and refinement. *Xing*, then, denotes a human capacity for radical changeability that is qualitatively productive.

A corollary feature of the Mencian formulation of *xing* that contributes to this perceived dynamism is its pronounced physicality. For Mencius, becoming human is not the attainment of some internal psychical disposition, but the full consequence—psychic and somatic—of the achieved human being. But the physical aspect of human *xing*, like the psychical aspect, should not be confused with what is animal in him. When Tang Junyi, for example, equates *xing* and *xin* 'heart-and-mind' 即 心 言 性, he means that *xing* is the content of the cultivated and refined heart-and-mind as reflected in a person's countenance and demeanor.[25] It is the embodiment of personal development. But it is more than simply a physical expression of psychical achievement—the physical countenance can itself have a shaping influence on positive psychical attitudes and postures. In explanation of the role of the physical aspect in the development of *xing*, the *Mencius* states:[26]

What the exemplary person cultivates as *xing*[27] 性 is authoritative personhood (*ren* 仁), appropriateness (*yi* 義), ritual propriety (*li* 禮) and wisdom (*zhi* 智). These components are rooted in his heart-and-mind (*xin* 心), and the complexion that develops in the process is disclosed radiantly in his face, manifested in his posture and extended throughout his four limbs. His four limbs thus communicate effectively without speaking.[28]

In a related passage, Mencius again alludes to the intimate relationship between the psychical disposition and one's physical expression:[29]

> When enjoyment arises, it cannot be stopped. And when it cannot be stopped, one unconsciously taps it with his feet and dances it with his arms.

In addition to Graham's underscoring of the dynamic aspect of *xing*, there is his insistence that *xing* is realized contextually. *Xing* is "concerned with developments which are spontaneous but realize their full potentialities only if uninjured and adequately nourished."[30] The implication here is that *xing* must be understood as a dynamic process conditioned by its particular context. Stated more explicitly, the human *xing* is a process that can only be understood relationally.

Tang Junyi in his analysis makes this same point. In his general discussion of *xing*, he notices that *xing* often has two referents: it refers to the continuing existence of a particular thing itself, and also refers to that which in a thing, continues the life of other things.[31] He cites an example from the *Zuozhuan* in which the *xing* of the soil lies not only in its own conditions, but also in its propensity to grow things conducive to *human* life.[32]

Throughout his analysis, especially in reference to man, Tang Junyi highlights the fundamental relationality of *xing*:[33]

> It is my opinion that in looking at the beginnings of a theory of *xing* in China's early philosophers, the basic point was not to take man or his *xing* as some objective thing that can be looked at and discussed in terms of its universal nature or its special nature or its possibilities. As man viewed the myriad things and heaven and earth, and as he moreover viewed the internal ideal of the human being which he embodied, what was important for him was to reflect on what the *xing*

of this human being is, and what the *xing* of heaven and earth and the myriad things is.

Tang's definition of man's *xing* in terms of his ongoing relationship to his several environments challenges the common interpretation of *xing* as a 'given' essence—some innate endowment present in us from birth.

Perhaps the most frequently cited passage that has encouraged the problematic notion that *xing* is an essentialistic 'given' is the opening line of the *Zhongyong*:[34] *tian ming zhi wei xing* 天 命 之 謂 性 . This passage is often conceptualized and translated with strongly essentialistic assumptions to assert that "What is decreed by Heaven is called the *xing*." As a prominent example, Donald Munro, having translated this *Zhongyong* passage in precisely these terms, concludes:[35]

> This means that a person's nature being so decreed, cannot be altered through human action: it is a "given" that exists from birth.

In his interpretation of this passage, Tang Junyi shies away from importing the notion of an irrevocably determinative principle—call it Fate or Destiny or Heaven or God—to the classical Chinese tradition. Rather, he understands *tian ming* in terms of the mutual relationship between Heaven (*tian*) and man:[36]

> The term *"ming"* represents the interrelationship or mutual relatedness of Heaven and man. . . . [W]e can say that it exists neither externally in Heaven only, nor internally in man only; it exists rather, in the mutuality of Heaven and man . . .

We can couple this mutuality of Heaven and man implicit in '*ming*' with the relationality of man's *xing* as it is made explicit in the *Zhongyong* itself:[37]

> The completion of oneself is "authoritativeness" (*ren* 仁); the completion of other things is "realization" (*zhi* 知). The virtue of *xing* lies in fusing the course of what is external and what is internal.

Now, if we take Tang Junyi's counsel on *ming* to the opening passage of the *Zhongyong* cited above, the phrase "what is decreed by Heaven is called the *xing*", might be more appropriately rendered "the relationships that obtain between man and his world (*tian ming*) are what is meant by *xing*". While the process of becoming human might be somewhat predictable in terms of tendency or direction, *xing* nonetheless reflects the mutuality of man and his various environments by being ever open to and reflective of negotiation.

I do not see how it is possible to make sense of the Mencian conception of *xing* or the vocabulary which defines it without taking account of the interdependence of man and his environments, both social and natural.[38] For Mencius, the human being emerges in the world as a spontaneously arising and ever changing matrix of relationships through which, over a lifetime, his *xing* is defined. At birth, his relationality is described as only faint 'stirrings' or 'germinations' (*duan* 端), tying him into the world in a way analogous to his physical form.[39] Just as a person enters the world 'embodied', so he has these 'stirrings' from the outset (我 固 有 之).[40] They are not, however, some internal fixed and unchanging endowment any more than one's physicality can be so construed. In fact, these 'stirrings' are profoundly more delicate and tentative than one's physical identity in that, without due care, they can easily be lost.[41]

These 'stirrings', then, are the initial defining conditions of a human being which are then available to him for development. Importantly, and often overlooked, these four 'stirrings' are as much social as personal, knitting a person into a particular context as well as defining his initial dispositions. This initial relationality is captured conceptually in the four categories of interpersonal bonds (*ren*), societal bonds of deference (*li*), meaning and value disclosing bonds (*yi*), and intellectual bonds (*zhi*), all of which are open to cultivation. These initial bonds provide him with a heading in the development and expression of his *xing*.

When Mencius states that these fours 'stirrings' are not fused into me from outside",[42] he is saying that they are not wholly appropriated from some external source. But this usage of 'inner/outer' cannot be understood dualistically.[43] In fact, the 'inner/outer' (内 外) distinction that we find in Mencius must be qualified by the fundamental relationality of *xing*. It is precisely because *xing* has both inner and outer aspects that Mencius can insist "a person who realizes his *xing* realizes

Heaven" and "all of the myriad phenomena are here in me".[44] Making a conscious effort to avoid internalizing or 'psychologizing' *xing*, we must say that it would be problematic in the Mencian tradition to describe a person at any stage—even infancy—as a discrete and isolated 'individual'. To call a person an 'individual' in the atomistic sense that we associate with some liberal democratic traditions would be to abstract him from the value-invested network of particular familial and cultural conditions and the immediate cognitive and practical relationships that define him initially, and which make possible his continuing growth.

Du Weiming, as an example, seems to overstate the role of the initial conditions when he says that[45]

> For Mencius, there is something in each human being that, in the ultimate sense, can never be subject to external control. This something is neither learned nor acquired; it is a given reality, endowed by Heaven as the defining characteristic of being human.

In so describing Mencius, Du makes the distinction between 'external' and 'internal' too severe. Further, he exaggerates the importance of the *initial* endowment by making it the defining characteristic of being human. In fact, what is most fully human is the protean *xing*, not the incipient *xin*.

Yet another insight that can be gleaned from Graham's conceptual reconstruction is his suggestion that *xing* seems to be fundamentally normative: the 'best' way for anything to grow. As he states, "the *xing* of a thing, then, is its proper course of development during its process of *sheng*."[46] Bearing in mind the fundamental relationality of *xing*, it would follow that *xing* could not in its most primitive sense mean simply 'good in itself', but must mean relationally good as in 'good at' or 'good for' developing for oneself those bonds which tie one into family and community. Graham is making this same point in his insistence that we distinguish the Mencian understanding of the human *xing* from its later Neo-Confucian reformulation as a metaphysical concept which construes humans as being good in themselves. The locus of *xing*, then, is not some isolatable self, but one's self as the center of relationships that are, over a lifetime, deepened, nurtured and extended with varying degrees of deftness and facility (*shan* 善).[47] It is the effort invested in cultivating these bonds that sustains one as a human being and elevates one qualitatively above the animal world.[48]

'Proper' (L. *proprius* 'one's own') conduct normally is thought to mean conduct consistent with one's own kind. But if I am correct in claiming that for Mencius the assumption is that phenomena are ultimately *sui generis*, then 'proper' must mean consistent with one's own particularity and uniqueness—making one's conduct most fully an expression of one's own self.[49] That is, as a normative concept, the 'best' *xing* is one that is able to maximize its possibilities, maintaining its own integrity and, at the same time, realizing the fullest degree of integration. The 'good' is not the actualization of some given potential, but the consequential optimization of the conditions defining of a particular thing over its history. These defining conditions of course include one's particular physiology and anatomy as the less important and yet more obvious constraints on one's humanity, and extend to one's cultural opportunities and consequent refinement as the more important ingredients.

Xing in the human context then, only minimally involves the animal satisfactions (*ming* 命) and incipient 'stirrings' of the heart-and-mind (*xin*). More significantly, it is a cultural product dependent upon the quality of its particular conditions. This is Mencius' point in rejecting Gaozi's naturalism.[50] Gaozi wants to equate 'everything that is born and grows' (*sheng*) with *xing*. This would, of course, dissolve the normative force of *xing*. Since *xing* is normative, it clearly cannot be everything that a person does (or derivatively, *is*), but only those things which can be construed as achievement, as a refinement of the bare stuff, as that which can be designated *shan*.[51] It is not so much that human 'nature' is *shan*, but more importantly, what human being does that is *shan* becomes human nature. This association between cultivation and *xing* is underscored in the *Mencius*:[52]

> The mouth's propensity for tastes, the eye's for colors, the ear's for sounds, the nose's for smells, and the four limbs' for comfort—these are the *xing*, yet basic conditions (*ming*) also have a part in it. That is why the exemplary person does not refer to these as *xing*. The relevance of authoritativeness (*ren*) to the father-son relation, of appropriateness (*yi*)

to the ruler-subject relation, of ritual action (*li*) to the guest-host relation, of wisdom (*zhi*) to the good and wise person, and of sages to the way of Heaven, are basic conditions (*ming*), yet the *xing* also has a part in it. That is why the exemplary person does not refer to these as basic conditions.

Mencius makes at least three important points here. First, as a cultivated product, *xing* is always *shan*—something achieved—whereas man's basic conditions (*ming*) are not necessarily so. Then there is a fundamental difference in importance—*xing* belongs to what is centrally important (*da ti* 大 體), while man's basic conditions (*ming*) are much more of a peripheral concern (*xiao ti* 小 體).[53] This means that human beings are unimportantly similar, and importantly distinct cultivated achievements. Finally, that which human beings attain and animals have no claim on is *xing*; what humans have in common with animals are certain basic conditions (*ming*). The cultivated product of the "four stirrings" is human; mere consciousness and desires are animal.

It is interesting that the physical senses, once cultivated as 'tastes', also extend into the notion of *xing*. Hence, Mencius perceives them to be an admixture of *xing* and *ming*. Even so, when measured against man's higher achievements—moral, aesthetic, religious, and so on—the exemplary person is not inclined to place them among the most important, and so regards even the educated physical senses as primarily *ming*. *Xing* as a category is saved to designate the highest products of human cultivation.

One clarification should be mentioned in the application of 'normative' to this notion, *xing*. What is 'best' is only retrospectively understood. The norm comes into being *pari passu* with the process. That is, the norm is itself an emergent product.

A second caution that we need observe arises from the frequent use of 'cultivation'—a term which suggests the organic metaphor. Although there are instances in which 'nurture' (*yang* 養) is used of *xing*,[54] 'cultivation' usually translates the character *xiu* 脩, as in 'cultivating oneself' (*xiu ji* 脩 己)[55] or 'cultivating one's person' (*xiu shen* 脩 身).[56] The character *xiu* translated 'cultivate' is most commonly glossed as 'effecting proper order' (*zhi* 治) in a sociopolitical rather than an organic sense. The point that I want to make is that the cultivation of humanity as a cultural product allows for a greater degree of creativity than a more restricted horticultural or husbanding metaphor might suggest.

Further, Aristotelian associations with this 'cultivation' metaphor conjure forth a potentiality/actuality distinction that is not appropriate. Such a distinction is fundamentally progressive, entailing as it does an efficient, a formal, and a final cause. By contrast, there is a real question as to whether the classical Chinese *xing* can be most clearly understood by appeal to systemic teleological models. It is the degree to which this Confucian model of humanity is free of any definite and specified goals that gives it its flexibility and creative range. In describing the emergent order that is humanity, one must distinguish between a posteriori generalizations and goal-direction. The physiological functions of the human being can, perhaps, be discussed in terms of some predetermined behavior-regulating 'program' that controls a process and leads it toward a given end. This would appear to be goal-directed and hence teleological. But as we have seen, Mencius is explicit and emphatic in excluding what humans share in common with other animals from his conception of *xing*. It is precisely the contrast between such programmed behavior and the creativity of the human being that Mencius is appealing to as being distinctively human.

Perhaps another way of making this point is to suggest that *xing* is an 'inspirational' rather than an 'aspirational' notion. *Xing* is not a preestablished normative standard to which one aspires. Rather, the heading that any person steers lies between the lure of 'inspiring' models and the contingencies of his own *sui generis* particularity in its ever changing circumstances.[57] Thus, where it might be appropriate to discuss *xing* in the language of generalizable similarities, it would be a distortion to assume any formal identity.[58] Since *xing* is a process realized within an always *specific* context, it is a generalization grounded ultimately in and derived from the historical particular. Any strict sense of identity or universality—and that notion of equality that attends it— is ultimately inapplicable.[59]

Mencius' appeal to Yao and Shun—concrete historical exemplars— as architects of an inspiring model of humanity reflects the ultimate specificity of *xing*:[60]

> Yao and Shun 'xing-ed' it; Tang and Wu embodied it in their persons; the Five Hegemons imitated it. Where a person imitates something resolutely over an extended period, who is to say that it is not his? In Mencius' discussion of the goodness of xing, his words invariably extolled Yao and Shun.

The not-uncommon verbal use of xing in the first passage is significant—xing is not a given, but an accomplished project.[61] The boundary conditions on humanity are in important measure the historical models available to a particular culture rather than some inherently programmed 'nature'. Further, what it means to be human is not a product of popular compromise, but what emerges as socially authoritative in hierachical patterns of deference to perceived worth. The more an exemplar is appreciated, the more he appreciates in cultural value. This passage is explicit in the suggestion that what is important in becoming human is not to be constituted by force or coercion, but is a function of willing deference to authoritative achievement.

There is another passage which makes a similar point: "When the world speaks on xing, it has nothing other than historical precedents (gu 故) to go on, and in appeal to these historical precedents, it takes facility as its fundamental criterion."[62]

One way of articulating the relational and inspirational conception of xing is to reflect on the shared implications between it and its cognate, xing 姓 which denotes 'family or clan name'. A family or clan name is a dynamic, meaning-invested generalization distinguishing a particular group of people over time that both inspires them and is inspired by them. It is a generalization ultimately grounded in historical particularity rather than some a priori conception of humanity. It is also elitist in that the possession of a family or clan name was itself a social distinction—not all persons were so distinguished.

Xing as family or clan name certainly signifies a set of shared conditions and tendencies, but more importantly, it is the opportunity for each member to cultivate himself and contribute in his own particular way—an opportunity to transform one's family name through the incorporation of one's personal name (ming 名) and its achieved meaning. One's xing, then, is no more an essential or innate faculty than is one's family name; both are a focus of relationships that one participates in and which becomes a repository for one's achievements over a lifetime.

This cognate relationship between *xing*—clan name—and *xing* is also of service in understanding what Mencius means by "the sage and I are the same in kind (*tong lei* 同 類)."[63] He is referring to a 'family resemblance' rather than some essential identity.

A way of restoring the cultural side of the Mencian conception of *xing* is to challenge the appropriateness of the 'nature'/'nurture' distinction often invoked to explain Mencius' conception of *xing* as 'nature'. Joseph Needham appeals to this nature/nurture distinction, ascribing to Mencius the position that, though human nature is necessarily good, nurture can be either good or evil, depending on the extent to which it is shaped by those impulses traceable to the original nature.[64] While Needham attributes this nature/nurture distinction to Mencius, Xunzi on the contrary criticizes Mencius specifically for having failed to distinguish what is given at birth from what is the consequence of a person's conscious activity. In Xunzi's words:[65]

> Mencius says that man's being able to learn is because his *xing* is good. I say that this is not so. This is failing to understand the *xing* of man and not discerning the distinction between the *xing* of man and man's conscious activity (*wei* 偽).

Given the boundary that Xunzi draws between *xing* and conscious human activity, he is justified in saying that Mencius does not understand the distinction between these two. But one can also turn this the other way and say that Xunzi did not understand that what Mencius meant by *xing* is that which is distinctively human, and which cannot be resolved into a nature/nurture distinction. D. C. Lau makes this point:[66]

> . . . Mencius and Hsün Tzu [Xunzi] took a very different line in the matter of the definition of the nature [*xing*] of a thing. Mencius was looking for what is distinctive while Hsün Tzu [Xunzi] was looking for what forms an inseparable part of it.

Graham makes this same observation in a different way. In isolating what distinguishes this early Chinese notion of *xing* from typical Western theories of human nature, he points out that Mencius is not moved to establish a distinction between *xing* as the actual process of being human, and *xing* as some capacity or faculty or set of categories that underlies and determines the process of becoming human:[67]

> [I]s the *xing* of man the process of physical growth and decay tending towards longevity, of changing passions tending towards the moderation favourable to longevity, and so forth, or is it the tendency itself abstracted from the process? We need not look too closely at this distinction, because Hsün-tzu [Xunzi] in the 3rd century BC seems to have been the first to recognize it, and he tells us that the word is used to mean both.

It is not at all surprising that Graham's analysis identifies Xunzi as the first classical Chinese philosopher to insist on separating 'nature' from 'nurture'.

For Mencius, then, *xing* refers to those special characteristics which make man different from animals. Said the other way round, those characteristics which we share with animals are not *xing*. Mencius' question, then, is not: is *xing* 'nature' or 'nurture'? Rather, in the absence of this distinction, the question is: in what proportion is that which is distinctively human a given, and in what proportion is it a cultural achievement? First, even with *xin* (heart-and-mind)—the basic 'ground' in which the *xing* is 'rooted' (*gen* 根)—there are human beings who, having failed to cultivate what is an incipient and fragile emblem of their humanity, do not qualify as human persons. They are inhuman (*fei ren* 非 人). When Mencius says that "no man is devoid of a heart sensitive to the suffering of others",[68] he is also saying "any man who does not have a heart sensitive to the suffering of others is not really human." When he says "there is no human being who is not good," he is also saying that "any one who is not good is not really human."[69]

The illustration that Mencius appeals to in defense of his claim that a person-who-is-human will feel sensitive to the suffering of others is his famous example of a child falling in a well. While scholars, following Zhu Xi, have focused on the 'innocence' of the child who is saved, it is also significant that the person moved by the plight of the child is himself an adult with experience in the world. Would another child in his innocence be provoked in the same way? Without cultivation, man's distinction from the animals is only 'infinitesimal' (*xi* 希).[70] As Mencius says,[71] "where man goes without education, he is close indeed to an animal."

Since the sage is most human, it must follow that the *xing* of man is predominantly what happens between birth and the possible achievement of sagehood, and is only in the most marginal way, what one begins with. For Mencius, although there is no nature/nurture distinction, what is most important about *xing* occurs as a consequence of cultivation and growth. It is negotiated in the process of socialization and enculturation.

Xing should thus be understood as having an inseparable relationship with culture; we might even extrapolate from what Mencius says to claim that for him, *xing* is culturally specific: there are different 'kinds' of human beings. We can define 'ritual action' (*li*) as the formal language through which interpersonal meanings are developed and expressed, and we can construe these same patterns of deference as the substance of culture. Such being the case, *xing* does not stand as the boundary conditions on ritual conduct; rather, ritual conduct is constantly reconfiguring what it means to be human. And ritual in turn is itself being reformed as a consequence of those specific actions which attract deference in the society.

We need now to highlight some of the implications of this interpretation of *xing*—implications which, though potentially positive, often have a rather familiar down-side in the opportunities they provide for abuse.

One of the historical consequences of the Mencian distinction between 'basic conditions' (*ming*) and *xing* and his construal of *xing* as an achievement concept is the cultural elitism that is one of the defining characteristics of classical Confucianism. For Mencius, an undeveloped human being—someone who is resolutely uneducated and uncultured—is not in any important sense 'human'. *Xing* is the signature of participatory and contributory membership in a culturally informed community. To be without culture is to be less than human, for a 'human being' who acts like an animal is not figuratively, but literally, a beast.[72] There is a qualitative distinction between the kinds of people who constitute our society, ranging from 'humans' who are not human at all to the sagacious who in their example redefine and improve upon humanity itself. This notion of *xing* then insists that some humans are considerably more 'human' than others.

A further consideration would be that since humanity is in important degree culturally determined, not only is the qualitative distinction between 'kinds of people' applicable to numbers of a particular community, but further, this same distinction separates one community from another. Perhaps reminiscent of the Dustin Hoffman film *Little Big Man*, there are from an internal perspective, the 'human beings', and the others.

Another implication of *xing* so defined would be that the meaning of 'humanity' is open to profound revisioning. In the classical tradition, there is a presupposition concerning the profound transformability of the human being, as is witnessed in its commitment to education generally, and in models of 're-education'. At the same time, there is also the perception that transformability becomes increasingly unlikely as a human being becomes set in his ways. In the *Analects*, while Confucius prides himself on nothing with more verve than his enthusiasm for learning. (*hao xue* 好 學), there is nothing more frustrating for him than the recalcitrance of people to overcome difficulty with learning.[73] Quite contrary to the stereotypical perception of Confucius as conservative, he says:[74] "The young ought to be revered. How do we know that their future accomplishments will not go beyond our own? On the other hand, there is certainly nothing worthy of reverence in one who reaches forty or fifty years of age without distinguishing himself in any way."

Given the contextuality of *xing* thus interpreted, the effects of environment upon one's humanity would be profound and inescapable. Success or failure in the project of becoming human would largely be a function of the quality of one's social background. In fact, in a crucial sense, *xing* is the particular focus of one's social rather than individual character, making the study of person a distinctly social science.

This interpretation of *xing* as the coordination of one's unique defining conditions into some optimal relational harmony accounts for the familiar correlativity of the personal, social, political, and even cosmic order in the classical Confucian corpus. It is under the sway of this relational understanding of becoming human that the coextensive-ness of personal, societal, and 'cosmic' realization is almost everywhere assumed.[75]

In summary, we can characterize our elaboration of the Mencian notion of *xing* in the following terms. *Xing* is:

1. a dynamic process which covers initial dispositions, growth, and ultimate demise

2. holistic, inclusive of both those psychical and physical conditions which are distinctly human

3. describable in genetic terms as an emergent order which, from initial 'stirrings', is cultivated by appeal to historical models to constitute onself through enculturation as the center of a centripetal field of unique, particular, and concrete circumstances

4. describable in morphological terms as a relationally defined matrix of conditions

5. an achieved order which pursues a harmony defined through the maximization of the participating conditions

6. an 'inspirational' rather than 'aspirational' process involving an appeal to the achieved quality of historical models rather than the realization of abstract ideals or principles, and hence characterizable more in terms of 'poietic' than practical or theoretical production

7. correlative with sociopolitical and ultimately, cosmic order

8. generalizable (like a surname), to identify the participation and contribution of a group of similar particulars

Although in the articulation of this classical conception of person-making, we have relied primarily on Mencius, I would argue that the dynamics of the same basic model can be reconstructed through an alternative cluster of concepts from the other classical Confucians—both Confucius himself, and, with qualification even Xunzi.[76]

If this analysis is a fair appraisal of the Mencian definition of *xing*, and if this definition of *xing* has had the enormous impact on the tradition that has been claimed for it, then it should be in evidence in the presuppositions that underlie not only the classical Chinese community, but contemporary society as well. This, I believe, can be demonstrated.

Above I have suggested that in classical Confucianism ritually constituted relationships are constantly reconfiguring what it means to be human. An interesting and appropriate analogy can be drawn between the codified ritual structures in the tradition and their contemporary equivalent—the Chinese constitutions of this century.[77] The constitutions seek to define the 'constitution' and character of the person-in-society. As such, one touchstone to test the ubiquity of this notion of *xing* as an achievement concept can be its relevance to the way in which 'person' is defined as a matrix of rights (in place of 'rites') in the contemporary series of Chinese constitutions. Such a definition can be readily abstracted from Andrew Nathan's analysis of human rights in the eleven, twelve, or thirteen Chinese constitutions that have been enacted and ratified during our present century.[78]

In articulating the "deep differences in values and practices" that stand behind the "broad rhetorical similarities" shared by *the* American constitution and the Chinese *constitutions*, Nathan focuses attention on six distinctive characteristics that make the Chinese 'rights' experience different from our own. Interpreting Nathan's six characteristic differences to make my own argument, in the Chinese constitutions, rights (1) are granted only to progressive, achieved classes, (2) are variable from one constitution to the next, (3) are programmatic—open-ended and reflective of emerging goals, (4) are always malleable—open to legislation that records changing cultural and sociopolitical values, (5) are enforced by immediate social relations rather than formal judicial institutions, and (6) are dependent for their execution upon hierarchical patterns of deference to achieved worth rather than popular sovereignty. In counter-distinction to this Chinese construal of rights as historical, culturally determined, progressive, and elitist, a standard perception of the American constitution is that it is a document based upon 'discovered' rights—rights which are ahistorical and acultural—which can be applied universally to discipline all social orders. In the Chinese context, the changing and fluid constitutions register an emergent, participatory order rather than a set of given criteria around which order can be effected.

To put the argument of this paper into perspective, I do not want to overstate the personal creativity entailed by the Confucian practice of self-cultivation. It might well be asked: if there was this emphasis on creative transformation, where is it celebrated in the tradition? Where is the avant garde?[79] Certainly in the rituals and institutions of society we witness a profound reverence for past achievements. But in the classical Chinese tradition, history is not simply an accurate account of past events. It is didactic. Creativity is expressed generally as refinement rather than novelty, and those historical exemplars who function as models do so by virtue of their creative transformation of their cultural legacy. Truly creative thinkers are ultimately commentators. Where Confucius was unwilling to speak on *xing* as an abstraction, neither he nor any of his early followers were reluctant to celebrate selected historical models of humaneness. It is perhaps ironical at least to us that reverence for history is not necessarily conservative, but in fact, can also register and reflect a profound respect for the creative as an extension of the authority of the past.[80] As Gadamer in defining 'tradition' observes:[81]

> The task involved in bringing together the petrified remnants of yesterday and the life of today provides a vivid illustration of what tradition always means: not just the careful preservation of monuments, but the constant interaction between our aims in the present and the past to which we still belong.

NOTES

I am grateful to my colleagues and graduate students at the University of Hawaii for their comments and suggestions, and particularly to Henry Rosemont, Jr., and David L. Hall whose criticisms have caused me to refine my position considerably.

1. See A. C. Graham, 'The Background of the Mencian Theory of Human Nature', in *Studies in Chinese Philosophy and Philosophical Literature*

(Singapore: Institute of East Asian Philosophies, 1986). Hereafter, 'Background'.

2. Donald J. Munro, *Concept of Man in Contemporary China* (Ann Arbor: University of Michigan Press, 1979). Munro's analysis of the classical Confucian conception of self is dependent on this explicit notion of an innate and unchanging nature. See especially pp. 19–20 and p. 57.

3. Our recently published *Thinking Through Confucius*, building on Herbert Fingarette's *Confucius: The Secular as Sacred* (New York: Harper, 1972), is an extended argument for a more liberal understanding of Confucius. See David L. Hall and Roger T. Ames, *Thinking Through Confucius* (Albany: SUNY Press, 1987).

4. See Xu Fuguan, *Zhongguo renxinglun shi* (Taizhong: Donghai University Press, 1963). The contemporary Chinese scholar, Zhang Dainian, has provided a summary statement on *xing* that can serve as a useful reference for laying out the key distinction between Mencius' notion of *xing* and the several rival positions in the tradition. He does so in such a way as to give proper notice to the extent to which the Mencian conception of *xing* is a cultural product. Like Xu Fuguan, Zhang Dainian is concerned that although each of the philosophers who join the discussion on *xing* is using the same locution, they certainly do not intend the same thing by it. He distinguishes three fundamentally different meanings:

1. that which is so at birth: what one can do without learning and what does not emerge out of practice
   a) that which is complete at birth (Xunzi)
   b) that which, although not complete at birth, is completed naturally in maturation (Gaozi)
   c) those possibilities or tendencies that one has at birth, but which require practice for development and completion (Neo-Confucian)
2. that cosmic nature from which man is endowed (Neo-Confucian)
3. that which makes man distinctively man (Mencius)

Clarifying this last category, Zhang Dainian insists that *xing* for Mencius is not simply what makes man different from animals, but what makes man more noble and special. What distinguishes this Mencian category 3 from category 1 is that in 1, the distinction turns on what are man's initial conditions and what are not. In 3, *only* those characteristics which are distinctively human and which are *not* shared with animals are *xing*. There are, on this model, many of man's initial conditions that are not *xing*. See Zhang Dainian, *Zhongguo zhexue dagang* (Peking: Chinese Academy of Social Sciences Press, 1982) pp. 250–253.

5. Benjamin Schwartz in *The World of Thought in Ancient China* (Cambridge, MA: Harvard University Press, 1985), especially pp. 175–79, makes a persuasive case that the 'problem' of human nature in the classical Chinese tradition goes back into our earliest sources, and that we do well not to confuse the relatively late discussion of the term *xing* with the perennial issue of what it means to be a human being.

6. This problem is encouraged by a familiar passage in Mencius (7A/1): "One who exhausts his heart-and-mind (*xin*) realizes his *xing*." It is important to appreciate the performative implications of the character that I have rendered 'to realize' (*zhi* 知)—conventionally translated as 'to know'. See my 'Confucius and the Ontology of Knowing' in Gerald J. Larson and Eliot Deutsch (ed.) *Interpreting Across Boundaries: New Essays in Comparative Philosophy* (Princeton: Princeton University Press, 1988).

7. Zhang Dainian p. 185.

8. A similar distinction that highlights the creative side of *xing* is made in *Mencius* 4B/19 where he says of Shun that "he understood clearly that way of things and was circumspect in regard to human relations. He acted from authoritativeness (*ren*) and appropriateness (*yi*)—it was not just that he put them into practice."

9. *Mencius* 6A/15.

10. *Mencius* 6A/8.

11. I am grateful to Thomas P. Kasulis who has pointed out to me that Ito Jinsai and other Japanese critics of the neo-Confucian interpretation of classical Chinese sources were, in a way analogous to the project of this study, anxious to get behind the metaphysics of neo-Confucianism and return to a reading of a more historical character. Ito Jinsai's interpretation of *xing*, as an example, seeks to disassociate it from 'principle' (*li*) and to revive what he refers to as 'movement' in the concept. Although his conclusions are markedly different from my own, it is clear that his problem is the same. See Yoshikawa Kōjirō, *Jinsai Sorai Norinaga: Three Classical Philologists of Mid-Tokugawa Japan* (Tokyo: Tōhōgakkai Institute of Eastern Culture, 1983) pp. 9–77.

12. Graham, '"Being" in Western Philosophy Compared with *Shih/Fei* and *Yu/Wu* in Chinese Philosophy' in *Studies*, pp. 357–359.

13. I am using the term 'poietic' throughout this paper in the Aristotelian

sense of '*poeisis*': relating to production or the arts of production, productive of a kind of knowing distinct from practical or theoretical knowledge.

14. See Fu Sinian, *Xingming guxun bianzheng* (Shanghai: Commercial Press, 1940). Xu Fuguan, in his *Zhongguo renxing lun shi*, is critical of Fu Sinian's attempts to excavate a fundamental meaning of *xing*, insisting that *xing* as a concept must be defined from context. I would argue that their positions, however, ought to be complementary rather than mutually exclusive.

15. Graham, 'Background', p. 8.

16. See Benjamin Schwartz, *The World of Thought in Ancient China*, p. 175.

17. See Jonathan Barnes, *Early Greek Philosophy* (London: Penguin, 1987) for a discussion of the cosmological vocabulary of the classical Greeks.

18. See *Analects* 18/6, which needs to be qualified with 5/10, 4/25, 4/3 and so on.

19. Graham, 'Background', p. 43.

20. In deciding on an appropriate translation for *xing*, it should be borne in mind that the etymology of the English word 'character' (Gk. *charakter*: instrument for marking or inscribing) is similar to the Chinese word for 'culture' (*wen* 文: patterning). While abandoning 'nature' in favor of 'character' would emphasize the 'cultivation' side of *xing*, the fact remains that *xing* covers much of the same ground that 'nature' does in our tradition. An adequate translation would thus have to combine both 'nature' and 'character' in a single term.

21. Even 'birth' in this context is different from the cosmogonic model. Where the *creatio ex nihilo* model generates a severe creator/creature distinction, the contextual ontology that we extrapolate from classical Confucianism makes each phenomenon both creator and creature.

22. Tang Junyi, *Zhongguo zhexue yuanlun: Yuanxingpian* (Hong Kong: New Asia Press, 1968) p. 10.

23. See Tang, *Yuanxingpian*, pp. 3–4.

24. Tang, *Yuanxingpian*, p. 6.

25. It should be noted in fairness to Tang Junyi, where he does equate heart-and-mind (*xin*) for *xing*, he insists that by "heart-and-mind means *xing*" 即 心 言 性 he intends that "it is the growth and development of heart-and-mind that means *xing* 即 心 之 生 言 性." See *Yuanxingpian* p. 28 and p. 10.

26. *Mencius* 7A/21. See Graham's translation and discussion of this passage in 'Background', p. 32. See also *Mencius* 7A/38.

27. It is both interesting and important that in this passage and elsewhere, *xing* is used verbally—"what the exemplary person '*xing*'s'".

28. One recollects the "Great Preface" to the *Book of Songs* which states: "One's feelings stir within his breast, and take form in words. When words are inadequate, they are voiced in sighs. When sighs are inadequate, they are chanted. When chants are inadequate unconsciously, the hands and feet begin to dance them." James Legge, *The Chinese Classics*, 5 vols. (Hong Kong: London Missionary Society, 1861–1873) IV:34–35 (my translation).

29. *Mencius* 4A/27.

30. Graham, 'Background', p. 8.

31. Tang, *Yuanxingpian*, pp. 10–11.

32. *Zuozhuan* Duke Zhao 25. Tang also cites the example of medicine which is most often defined in terms of its effects on the human subject.

33. Tang, *Yuanxingpian*, p. 3.

34. *Zhongyong* 1.

35. See note 1 above.

36. See Tang Junyi (Tang Chun-i), 'The T'ien Ming (Heavenly Ordinance) in Pre-Ch'in China', *Philosophy East and West* 11:4 (1961) 195–218; 12:1 (1962) 29–50, especially p. 195.

37. *Zhongyong* 25.

38. One of the most persistent and influential commitments of the classical period (and beyond) is the mutual determination of Heaven and man, variously captured as *tianren ganying* 天 人 感 應, *tianren gantong* 天 人 感 通, *tianren heyi* 天 人 合 一, and so on. In fact, it would follow that the pace and quality of change in man's environment would have a direct and transformative affect on his *xing*.

39. See *Mencius* 2A/6: "A person's having these four stirrings (*duan*) is like his having four limbs."

40. *Mencius* 6A/6.

41. For example, see ibid., 4B/12.

42. Mencius 6A/6.

43. See David L. Hall and Roger T. Ames, *Thinking Through Confucius* pp. 17–21 for a discussion of the difference between a conceptual polarity and dualism.

44. *Mencius* 7A/1 and 7A/4.

45. Tu Wei-ming (Du Weiming), 'On the Mencian Perception of Moral Self-Development' in *Humanity and Self-Cultivation* (Berkeley: Asian Humanities Press, 1979), p. 63.

46. Graham, 'Background', p. 10.

47. In fact, just as 'rightness' (*yi* 義) as a norm emerges out of deference to personal achievements of appropriateness in ritually constituted relationships, so 'goodness' (*shan*) as a description of character derives from deference to perceived facility in the cultivation and coordination of these same defining relationships. In both cases, they are fundamentally an aesthetic and derivatively a moral achievement. The *Shuowen* lexicon defines *shan* as "synonymous with 'appropriateness/rightness' (*yi*) and 'beauty' (*mei* 美)." This aesthetic sense is also apparent in the cognate refinement of *shan*, *shan** 繕 (to make good =) 'to repair', 'to put in order'.

48. Mencius observes that (4B/19): "What distinguishes man from the brutes is ever so slight, and where the common run of people are apt to lose it, the exemplary person maintains it." This notion that what defines a person as human being is ultimately cultural is an integral part of the tradition. See, for example, the *Book of Songs* 52:

> See the rat—it has skin;
> A person without dignity;
> A person without dignity;
> Why does he not die?

> See the rat—it has teeth;
> A person without proper deportment;
> A person without proper deportment;
> Why does he wait to die?

> See the rat—it has a body;
> A person without ritual conduct;
> A person without ritual conduct;
> Why does he not make haste to die?

49. See Graham, 'Background', pp. 59–65. Graham's interpretation of the cognate term, *qing* 情 as 'what something essentially is', 'the genuine', is an attempt to come to terms with one of the most elusive of the classical philosophical terminologies. In rejecting the common renderings of *qing* as 'passions' in favor of what is 'essential' to any given thing, Graham seems to want to reserve this concept for the genetic conditions of *xing*. But even if Graham is right (which I suspect he is not), it is important that *qing* in the

classical corpus has several connotations and associations which are clearly suggestive of relationality: facticity, circumstances, emotions, feelings, desires. Wang Chong in his *Lunheng* 'Beginning Endowment' (*chubin*) chapter in fact distinguishes between *qing* and *xing* in precisely these terms: "*Qing* is what is so morphologically; . . . *xing* is what is so genetically." In the *Hanshu* biography of Dong Zhongshu (Shanghai: Zhonghua shuzhu, 1959, p. 2501) it states that "*xing* is the basic stuff of life; *qing* is human desires." In the *Yijing* it states that (Harvard-Yenching Index Series 20/31) "each of the myriad things has its nature. If one observes what each of them responds to, one can see the *qing* of heaven, earth and the myriad things. This means that *qing* is what responds and moves."

50. *Mencius* 6A passim.

51. Ibid., 6A/3.

52. Ibid., 7B/24.

53. Ibid., 6A/14, 15.

54. Ibid., 7A/1.

55. *Analects* 14/42.

56. *Mencius* 7A/1, 7A/9 and 7B/32.

57. This language is borrowed from A. S. Cua's *Dimensions of Moral Creativity* (University Park: Pennsylvania State University Press, 1978). Cua makes a careful distinction between an ideal *norm* and an ideal *theme*, and between an *aspirational* and *inspirational* standard. I want to use aspirational as indicating a predefined standard that is to be replicated, and inspirational as indicating an analogous model that inspires one's own unique development.

58. See *Analects* 17/2 and 5/13, and *Mencius* 2A/6. Even when Mencius says "the sages and we are of the same species," he prefaces this abstraction with the qualification that "all things of the same species *resemble* (*si* 以) each other," echoing Confucius' position on *xing* that human beings are only 'close' (*jin* 近), not the same.

59. The notion of 'equality' operative here is one of parity rather than sameness. It means forbearance on the part of other things to allow something to be itself and not something else—an accommodation. See my 'Rites as Rights: The Confucian Alternative' in Leroy S. Rouner (ed.), *Human Rights and the World's Religions* (Notre Dame University Press, 1988).

60. *Mencius* 7A/30 and 3A/1; see also 7A/21 and 7B/33.

61. Ibid., 7A/21.

62. Ibid., 4B/26.

63. Ibid., 6A/7.

64. Joseph Needham, *Science and Civilisation* (Cambridge: Cambridge University Press, 1954) vol. 2, pp. 17ff.

65. *Xunzi* 17.

66. *Mencius* (Hong Kong: Chinese University of Hong Kong Press, 1984) Vol. I, p. xx.

67. Graham, 'Background', p. 15.

68. *Mencius* 2A/6 (D. C. Lau's trans.).

69. Ibid., 6A/2.

70. *Mencius* 4B/19.

71. *Mencius* 3A/4.

72. See Mark Edward Lewis, *Sanctioned Violence in Early China* (Albany: SUNY Press, 1990), for a detailed discussion of this presupposition.

73. See *Analects* 16/9.

74. *Analects* 9/23.

75. See *Analects* 6/30, and the *Daxue* (Great Learning) which is the classic statement for this coextensive relationship.

76. The model we find in Confucius is rather simple: *xing* represents the basic conditions, and *ren* is the achievement concept. For Mencius, *xin* and *ming* are the basic conditions, and *xing* is the achievement concept. In Xunzi, *xing* as a concept captures the initial animal conditions—comparable to Mencius' use of *ming*. For him, *xin*, the moral mind, is the achievement concept, comparable in many ways to Mencius' use of *xing*.

77. See my 'Rites as Rights: The Confucian Alternative'.

78. See Andrew J. Nathan's chapter on 'Political Rights in Chinese Constitutions' in Andrew J. Nathan et al, *Human Rights in Contemporary China* (New York: Columbia University Press, 1986), pp. 77–124.

79. In fact, I am indebted to Henry Rosemont for posing precisely this question.

80. This historiographical point can be illustrated any number of ways. Contrast, for example, the Freudian model of a son achieving his own identity through the rejection of the father, with the Confucian model of a son expressing his uniqueness through the embodiment and extension of the

values and importances of the father. (See *Analects* 1/11 and 4/20). Again, there is the underlying dynamic of ritual practice in classical Confucianism in which a person pursues authoritativeness (*ren* 仁) through embodying the cultural authority of the past and authoring it for his own time and circumstances. History as tradition is understood to be transmission rather than either simple conservation or rejection and innovation.

81. See Hans-Georg Gadamer, *The Relevance of the Beautiful*, trans. N. Walker, ed. R. Bernasconi, (New York: Cambridge University Press, 1986) p. 49.

PHILOSOPHICAL
ISSUES

Should the Ancient Masters Value Reason?

Chad Hansen

A. Irrationalism: Plus and Minus

Students of Chinese thought fall into two groups with fundamentally different attitudes toward Western rationality. Some champions of Non-Western Philosophy denigrate reason. Their stale litany has it that the Western Rational Mind simply cannot fathom a non-rational philosophical insight. Elaborations of this fable may sort mental processes into rational (linear, left-brained) and intuitive (aesthetic, emotional, right-brained). They treat *irrational* as a compliment. We shall call this attitude, whatever the content, the **+**.

Other equally zealous patrons of Chinese philosophy prize rationality. They find themselves comprehending and savoring the texts—at least part of the time. They regard the charge of irrationalism as a condemnation. It devalues Chinese philosophy. We shall call this attitudinal set the **−**.

How can we explain these opposite reactions? I propose to distinguish three questions:

(A) Is Chinese philosophy[1] rational?

(B) Does Chinese philosophy have a concept of reason?

(C) Do Chinese philosophers give reasons for their views?

(A) is the formulation that excites the conflicting attitudes among partisans of Chinese thought. They express their attitudes in their answer to this question. But their answers to the other two questions may be less easy to predict. The question is how to relate our answer to (A) to our answers to (B) and (C).

The − are most impressed that the answer to (C) must be positive. This fact makes understanding possible when we do understand. Absent this fact, it would be hard to verify that we have understood. Without a positive answer to (C), claims to understand become subjective warm feelings to comfortable insights. These are mysteriously evoked in us as we stare at the pages. The − think (C) is an appropriate translation of (A) and that both get a positive answer.

The + must find (C) a mildly troubling question. They do claim to understand the texts. They routinely try to give us the textual basis for their claims. That seems, on the surface, to suggest the texts contain reasons for those claims. Chinese philosophers seem to the + to give reasons for not being rational. I assume those who seriously give a negative answer to (C) will not be reading this book or article. They will be meditating somewhere waiting for insight. So pragmatically, those engaged in trying to prove something about Chinese thought, cannot answer (C) in the negative. The + who are still willing to go on reading, therefore, cannot treat (C) as a translation of (A).

The − are more embarrassed by (B). No clear counterpart of *reason* emerges from among the common terms of Chinese thought. Translation proposals for reason never seem to gain currency. The first to come to mind is the Medieval Neo-Confucian term *li*.[2] 'Principle' has become the accepted translation. The lingering controversy about *li* turns on whether 'pattern' might not be better than principle. In any case, *li* plays only incidental roles in classical thought. It did not become a central philosophical concept during the creative classical period. Carus has proposed *reason* as a translation of *dao*.[3] That made no headway at all against the thoroughly entrenched *way*. In any case, the orthodox view is that Daoists are prototype irrationalists and they worship *dao*. This makes the translation at best mildly paradoxical. (Perhaps the only (in)consistently irrational way to be an irrationalist is to worship reason!)

Could the + be happy with a negative answer to (B)? It is not a translation of (A)—at least it is not what they could have meant when they give their negative answer to (A). Routinely, when they argue for (A) they implicitly accept (B). Chinese philosophers have good reasons, they insist, for rejecting reason. The + usually credit some minor, ill favored schools with being rationalist. The dominant schools must have had the concept to reject it using deliberate proofs. It would not do for Chinese philosophers to reject reason irrationally—without having mastered the concept!

Let us call the view that Chinese philosophers had a concept of reason which they deliberately rejected, contrastive irrationalism. [(B) = Yes and (A) = No—perhaps with the word *dominant* inserted.] Nietzsche is an archetype of contrastive irrationalism. Contrastive rationalists, by contrast, would hold that Chinese thinkers had a concept of reason which they embraced.

Non-contrastive irrationalism confuses me. *Irrational* depends for its meaning on a contrast with *rational*. If Chinese thinkers are irrationalists who never explicitly reject reason, then we must say that somehow their doctrines entail that one should reject reason. But it is hard to see how an intelligible doctrine that does not use a concept of reason could entail that we ought not use reason in general.[4] Non-contrastive rationalism is mildly better off. The interpreter could argue that the theory, which does not use the concept of reason, would be compatible with a doctrine that prized reason. In either case, the mention of reason seems an uninformative aside. We cannot evaluate either position until we see what positive account they give of the content of Chinese theories.

Professor Graham has waded into this issue repeatedly in his many works. The themes of reason, is-ought, fact-value are consistent and sustained concerns that informed many of his creative projects. He would probably come to mind along with Hu Shih if one asked for the pacesetter of the − faction. His answer to all three questions seems to be yes. But his position has always been more complex and subtle than we would suppose. He argued in 1964 with a − tone but with a + twist. Over the years he has filled in and corrected many of the details, but the outline of his position has remained remarkably stable and consistent. The Chinese tradition has an important place for reason and had powerful rationalist schools. The Daoists, however (and especially Zhuang-zi) were self-conscious, deliberate, contrastive anti-rationalists.

His attention to the school of names was central to this guarded hybrid view. The discovery of the concept of reason by the school of names makes Zhuang-zi's conclusion possible. Graham's obvious fondness for Zhuang-zi therefore gives a surprising **+** cast to his views. It is only by having a relatively focused conception of reason that one can give reasons for abandoning it. Chinese philosophy is not irrational, but its best philosopher is a contrastive anti-rationalist.

Equally consistently throughout his writings, Graham develops the issue by reference to the fact-value, nature-morality, or is-ought distinctions. These classical Western distinctions and the concept of reason fit neatly into a familiar concept cluster. The structuring concepts include the contrast of reason-emotion, belief-desire, intellect-appetite, idea-feeling and, therefore, mind-body. Graham has stood for the view that Chinese thought, especially the Daoism of Zhuang-zi, reduces or eliminates the gulf between *is* and *ought*.

I want to explore this conceptual melange and pursue these general characterizations of Chinese philosophy. (B), I shall argue, is false. (C) is true. Chinese philosophers do conceptually collapse the fact-value distinction. However, the is-ought distinction differs structurally from the fact-value distinction and Chinese philosophy seems not to deal with it at all. The fact raises questions about whether it has a radically different concept of morality (or perhaps none at all).

B. The Concepts of Reason

Giving an account of the concept of reason is almost like giving the history of Western philosophy. I have no intention, therefore, of being comprehensive. I hope to give as accurate a capsule treatment as possible and beg the indulgence of those who know how much more we could say. My purpose is to outline the concept enough that we can fix what would make the claim, "Chinese thinkers have the concept of reason and rationality", true. Serious Chinese scholars usually accept

Graham's views on this cluster of concepts and their role in Chinese thought. That near unanimity is only partly due to the nonpareil respect in the field for the soundness of his scholarship. The other source lies in a widely shared set of assumptions about rationality, morality, and individuality. The accepted view of Chinese thought drags these assumptions in its wake. That, I shall argue, is the mistake.

Reason comes as close as any term to being a Western philosophical primitive. That tempts us to treat it as a natural kind. If it is a natural kind, then, whether they have a specific term for it or not, Chinese thinkers are likely to refer to it regularly. If it is not a natural kind, then, absent the theories in which it functions so centrally, we should avoid treating their language as referring to it.

The kinds of theories in which reason functions include (prominently) psychology, epistemology, logic, and ethics. Among some Hegelians and Platonists (hardcore rationalists), it functions in metaphysics (idealist psychology must spill over this way). The psychological role is most popularly known. We class reason and rationality among the faculties or skills that distinguish us from other animals. The reasoning ability enables us to employ and complete a reasoning process. Explaining the process draws on logic. My discussion here, however, should not require more logic than learning basic Euclidean geometry requires. Euclidean deduction still stands as the most influential model of this reasoning process. Rationality enables us to generate theorems or conclusions from axioms. Or, if we are not so good at it, at least to follow Euclidean demonstrations or proofs. A proof is a series of sentences. Some have special status (axioms, assumptions, definitions, previously proved theorems) and the rules of reasoning produce the others. Reasoning is thus a source of knowledge.

We would not be reckoned rational if we generated sentences that did not follow. Nor would it be acceptable if we merely generated them and did not believe them. Reason is the ability to recognize validity and to be cognitively motivated by valid arguments. Rational creatures will alter their systems of beliefs by this process. Their psychological makeup is such that sound arguments affect their beliefs.[5]

The Euclidean model explains one of reason's grammatical shifts. *A reason* is a premise in a proof. Reason*ing* is processing reasons (sentences) according to deductive principles then constructing, displaying, storing, and acting on the result. When we have reason, we also have reason*s*.

Reason, in this core Euclidean sense, thus presupposes an 'arguments on paper' view of the mind.[6] The Euclidean model explains why we are tempted to the view that computers might be rational. Computers can produce arguments. We imagine programming 'in' the counterparts of sentences—the premises. The computer screen, like our conscious mind, lights up with a new sentence—the conclusion.

Our conception is analogous to our view of grammatical ability. We have the capacity to process words and construct, recognize, and produce grammatical sentences. Validity is a kind of grammar of arguments. The tendency to respond to valid logical form is the core of the concept of reason.

The interesting twist is that this tendency, applied to both sentences and proofs, intimately involves the notion of truth. Our sentence-producing ability requires more than merely producing grammatical sentences. We must know what it would be for those sentences to be true. Valid argument form preserves truth. If the premises are true and the form is valid, the conclusion is true. Our psychological capacities include being able to recognize true sentences and recognize inferences that transmit truth.

So our Euclidean computer not only generates grammatically correct sentences, it picks out those which are true. These constitute the beliefs of the reasoning apparatus. The faculty concept of reason seems to require this companion concept of a special set of sentences—the beliefs which we organize in valid form to generate new sentences.

Euclidean reason thus generates a characteristic form of skepticism—belief skepticism. Euclidean skeptics worry that some of the unit's initial processing set may be false. Reasoning, in that case, would not be a reliable way of producing new true beliefs. Euclid himself required that we start with self-evident truths—axioms and definitions. That his self-evident truths were not true is one of the shocking bases of modern relativist skepticism.

Finally, the Euclidean model bequeaths to the concept of reason a descriptive or representative function. Reason aims for true beliefs. The rational mind constructs a sentence based map of the way things are.

Knowledge is the goal. If the internal sentences accurately map states of affairs and reliable, rational processes produce them, they constitute knowledge. Much of our past philosophical tradition has assumed that if reason could lead to ethical knowledge, it entailed that ethics was real.

1. Natural Extensions of Euclidean Reason

a. Rational intuition. Western use of the concept of reason never stops merely with the deductive process model. The model itself requires an additional function of reason. We require a special twist on the ability in order to know what would count as making a sentence true. We must know some sentences without using Euclidean reasoning or we would face an infinite regress. This could make knowledge seem impossible. In particular, we require insight into the truth of the presupposed axioms. Some sentences must be self-evident to reason and our reason must be able to provide those sentences independently of the Euclidean process. Reason must be able to recognize, accept, and store some sentences without relying on proof process.

Western thought thunders with the battles of two schools of thought about the source, nature, and content of these foundational beliefs. Empiricists held they come from sense experience. Rationalists used to argue that they were innate—hard-wired in the circuitry of the mind. Later they argued that the sentences are the natural outputs of any circuitry capable of operating rationally. Empiricists may not require that the senses themselves are rational, but must allow that it is rational to accept non-processed perceptual beliefs. That premise must be hard-wired along with the senses themselves. The mere transmission of data about the world is not enough to get Euclidean reasoning off the ground.

The notion of rational process thus motivated the notion of rational intuition. Without the latter, the process could hardly justify the adoration typical of Western thought. And Reason was adored! The light of reason became hard to distinguish from the light of intuition except that rationalists rather than mystics proclaimed it. The pure intuitionist was going to rest with the insights alone. The rationalist was going to use them in the Euclidean reasoning process.

b. Practical reasoning. Rational intuition becomes crucial in the second extension of the Euclidean process model—practical reason. Socrates first insisted on employing reason for guiding our lives. Aristotle formulated a specialized argument form—the practical syllogism. He adapted the Euclidean model to explain our actions as well as our beliefs. The premise-conclusion structure remains in place but the interest is now in guidance, not mere descriptive truth. So, to be valid, at least one premise must have some prescriptive force. The conclusion, notoriously, is an action.

Following the belief model, we again call any of the premises a reason for the action. This model was fecund enough to fuel several thousand years of ethical disputation and analysis. But it bequeaths to Western philosophy a problematic motif—the priority of the descriptive model and the descriptive sentence. We see the effects in our primary school assumptions that a complete thought is a sentence. A complete sentence has a subject and a predicate. An imperative sentence lacks a subject.[7] Similarly, a practical syllogism lacks a sentential conclusion. We represent the action, however, as another prescriptive sentence—an ought-sentence. If we do that, then the valid form becomes explicit again. However, the link to truth that rationalizes sentence and argument construction becomes problematic when we deal with oughts. We would use *true* of neither the imperative sentence nor the action. Is the ought-sentence true or false? Here, we branch to two hundred years of Western meta-ethics.

We will not follow that branch far. The important thing for my present argument is this. It is from reflection on the practical syllogism that we derive our familiar contrast of *is* and *ought*. We were able to recapture the explicit sentential structure of practical reasoning by making the conclusion an ought-sentence—one containing the word *ought* or *should*. Then, as Hume insisted, there must be at least one ought-sentence in the premises for the moral argument to be valid.

This puts two more wrinkles in the fabric of reason. First, rational creatures once again need access to rational insight—now a moral version. Some a priori categorical imperative is presupposed by the process. Again, either it can be hard-wired in the moral-rational structure of the mind or a necessary moral output of any circuitry capable of behaving rationally, that is, in accordance with some version of practical Euclidean reasoning. Second, a rational actor requires something beyond merely flashing the ought-conclusion on the screen. Just as it must have some attitude of belief-acceptance, so it must have some motivation to act on the conclusion. If we merely display and store the conclusion we are not rational actors. Of course our science fiction robots and vulcans are fully rational in this practical sense. But it clearly requires more intricate programming than is available for a word processor with a grammar and logic checker. This is why Aristotle first insisted the conclusion of a practical syllogism was action.

Again we have the counterpart of a rationalist-empiricist split. For empiricists, desires are to basic motivational premises as sense experience is to perceptual beliefs. So they argue, desires are the little extra the computer needs to be a rational actor. But the analogous presupposition that it is rational to fulfill the desires seems problematic at first glance—more at least than it was in the case of perceptual beliefs. Moral empiricists seem to require a distinction between rational and irrational desires that they did not need with perceptions.

If we can separate rational and irrational desires, then the practical syllogism allows us to put rationality to work in guiding our behavioral output. The desires are the dispositions structured in the hard-wiring of the entire unit—not merely its rational processing module. By selecting rational ones, the Euclidean process should produce rational actions. It also allows the generation of new desires just as it does new beliefs. Desires for an end rationally generate desires for the means.

Practical rationality thus embraces the behavioral capacity to adjust means to ends. When Westerners living in China fume that Chinese are irrational, they are usually assuming that we share ends and that Westerners have found the uniquely rational way to achieve them. Our familiar economic concept of rational action develops the empiricist view with an assumption (rational?) that self-interested desires of accumulation are rational. Philosophers, as opposed to economists and political scientists, typically insist that moral actions are at least as rational as self-interested actions.

The Euclidean prototype applied to practical rationality becomes our main explanatory model for human (and frequently animal) behavior. We assume the process is psychologically real. Rational beings produce such 'arguments on mental paper' in guiding their behavior whenever they act deliberately and voluntarily. The explanans are beliefs and desires and the hard-wired capacity for rational processing. The outputs are voluntary human actions—the stuff of normative theory. The Greek psychology of beliefs and desires constitute the electrical potential counterparts of is- and ought-sentences. These concepts all lie near the core of our definition of ourselves as rational animals.

It will not do to characterize this as merely Western folk psychology, however, since the Greek influence extended east to India. We can find the central elements of this model of human functioning—the psychology of rationality—in Buddhism and Hinduism. But the only undisputed component of this cluster found in ancient Chinese psychological theory is desire.

c. Miscellaneous uses of *reason*. The Empiricist's requirement that we be able to derive rational perceptual beliefs from our senses led them to derive another function for reason. Language learning presupposes the mental process of rational abstraction. Our Euclidean processing requires sentences or beliefs—their mental counterpart. The sentences have a syntactic structure that minimally includes general nouns and adjectives. There must be some way of linking these words with sensations so reason can derive the true belief from the sense data. This function of reason is abstraction. From an accumulation of data, reason pares off individualizing detail and thus produces the abstract idea. In our tradition, this is a pre-linguistic process just as recognizing self-evident truths is. Abstraction does not use the Euclidean process. But, again, Euclidean process seems to require this abstraction activity. We need this ability to be able to detect the truth of perceptual sentences, and we need that ability, in turn, to engage in Euclidean processing. If we are to class the outputs of that processing as rational, we must similarly characterize both these essential prior processes.

The early rationalist simply has these rational concepts as components in innate truths. We still call them concepts of reason. Their respective theories push both schools to the corollary that language has a rational basis. Of course languages have different sounds and structures, but behind that is a rationally pure language of the mind—mentalese. Rationalists would hold that all humans think the same idiolect of mentalese. Empiricists could allow for differences arising from the range of environmental experiences. Eskimos may have concepts for more varieties of snow than Amazons. Languages can differ, but they mean the same thing. Meaning, like truth, is a close associate of reason (and another in the cluster that is hard to identify in Chinese thought).

Consequently, we interpret something as language only when we impute rationality to the creature. To interpret is to presuppose some shared pattern of processing of beliefs and desires. If these were crucially different, we could never come to understand each other. Interpretative principles such as the principle of charity and the principle of humanity attribute rationality to those we interpret. We assume minimally that they can recognize validity and tend to believe the valid consequences of their prior beliefs.

Finally, therefore, we use reason as the opposite of convention. Probably this use stems from the assumption that reason is part of our essence and thus transcultural. Reason gives us access to pan-human concepts and pre-linguistic truths. Reason gives us access to pan-human a priori moral axioms. Conventions, we easily discover, can differ widely. Thus universal reason becomes an enemy of partial, limited, local convention. This is the impact of the use of this term in moral theory.

C. Is-Ought and Fact-Value

As I argued above, the structure of the concept of reason when used to provide practical guidance draws our attention to the *is-ought* distinction. We distinguish the different roles sentences play. Those that guide action may do so because of imperative form (commands) or the presence of some crucial word—typically *ought*. We distinguish those that describe or predict as *is*-sentences. They function in guidance. They are frequently crucial premises in practical syllogisms. Consider the abortion argument.

1. We ought not cause the death of innocent persons.

2. Aborting births cause the death of fetuses.

3. Fetuses are innocent persons.

4. We ought not abort births.

Each of the premises (the reasons) is equally necessary for the conclusion. The Humean slogan, "You can't get an *ought* from an *is*," insists that (1) plays a peculiarly important role. It warns us that we cannot complete the argument merely by information available to doctors or geneticists.

Hume's prejudice has been transmitted to modern times along with his logic. He took the is-ought slogan as grounds for his famous claim that reason is (and ought to be [?]) the slave of the passions. Ought-sentences, we commonly suppose, are matters of feeling where is-sentences have their basis in reason plus experience of the world. Is-sentences constitute the objective, determinable issues. In principle, we can assign truth or falsity to these sentences using scientific method. Ought-sentences, by contrast, are matters of feeling, subjectivity. Thus, though they function in rational argument, some may argue that their basis is pre-rational. They rest in crucial ways on subjective states of individuals—desires, feelings, passions.

The notion of subjectivity, used in this package of conventional Western philosophical wisdom, smuggles in another set of assumptions. The subject of subjectivity is an individual. Desires belong to individuals. Cognitive states, of course, also belong to individuals.[8] But cognitive states are caused by external objects through sense perception. Other individuals can arrive at agreement by using their eyes and ears (tongues, skin, and nose!). Emotive states, our folk psychology says, are irreducibly individual.

Individualism in our culture is popularly thought to be a companion to the concept of reason. The faculty is a faculty of individuals. One paradigm of rational action is individual prudence. The desire input in practical reasoning is irreducibly individual. Nothing in the pure concept requires these results. We could regard reasoning as a capacity of a community—as sociological rather than psychological. For example, it may be a sociological property of a scientific community as much as a psychological property of the individuals who make up that community.

We have come to regard desires which we know to be instilled by social means as rationally suspect. They suffer from association with social conventions. Similarly, we regard conventional wisdom as a derogatory term. On the face of it, that a belief happens to be mine and that my community happens share it, should make no difference to reason.

Associating individualism with reason has affected both our morality and our moral skepticism. Skepticism arises because we doubt that reason can justify moral axioms. The alternative seems to be subjectivism. Moral realism—essentially the Kantian version—takes the respect for reason to entail respect for the dignity of individuals.

The fact-value distinction seems to be merely different terminology for the same phenomenon. The focus has shifted from the type of sentence to that which makes the sentence true. The world of facts makes an is-sentence true. Values make an ought-sentence true. However, we can make a worthwhile distinction between values and obligations. The popularity of utilitarianism, which defines the right in terms of the good, contributes to blurring this distinction. Roughly value is to terms as obligation is to sentences. Just as we distinguished between a descriptive and prescriptive sentence, so we can distinguish between an evaluative term and a descriptive term.

The paradigm descriptive term is the natural kind term—the scientific classification. These terms divide nature at the joints. Evaluative terms divide nature at points that are important in schemes that guide our choosing and rejecting. A brown bear is brown whatever our involvement may be in the situation. A nice bear counts as such because humans are involved with bears in ways ants are not.

The link to reason comes from the role of reason in abstraction. The Western tradition treats natural kind abstraction as a rational process based on experience. We treat evaluative classifications as stretched over natural kinds by the subjective bias of desires. Although our theories of mind cannot give us much reason for it, we regard the natural kind classifications as objective and the evaluative ones as subjective. We suppose our values differ but our sensible experience is more constant.

Some recent philosophical discussions have questioned this close association of is-ought and fact-value. They argue that the is-ought distinction is real while the fact-value distinction may be spurious.[9] All terms help guide our behavior. All use of terms involves making distinctions—projecting a line of demarcation on the world. Where the line falls depends both on the world and on us. The distinction between colors and values seems to shrink when we consider the matter this way. There is no more a natural joint between brown and orange than between nice and mean. We can learn to apply both distinctions. We apply them with a high degree of interpersonal agreement. Both are world-guided.[10] Neither is fully independent of our nature.

Both distinctions guide our behavior. The difference lies in the relative constancy of the direction of guidance. We may use brown and orange to guide a preference in many different ways. Nice and mean exhibit a constant pattern guiding our choosing and rejecting. Normally we choose nice and reject mean. The man with the tranquilizer gun and a rare, special, social role chooses the mean bear.

The relation of reason to the fact-value distinction is tenuous. It rests on the use of reason in the theory of abstract ideas. This process is prior to the core Euclidean reasoning process. The is-ought distinction arises within the proof model.

D. The Classical Chinese Conceptual Framework

What I want to claim about classical Chinese philosophy is this. It does not generate any theory of something resembling the Euclidean process. Thus it has no basis for using a concept strongly similar to the core concept of reason. It does exhibit suggestive counterparts of some of the peripheral roles. But without that core, using *reason* as a translation obscures some vital and interesting differences between our respective philosophical traditions. We will find ourselves projecting

Euclidean assumptions about reasoning structure on those thinkers on the most tenuous shreds. Given the uncontroversial assumption of no Greek influence on the classical period of Chinese thought, we will have to accept the innateness aspect of Greek rationalism to explain its presence in China. Further, attributing a theory of rationality will tempt us to project our optional associated views about individuals, subjectivity, desires, and beliefs into Chinese theories.

The important conceptual differences are these. The Chinese zi ('masters') viewed language as playing essentially a guiding role, not a descriptive one. (They were interested in ethics, not metaphysics). Their interest in language centered on the word, not the sentence. They based their analysis of disagreement on how we project distinctions on things, not on our proofs and presuppositions. Thus, they had no sentence-based is-ought distinction.

They did not have an implicit belief-desire psychology. (They had no mind-body dualism.) The concept of knowledge is closer to skill than to belief. (They had no classical epistemology.) With regard to fact-value, they had no individualist theory of abstraction. The patterns of projecting lines of demarcation in guiding behavior, Chinese philosophers mainly regarded as learned, conventional patterns. If the individual had any inner basis for his projections, it was a matter of natural dispositions. No one appealed to a faculty whose initial purpose was appreciating argument validity.

I remind the reader that none of this entails that Chinese philosophers did not give reasons for their philosophical views. I direct these observations at undermining claim (B) above, not (C). The issue comes because serious students disagree with each other about the proper interpretation and the import of some phrases, terms, or passages. It is only because we can plausibly reconstruct their reasons for writing those passages that we can attribute one or the other interpretation to them. My claim is that the reasons they give for the disputed claims are good reasons if we attribute to them the conceptual scheme I have outlined. If we attribute classical Greek psychology and rationality theory, their reasons become obscure, irrelevant, or philosophically silly.

1. Chinese Candidates for the Concept of Reason

Now we can find some counterparts of the Western conceptual roles reason plays in classical Chinese philosophy. These undergird the confidence that the Chinese tradition has a concept of reason. But that conclusion fosters confusion unless we distinguish which role of reason we are attributing to them. What we find in Chinese thought are counterparts of the extended uses of reasons—not of its Euclidean core.

One example is Mencius' theory of the innate knowledge of the heart-mind. Mencius credits the heart-mind with reliable intuitions about *shi-fei* ('this:right–not this:wrong'). The dominant interpretive line also credits him with a familiar Platonic rationalist assumption. This knowledge is innate.

Another example is Mozi. Mozi rejects convention or tradition as a moral standard and constructs a utilitarian, maximization moral theory. The first move reminds us of Socrates' contrast of hearsay, conventional wisdom, and reason. It recalls the basic contrast of culturally relative social mores and objective rational morality (positive versus critical morality). The second prompts comparisons with such giants of our analytic reasoning tradition as Hume, Bentham, and John Stuart Mill. His political theory, further, reminds us of Hobbes for whom the concept of rational egoism is the crucial pivot. It undergirds his rational alternative to the essentially religious divine right of kings.

But lacking the core concept of a Euclidean faculty, treating these counterparts of peripheral meanings of reason (rational intuition and practical maximizing) as appeals to reason distort as much as they explain.[11] Mencius' intuitions, for example, have little in common with Plato's beyond innateness. Plato's theory of innate knowledge is integral to the Euclidean project. Plato credits the slave Meno with knowledge of axioms together with deductive abilities. These work together to help him do a geometrical derivation. It is not that the slave remembers the answer to the problem. He has innately whatever is necessary to solve it. The innate contents are relative to the Euclidean deductive process.

Mencius does not use his *shi-fei* judgments as first premises in a deduction of moral truth. The outputs of intuition are different in content and use. The *shi-fei* reactions are non-sentential and more evaluative than descriptive. They are direct motivations to action (knowledge is action)—like the action conclusions of practical syllogisms.

There may be a process of cultivation or growth which involves an emotive transfer or extending. Mencius scholars typically liken this to analogical reasoning. But it is not a reasoning process. It is a cultivation process. Mencius does not assume, as Greek thinkers do, that rational justifications will change our desires and beliefs directly. Drawing the conclusion is not having the motivation. Having the proper *shi-fei*, if not innate, is a lengthy process of cultivating moral motivations. They play no role in logical deduction.

The moral impulse to do this rather than not-this does come from within for Mencius. But, it is not a deduction from principles. Its essence is as a response to a situation. The innate knowledge would not be available to its owner as an abstract content. It comes only in a situation requiring moral choice and action. It cannot present itself as a sentence (unless the situation is wondering what to write or say).

Mencius thinks the intuitions are natural, reliable, and the authoritative standard of what is right and wrong. That, however, is not enough. Rationalists do claim these advantages for reason. But that merely makes Mencius' a rival theory of natural moral authority. Mencius claims for intuition what rationalists claim for reason. That does not make his theory a theory of rational intuition. He proclaims natural, emotive instincts. Rationalists proclaim the faculty of reason. In the absence of any link to deductive process, there is no reason to class Mencius' concept of intuition as *rational* intuition.[12]

But the game is not lost. Mencius' appeal to the standard of intuition is a reaction to Mozi. We could still credit Mencius with a nativist response to Mohist rationalism. The Mohists criticize Confucian conventionalism and propose a maximizing moral standard. They thus highlight practical means-ends processing. That looks familiarly rational. We could, thus, say Mencius' is a rival theory in the necessary contrastive sense. That saves the premise that the tradition has a concept of reason. Mencius, on this account, deliberately rejects Mohist deliberative reason for non-rational, non-calculating, intuition.

This strategy puts the burden of proving the contrastive irrationalism interpretation on the interpretation of Mohism. A similar result flows from studying the case of Zhuang-zi and Neo-Mohism. Here, without Graham's work we would be totally at sea. The orthodoxy had treated Zhuang-zi as little more than a rhetorical variation on Mencius. Zhuang-zi, the Neo-Confucian line went, advocates following a natural, intuitive, reliable, authority, to wit, the mystical *dao*. What making the intuition mystical does to distinguish Zhuang-zi from Mencius is, of course, mystical. It certainly shrinks their difference to a narrow band on the philosophical spectrum. The Neo-Confucian line, conveniently, allowed the bromide that Confucianism and Daoism were perfectly harmonious.

However, explicitly calling the intuition mystical and adding the contrastive theory that *dao* is inaccessible to reason, makes a rhetorical difference. Where for Mencius the contrast with reason was merely implicit, with mystical intuitionism it is explicit. Whatever mystical intuition is, it is not rational intuition. But since Mencius' intuition is not rational, we have no insight into how the two forms of intuition differ.

Graham's great contributions lie in his reconstruction of Neo-Mohism. He shows that Zhuang-zi's foil is the School of Names.[13] Graham argues that the Neo-Mohists studied and advocated logic. Zhuang-zi, relying on his school of names resource, Hui Shi, turns analytical reason into its own critic. He is thus a fully self-conscious anti-rationalist. Graham's Zhuang-zi is a contrastive anti-rationalist.

However, in Graham's reconstruction, Zhuang-zi's irrationalism does not rely on Mencius' question-begging initial appeal to mystical intuition. Zhuang-zi first refutes reason rationally. He uses reason, while maintaining a theoretical and stylistic neutrality. Zhuang-zi shows his freedom from reason while putting reason to work. He engages in frequent flights of hyperbolic imagination, puts his arguments in the mouths of fantasy creatures and injects startling or humorous twists in the direction of his exposition. He embraces mystical intuition after having rationally disposed of reason. Intuition is the surviving alternative, not the authority in a question-begging attack on reason.

The upshot is, we seem to have to look to the Mohist school, early or late, for our contrastive foil. Do Mohists construct theories that would allow us to credit them with a concept of calculative reason? If they do then we can treat Mencius and Zhuang-zi respectively as anti-rationalists in the full sense. If they do not, then we must conclude that such characterizations are likely to be misleading at best.

2. *Reason in Mohism*

For the synoptic Mozi, this question turns mainly on his ethical theories summarized above. He ethics is anti-traditionalist as rational ethics is. He gives reasons for doubting that tradition can be an acceptable moral standard. He also suggests that his words "are like rocks." But he does not claim that we have a reasoning faculty that recognizes reasons as reasons. He does not identify it as the source of moral authority. We implicitly supply those corollaries from our own conceptual scheme. The morality with which we contrast positive traditional, social morality is rational morality. We project, not discover, that concept in Mozi.

Mozi also gives a maximization ethical standard that looks similar to Western Utilitarianism—a model of calculative rationalism in ethics. But what impresses Mozi is that the utilitarian standard is measurable, easily projectible, and therefore accessible to those outside the literati. The appeal to the *li-hai* ('benefit-harm') distinction gives widespread access to a standard for practical application of terms used in moral guidance. He does not think of utilitarianism as a powerful way to give a deductive justification of ought-sentences. The distinction between *li-hai* is like a measuring tool for the application of moral guiding terms. It is not an axiom for the deduction of moral truths.

When it comes to justifying the reliance on the *li-hai* ('benefit-harm') distinction as a public standard, Mozi does not appeal to reason, but like Mencius, to *tian* ('nature:Heaven'). The point about the *li-hai* distinction is that it introduces a natural source of guidance—the natural, Heaven-given tendency to choose *li* ('benefit') and reject *hai* ('harm'). This contrasts Heavenly or natural will with cultural, historically conditioned will.

The orthodoxy always finds this appeal to Heaven to be evidence of religiosity in Mozi. This created a paradox for them since he has also to play the role of rationalist for the contrastive interpretation. And, in our conceptual scheme, reason and religion are not fast friends. Graham's 1964 survey of Chinese thought remarked on this same paradox. But by

1981 he had realized that the appearance of religiosity in Mohism was misleading.[14] Despite the fundamental appeal to the concept of *tian* ('nature:Heaven'), we find little of the emotional character of religiosity in the writings. We find even less in the Neo-Mohist writings. They had abandoned appeal to *tian* ('nature:Heaven') and Heavenly will like abandoning an old wrinkle in their theory, not like religious deconversion.

The paradox disappears entirely if we accept the hypothesis that Mozi appeals to *tian* ('nature:Heaven') as the authority for making *li-hai* ('benefit-harm') the base distinction. He does not appeal to a rational faculty capable of making transcultural judgments. He appeals to a transcultural basis of willing—the preference for benefit over harm. Graham again sees what the orthodoxy distorts. Mozi's appeal is not to egoistic benefit and harm.[15]

If we think of Mozi's position as measurement utilitarianism, then we could contrast Bentham's 'Moral Calculus' as arithmetical utilitarianism. Arithmetical utilitarianism calculates a complex set of pluses and minuses to get a sum. Measurement utilitarianism just applies a gauge to sight along to find what to do. The natural arithmetical extension of Mozi's measurement utilitarianism had to await the Neo-Mohists. Even they explain it more with the balancing apparatus than as a calculation. We find little evidence that Mozi's utilitarianism was ever a calculus as it was for Bentham.

Mozi's theoretical structure as reflected in utilitarianism thus makes no appeal to the Euclidean faculty of reason. His utilitarianism is not a definition of ought in terms of the good nor a derivation proof structure in any sense. It does not involve the Western model of practical or moral reasoning. He doesn't have a moral axiom—a fundamental moral truth—that we ought to maximize utility. His appeal is to a basic *bian* ('distinction') between *li-hai* ('benefit-harm') that serves as a natural motivational split. Mozi wants that one to motivate us to other motivational splits.

The Western goal is to show that an axiom of practical reasoning is: 'we ought to maximize good'. That goal fits into the Euclidean model of practical rationality. They want to establish a rational moral axiom to start a proof of potentially many theorems containing the word *ought*.

Mozi's concerns are directly with the measurement standard for assigning evaluative contrasts such as good/bad. That such term contrasts guide our behavior was an unstated assumption that all the classical thinkers share. His focus is on *bian* ('distinctions') not sentences—certainly not sentences arranged in proofs.

This term-based focus, however, reminds us to look at another of the roles of reason. Rational abstraction is the application of reason to subsentential units—terms, names, adjectives. Here the faculty of reason underlies the rational process of abstraction which generates the meaning, concept, or idea. That, in turn, determines what things we refer to with words. Thus, implicitly, this component of the rationalist doctrine has it that reason determines where the discrimination between what is and what is not the thing in question falls. Mozi's theoretical concern with where a word's boundary will fall seems like an interest in one of the functions of reason.

Here again, however, the assimilation will be misleading. His is a rival theory of the process. He sees categorization as depending on the social acceptance of a pragmatic standard to guide the range of social uses of terms. Classification is not the output of some transcultural human faculty. We could easily argue that his is a more rational theory of the process, but not that it is a theory of rational abstraction. And it does not, as the Western theory does, borrow a Euclidean concept to give the process a realistic, extra-cultural basis. The extra-cultural basis comes from the natural or Heavenly will to prefer benefit to harm.

His theory of term scope is more radically pragmatic than almost any traditional Western theory. Pragmatic, historical, or social standards guide the use of language—which in turn guides human behavior.

Here Graham's early view and his late view misses the point of Mozi's three standards of language. Mozi proposes three standards for the correctness of distinctions and the applications of terms that make them up. He calls these standards of language because he assumes words make up language. The three standards are historical conformity, social conformity and ease in application, and pragmatic usefulness. In 1964 Graham introduces the standards by saying that the "pressure of controversy forces" Mozi to give "reasons".[16] He imposes the

Euclidean model of argument on the text. This yields three premises of the form 'if a sentence (theory, belief, doctrine etc.) is X then it is true.' As I argued, this construal removes the motivation for the standards.[17] They are bad tests of truth. They are perfectly reasonable standards for determining the appropriateness of someone's use of a word.

Still in 1981, Graham sees this doctrine in the *Mozi* as "crude" argumentation.[18] However, he clearly is focused more on making sense of the Later Mohists than their founding master. And in his analysis of their works he is very clear that the issues concern the application of terms in describing the world. The focus of this semantic concern is on the concept of *bian* ('discrimination'), the relations of opposite terms and the appropriate standards for collecting things into *lei* ('similarity categories'). If Mozi had the basic Euclidian idea of arguing for the truth of a conclusion, his most logically inclined disciples had forgotten or ignored it.

3. The Later Mohists' Logic

Graham's analysis of the Later Mohists is correct. But we have to explore how it undermines the orthodox view of Mozi. He points out that the Later Mohists abandon any reference to Heaven's will. This is not, as I argued above, a religious movement become irreligious. It is a theory change. The appeal to Heaven's will was Mozi's basis for making *li-hai* ('benefit-harm') the distinction to guide all other distinctions. He saw the process of social agreement on distinctions as pragmatic, historical, and social (as implicitly, Confucius had).

The later Mohists, Graham sees, do respond to what he calls the "metaphysical crisis" stemming from the beginnings of Daoist theorizing. The question is what should be the base distinction in a pragmatic program of rectifying names. The crisis confronts them because of Yang Chu and Mencius. Clearly the appeal to a natural basis for making distinctions gives no determinate answer.

The benefit-harm distinction itself has two natural forms. One in which we consider the benefit to a social group, the other where we focus on benefit for ourselves. Mencius argues effectively that the prejudicial bias in favor of our own kin is as natural as is universal sympathy. The appeal to nature can lead to nothing except a non-cognitivist relativism. The natural historical fact of my commitment to some root distinction generates my scheme of guiding concepts. My neighbor's history generates his conflicting scheme.

So the Later Mohists abandon the notion of a core natural willing or choice. But they still want a natural standard. They need one that yields a unique place to mark the distinction between opposite terms. This leads them to attempt to formulate semantic realism. The basis for our distinctions must lie in objective, external similarities and differences. Graham again finds evidence of our familiar conceptualist account of rational abstraction. I have argued that it is a mistake to assume that the presence of terms like *i* ('idea') allows us to impute the entire apparatus of British empiricism to the Later Mohists—ideas, properties, inner pictures, subjective meaning theory.[19]

But even if we were to accept a mental pictures account of the Later Mohists' semantic theory, we would still look in vain for rational abstraction theory. We find no appeal to a reasoning faculty which constructs this idea out of the multitude of experiences of concrete things of the class, no epistemological metaphysics of a particular with repeatable properties nor of a mind that stores visual images, no account of an operation of abstraction-subtraction, generalization to produce abstract ideas. The mind surveys the output of the senses and then *bian* ('discriminates').

Despite correctly analyzing the focus on Later Mohists' interest in language, and their influence on later philosophers, Graham's study of the Later Mohists did not dislodge his orthodox view of Zhuang-zi. This is because Graham still describes the School of Names as logicians. The interest in logic is the concern that links the Later analytic school with Mozi's three tests of truth.

The instinct is right, any concern with logic must implictly deal with truth. And any study of truth must implictly presuppose the concept of the sentence—the bearer of truth. Graham argues that the Later Mohists discovered sentences as their latest and most difficult discovery.[20] In that case, we have another reason to doubt the orthodox view of Mozi's tests. If the cognizance of sentences was so deeply and enigmatically hidden from view, we shouldn't make the tests apply to sentences.

Graham preserves the orthodox line by a rhetorical assimilation of *bian* ('discriminate') to logic. The key error common in the orthodox line is—the failure to see that the English word *argument* is equivocal. In one sense it is synonymous with *proof*. In the other sense it is synonymous with *quarrel*. We tend not to distinguish them outside of logic classes. When we disagree or quarrel, we assume it is because the parties give different arguments with different premises. Thus the study of the arguments we give helps us improve our performance when we have arguments.

An engrossing and instructive parallel in ancient China helps that confusion along. The School of Names equivocated in its use of *bian* ('discriminate'). They used *bian* in the sense of *dispute* or *disagreement*. All disagreement, they suggest, is based on differences in how we assign words and discriminate. (This is the Mohist version of the philosophers' adage that all questions are semantic.)

So the Later Mohists are still talking about *bian* ('discriminate') when they come to their paradox. Thieves are people but killing thieves is not killing people. The Mohists defend this incongruity by considering a host of examples with similar structure. That certainly makes it look as if they are interested in the inferential form. This dialogue is the best hope for finding logic in classical China. But only a hope. The Mohists do not generate any theory along with the examples. They take the issue to be about reliability of language, not a faculty of thinkers. They don't identify the sentence pairs as proofs or arguments. And, finally, their conclusion is negative. The point of the examples appears to be that formal operations on language are capricious.

Had they discovered logic, had they arrived at a concept of proof or argument structure, they would hardly have given in so easily to pessimism. But they were looking for stable compositional principles for words. Their citing of examples convinced them that hope was illusory. Matching phrases is an unreliable process. They embrace their paradox defiantly. Many other examples of the anomalous effects of compounding phrases are routinely accepted. This one presents no special difficulty.

In any case, Zhuang-zi's arguments focus on names and shifting reference. It is hard to find any text in which he deals with inference or argument form. Similarly, Xunzi treats the paradox as "using names to confuse names". If the Mohists had discovered argument form, the secret did not get far out of their inner circle.

The core assumption that philosophers from Mozi to Zhuang-zi share is this: All disagreement stems from disagreement in how to use terms of parts of the world. We *bian* semantically when we disagree with others. Similarly, they treat *bian* ('discriminate') as the base of all intellectual activities. Disagreements all have a semantic basis. Their attention is not riveted on premises, but on the alternative roots from which we generate distinctions. Because those base distinctions are different, our outputs are different and we disagree.

Xunzi develops this view in a way that further explains Mozi's scheme. Humans do have a defining faculty. It is not, however, reason. Nor is it intelligence. *Zhi* ('intelligence') distinguishes animals in general from other living things. The distinguishing faculty of humans is the ability to *fen* ('divide') or make distinctions. This is what makes *i* ('morality') possible. We divide ourselves into morally functional groups and organize our behavior by using conventions of discrimination and choice to guide our behavior. Agreement on these guiding discriminations preserves social cooperation.

Mozi had described his state of nature as a state in which people had different *i* ('moralities'). They divided and described in different ways and so they acted in different ways. This led to friction and war. His theoretical and political goal was to give a harmonious way of basing prescriptive guidance on language.

That is the goal that links the founder of Mohism to the Later Mohists. Their focus is not logic, not argument, not proof, not the Euclidean model of reason. That goal of reliable prescriptive language, and not logic, is what Zhuang-zi rejects.

E. Conclusion: Non-contrastive Rationalism

What then of Zhuang-zi? If my argument of the previous section is correct, then he does not have the concept of logic or any rationalist theory to kick around. He cannot, therefore, be a contrastive anti-rationalist. Given Professor Graham's observation of his knowledge of the School of Names and assuming his antagonism to them, we can say, at most, that he is an anti-realist in semantics. He is anti-*bian*.

This turns out to give the best account of Zhuang-zi's own arguments as well. His argument is that we lack any real basis for our discriminations. We make them from incommensurable points of view and we index the terms we use to our point of view. This insight weaves both the skeptical and the relativist threads in Zhuang-zi. No way, he argues, can we make a perspective-free term assignment. Now if there is no way to settle disagreements based on *bian* ('discriminate'), then presumably there is no *rational* way to do so. Of course, Zhuang-zi does not put the point using the concept of rationality. Even if he did, we would not normally call him an anti-rationalist. It is hardly infrequent that people who cling to reason draw skeptical or relativist conclusions. A non-cognitivist is an anti-rationalist only in the sense that an empiricist is—not in the sense a mystic is.

We could also put Zhuang-zi's point (though he does not) by saying there is no reason to prefer one perspective to another. But this tempts us to elaborate by saying the different schools start from different axioms, reasons, premises and thus arrive at different conclusions. Since they share none of the presuppositions, they cannot settle their dispute by argument. Again Zhuang-zi's point is interestingly different from this familiar Western one. Indeed he holds that our prior commitment to doctrine explains our current disagreements. But in his view, a doctrine is a conceptual perspective, not a body of beliefs with term-meaning taken as fixed.

We have an investment in a *shi-fei* system. That past pattern of assigning *shi-fei* fixes our point of view as surely as our perceptual perspective does. He sees them as perfectly analogous. But these prior commitments are not to sentential premises, but to other key distinctions. Prior selection of a base distinction determines our subsequent application of *shi-fei*. Our disputes about them are pointless because we have no way to get to a common base distinction. Euclidean reason plays no role in his skeptical argument.

Thus the warring voices are incommensurable and the disputes between various schools, practically speaking, irresolvable. He presents a rational scheme for semantic non-cognitivism. That, given the shared assumption that language guides behavior, yields moral and political non-cognitivism. He is thus diametrically opposed to Mencius—not an irrationalist twin. Zhuang-zi is that frequent and familiar product of philosophical reasoning—a skeptic.

Now I have said nothing to question Graham's positive account of Zhuang-zi's position. Zhuang-zi does outline an inspirational ideal of 'getting the knack' of things and acquiring practical know-how. He revels in the clear awareness that it has little to do with mastering a system of prescriptive concepts. Graham's treatment of Daoist spontaneity is essentially correct except for the contrastive 'anti-rational' portrayal. Zhuang-zi says nothing against the giving of reasons, against logic. I would not even object to calling getting the knack *mystical* if we dropped the contrastive connotations of that word. Of course, that would leave us with the always daunting task of making sense of what Chinese mysticism was.

So what is the answer to (A)? Chinese thinking is non-contrastively rational. Chinese thinkers certainly are rational. But no classical Chinese theorist is either a rationalist or an anti-rationalist. There are excellent reasons for their philosophical views. However, these views do not concern the core concept of reason—pro or con. Zhuang-zi himself is the model of a non-contrastive rationalist. Classical Chinese philosophy has no rationalists, and so no anti-rationalists.

REFERENCES

Bruce, Percy. 1923. *Chu Hsi and His Masters* (London:Probsthain).

Carus, Paul. 1913. *The Canon of Reason and its Virtue* (Chicago: Open Court).

Dawson, Raymond. 1981. *Confucius* (New York: Hill and Wang).

Graham, Angus. 1964. 'The Place of Reason in the Chinese Philosophical Tradition,' Dawson, (ed.) *The Legacy of China* (London, Oxford University Press), 28–56.

————. 1981. *Chuang-tzu: The Inner Chapters* (London: George Allen & Unwin).

————. 1978. *Later Mohist Logic, Ethics and Science* (Hong Kong and London: Chinese University Press).

Hansen, Chad. 1983. *Language and Logic in Ancient China* (Ann Arbor: University of Michigan Press).

————. 1985. 'Chinese Language, Chinese Philosophy, and "Truth"' *Journal of Asian Studies* Vol XLIV, No. 3, May.

Mozi. 1973. *Harvard-Yenching Institute Sinological Index Series* (Taipei: Chinese Materials and Research Aids Service Center, Inc.).

Schwartz, Benjamin. 1985. *The World of Thought in Ancient China* (Cambridge: Harvard University Press).

Wiggins, David. 1976. 'Truth, Invention, and the Meaning of Life', *Proceedings of the British Academy,* LXII.

Williams, Bernard. 1985. *Ethics and the Limits of Philosophy* (Cambridge: Harvard University Press).

Xunzi. 1966. *Harvard-Yenching Institute Sinological Index Series,* no. 22 (Taipei: Chinese Materials and Research Aids Service Center, Inc.).

NOTES

1. I shall use this term to refer to the Hundred Schools period of classical philosophy only.

2. See especially Bruce, 1923.

3. Carus, 1913.

4. It is easy to imagine a doctrine that entailed that we should not use reason in particular circumstances—say in intimacy or in learning grammar or in skillful performance. If we imposed a strict definition on reason—say, required that it must include some processing or calculation—then certain forms of immediate intuitivist positions would be irrationalist positions whether they mentioned reason or not. That could (see below) include Mencius and even some Western thinkers who would describe themselves as rationalists.

5. This way of putting the matter makes it look as if the concept of reason is parasitic on the concept of belief. I have already argued (Hansen 1985) that Chinese philosophers had no concept of belief. But, since reason, practical reason (see below), also affects our affective attitudes, we should be satisfied with a concept of reason that linked it to changing our cognitive-affective attitudes in an appropriate way.

6. I learned this phrase and this insight into Western philosophy of mind from my colleague, Hilary Kornblith. See his 'Beyond Foundationalism and the Coherence Theory', *Journal of Philosophy* LXXII (Oct. 1980).

7. Of course we all know that it has a logical, or imaginary, or implied, or deep structure subject. That is required by our calling it a sentence!

8. See Sandel, 1981, especially chapter 1, for a detailed tracing of these assumptions of deontological individualism in the West.

9. See David Wiggins, 1976.

10. This has been argued especially for what he calls "thick" moral terms by Williams.

11. Of course the reasons for such parallels may not be accurate explanation as much as getting a favorable hearing and reaction. Typically translators suppose we will have a higher opinion of Chinese philosophy if it has all the familiar apparatus of our own tradition. That may be politically correct. Philosophers, however, are more likely to be interested if there are conceptual novelties, an opportunity to study a different way of thinking about our minds and our natures.

12. Of course, given the virtually unrestricted use of the Western philosopher's appeal to rational intuition, the light of reason, and so forth, nothing would prevent Mencius from identifying his heart's *shi-fei*-ing as the operation of rational intuitions. It should embarrass him that there is literally no calculation or deliberation involved. But it should equally have embarrassed Bishop Butler whose rationalist position is close to that of Mencius.

13. He also shows a crucial place where Zhuang-zi rebuts either Mencius or some analogous Confucian position. But Graham doesn't develop this contrast as thoroughly as he does the one with the School of Names.

14. Graham, 1981, p. 14.

15. This lesson has still not been absorbed by other interpreters. See Schwartz, 1985, p. 146.

16. Graham, 1964, p. 33.

17. See my 1985.

18. Graham, 1981, p. 15.

19. Hansen, 1981.

20. I have expressed doubts about this. The doubts are not that Graham has no argument for the view. He has an interpretive argument for the claim that they had discovered the sentence. I think there is a better argument that they did not. What Graham has no argument for is the claim that after having made this discovery, the Mohists decided to use *ci* ('phrase') only to refer to phrases that happen to be complete, truth-bearing sentences.

Reason, Spontaneity, and the *Li* 禮 — A Confucian Critique of Graham's Solution to the Problem of Fact and Value

Herbert Fingarette

"At seventy—spontaneous, yet on the mark." So spoke Confucius,[1] running through the sequence of decades of his life. While he stops with age seventy, the consummatory phase of spiritual development, his remark implies that age seventy is a beginning as well as a terminus. It begins the fully liberated and creative life; but it is also a vantage point from which to look back and to reflect appreciatively on what has gone before. From a Confucian's standpoint, then, how apt it is that on this occasion we celebrate Professor Graham's seventieth year: We reflect on the many profound and creative intellectual works that have filled the past years in his remarkable career; and we look forward to the ripened fruits yet to come from his wisdom.

There is a double justness in associating Confucius' remark with Professor Graham. In *Reason and Spontaneity*,[2] a recent major work that proposes "a new solution to the problem of fact and value", Professor Graham places spontaneity at the heart of this solution. Continuing the coincidence even more strikingly, we see that Confucius stresses the "attentive ear"[3] at the stage of life—the decade before seventy—that precedes and culminates in the spontaneity of age seventy, while Graham places "Be aware" as the precondition for spontaneity. Given the absence in Confucius' Chinese language of any concept exactly corresponding to our 'awareness' or 'consciousness', Confucius' metaphor of the "attentive ear" is as close as we should require to justify the claim that Confucius was placing sensitive, direct awareness as the precedent condition for spontaneous action that is on the mark. And this corresponds to Graham's grounding formula for all choices of ends.

But, as we see in this passage from Confucius as well as other remarks of his,[4] all this is grounded in turn on learning the *li*, thereby being able to take one's stand in life.

In this essay, I aim to examine the relation between *li* and spontaneity. More particularly, I want to show why Confucius is right in emphasizing the role of *li* as the ground from which springs the awareness and spontaneity of a truly human life, and why Professor Graham's emphasis on the formula, "Be aware", important though it is, nevertheless fails to take into account the true significance of the Confucian insight.

My thesis, in a nutshell, is that we cannot acceptably account for how a person should choose ends by reference solely to that person's awareness as the ground of spontaneous conduct; we must include reference to something in the nature of Confucius' *li*, and we cannot do this by somehow incorporating the role of *li* in the concept of awareness or in the concept of spontaneous act. If one likes, this paper may be viewed as a Confucian critique of Professor Graham's formula and theses.

One might at first glance suppose that this is a Confucian versus Taoist controversy. Professor Graham's focus on spontaneity, taken together with his renown as a scholar of Taoism, seem inevitably to define the target of my critique as, at least in spirit, a Taoist doctrine. But not so. This would entail a serious misunderstanding of the Graham theses, as he himself warns us, and as we will shortly see.

So let me set out more fully the grounding formula proposed by Professor Graham in his remarkable book, and let us explore its significance as he explains it. And in so doing let me remark here at the outset that we will be by-passing the richly informed and amazingly broad-ranging analyses of many specific topics that are discussed in this book. My concern here is focussed narrowly on the highly generalized philosophical thesis enunciated in chapter 1 of the book.

I

Professor Graham's grounding formula tells us to act in the way we spontaneously would be inclined to act were we aware of what is relevant.

Formulated in a more syllogistic-looking way, the formula is expressed by Graham this way:[5]

> In awareness of everything relevant to the issue (= everything which would spontaneously move me one way or the other), I find myself moved towards X; overlooking something relevant I find myself moved toward Y.
>
> *In which direction shall I let myself be moved?*
> Be aware.
> Therefore let yourself be moved towards X
> (= choose X as end).

Before examining the larger scope of this formulation, we need to take into account the meaning Graham assigns to some of the terms. Graham contrasts the 'spontaneous' with the 'deliberate'. Spontaneous choice is choice that is not deliberate, not "considered choice".[6] More specifically yet, considered choice "requires the operation of verbal or other symbols" and this requirement is the criterion for distinguishing the deliberate from the spontaneous.[7] The spontaneous includes what is "not initially chosen" by us—"birth, breathing, digestion, orgasm, death; the emotions; the desires and aversions which are independent of our principles, dream, reverie and fantasy; ecstasies of love, mystical illumination, intellectual discovery, artistic creation and contemplation".[8]

What Graham appears to be getting at is a distinction between reason and will on the one hand, and on the other hand that within us which "belong(s) to the realm of the caused".[9] Reason and the will, then, *interrupt* or *intervene* in spontaneous action.[10]

Rational reflection is allowed as means to achieve adequate awareness. But the point is that in any particular case we are to be aware of all relevant facts, that is, all facts that would causally influence our inclinations, and then, being aware, we should let our inclination cause our choice and action rather than deliberately choosing.

The other key term whose use we at once need to understand better is 'aware'. In its primary meaning, 'aware' means, ideally, a full-blooded imaginative or actual perceptual consciousness, an experiencing of the reality in question.[11] It is not mere 'knowledge about' something, or a mere glimmering of recollection, or the pale and largely conceptual entertainment of a future possibility.

So, for example, a child may initially have no awareness at all—no knowledge or experiential recollection—that eating so much of the candy will cause misery later. So the child's spontaneous inclination is to eat all the candy. Later the child may have a faint memory, both conceptual and feeling-like, of the misery that followed, but it may not be 'the fullest attainable awareness', and may therefore not be psychologically strong enough to outweigh, causally, the vivid and intense awareness of the fresh desire for more candy. At still a later stage, the child may be able to imagine vividly, full-bloodedly, the misery that resulted from overeating candy, and this imaginative full awareness of the future potential misery will now at last have greater current causal power than the current felt appetite for candy. Now, with full awareness, the spontaneous inclination will be to refrain.

Such full awareness is a profoundly important desideratum in moral choice, choices where, unlike that of the child's purely self-regarding appetite, the welfare of other persons is at issue. Here, ideally, full awareness calls for a full and exact empathy with the others who are involved. One must seek to experience the other person's situation as if one were that very person. Here Graham alludes to variations on the Golden Rule; and Confucians will think of the central role of *shu* in the Master's teaching,[12] a concept that calls upon us to use imaginative empathy.[13] And one should ideally be aware of all else that is relevant (that could influence one's inclination), including of course such things as one's own relevant desires, feelings, and beliefs. Then, being fully aware, one should cease rational reflection, or deliberately willed action, and should let oneself be moved to those ends to which one is then spontaneously inclined.

These remarks about the meaning of 'spontaneity' and 'awareness' as defined in the context of Graham's formula suggest plainly that problems for that formula lie ahead. Obviously, the task of achieving ideal awareness in moral matters would be no easy task, indeed the ideal is unachievable. But Graham confronts some of these problems by refining and qualifying the formula for use in real life.

If we charge that the demands of ideal awareness are too great for mortals, Graham responds by telling us, first, of several ways in which the ideal is less demanding than may at first seem; and then he also postulates that his formula, properly applied, does not demand that we actually achieve the ideal.

One important mitigation of the apparently strenuous demand of the formula is that it is not intended as a formula to guide *all* choices. That is why this is not Taoism, whatever the Taoist inspiration behind it may be. The grounding formula is to guide our choices of ends only, but not of means. So, if the child chooses to eat more sweets, this is an end, but it will be achievable only if the child carefully calculates the coins in his pocket, the means of getting additional money from his parents, and the means of getting to the one store where what is desired can be bought for the money available. Calculations of this kind—"operations of verbal and symbolic kinds"—are just what distinguishes the non-spontaneous from the spontaneous. But here they pertain to the means, not the selection of the end.

Not only does the formula apply only to choice of ends, the requirement of awareness applies only to what is relevant. One need not be aware of *everything*; indeed there may not be much that is relevant to the issue. The prospect of getting sick, and of satisfying the appetite for candy, and the availability of money and a store are all relevant; for awareness of them in fact causally affects the child's inclination to choose to eat the sweets. But not much else is relevant for the child. Perhaps the parents' expressed approval or disapproval would be the only other relevant factor. To pick an example at random of what is not relevant: The child's awareness of the fact that the candy in question is sold only in the U.S. would in no way cause the inclination to eat it to change, so it is irrelevant.

Let us note for future reference that in real life relevance will depend not only on what we might call objective relationships between act and consequences, but also—and at least equally crucially—on the subjective, on what that particular individual brings to the experience. Vividly imagining a particular future situation will have a different causal effect on a child as compared to an adult, on a person of high culture as compared to an improverished peasant, on an American as compared to a Frenchman or a Chinese, on a physician as compared to an artist. Unless we are to conceive a God-like awareness that ranges over all possible individual awareness and particular situations, human awareness must ultimately be limited in its perspective by the individual's unique angle of vision.[14]

In matters of real moment then, for example, in moral or other complex life situations, far more is relevant to the choice of ends than in the case of the child's hunger for more candy. Vividly and accurately imagining oneself being sick from overindulgence is a vastly simpler matter than full-bloodedly and accurately, yet perforce vicariously seeing and feeling the world as another person does, a person who is perhaps one's rival, or one's hated enemy, or the object of one's love.[15] And even if one accurately perceives the present, it can be enormously difficult to accurately and vividly imagine the subsequently reshaping of the intimate relevant personal relationships and sensibilities that will gradually evolve out of new choices of ends.

Especially because of the vast range of the possibly relevant, one of the great problems posed by the grounding formula is that of determining the relevant range of topics or areas of awareness, and, in each area, the amount and kind of detail that ought to be explored.

In response to this sort of problem, Graham suggests in a slightly different context that 'awareness' need not in practice be awareness of *all* that is relevant but need only be awareness of as much as the constraints and urgencies of action allow.[16] He recognizes that where prompt decision is essential, awareness must be limited, and too obsessive a concern for full awareness may be self-defeating. To acknowledge this is good common sense. But where does this acknowledgement leave the theory? Does it provide criteria for assessing the appropriateness of the limited selection attainable to the person under the real-life conditions of limited time, skill, and access? It does not.

What can we reasonably do in the face of such limitations? It would be easy to answer this if one were assured—as Professor Graham at times seems to suggest we are[17]—that the more fully aware the actor is, the closer would that actor's actual choice be to the ideal choice. But there is no warrant whatsoever for such an assumption; indeed it is plainly false at times. It needs no belaboring that, as the saying goes, 'a little knowledge is a dangerous thing'. How familiar a thing it is, for example, that having explored the relevant features of the situation conscientiously, one discovers after the choice, to one's chagrin, that one did not know the one right question to ask and so one had failed to appreciate correctly the one point that would have changed the impact of one's awareness on one's choice. Surely this and other variations of the ignorance of crucially relevant factors are obvious to all, and too common to be ignored here. Thus in real life a fuller but incomplete awareness may lead one astray from where ideal awareness would have led one. From this perspective one can see that a wider awareness is not always a better guide to choice.

On the other hand if Graham were to argue that the phrase 'led astray' has no meaning here, or represents the very kind of value-dogma he means to criticize, and that the criterion of 'right choice' is precisely that one acted spontaneously on the basis of one's best attempt at awareness with the constraints of action, then we have to ask: Why should we accept the dogma that the latter should be the overriding criterion for all choice of ends? It seems difficult to know how Graham would argue for our adopting his rule if there is no independent criterion of its propriety. Its claims to being the essence of a rational and realistic principle of choice is not self-evidently valid in view of the sorts of practical outcomes and limitations to which I have been calling attention.

In another related respect, Graham says the formula is less demanding than it may seem because not only does it not require awareness of *all* relevant factors, it does not even require "fullest attainable awareness" of each particular item that one is aware of. It suffices if one has ever attained fullest awareness, and if one now has a current recollection in paler form. So far as experiential imagination, then, surely we are no longer entitled to let ourselves be moved by the totality of these causal influences on my inclination. So far as causal efficacy goes, surely the vivid experience will outweigh the pale recollections, even if, under ideal conditions, the latter recollections would far outweigh the former ones in their causal power. And if the less vivid, weaker recollections are to play their proper role, and to have their proper weight, it will have to be because I weigh the issues in a very different way, introducing elements of reason, deliberateness, and 'will' into the choice process rather than allowing 'mere' causality to operate.

By now we not only have abandoned *full* awareness as the basis of spontaneity, but have frankly abandoned spontaneity itself. Thus, as I have said, and as Graham has said, this is not Taoism. Indeed, the further one goes into the matter, the more suspect is the concept of 'spontaneity': it is either an ideal concept, unreachable, that in practice leaves one confronting the harsh reality of having to choose deliberately according to what one believes would be one's spontaneous choice under hypothetical conditions; or else this spontaneity does operate in real life, but does so under conditions of limited awareness, and thus leaves us with a variety of grave questions about the universal appropriateness of it in the realm of choices of ends.

I believe that Graham himself reacts to these problems by wavering, unwittingly, between several interpretations of his formula. In reacting to the implications that I have emphasized above, Graham writes at times as if the formula calls for actually spontaneous decisions about ends, in which our inclinations are caused and our choice is a direct manifestation of our inclinations.[18] At other times he writes as if it requires that in choosing we should deliberately direct our choices, using "symbolic" operations and "will", so that the choices conform to what, hypothetically, we would spontaneously choose if, ideally, we were fully aware of all that is relevant.[19] In short, it is not clear whether spontaneous choice caused by awareness is an actual process by which choices should be made, or is an unachievable ideal standard by which we should deliberately will our actual choices.

Sometimes, indeed, Graham seems to be arguing for still another role for the awareness-spontaneous thesis. On pages 8 and 9 (especially page 9) of *Reason and Spontaneity*, Graham seems to be talking about what he labels "ultimate" goals, where "ultimate" seems at least to mean logically ultimate. In the end, as he argues, there is no logical way to pass from *is* to *ought*. At some point—"ultimately"—we must simply move, spontaneously, from awareness to the choice of the end, that is, we must be moved by inclination inasmuch as reason will not provide the final link between *is* and *ought*, between awareness and choice. Graham puts it this way: " . . . we are not advising [the rational man] to be any more spontaneous than he already is, merely inviting him to continue reasoning about means, ends and principles as before, with his mind at rest about that little puzzle about passing from 'is' to 'ought'."[20] Graham's aim is to persuade the rational man "to be intelligent as well as spontaneous".[21]

In all this, Graham seems to be saying that the point of his formula is not to tell us how to choose—for spontaneous choice is logically inevitable—but to tell us how to be, that is, intelligent, rational, aware. The practical point of the formula, then, is to urge that we at least be "*intelligent*",[22] which in turn translates as 'awareness'. But read this way, the grounding formula encounters all the questions, practical limitations, and challenges that I have already raised in connection with 'awareness'.

These problems and questions are not evidence that Professor Graham's thesis is radically wrong. On the contrary, the thrust of his arguments, as the rest of his remarkable book reveals, can generate richly detailed and illuminating analysis of the role of spontaneity in morals and in art, and of deep trends in our culture and art, as well as of many aspects of the human psyche. What I maintain is that problems arise in connection with the incompleteness of the grounding formula, along with his universalistic claims for it. Taken as a universally valid ground for all choice of ends, it obscures rather than illuminates. It does not clearly and adequately capture the interplay of reason and spontaneity in human life. I want in the remainder of my remarks to focus on one major respect in which the generalized emphasis on 'awareness' as the ground of action is radically incomplete, and I want to fill in the gap.

II

The ground formula cannot serve as a sufficient guide as to how to choose ends for at least one profoundly important reason: It lacks an adequate representation of the essential roles of the *li*.[23] This gap leaves the formula, as it were, inadequately rooted in human nature. For the "ultimate" impulses that give rise to our choices of ends are rooted not only in our biological constitution but also—pervasively and essentially—in the conventions and traditions we inherit from our culture.

This is a theme that I take to have been a central insight of Confucius' as it pertains to the present context. The *li*, he saw, provide the essential foundation not only of habit but also of ultimate standards that, jointly, give shape to our original nature and make a truly human life according to the Way possible. This is indeed a life in which, in the spirit of Graham's suggestion, spontaneous conduct issuing out of a well-tuned sensibility will mark the fruition of truly human development. Confucius, as we recalled at the outset, sees the fully ripened personality as aware, spontaneous, and on the mark. But he sees the *li* as the essential precondition.

We can consider each of these points more fully.

There is no reason in the abstract why the Chinese should have many of the customs and proprieties that they do, rather than those of the Germans, or pre-colonial native Americans, or Sikhs. Our original nature (physical and biological) does not suffice to render human conduct or experience determinate. This original nature, though it sets physical-biological and psychological limits, still leaves open innumerable opportunities for specific response by the individual, and it is a platitude that culture, largely through the lore and the practice of the *li*, defines for the members of a particular culture those specific forms of response which are to be valued and learned, and those which are not. Thus, we learn and practice the *li* of our culture not because we find it to be right, but by virtue of its defining for us what we are to value as right.

Therefore even the most complete awareness of particular circumstances, if it be somehow independent of the forms and values presupposed in the *li*, cannot even in theory suffice to guide us to truly human ends. There must be a prior education in, and 'internalization' of, the *li*; only then can particular circumstances be *given* a meaning that then enables us to make the sorts of choices essential to a truly human life. Of course our animal nature will suffice to guide us spontaneously toward such things as food when we are hungry, and warmth when we are cold. But such promptings alone can only produce a brute, a human animal, and not the truly human being who is the subject of both Confucius' and Graham's inquiry.

It will not do to argue—as Professor Graham's theses might incline one to do[24]—that what I have said, if true, merely entails that adequate awareness of relevant factors must include awareness of the relevant *li*. This line of argument fails for several reasons. One reason is that it stretches the meaning of 'awareness' to the point of unusability: We are not in general *aware* of the *li* by which we act, but rather we have learned to act that way without having to be *aware* of it at all—we do so spontaneously. The more apt formulation is that the *li* help determine how we will become aware, and of what. In short, the *li* are in this respect the shapers, not the content, of awareness. And indeed the element of spontaneity, so central to Professor Graham's theses—comes into play centrally. For the *li* establish habitual response *to* what we are aware of.

A second and more fundamental reason why we cannot treat the *li* simply as that which we are to be aware of is that it is reasonable, necessary, and common practice for individuals not even to attempt to become maximally aware of the relevant circumstances, but *instead* to base their decision upon familiar and accepted moral or prudential principles that inhere in the *li*. Thus, in a certain situation I may become aware of some immediate apparent incentive for me to betray the trust of my wife or a friend, but I simply ('spontaneously') don't do it. The principles, maxims, character dispositions, and habits that constitute the internalization of the *li* suffice without any inclination or need for me to become more fully 'aware'. The choice to keep faith is made almost before the question of exploring the issue arises. Indeed it is a mark of moral maturity that, typically, I do not seek and have no need to seek further awareness—not even awareness of what I *would* do if I *were* 'fully aware'. The merit of *not* pursuing further awareness arises from the two roles played by the *li*: They serve as powerful prudential guides— without need of further "awareness", indeed more reliable than awareness of particularities of the moment would be. More fundamentally, they define for me what I am to find good and worthy, and thus preclude the need for further awareness, for they have their own autonomous authority independently of consequences.[25] Keeping faith with my wife or friend may in some circumstances engender much suffering on my part: It is because I have made the *li* a part of me that, in spite of such consequences, this goal is worthy in itself. No awareness of facts engendered this commitment; it is the commitment that colors and structures my awareness and my response to what I am aware of.

Of course consistently with all this I might want to become further aware about aspects of the situation having to do with means and methods, or with interpretation of the relevant guiding principles as they apply to this case. But I do not try to expand awareness in regard to the basic question of ends, the question whether I should keep trust or not. That issue is settled by prior principle and disposition, not by expanding current awareness.

The issues raised here warrant a more substantive, illustrative discussion. I would like to elaborate on a contrast that Graham himself introduces.[26] He alludes to the reverence for family, especially parents, that so imbues traditional Chinese and much of Asian life. This value-orientation of course plays a far lesser role in the modern Europeanized world. Let us suppose that a parent demands that the son perform some filial service which, as it happens, entails frustrating some well-established expectation on the part of the son's wife. Here are 'facts'. But what they mean, and how they bear on choice will obviously depend on the set of general commitments and standards of the son. A traditional Chinese son, 'facing the facts', will not hesitate to comply with the demand. A young American of today may just as unhesitatingly give priority to his spouse.

Graham suggests that perhaps the Chinese son might with fuller awareness take account of the 'damage' to the community as a whole that would be done (in a Confucian community) by being disobedient to the parent. But this misses the basic point: There is no way of assessing 'damage' independently of one's prior value commitments. To the son strongly imbued with Confucian values, the shame and anger of the parents is 'damage' of the worst sort, whereas the frustration and suppressed anger of his spouse are signs of *her* moral defect, not 'damage' done by him. But once the Confucian *li* weaken their hold on the son, the spouse's suffering may be seen as 'damage', and the erosion of the Confucian family, the feelings of his parents, will be seen as unhealthy remnants of a 'damaging' social system.

Thus, 'awareness of the facts' is a concept that cannot give adequate recognition to the necessity for, and the reality of, the *li* which are constitutive of the enduring self-identity of the agent. The generalized commitment to reverence for parents, or to devotion to spouse, is not derived from awareness of the facts or from prior experiences; it is, as it were, imposed on the particular factual situation.

All this conflicts with the central thrust of Graham's thesis, which is designed to preclude the decisive imposition of general principles or commitments and to treat them as mere generalizations from prior experiences.[27] But to a son who does not give priority to parental authority, no series of past experiences could reveal this to be the best prudential principle.

Seeking to adapt Graham's thesis to these considerations, one might say that the son can be said to 'be aware' that parents are *entitled* to respect, that he *ought* to respect them; he might be said to be aware of being *obligated* to respect them. These ways of expressing the matter make good English and conform *verbally* to Professor Graham's thesis that 'awareness' is the sole ultimate condition of rational conduct. But here the verbalism obscures the substance of the matter: If Professor Graham's use of the term 'awareness' is to make his thesis significant rather than empty, it cannot include as its content the very things Graham means to attack: the idea that there are moral and other principles having autonomous general authority, principles that obligate us independently of particular circumstances. Therefore the role of the *li* as giving definition and significance to particular 'facts' cannot be conceived as simply one form of 'awareness' of particular facts.

In arguing as I do, I by no means intend to exclude the possibility that awareness of *li* may in turn lead us to a richer appreciation and even revision of our *li*. Confucius certainly saw the appropriateness of critical awareness for revision of the *li*.[28] Confucius, however, had some of the limitations of his time, place, and culture: He did not appreciate that awareness of the *li* of other cultures than one's own may also enrich one's appreciation of one's own, and may lead to critical evaluation and reform of one's own *li*.

None of this is inconsistent with my assignment of ultimate logical priority to the internalized *li* rather than to awareness of 'fact' or *li*. How, for example, could the Chinese son or the American son consciously question the *li* governing parental authority and spousal loyalty unless there were a larger context of norms, unquestioned within this context, by reference to which the parental and spousal *li* come into question? How, in the end, could either son make a final judgment as to the legitimacy of a specific element of the *li* except by bringing into play other, accepted values in terms of which to make the judgment? Whether it be awareness of 'fact' or awareness of *li*, the perceived significance of the fact or the *li* has as its precondition a wider context of what is at the time unquestioned *li*. If, on the other hand, awareness of our *li* could bring the totality of our *li* into question, we would be morally paralyzed by a total and irremediable normative skepticism.

Thus the possibility of awareness transforming the *li* is an important—but special—phenomenon that is itself a derivative of the more ultimate logical priority of the *li*.

Nor should we suppose that insofar as we invoke the *li* without self-awareness of this, we are somehow less than consummately human, mere slaves of habit or automatons. We should remember that one of the distinctive marks of mastery of the *li* is that the conduct is *not* 'mechanical'; instead it is intelligent, sensitive, spontaneous. As Confucius said, the person is 'present', the feeling is genuine.[29] The truly gracious host is not the one who mechanically utters the standard formulas of politeness. On the contrary, there is a freshness, creativeness, context-responsive genuineness and spontaneity that makes the guest feel truly welcome. And typically the genuinely gracious host—the master of the *li*—is *not* aware of (that is, not explicitly conscious of) the conduct as being 'the *li*' or as being 'proper'. 'Spontaneity' here implies just the contrary: unselfconsciousness. This is a fundamental kind of spontaneity whose nature, I fear, is not well accounted for in Professor Graham's analysis.[30]

In sum, then, we need to precede the emphasis on awareness by emphasizing positively the normative role of the *li* as the context of meaning that initially defines for a culture and its members what life is all about. This role combines with the more practical role I discussed earlier—that of providing normative guidance to choice, enabling the person to forego seeking greater awareness of the facts, especially in human relationships where the facts are so complex and subtle. I repeat: This practical role has value not because such principles are symbolic shortcuts to appreciating what 'full awareness' would reveal, but because they are alternatives to awareness, or co-necessities along with awareness, and because the very concept of 'full awareness' is not coherent when we try to spell out fully what it would entail.

Conclusion

As I have written elsewhere, [31] I do not mean to imply that the concept of the *li* alone suffices to account for rational and humane choice. As Confucius said, *shu* and *chung*, mutual empathic identification along with mutual commitment to the integrity of the other, form a main-thread of the truly human life. There is no substitute for generalized commitments; neither is there a substitute for sensitive and empathic awareness or 'listening' to the nuances and particularities of persons and circumstances. There is no substitute for a learned repertoire of habits and values embedded in action—the *li*. There is no substitute for occasional rational deliberation about particular matters of fact and their relation to general principles. And, finally, there is no escape from the reality that, in the end, we take the leap, we choose— 'spontaneously', if you will.

We must not blink the complexity and variety of the dimensions of the process by trying to bring all under one formula. Certainly I do not by any means claim to have here exposed all dimensions of the matter in a balanced way.

I might say by way of conclusion that I think the Taoist teaching (which hovers in the background here, even though Graham's thesis is not Taoism) is profoundly important, but it is also gravely incomplete if taken as theory rather than as a collection of evocative, situationally relevant remarks. Nor do I think Confucius purported to offer, or did offer, a fully rounded account of how we should shape our conduct. And for the reasons I have given, I think Professor Graham's account, while highly suggestive and in many ways to the point, yet does not suffice to tell us how rational and humane choices are to be made. But how impoverished we would be without the insights these teachers have given us!

NOTES

1. Englished in a way that seems fair, though it is a bit free and unorthodox. *Analects*, Chapter II, 4 (5).

2. A. C. Graham: *Reason and Spontaneity: A New Solution to the Problem of Fact and Value* (London and New Jersey: Curzon Press [Barnes & Noble], 1985), hereafter referred to as *R & S*.

3. *Analects*, Chapter II, 4 (5).

4. *Analects*, Chapter II, 4 (2) ["At thirty I took my stand"]; and Chapter XX, 3 (2) ["*Li* not being known, there is no taking one's stand."]

5. *R & S*, p. 7.

6. Loc. cit.

7. Loc. cit.

8. Loc. cit.

9. Loc. cit.

10. Loc. cit.

11. *R & S*, pp. 16–17.

12. *Analects*, Chapter V, 11; VI, 28; XV, 23. And for full discussion see: Fingarette: 'Following the "One Thread" of the *Analects*', in: Rosemont and Schwartz, eds., *Studies in Classical Chinese Thought* (JAAR Thematic Studies), September 1979, pp. 373–404, especially pp. 377–387.

13. As Graham recognizes, e.g., on p. 29, *R & S*.

14. Ibid, p. 8. Plainly, relevance is context-dependent: In a household where "Buy American" is a lively issue, the matter of the candy's provenance would be relevant for the child.

15. *Analects*, Chapter VI, 28 (3) [*neng chin ch'ü p'i*]. And see Fingarette, (fn. 12), pp. 382–387.

16. *R & S*, pp. 9, 47.

17. The key formula strongly suggests this: *R & S*, p. 7.

18. See, e.g., *R & S*, p. 17, where it is enough to identify which *would* be the stronger inclination *if* one were fully aware.

19. *R & S*, p. 9.

20. Loc. cit.

21. Loc. cit. [" . . . ultimate goals are spontaneous . . . *are*, not ought to be . . . "]

22. Loc. cit. [" . . . what (ultimate goals) *ought* to be is intelligent as well as spontaneous . . . "] (Emphasis added.)

23. I have discussed the role of Confucius' concept of *li* at some length in the following: *Confucius: The Secular as Sacred* (Harper, 1972); 'Following the "One Thread" of the Analects', op. cit.; 'The Music of Humanity in the *Conversations* of Confucius', *Journal of Chinese Philosophy*, May, 1983. I am presuming here the general outlines of those analyses.

24. See his discussion of "decision and Principles", *R & S*, pp. 41–52, especially at 44–45, where principles are assumed to be merely generalizations of awareness of particulars, and so to have no inherent authority, and to be mere means to wider awareness of particulars.

25. Graham (*R & S*, p. 44) begs the enormously important question as to whether the authority of moral principles is solely prudential, based on generalizing from prior experiences, or whether they have authority beyond that. He says—but never argues—that they are merely prudential generalizations. This is dubious psychology and perennially arguable as moral theory.

26. *R & S*, p. 44.

27. Ibid, pp. 44–45.

28. Cf. *Analects*, Chapter III, 12, 26.

29. Cf. *Analects*, Chapter IX, 3.

30. I am grateful to Henry Rosemont for calling to my attention the need to address the several important questions that I attempt to answer in the preceding four paragraphs.

31. 'Following the "One Thread" of the *Analects*', op. cit.

Who Chooses?

Henry Rosemont, Jr.

Introduction

Angus Graham has long been concerned with the problem of value. Such is the title of a book he published early in his career,[1] and it is the focal point, twenty-four years later, of the recent *Reason & Spontaneity*, which, according to the subtitle, proffers "A new solution to the problem of fact and value".[2]

This subtitle may seem bold, but is actually rather modest, for there are several theoretical problems associated with the relation(s) between facts and values in modern Western moral philosophy, and *Reason & Spontaneity* (hereafter *R & S*) comes to grips with all of them in an altogether original manner. Moreover, his "solution" to the problem—I will argue that it is more a *dis*solution—provides a basis for him to view a host of other topics in a radically different light, topics ranging from science to the sacred, from sadism to Surrealism; and much more.

I believe *R & S* is a very important philosophical book, and is a milestone in the historical development of comparative philosophy. Yet up to the time of my writing these lines, the book has attracted little scholarly attention, and almost none at all from philosophers. Probably the most important reason for this neglect comes from the conservatism inherent in all scholarship, philosophy included: if Angus has gotten things *right*—and I shall be arguing that on many issues, he has—then much of what the rest of us have thought about those issues has been *wrong*; a humbling confession not at all easy to make.

There are other reasons why *R & S* has not received the attention it deserves. A part of the neglect may be due to the non-standard philosophical style Graham employed in writing it: while he is consistently sensitive to the demands of logic, *R & S* is not a rigorous argument moving progressively from beginning to end. On the contrary, after setting forth his major thesis, Graham develops it by applying it to a wide variety of other topics, some of them unexpected in a work of this kind. This style is deliberate (he follows it "without the least humility", as he says on p. vii), and it is not only often refreshing, it is regularly effective; but it is unusual (and at times frustrating, because the book does not have an index, which makes cross-checking very difficult).

R & S is also unusual in another way: Graham derives his *problematik* from the writings of Hume, and was himself trained in the tradition of modern British empiricism and linguistic analysis (references to Ryle's *The Concept of Mind* are sprinkled throughout *R & S*). Yet Graham himself does not rely on either logical or linguistic analysis in setting forth his position. Very rarely does a variable occur in *R & S*, there are no formulas in canonical notation; nor does Angus ever tell us "We do say this", or "We don't say that"—*à la* Ryle—in presenting his case(s). On the contrary, he argues from descriptions of human experience, as my quotes from his text will show clearly, and this is not at all the style of analytic philosophy, but the style of phenomenologists—who do *not* take their *problematik* from Hume, but from Descartes.

Moreover, Graham has devoted the large part of his sholarly life to the translation, interpretation, analysis, and evaluation of Chinese texts. It would be incomprehensible that a person would do this unless he thought those texts had something important to say. We should therefore not be surprised that there are distinctive Chinese influences in *R & S*, yet if there is one area in which analytic and phenome-nologically-oriented philosophers come together, it is as chauvinists, in ignoring, or dismissing, Chinese thought.

Further, I believe that in addition to its many strengths, *R & S* has some weaknesses as well, but the book is sufficiently dense, rich, and varied that I hold the latter belief with diffidence; it may well be that I (and probably others) simply have not understood what Graham was about at times. For all these reasons, it seemed appropriate to address *R & S* directly and at length in a *Festschrift* of this kind, so that he can comment on where, how, and why he may have been misunderstood, and respond to criticisms he sees as well taken. Hence the present essay can be read more or less as a lengthy review article of the book.[3]

In what follows, then, I will first give a fairly detailed exposition of the fundamental philosophical claims on which Graham rests his several analyses in *R & S*. I will then explore a number of implications of those claims as I see them, some of which he does not directly take up in the work itself. Finally, I will offer arguments to suggest that some of Graham's fundamental views will have to be revised before his solution to the problem of value can command our conviction.

Exposition

What, exactly, is the "problem of fact and value?" According to Graham (p. 2), human beings are not simply self-conscious and capable of reason, they are *agents*, which means they can act *purposefully*, and will act in different ways depending on what purposes they have. Purposes are ends, and there is a great multiplicity of possible ends one might strive to achieve. The problem arises when we ask how we can decide which ends we ought to strive to achieve, because of the persuasiveness of Hume's argument that no imperative statement (encompassing values) is logically derivable from any set of declarative statements (encompassing facts). "It has long remained unquestioned," Graham says, "that to decide how to act it is not enough to be aware of things as they objectively are." (p. vii). Something more is needed to get to values, but what? And from whence can it come?

Hume's position (in the *Treatise* and the *Enquiry*, at any rate)[4] entails that the answers to these questions must be "nothing", and therefore "nowhere"; our values are ungrounded. On this account, according to Graham ". . . although codes of more or less articulated principles are a practical necessity for everybody, they seem to hang in a void without anything to support them" (p. 2). Because ". . . I am not an instinctive being like an animal, I have to choose, and on the [Humean] position we are considering, all imperatives are ungrounded . . ." (ibid.).

The spell of this problem of the gulf between facts and values was indeed first cast by Hume, but its enchanting powers derive from Descartes' view of what it is to be a human being, Hume's anti-Cartesianism notwithstanding. The plausibility of this form of scepticism about values requires that we see human beings as having bodies, each with a specific shape, weight, color, and spatial and temporal location, bodies which generate a mixed set of impulses, emotions, passions, attitudes, and so forth. Hovering over and above each of these lumps of matter and messy assemblages of psychological states is a pure (because disembodied) mind, supremely competent to ascertain how things *are* (the objective world of fact/science), and how things *must* be (the necessary world of logic/mathematics), but—Hume's contribution—altogether worthless for determining how things *ought* to be (the world of ends/values). The break between mind and body is total. Moreover, the bodies we have are obviously contingent upon the way the world happens to be, and are subject to all of the causal laws which govern this contingent world; and how could such contingently existing, causally determined lumps of matter have value, be the source of value?

It is philosophically irrelevant whether we accept this picture of human beings as literally true, or simply as a Western conceit useful for theorizing about basic issues, akin in large measure to Hobbesian capitalists in a state of nature, or Rawlsian statesmen behind a veil of ignorance, or Quinean linguists who can never be certain of the meaning of 'gavagai'.[5] Whether seen as fact or fiction, the picture is one of a sense-absorbent and logically calculating mind altogether discontinuous with an emotively-evaluating (but probably valueless) body, with no moral, aesthetic, or spiritual equivalent of the pineal gland to bring them, or facts and values, together.

This Cartesian picture of what it is to be a human being has dominated Western moral, aesthetic, and religious thinking for almost three hundred years. Kant accepted much of the picture, but recoiled from a major inference Hume drew from it, namely, that reason had to be the *slave* of the passions. Instead, he endeavored to ground ends (and values) on purely rational grounds, insisting that reason be the *master* of the passions. Graham—although he does not discuss Kant at length in

R & S[6]—rejects all such efforts as wholly inadequate for dealing with the facts of human life (a theme stressed throughout the book), and worse, as all too easily eventuating in a "moral nihilism" (p. 1).

Even within the Cartesian picture, the mind must obey the imperative to face facts, and Graham's solution to the problem of value lies in calling our attention to certain salient facts, phenomenologically confronted. The first of these is that human beings do in fact have ends, and are bestowers of value; this is what it means to be an *agent*, as opposed to an animal or an automaton (p. 2). Second, we must face the fact that all of our ends—and hence values—are derived from our *inclinations* (Graham's blanket term for what is generated by our psychological states). These inclinations are the grounds of human ends, and consequently there can be no question for reason about *how* or *whether* to ground them, for they are already grounded. Let us suppose, Graham says, that:

> . . . I continue to insist that at the centre of me I differ from the child in having escaped being restricted to choice between spontaneous goals. But when and how did I make this escape? The most rigorous deduction of new ends cannot release me, as long as it was from spontaneous goals that the ends from which my system grew were themselves originally chosen. A stream of spontaneous desire and aversion continues to pour into the centre of me, and I never cease to choose new ends from among its goals. Indeed, as far as my self-interest is concerned, on what principle could I choose as an end sufficient in itself something which I do not spontaneously want? (pp. 8–9)

This quote also calls our attention to a third fact Graham will have us face: our inclinations are *spontaneous*, in the sense that reason alone cannot give rise to them, or make them go away. Our inclinations stand in a deterministic relation to our bodies, which in turn stand in a deterministic relation to the external world. But the inclinations are nevertheless spontaneous. We can neither think nor will ourselves to be attracted or repelled to something or somebody; these and all other inclinations arise spontaneously. Graham again:

> . . . [A]lthough you can choose to think about a problem, be considerate to your wife, distribute pamphlets for a cause or pray for forgiveness for a crime, you cannot by mere exertion of will hit on a new thought, love

your wife, have faith in the cause, or repent the crime. Someone may ardently desire to create, love, believe, repent, but if the hope is fulfilled it will be because of a spontaneous process of maturation or crisis of conversion, which reason and will can coax but not force. (p. 13)

Nor can reason be employed to weigh (evaluate) our spontaneous inclinations as they move us towards ends, for our inclinations are the grounds of *all* evaluations of ends; only with respect to means can reason unaided lead us to conclude that it is better to do *x* than *y*. "If we are to use the metaphor of weighing, in choices of means the agent is the weigher, but in choices of ends he is the arm of the balance itself" (p. 6). Or, put metaphorically: ". . . all valuation starts from how you *do* react when aware, and to confuse it with how you suppose that you *ought* to be reacting poisons valuation at the source." (p. 69; italics in original)

Thus Graham's picture of what it is to be a human being differs somewhat from the Cartesian. Bodies exist, and so do values, which arise from psychological states determined by the interactions of our bodies with the external world. We also have minds, which are inextricably linked to our bodies because of the contribution they make to our psychological states by the ways they organize our perceptions of the world. But our minds alone cannot cause us to have any psychological states, and hence cannot either generate or suppress the inclinations which come from those states; the inclinations arise spontaneously.

There is, however, another task which our minds (reason) can perform: assist us in acting on the basis of one spontaneous inclination rather than another. Even though reason can neither force an inclination to come or go, nor evaluate inclinations as ends, it is not irrelevant to what we do. Over and above the epistemological functions reason serves—as alluded to above—and the role it plays in selecting means, reason can also contribute to our being moved by one inclination rather than its competitor(s). Unlike animals, Graham says:

. . . I am self-conscious, can detach myself from spontaneous process in order to analyze and criticize perceptions, analogies and reactions, choose ends from my spontaneously emerging goals, choose means to my ends. In becoming self-conscious I require an imperative by which to choose between spontaneous tendencies as they veer with changing awareness, but only one, "Be aware." (p. 151).

Thus Graham claims strong empirical support for his basic views. From the several salient facts about human beings he will have us face, and his analyses of them, he concludes that neither Kantian 'Reason as Master' nor Humean 'Reason as Slave' views are, or can be, faithful to the reality of human life, and consequently we can only solve the problem of value by adopting the 'Reason as Guide' position embodied in the above quotation. Reason cannot lead, for it must needs be directionless, and to ignore the body and its attendant psychological states—the only possible source of direction(s)—would leave us incapacitated. Nor can reason simply follow: if reason were seen as no more than a means-developer, this would ignore the mind's ability to check our bodily drives (directions), which would leave us as no more than clever animals. In neither case would we be truly human agents.

But how can this work? If reason does not *cause* any inclinations-as-ends to come or go, and it is incapable of *evaluating* inclinations-as-ends, how can it guide us? What, exactly, is reason supposed to do? Or, more specifically, of *what* are we supposed to "Be aware?"

First, we should be aware of those facts about the world (including the psychological states of other people) that might spontaneously move us to action one way or another in any given situation. And "The test of relevance will be whether awareness of a fact does act causally on spontaneous inclination" (p. 6). I am offered an after-dinner drink. It is good cognac. I enjoy good cognac. A glass of good cognac has seldom caused me 'morning-after' headaches, and has regularly helped to settle my dinner. I am strongly inclined to have a glass of good cognac, and hence moved to say "yes, please". But I also have another, albeit much weaker inclination: to refuse, which is caused by my awareness that I must drive home. Now other facts come to awareness: I have already had wine with dinner, which, when coupled with a glass of cognac, will very probably impair my driving skills; I might get a ticket, or much worse, cause an accident that results in the injury or death of innocent others, and/or a not-so-innocent myself. With this fuller awareness, I am now moved to say, ruefully perhaps but clearly, "no, thank you".

Now this example should not be construed as suggesting that my reason will tell me I *should* act on the weaker of the two inclinations.

Again, Graham argues on empirical grounds, and will say, entering a
ceteris paribus clause and a caveat to the effect that I am not an utter fool,
that I *will* spontaneously tend to refuse rather than accept the cognac
when I am fully aware of the facts of the situation (especially including
those facts which have caused my differing inclinations). He must also
say—less empirically now and more purely philosophical—that if I
have *no* inclination, however weak, to be moved to refuse the cognac,
unaided reason could not provide one. That one of my spontaneous
inclinations may be stronger than another is in one sense irrelevant; it is
only necessary that I indeed have more than one spontaneous inclination in order for reason to perform its function as guide:

> My fear of a remote danger may be almost driven from mind by current
> emotions; but to decide to take precautions I need no more than the
> faint tremor as I glimpse what the consequences of neglect would be
> like . . . Similarly, it may take no more than a momentary pang of
> empathetic distress to convince me that if I could become as aware from
> the sufferer's viewpoint as from my own I would be spontaneously
> moved to help him even to my own cost. (p. 17)

It may well seem that my example is not at all convincing. All I have
done on Graham's behalf, it may be argued, is describe a prudent man
who drinks in moderation, an exemplar not only of the liberal English
bourgeois tradition which nurtured Graham, but an exemplar as well
of the Chinese intellectual tradition which he has devoted the bulk of
his scholarly life to studying. I believe, however, the example should be
taken quite seriously, and to show how this is so, let us consider that we
are not dealing with a prudent man, but an alcoholic, and see what
further might be said on Graham's behalf.

Of course we must admit immediately that the alcoholic will in all
probability not obey Graham's imperative to be aware. Unfortunately
for everyone in an automobile on the relevant roads at this particular
time, it is equally improbable that the alcoholic will obey Kant's
categorical imperative, or the utilitarian imperative to calculate the
greatest happiness for the greatest number, or any other imperative put
forth by any other philosopher; if he is indeed an alcoholic *no* theory of
value can *guarantee* his sobriety (until and unless an inclination arises in
him spontaneously to change his ways). Relatedly, Graham can also

point out that even those philosophers who more or less accept the Cartesian picture of human beings have to insist that it is *irrational* not to attend to those causal factors which affect our psychological states, and when irrationality advances, philosophy must retreat. With those who flatly refuse to acknowledge otherwise agreed-upon facts, or obvious inconsistencies, we cannot sustain philosophical dialogue, debate, or discussion.

Graham can also make a third reply, namely, that his picture of what it is to be a human being, and his 'Reason as Guide' perspective, provide us with the means to give a far more accurate empirical description of a prudent man who drinks in moderation, and the alcoholic who doesn't, than any other value theory can offer. (Much of *R & S* is devoted to giving a variety of such descriptions, and more will be said on this point below.)

The single imperative "Be aware", Graham claims, is both universal and has a priori validity, ". . . since it would be inconsistent to say of anything that it exists yet is irrelevant to any possible choice" (p. 6). To flesh out his 'Reason as Guide' perspective, he embeds the imperative in a 'quasi-syllogism':

> In awareness of everything relevant to the issue (= everything which would spontaneously move me one way or the other), I find myself moved towards X. Overlooking something relevant I find myself moved towards Y.
> *In which direction shall I let myself be moved?*
> Be aware.
> Therefore let yourself be moved towards X (= choose X as end.)
> (p. 7; italics in the original)

To instantiate Graham's schema with our earlier example:

1. In awareness of everything relevant to the issue of whether to drink cognac or not, I find myself moved to say "No, thank you".

2. Overlooking the facts that I've already had wine, will impair my driving skills by drinking more, perhaps causing an accident, I am moved to say "Yes, please".

3. I believe I am aware of all the facts relevant to the issue.

4. "No, thank you".

In normal circumstances, whether or not one has a glass of cognac is a personal, and not a moral issue (I could have replaced "a glass of good cognac" with "a second helping of dessert" in the example, in which case other facts would have been relevant, yet the example would still stand). But as the specific example shows, moral issues involve others directly, and consequently Graham must give us a more concrete version of his quasi-syllogism if "be aware" is to be as significant for understanding morality as it is for understanding the nature of personal preferences:

> In awareness from all spatial, temporal, and personal viewpoints which are relevant to the issue (= viewpoints from which I do find myself spontaneously moved in one direction or the other) I find myself moved towards X. Overlooking a relevant viewpoint I find myself moved towards Y.
> Be aware.
> Therefore let yourself be moved towards X (a goal which may be here or there, now or then, yours or mine). (p. 16).

Becoming aware from another's personal viewpoint does not mean that I must merely *imagine* what the world is like from your viewpoint, because the exercise of our imagination is a purely cognitive act, and as we have seen, purely cognitive acts—the employment of reason—cannot generate inclinations, the source of our goals and values.[7] But here Graham calls our attention to additional facts about human beings: we all know that we resemble others in the ways they resemble each other (p. 16), and all of us do have the capacity, weak or strong, to be genuinely empathetic, sympathetic, compassionate, and so on (p. 165; I shall have more to say about this capacity below). Consequently the imperative to be aware demands that I let myself be moved not only from my own standpoint, but from yours as well, which is necessary for my becoming more fully aware from *either* standpoint (p. 20). In this respect at least, Graham seems to be of a piece with Hume: "Morality, therefore, is more properly felt than judg'd of."[8]

But how could it be possible for me to *feel* (what generates) *your* inclinations? If such feeling is necessary for achieving awareness from your viewpoint, and hence for allowing myself to be spontaneously moved on the basis of your inclinations, it would seem that awareness from your viewpoint is not possible for me. *Ex hypothesi* I cannot feel *your* pain, because it is in *your* body, and *my* body is distinct from your own. Empathy I might have, but how could *I* be spontaneously moved by *your* inclinations?

Such questions, however, are not directly relevant to the points Graham is attempting to make. They are carryovers from epistemological puzzles of the early decades of twentieth-century analytic philosophy, and at the heart of the 'private language' arguments made famous by Wittgenstein. With such issues Graham is not concerned: it must be *possible*, he will insist, for me to feel (what generates) your inclinations, because as a matter of fact, we *actually* do so, as normal human beings:

> . . . [I]f [a person] tells me he has just learned he has cancer I may hear in imagination the doctor's grave voice, but I do not imagine the fear, I feel the chill of it; if I see him cut his finger I do not imagine the pain as something objective before my "mind's eye," either I look on as though the knife were cutting through cheese, or I incipiently wince. . . . If I explore in imagination a coming danger, I cannot simulate my future fear without already being afraid, and moved to avert the danger. (p. 17)

These, then, are the salient facts about human beings as purposeful, goal-seeking agents that Graham would have us see. We have both minds and bodies, linked together by the activities of the former which organize the perceptions of the external world that causally affect the manifold psychological states that arise from the latter. But causally affected though these psychological states may be, they are nevertheless truly spontaneous, because we can neither reason nor will them into or out of existence; and it is from the spontaneous inclinations arising from our psychological states that all human values are, and must, be grounded. To denigrate this human spontaneity and celebrate reason alone, as some rationalists would have it, leaves human values ungrounded, and leads straightforwardly, if not necessarily, to a radical moral relativism, or worse, nihilism. To denigrate human reason and celebrate spontaneity, as many of the Romantics would have it, leaves human rationality irrelevant to human values, and leads straightforwardly, if not necessarily, to a radical moral relativism, or worse, nihilism. If we wish to truly understand human agency and—more concretely to the point philosophically—if we wish to lead meaningful lives, we must come to understand, and appreciate, the importance of both reason and spontaneity for *homo sapiens*.[9]

If I have given an accurate description of Graham's position, it should be clear that the overall argument is in the form of still another conditional: if the Cartesian *cum* Humean arguments are correct, then truly human agency is impossible. Many moral theorists have accepted the antecedent, but have gone on to introduce additional premises in order to obviate the consequent; but these additional premises, on Graham's view, all too easily lead to a radical relativism, or worse, nihilism. Instead, Graham will simply deny the consequent—human agency *must* be possible—and, *modus tollens*, thereby deny the antecedent. What, precisely, is wrong with the Cartesian/Humean picture Graham does not analyze at length, and in this way it can be seen that he has not *solved* the problem of value. On the contrary, by showing how salient facts about human life cannot be made to square with the Cartesian/Humean picture, he *dissolves* the problem of value in its traditional formulation. On the basis of this general description of Angus's position, which I hope he will correct if it is mistaken, I now want to elaborate how he dissolves the problem, and to defend his dissolution thereof, by drawing out a few of the major philosophical implications of his views on the close relationship between reason and spontaneity.

Implications

If my description of Graham's 'Reason as Guide' model of human agency is at all accurate, it should weaken the tendency we might have, arising spontaneously or in full awareness, to get caught up in the major controversy which has exercised Western moral philosophers for well over a century. That controversy, simplistically stated, centers on whether contractarian principles (roughly Kant, and more recently, Rawls), or consequentialist principles (roughly Bentham, Mill, and their successors), are the more logically correct for autonomous individuals to employ in freely choosing their actions as moral agents. We will not become enmeshed in this controversy because if Graham is correct, individuals are not altogether autonomous, they are not free in the sense intended by modern Western moral theorists, and, in a very important way, individuals do not make moral (aesthetic, religious) choices in the strict sense of the word. If Graham, in essence, rejects the Humean statement of the problem of value, we should not be surprised that he simultaneously must reject the conceptual framework within which all the solutions to the problem have been proffered.[10]

On the Cartesian/Humean picture of human beings, it is clearly the mind that is autonomous, but for Graham, this is simply false. Our minds are linked to our bodies by the ways in which they organize our perceptions of the world, they are not autonomous ('self-governing') generators of perceptions themselves. And our minds cannot tell us how we *ought* to respond to those perceptions, because our responses are causally determined in accordance with physical principles. Again, our minds—reason—can neither cause a spontaneous inclination to arise, nor to go away. Hence human agents cannot be described as fully autonomous.

A similar argument shows why human beings are not free in the sense needed for standard responses to Hume to have force. To say that the mind is free to choose anything whatsoever, unencumbered by spontaneous inclinations arising from our psychological states, is to say that the mind can't be free at all, because the mind alone cannot generate any goals from amongst which it might choose. On this score, the mind is simply helpless on Graham's view, and if helpless, then surely not free in any meaningful way. (Note that this argument is clearly distinct from any arguments about free will versus determinism, an altogether different philosophical issue (cf., p. 13).

Turning next to the concept of choice, it may appear as if I do Graham no favors by interpreting him as basically ignoring the concept, because choice has been at the very center of modern Western moral theory: if it is not my fundamental moral task to *choose* an action I deem good or right on the basis of certain theoretical principles, then what is it to be a moral agent? Isn't my most basic obligation to *choose* the right course of action, and then endeavor to follow that path?[11]

Not exactly, says Graham: "We shall not linger over what we mean by choice, which even when narrowed to considered choice is a concept with blurred edges" (p. 7). To be sure, he often uses the word 'choice' in his exposition (e.g., pp. 15, 21, 35, 37, et sup.), but the term is just a convenience, in keeping with standard English usage; the concept associated with the term plays no philosophical role in Graham's theory.

To illustrate, let us take a personal preference example of the sort Graham himself regularly gives. Did you ever *choose* to have a taste for pizza? Note first that the question has not been loaded by including the words 'taste for', because if you ever chose simply to have a pizza without any gustatory inclination—'taste for'—whatsoever to do so, your 'choice' would be absolutely arbitrary, no more the subject of *rational* choice than electing instead to clean your glasses, light a candle, go fishing, or write philosophy instead of having a pizza. Again, then: did you ever *choose* to have a taste for a pizza? Highly doubtful. Much more likely is it that at certain times when you haven't eaten for awhile you have smelled pizza cooking, or seen a coupon announcing a two dollar discount on all pizzas, and/or had a friend who allowed that she would like some pizza; any or all of which caused a spontaneous inclination in you to have some pizza. It is surely counter-intuitive to suggest that a rational agent first *chooses* to be hungry, and thereafter *chooses* a particular dish on the basis of we-know-not-what considerations that have been considered solely in the lights of pure reason. You might have some inclination not to eat at all—you are on a diet—or you might, if hungry, have an inclination toward Chinese food. But absent *any* inclinations, what is there to choose? And if inclinations narrowly constrain the parameters of choice, how purely rational—except as means—can choice be?

We may better appreciate Graham's position, which basically does away with the concept of choice, by considering another example. It would appear altogether straightforward to say "I didn't choose my parents, but I surely chose my friends." I want to suggest that such a statement, straightforward or no, is false, and that Graham's dual attentiveness to reason and spontaneity helps us understand why it is false.

I have met many people in the course of my life: other children in the neighborhood, classmates, fellow Marines, fellow students, colleagues, neighbors, and so forth. I have met them in classrooms, barracks, on the job, at conferences, parties, and other kinds of gatherings too many and varied to recall. A number of these people I enjoyed being with right from the start, and after our initial meeting we agreed to play together the coming weekend, or have coffee together after class, or lunch, or visit each other's homes for dinner and conversation. Some people I saw only a few times, after which, for one reason or another, our ways parted. With some people the relationship continued, but remained at the (pleasant) level of acquaintanceship. But with (fewer) others the visits grew more warm and numerous, more confidences were shared, mutual respect and affection grew deeper.

These latter people are my friends. But upon reflection, it seems that at no time did I consciously *choose* them as friends. At no time, that is, did I sit down and say that now that I have seen candidate-friend eight or eighteen times, I must now tot up his/her virtues and vices, make calculations, and *decide*—choose—that he/she would be a friend. Nor do I believe that I am in the least bit unusual in this regard. To carefully weigh virtues and vices, and then come to a conscious decision on the basis of one's calculations, may be perfectly appropriate activities when buying a used car, but it is surely not an account of how we come by our friends. (It isn't an account of how we come by lovers and spouses either.)

Indeed, I would venture to say that virtually all of us would be deeply hurt and offended to learn that a 'friend', spouse, or lover had made such calculations with regard to ourselves. Friends and lovers are ends, not means, as Graham's work reminds us. Meeting someone, I may be spontaneously inclined to want to get to know him better. After a few visits—'fuller awareness'—my inclination may grow stronger. I might have a counter-inclination toward not becoming vulnerable, maintaining my privacy, or whatever. More visits, ever fuller awareness. But if these inclinations continue, and are enhanced, then one day—although almost surely neither of us could specify it—we are no longer acquaintances, but friends. There is nothing mysterious here. Surely Graham is right that reason guides me with respect to friendship: what people say and how they behave influence my inclinations profoundly. But inclinations they are, and not *choices*; there is all the difference in the world between an old friend and an old Ford.[12]

It must be noted that in drawing out this implication of Graham's views—the implication that the picture of human beings as purely rational, as freely-choosing autonomous individuals, must be given up if

we are to understand human agency—I have in part adopted his
methodology: I have not argued, with respect to friendship, that this is
the way things *ought* to be, but that this is the way things *are*. Like
Graham, in other words, I have made some empirical claims, phenomenologically argued. It is therefore not out of place to adduce additional
empirical evidence, experimentally argued, in support of Graham's
and my own views, especially on the supposedly central concept of
choice, even if the clear philosophical waters have to be muddied
somewhat with experimental data from the behavioral sciences. Here-
with one example, taken from a recent integrative work in cognitive
science by Howard Margolis; the parallelism with statements from
Graham in *R & S* is particularly striking:

> The answer I will come to on this is that conscious judgements probably
> do always *follow*, never determine, choices; conscious reasons neverthe-
> less play an essential role, but that role concerns how judgements are
> sometimes revised, not how they are made in the first instance.
>
> An experiment illustrating the problematic relation between choice
> and conscious volition asks subjects to decide when they will make some
> simple movement (something like, wiggle a finger) and note the
> position of a clock hand when they do that. At the same time, brain
> currents are monitored, looking for certain "readiness" potentials
> which invariably precede movements. The result is striking evidence
> that the readiness potentials precede consciousness of a decision by
> about a half-second, so that the "decision" *follows* the physiological
> signals that the movement is being organized, not the reverse. It
> appears, then, that the unconscious beginnings of the act cause both
> the movement and the conscious sense that a decision has been made to
> move.
>
> The significance of these results is disputed (Libet 1985). On the
> argument here, though, a certain aspect of Libet's interpretation is
> particularly appealing, namely, that *the function of consciousness concerns
> reviewing or checking intuitions and volitions, which sometimes prompts a
> halting of what is underway. But we do not decide to have a volition or
> intuition, and only a small fraction of what occurs in the brain that we suppose
> might prompt a conscious intuition or volition actually does so.*[13]

Evidence of this kind, plus the evidence of reflection on the histories
of our friendships and love lives, surely do not *prove* that concepts of

autonomy, choice, or 'Reason as Master' views are wrong-headed in coming to grips with the problem(s) of value, and they do not *prove* that we must acknowledge spontaneity as the source of human valuation, aided and abetted by human reason, while never replaced by it. But this evidence does, I believe, make Graham's views eminently reasonable at the very least; and if they do not command conviction, it will probably be due in some measure to a distrust of spontaneity that is deeply rooted in the modern Western philosophical tradition. Resistance to Graham's position might well take the following form: it is one thing to *acknowledge* that we have spontaneous inclinations, be these described as impulses, passions, desires, our will, or whatever; virtually all philosophers have been aware of such inclinations. It is something else altogether to *celebrate* this spontaneity, as seems to be the case in much of *R & S*. For it is human reason that links all human beings, and spontaneous inclinations that divide them. It is the passions and not reason that lead to racism, rape, war, genocide, and most all else that we regard as evil, from long before the execution of Jesus to the Holocaust and beyond; if there is any hope for morality, it must lie in human reason, not spontaneity. If, therefore, you embrace spontaneity, either you are a moral relativist sufficiently radical as to be indistinguishable from a moral nihilist (a loathsome position), or you must have an inordinate faith in the ultimate goodness of human nature (an implausible position).

Graham must indeed celebrate spontaneity, for a very simple reason: it is of the essence of our being human, and not only the source of our valuations, but of creativity as well. If we are not as autonomous as we thought we were, neither are we merely animals or automatons; and it is our spontaneous inclinations, guided by reason, but not led by it, that distinguish us from the latter groups.[14]

It is much more important to understand, however, that Graham: (1) does not embrace, nor does his position entail, moral relativism; and (2) does not believe in, nor does his position require, a theory of the goodness of human nature.[15] All attempts to pigeonhole *R & S* into one or another pat positions must fail if we read him carefully; we must be prepared to break with the regnant paradigms in modern Western philosophy if we are to understand him aright. (Which, given the years of his scholarly life he has devoted to Chinese thought, should come as no surprise [Cf. also p. 40].)

Mencius is very probably the first philosopher to argue for the goodness of human nature. Seeing a child about to fall into a well, he argues, we are spontaneously and immediately moved to render aid, before any thought of danger to ourselves, or reward, or anything else reason might suggest, enters our heads. From this deceptively simple *gedanke* experiment Mencius concludes *ren zhi xing shan*—'human nature is good'. As the text which bears his name makes clear, Mencius is not unaware that people regularly behave badly. He is no more naive than proponents of an aggressive (i.e., anti-social) instinct in human beings—Lorenz, Ardrey, Morris, Tiger, Fox, etc.—are unaware of numerous examples of noble, altruistic, or just plain decent actions in the histories of cultures.[16] As the former will attribute human mischief to environmental circumstances, so will the latter explain human decency; the nature versus nurture dispute once again.

Graham eschews both theoretical positions, and he obviously cannot give credence to the so-called 'neutralist' position, whether it be promulgated by Gao Zi or B. F. Skinner. But he doesn't need any of these theoretical positions. All he needs is an acknowledgement that human beings *do* regularly have spontaneous inclinations toward what we would call empathy, compassion, sympathy, pity, etc. He can allow (indeed insist) that human beings also have spontaneous inclinations toward extreme self-interest, or worse, being cruel to others. For as we have seen above (p. 234), it is not necessary that one inclination be stronger than another for us to act on it. Here is where 'Reason as Guide' can be seen most sharply: even if the sympathy for another, derived from awareness from her viewpoint, is not as strong as a sadistic inclination to see her suffer, so long as it is allowed that I have *any* inclination toward the former, Graham's quasi-syllogism provides a ground for defeating sadism, egoism, or, more generally, moral relativism.

Putting this point in another way, throughout *R & S* Graham not only acknowledges, he is often downright fascinated by the fact that many human beings frequently act, at best, oddly, and at times are downright perverse; *pace* his detailed analyses of Zhuang Zi, Nietzsche, de Sade, Futurists, Dadaists, and the Surrealists. What we would call non-, a-, or im- moral inclinations can be given their due, however, without surrendering to moral relativism, or nihilism. Again a salient fact to which Graham calls our attention: weak, attenuated, or whatever, human beings have some inclinations towards others that can only be described as moral, by anyone's definition of the term be they British, Bengali, or Bantu. It is this insight which invests Graham's account of Nietzsche with such originality. As he says:

> A point of interest is Nietzsche's implicit acknowledgement that the impulse to sympathy is inherent in all awareness from other viewpoints; you have to be spared the very sight of illness if you are not to risk mistaking it for your own. Here this most psychologically acute of philosophers agrees with a claim of the present book which readers much less committed than Nietzsche to the innateness of human selfishness may have found highly controversial (pp. 165–66).

Thus the overall goodness of human nature need not be assumed in any accounts that see spontaneity as not only actual, but desirable; all that is needed is the belief—hard to deny, even for Nietzsche—that we all have *some* inclinations blanketed by the term 'good', compete though they do with others we would all label 'evil'.[17] But if this be accepted, then we need not be moral relativists, especially if we are willing to allow that reason is a capacity shared equally by all human beings, and that it has the power to guide the ways in which we are moved by our inclinations.

Another way—somewhat less important, but by no means irrelevant—in which Graham's position is anti-relativistic can be seen by attending to aesthetic considerations. At all times Graham insists on our human attributes, especially our bodily constitution. By doing so, he must equally insist that while the kinds of things towards which we might be inclined is a very large set, it is not an infinite set; our anatomy and physiology place sharp constraints on what we can be attracted to, repelled by, or simply understand. Although Graham does not employ it himself, language is a primary example of this point. Over three thousand human languages are still in use today, the very great majority of them unintelligible to speakers of any others, owing to different patterns of syntax, phonetics, and phonology, and semantic variability.

Yet if the theory of generative grammar, in any of its variant forms, is correct, all of these three thousand plus languages will exhibit the same constraints; the set of possible languages naturally accessible to human beings is a highly restricted set.

Similarly, I may consistently be moved to tears by Beethoven's Ninth Symphony, while you hear it as romantic gushing, decidedly inferior to the works of Bach or Mozart. But neither of us will either be inclined toward, or away from, any 'symphony' composed solely of notes inaudible to the human ear—however much dogs might be moved by its melodies. The world of color may be indefinitely large; but *homo sapiens* is obliged to live within the spectrum from infra-red to ultra-violet. Some of us love more deeply than others, but it is highly unlikely that any of us would love in ways that are at all familiar if we were self-reproducing creatures. And even if it be allowed that beauty is in the eye of the beholder, the beauty beheld would surely be radically different if we had insect visual systems, rather than the visual systems we do in fact have.[18]

I should like to draw together the threads of this discussion of the implications of Graham's position by taking up one additional topic that he treats at length (the last third of the book, pp. 157–227): the difference between irrationalism and anti-rationalism. Drawing upon this distinction, we can see just how much Graham has distanced his own views on spontaneity from those other views which have so often been the object of philosophical fear, or opprobrium, or both.

To a friend I confess a very strong desire for a chocolate malted. I can easily imagine a multiplicity of responses: "Drink water instead, Henry, you're already overweight"; "What a coincidence, I've got a taste for a chocolate malted too"; "Your desire must go unfulfilled tonight, because the ice cream shop is closed"; "If you want one, go get one, but I'm too busy to join you right now"; and more. All of these and many other responses to my statement would be altogether normal, expected, appropriate. Unless my friend is a philosopher, however (or a psycho-analyst) I will be drawn up short if the response is simply "Why?" I will be puzzled not only about what reply to make, but what *kind* of reply to make. What would count as a rational reply? Why would anyone ask such a question? And if my answer is "I just do, that's all; why do you ask?" would we not all agree that this was a good 'answer'?

However, from the fact that I—you, anyone—do not proffer rational reasons for wanting a malted, it would surely be inaccurate to conclude that the want was *ir*rational. In the same way, and to return to an earlier example, it surely does not follow, from the (true) premise that I never deliberately weighed my wife's numerous virtues against her very few vices, that it was irrational to have asked her to marry me. In all such cases, intimately involving human agency though they do, the contrasting pair rational-irrational is simply out of place in our considerations, in the same way that a sunset might be moving or serene, uplifting or dispiriting, extraordinary or ordinary, but neither courageous nor cowardly.

In this light, we do not have to see Pascal as prefiguring the nineteenth-century romantics when he said "The heart has its reasons, which reason knows nothing of."[19] We should check the temptation to interpret Pascal as a champion of irrationality, for he was a first-rate mathematician, surely aware of the powers of reason and the joys attendant on the exercise thereof. Rather should we grant him the insight that reason has not been, and never can be, the be-all and end-all of human life. This view we may characterize, with Graham, as *anti-*rationalist. It acknowledges the place of reason, but insists that reason be in its place, and if it oversteps its bounds, the results may not only not be helpful, but downright harmful (pure reason alone will never secure friends or lovers, and may cause us to lose both). Anti-rationalism is consistent—hence rational—in ascribing important functions to reason, and providing reasons why reason should be distrusted when it is employed to serve other functions.

In contrast, Graham sees irrationalism as an arbitrary appeal to reason when it suits one's purposes, and a contempt for it when it does not—the most vulgar form of inconsistency. An example he gives (p. 159) is of the Nazi who fully subscribes to all the canons of logic, mathematics, and principles of scientific methodology when designing crematoria, but will abandon them in a moment when asked if the *Protocols of the Elders of Zion* might be a forgery. For Graham, the distinction between anti-rationalism and irrationalism is all important, because anti-rationalists (Zhuang Zi, Breton, Graham himself at times) neither disavow reason nor employ it arbitrarily, hence can celebrate spontaneity while yet subscribing to the quasi-syllogism and obeying the imperative to be aware.

Irrationalists, on the other hand (Nietzsche, de Sade), champion spontaneity at the expense of reason, are arbitrary and/or whimsical in obeying and neglecting the imperative, can only mount *ir*rational 'defenses' for their positions, and consequently stand indicted by Graham not for *moral*, but for *cognitive* defects (see pp. 15, 29, 159, and the analyses of Nietzsche and de Sade on pp. 164–183).

In sum, Graham both acknowledges and celebrates the role of spontaneity in human life, and places reason at its side, neither as leading nor following our inclinations, and on this basis proffers his "solution" to the fundamental problem of value. The importance of spontaneity for his position in no way unleashes the demons of egoism, sadism, skepticism, irrationality, nihilism, or a radical relativism. On the contrary, Graham's views provide powerful arguments against such demons, and, along the way, make us re-think a number of concepts central to modern Western philosophy, from autonomy to automatons, from choice to friendship.[20]

If this summary evaluation is correct, *R & S* is indeed a very important book. Before we can build philosophically on its manifold strengths, however, we must examine its foundational presuppositions closely to insure that they bear scrutiny, and will not lead to more philosophical puzzles than can be solved within its conceptual framework. I believe that some of those presuppositions—and consequent arguments—will *not* stand up to careful scrutiny, and it is to an examination of them that we now turn.

Critique

The examples and arguments which follow are fairly specific and detailed, and in order that the forest not be lost to the trees I want to begin by contextualizing my objections, describing at some length the basic *source* of the difficulties I see with Graham's position. Since at least the time of Kierkegaard, value theory has been seen to fall into three general domains: aesthetics (one's own tastes, preferences, personal goals, etc.); morals (one's relations to others); and religion (one's relation to the cosmos, to the sacred—"matters of ultimate concern," as Tillich would have it).[21] To any careful reader of *R & S* it will be obvious that this trichotomy is applicable to it.

It has been equally traditional in modern Western philosophy to see the Cartesian/Humean picture of human beings as an abstract portrait of an *individual self*. Such viewing is so altogether common and natural (what else *could* it be?) that we have difficulty appreciating that it is just that: a viewing; and hence, a view. Graham has altered the Cartesian/ Humean picture significantly—minds and bodies are not at opposite ends of the frame with nothing in between—but an individual self is still discernible, and more than that, is desirable: Graham" . . . supports, as beneficial to all, a certain kind of individualism" (p. 25). Herein lies the fundamental problem with his positions as I see it: his defense of a certain kind of bare individualism, even though the concepts of autonomy, complete freedom, and choice no longer apply to Graham's individuals as they do in the Cartesian/Humean picture.

To be sure, in most, if not all of aesthetics our focus will be on individuals. Whether I prefer tweed jackets to blazers, blondes to brunettes, Beethoven to Bach; in such cases, and others of a similar kind, what is central for description and analysis is my *individuality*, my *personal* tastes, preferences, and goals. The situation is similar in religion. Whether I lament that I am "alone and afraid/in a world I never made",[22] or pronounce with enthusiasm, as a born-again Christian, that "I have accepted Jesus as my Savior", the reference of the first-person singular pronoun is just that: *personal* and *singular*; an individual. Moreover, in both cases the individual is an *isolate*. This is precisely what the first statement says, and if we are Christians, or Jews, or Muslims—'born again' or orthodox—we do *not* meet our Maker accompanied by our parents, children, spouse, or friends; on Judgement Day we stand alone; isolated individuals.

Thus the concept of the individual self has been seen as natural, and central to reflections on aesthetics and religion in value theory. Within the realm of morals, however, the concept of the individual self is not so

natural, even though it has been equally central. Indeed, one might go
so far as to suggest that the concept of the individual self—and the high
value placed thereon—is so difficult to reconcile with the concept of
morality (one's relations to others), that the *real* problem of value in
modern Western philosophy lies in the unconvincing nature of all
theories which have attempted a reconciliation, from Hume himself to
the present.

Graham of course is not an American pioneer, robber baron, social
Darwinian type of 'rugged individualist'. He is not unaware of the value
and importance of others and of community. He acknowledges that
each of us " . . . belongs within a cosmos as within a community" (p. 83).
And he is sensitive to the fact that communities are held together by
customs, rituals, and traditions, which are necessary for our human
lives.

> . . . [I]f we consider what is left of our own traditional seasonal festivals,
> it appears perfectly comprehensible that someone should feel that to
> miss the reunion with the family at Christmas is not just a disappoint-
> ment, it is an interruption of his rhythm damaging to the sense of
> security which he annually renews by going back to his roots (p. 111).

But his awareness and sensitivity notwithstanding, Graham is an
individualist, who endorses, as quoted earlier, "a certain kind of
individualism". There is much additional textual evidence for my
reading of him on this score. Moral concerns are considered in several
places in the book, but only 15 of 227 pages of it are devoted to a close
analysis of moral issues, which is unusual, given the importance of
moral values to value theory in general. Further, of the four thinkers he
singles out for detailed examination (Nietzsche, de Sade, Zhuang Zi
and André Breton), all but the last are thoroughgoing individualists,
and even Breton's affinity with and for his small Surrealist circle is
mitigated by the fact that the members of the circle circumscribed it
with their antipathy to the larger communities within which they lived
their lives. And although Graham (correctly) maintains that we do have
feelings of sympathy, empathy, etc., nevertheless becoming aware from
another's standpoint must require a good deal of effort, for we are
essentially alone. A revealing quote: " . . . Birth, orgasm and death *are*

breaches of the fence between self and other . . . " (p. 144; italics added). But, keeping with the metaphor, I believe Frost was mistaken when he said that "Good fences make good neighbors."[23] Whether Graham would accept Frost's evaluation I do not know. Clearly he would endorse the description, which I believe to be the root of the conceptual difficulties with *R & S* as I see them, if not in aesthetics or religion, then definitely in the realm of morals; difficulties we must now examine in some detail.

Graham distinguishes private morality from public justice (p. 301 of this volume), but believes his 'Reason as Guide' perspective, made specific by his quasi-syllogism, is equally applicable in both cases (ibid.). As it stands, I don't believe it is applicable in either case. Consider public justice first. He says:

> For public justice on the other hand there is no problem about being equally aware from all viewpoints. I would be designing law from the viewpoint of *anyone,* as in Rawls' *Theory of Justice,* and would be tempted to confuse this impersonal creature with myself only if I were the dictator of the state (ibid., italics in the original).

Let us now recall the multiplicity of facts of which we should be aware: our own spontaneous inclinations, what causes those inclinations; your inclinations, what causes your inclinations; we must (should) be aware, in short, of "everything which would spontaneously move us one way or the other" (p. 16ff.). We must also recall the foundational premise of Graham's solution to the problem of value: all human ends, goals, hence values, are grounded in our spontaneous inclinations.

Perhaps we can truly advance public justice in this manner, but we cannot do it in a Rawlsian way. For Rawls, the veil of ignorance behind which we enter the 'original position' is a very thick veil indeed. Not only do we not know whether we are young or old, male or female, rich or poor, black, white, or whatever; *we also cannot know what our personal goals are, our concepts of the good, our inclinations or our aspirations.* Rawls is explicit on this issue:

> [The] original position is . . . understood as a purely hypothetical situation characterized so as to lead to a certain conception of justice. Among the essential features of this situation is that no one knows his place in society, his class position or social status, nor does any one know

his fortune in the distribution of natural assets and liabilities, his intelligence, strength, and the like. *I shall even assume that the parties do not know their conception of the good or their special psychological propensities.* The principles of justice are chosen behind a veil of ignorance.[24]

Equally explicitly:

We should insure further *that particular inclinations and aspirations*, and persons' conceptions of their good do not affect the principles adopted.[25]

We can allow that Graham and Rawls probably do not mean exactly the same thing in their use of the term 'inclinations', and allow equally that Graham might (should) be sceptical about principles of justice, public or otherwise, that will be selected by people so lacking in awareness as to be indistinguishable from thoroughgoing amnesiacs. With these allowances, however, Graham's apparent endorsement of Rawls is all the more puzzling, for the views of the two of them are flatly incompatible. Graham insists that we be maximally aware of (among other things), our own and the inclination of others. And because our goals and ends are grounded in our inclinations, to be aware of our inclinations is *eo ipso* to be aware of our (likely) goals and ends. That we will in all probability be aware of more than one inclination at any one time is not relevant here; we will have *some* awareness of (possible for us) ends and goals, and by not much extension, we will thereby have at least *some* concept of the good as we see it. But this awareness prohibits Graham from taking a seat in the original position. He would know (be aware) of much more than anyone else so positioned, and hence would clearly be, on Rawlsian grounds, cheating.

The other horn of this dilemma can be succinctly stated: if Graham believes laws or principles of public justice can be ascertained within a Rawlsian ('Reason as Master') conception, he must see his quasi-syllogism as superfluous, and his imperative of 'be aware' as out of place.

(Curiously enough, although Rawls on the whole accepts much more of the Cartesian/Humean picture for his philosophizing than does Graham, the former's agent is, in enforced ignorance, far less an individual self than the latter's agent is in enforced awareness. But perhaps this isn't—shouldn't be—curious at all.)

I am not arguing that Graham cannot give a satisfactory account of how we arrive at public justice within his conceptual framework. Nor am I arguing that it is logically impossible that he can give an account that might not be incompatible with the account given by Rawls. What I have argued is that *R & S* stands here, *A Theory of Justice* stands there, and Graham has erected a fence between them which he has not showed us how to breach.

More serious problems with Graham's position arise when we turn to the field of 'private morality' (p. 301 of this volume), by which I assume that he is referring to morals *per se*, rather than to the grounds of political obligation. On the basis of the Cartesian/Humean picture, enhanced by computer-driven work in artificial intelligence, a cottage industry has grown up attempting to state and then solve problems that are collectively known as 'prisoner's dilemmas'. Bowing to the Age of Technology, let us consider a variant on one such problem, and attempt to solve it utilizing Graham's quasi-syllogism, adopting his phraseology as well.

Confined involuntarily by others, I am told that if I betray a close friend, the fate that awaits me will be considerably less dire than if I do not. I am painfully aware of an inclination to betray him, because I am frightened. I am aware of another inclination not to betray him because he is indeed a close friend; we have jointly shared triumphs and losses, joys and sorrows, for a great many years. I am given a document which betrays me, a document written and signed in a hand that appears unmistakeably as my friend's. My inclination to betray him now grows stronger, fear being augmented by anger and resentment. But simultaneously—or almost so—I begin to suspect that the document is a clever forgery.

In standard 'prisoner's dilemma' puzzles, the interrogative formulation of the problem would be "What should I do?" But this would beg the more important question against Graham, so let us state it his way: "How shall I be moved?" To help answer this latter question, I overlay Graham's quasi-syllogism (in condensed form) on the statement of my problem, just as we have encountered it before:

1) In awareness of everything relevant to the issue, I find myself moved towards X.

2) Overlooking something relevant, I find myself moved towards Y.

Be aware

Therefore, let yourself be moved towards X.

Now this schema will, according to Graham, begin to enable me to solve my prisoner's dilemma as soon as I instantiate it (i.e., replace the variables with appropriate goal-stating phrases). Unfortunately, I cannot find a neutral way to do this. Much of the plausibility, indeed naturalness of Graham's descriptions and defenses of the quasi-syllogism vanishes when we move from second or third person accounts to an attempt to employ it in an actual first person situation. I cannot find, in other words, an isolated *individual self* into which awareness flows neutrally. I am either a frightened man, or a close friend. I first examine the first premise of the quasi-syllogism. If I am strongly inclined not to betray my friend (*ex hypothesi*) I will obviously be strongly inclined to instantiate X with 'Don't betray friend', and I will enhance this inclination by 'overlooking' the document. But if my fear, and the document, weigh heavily on my inclinations (*ex hypothesi*), they will weigh equally heavily on my inclination to replace X with 'Betray friend', and this will be so to the extent that I 'overlook' my suspicion. Yet it would appear that I must overlook either the document or the suspicion, and whichever one I overlook—rationally or spontaneously—*guarantees* what X will have to be, and consequently my instantiation of the quasi-syllogism formula will be altogether post hoc. Again, I am either a frightened man, or a close friend.

Nor do I seem to be helped in my instantiation problem if I try to work with the second premise, and endeavor to instantiate Y. Unless Angus has a description very different from my own, it seems proper to say again that I must 'overlook' either the document or the suspicion. Both the document and the suspicion are clearly relevant to the issue, as the quasi-syllogism demands. Suppose I overlook the document. Then Y must be replaced by 'Don't betray friend'. But it was only because I was inclined to overlook the document that I was inclined to replace X with 'Don't betray friend' in the first premise. So if I am consistent in overlooking the document, X will be 'Don't betray friend', and Y will be

'Don't betray friend'. In short, X = Y; which reduces the quasi-syllogism either to nonsense or tautology, useless for solving my prisoner's dilemma. The situation is not improved by coming the other way: being inclined to overlook my suspicion requires that Y be instantiated with 'Betray friend', but it was only because of my inclination to overlook my suspicion that I was inclined to replace X in the first premise with 'Betray friend', so again, X = Y. Something, I submit, is wrong here.

Now it may appear as though the exciting, original, and incisive picture drawn earlier of the grand vision(s) embodied in *R & S* I am now obscuring by narrow, nit-picking (i.e. English empiricist/analytic) methods. But Angus is not averse to close detail (*pace* his work on Chinese grammar as well as in *R & S*), so we may pursue this issue in even closer detail.

Crucial to my argument have been the terms 'inclinations' and 'overlook'. I believe I understand what Graham means by the former, and have felt comfortable in employing it in my exposition and defense of his views; he will correct me if I am mistaken in this regard. But I am troubled by 'overlook', evidenced logically by the way it is displayed in the prisoner's dilemma example, and evidenced grammatically by signalling my uneasiness with the term by placing it within quotes at relevant times.

There are a number of definitions of 'overlook' ranging from 'oversee', to the older 'to look upon with the evil eye'.[26] Ignoring these, Graham must be using the term as meaning 'not to take into account', but this definition unfortunately allows for ambiguity in employing the word, for things may be overlooked either by accident or design. I can either inadvertently or deliberately overlook something, and the concept of spontaneous inclination embedded in the quasi-syllogism allows either interpretation at any time. Further, it would seem perfectly acceptable to say 'I have a strong, spontaneous inclination to overlook fact A', the plausibility of which I have assumed in the example above.

Such prisoner's dilemmas are neither far-fetched nor counter-intuitive; nor, unfortunately, are they uncommon in human experience. I must confess, however, to constructing the example in a special, albeit straightforward way. In it, the other person 'relevant to the issue' is a close friend, and being a close friend is a reciprocal relationship: 'He's my close friend, although I'm only a bare acquaintance to him' is surely odd; if I *have* a close friend, I *am* a close friend. Moreover, in addition to this reciprocity, what it means for me to describe someone as a close friend is that I will overlook (in the sense of ignore) empirical evidence—even a great deal of evidence—that she or he is not worthy of the strong feelings of attachment I have toward her or him. Hence in the example, the viewpoint I take as my own cannot be that of an individual self. Rather is my viewpoint that of a close friend, which, owing to the reciprocity of the relation, makes it also the viewpoint of a close friend 'relevant to the issue'.

Consequently my reason will tell me that the document is a clever forgery, or that my friend must have undergone extreme torture in order to have written or signed it. If the other person relevant to the issue was a relative stranger, my reason would undoubtedly operate differently. But if we are focusing on the *concept* 'close friend', there does not appear to be any room for an 'individual self', and therefore no neutral reference for the first-person singular in the quasi-syllogism: being a close friend obviates the question 'How shall I be moved?' in its moral sense. The only question would be factual: 'How much pain can I endure?'

In short, it would seem that the example requires that 'I take the viewpoint' of a close friend both for myself *and for him,* and do not betray him until and unless I break under torture. The quasi-syllogism plays no role. On the other hand, if I betray him after the first verbal threat, I clearly do not understand the concept—and hence have no human feeling, or appreciation—of what it is to be a close friend; I will not only be a coward, but have cognitive and emotional defects as well, in the same way Graham indicts egoists and sadists. But again, the quasi-syllogism has no role to play.

And it does not seem possible for me to 'stand' anywhere else to 'take a viewpoint'. Angus will say

> What affects me . . . requires me to set it apart and keep my distance, above all when its reverberations are strong enough to shake self-control, foreign enough to threaten identity. If it lifts me above myself . . . (p. 136).

But to "keep my distance" from myself, or to be "lifted above myself", it would seem that I need a skyhook. What is suggested in the quote—and throughout *R & S*—is that, akin to Nagel, we take "a view from nowhere".[27] Unfortunately, the view from nowhere is just that, nowhere; in moral considerations I must always be somewhere, and, concretely for Graham, somewhere "relevant to the issue". Philsophers who accept the Cartesian/Humean picture of human beings as having minds and bodies altogether distinct from each other may be naturally inclined to believe they, and anyone else in a moral situation, can view the world *sub specie aeternitatis*. Graham correctly rejects the picture, but the manner of his rejection entails that the 'I' always has a specific spatio-temporal (and cultural) location; it is always somewhere, spontaneously tending this way and that in accordance with the specific ways our bodies are interacting with the environment, interactions mediated by the mind's activities.

This constant *somewhere* at which each of us is constantly standing is not, of course, only the viewpoint of a close friend. The specific somewhere that Antigone stood morally was in the role—which she *lived*, not played—of sister. Raised in the tradition of modern Western moral theory, we are tempted to describe her situation as one of conflicting inclinations of duty, sibling on the one hand, niece and loyal subject of Thebes on the other. But it is obvious from Sophocles' account that this is not the way Antigone sees things: from the outset of the play we know she is not going to abandon the body of Polyneices, traitor to Thebes though he might be, and despite Kreon's injunction.

Of what is Antigone unaware? In what sense might she be charged with irrationality? For myself, I do not see plausible responses to these questions coming from Graham's position, nor generated by attending to his basic question, 'How shall I be moved?' because if we re-phrase the question to '*Who* is to be moved?' it is difficult to find an appropriate answer. To see things from your viewpoint deeply enough to be spontaneously moved by the perceptions of them only seems possible to the extent that I abandon my own viewpoint, at least for the nonce, be my viewpoint that of sister, friend, or philosopher. Thus Graham's account gains plausibility only to the extent that we imagine an 'I' that is supra-aware, cognizant of the inclinations (towards being moved) from being in your shoes, and from being in 'my own' shoes. But who or where is this supra-aware 'I', and which shoes is this 'I' wearing? It becomes irresistable here to paraphrase Hume, who looms so large in the background of both *R & S* and the present essay:

> For my part, when I enter most intimately into what I call *myself*, I always stumble on some particular role or other, of son or father, lover or friend, student or teacher, brother or neighbor. I never can catch *myself* at any time apart from a role, and never can observe anything except from the viewpoint of a role. . . . If anyone upon serious and unprejudic'd reflection, thinks he has a different notion of *himself*, I must confess that I can no longer reason with him. All I can allow him is, that he may be in the right as well as I, and that we are essentially different in this particular. He may perhaps, perceive something simple and continu'd, which he calls *himself*; tho' I am certain there is no such principle in me.[28]

These considerations suggest that Graham is rather closer than he thinks to other modern Western moral philosophers, because this generalized 'Antigone problem' applies no less to those who see the basic question in terms of 'What should I do?' as it does to his own position. If Antigone stands as sister, the shade of Polyneices will loom very large in her attempts to formulate a universalisable maxim, and/or to calculate happiness benefits. If Antigone, *per impossibile*, stands as niece and loyal subject, Polyneices will be virtually invisible. In either case, we can bet on which maxim she will formulate, and/or how she will calculate benefits; there can be no genuine moral problem, for there is no supra-aware, philosophical 'I' to formulate the problem.

Can Antigone take a viewpoint (stand) other than that of sister, or niece and loyal subject of Thebes? I think not. Any other viewpoint should be *ir*relevant to the issue, and worse than that: it would be impossible. She would cease to be Antigone, becoming instead just one more 'ghost in the machine', which Graham no less than Ryle has struggled long and hard, but, in my opinion, ultimately unsuccessfully, to exorcise.[29] She stands as sister, in keeping with Greek custom, just as Confucian males stand as sons, in keeping with Chinese custom; and just as close friends stand as close friends, in keeping with universal custom.

In conclusion, I am sceptical that Graham can maintain his notion of the individual self as described in *R & S*, for that notion is too closely linked to all of the standard 'solutions' to the problem of value, solutions from which he otherwise wishes to distance himself. If we are to keep the manifold strengths and varied insights of *R & S*, Angus will have to be willing, in my opinion, to let himself be moved more toward the *Lun Yu* and the *Mencius*,[30] and even farther away from the modern Western moral tradition (and probably a little farther away from the *Zhuang Zi* as well). If he does not, then I do not believe the question which entitles this essay can be intelligibly answered, or modified, or rejected, in a manner consistent with an accurate account of human moral experience.

But perhaps I am mistaken. In any event, I trust that Angus will be able to see the issues raised herein from my friendly viewpoint as well as from his own—as I have attempted reciprocally to do—and that he will consequently be spontaneously inclined, with reason as his guide, to respond to these meditations on his considered solutions to the problem of value.

NOTES

1. *The Problems of Value*. London, 1961.
2. London and Dublin, 1985.
3. I cannot, however, begin to discuss the full range of topics explored in *R & S* without this 'review' exceeding the length of the book. Even among those themes I take up in some detail, it will be painfully obvious that volumes have been written on them which both Angus and I ignore, or pass over in a sentence or two. In extenuation, it can be argued that Graham is breaking with tradition, making most of the volumes that work within the tradition—rightly or wrongly—beside the point. I should note also that some of the themes I do address have also been taken up by other contributors to this volume (especially Hansen and Fingarette), but it seemed best to let these essays, and Graham's responses to them, stand on their own, without additional commentary from the editor in his own contribution. Relatedly, another editor might well have abbreviated the present essay considerably, for it is almost the longest piece in the volume, and may appear arcane at times. In extenuation, I can only say that I think *R & S* reflects not only *what* Angus has done as a scholar, but *why* he has

done it, as a human being; and it is simultaneously to a scholar, to a human being—and to a friend—that I have written this essay.

4. But not, of course, in *The Inquiry Concerning the Principles of Morals*.

5. Thomas Hobbes, *Leviathan*, Harmondsworth, 1968; John Rawls, *A Theory of Justice* (Cambridge, MA, 1971), pp 12–18; Willard Van Orman Quine, *Word & Object* (Cambridge, MA, 1960), esp. chapter 2.

6. And as a consequence, I will not take up herein the complex issue of the function(s) of the will in Kant, and in Graham. For the former, the will must be the executive which endeavors to realize (i.e. make real) the laws enacted by the legislature, reason. Despite Graham's dismissal of Kant's 'Reason as Master' position, however, it appears as though the will serves a similar function in his scheme of things; the 'Let yourself be moved' imperative which will be taken up below seems to require a will with at least some Kantian characteristics.

7. Entering the caveat that what is imagined not be purely imaginary: "Provided that an object is conceived to be real, reactions to it are the same in kind whether one happens to be perceiving or imagining it" (p. 17).

8. *A Treatise on Human Nature* (Harmondsworth, 1985), p. 522.

9. The 'if not necessarily' clauses in this paragraph are needed so as not to suggest that either Angus or myself holds that 'Reason as Master' and 'Reason as Slave' perspectives *logically entail* moral relativism, or nihilism. Both of us, however, are more concerned with the actual world than with logically possible or necessary ones, hence the strong form of the statements. That we live in an intellectual climate today dominated by relativism—cognitive as well as moral—should be obvious to anyone who hasn't spent the last decade living in a clothes closet, and for nihilism, we don't need to cite neo-Nazis, 'skinheads', or the scourge of drugs: rather we can note that the most recent Attorney General of the United States, Edwin Meese, claimed moral stature simply on the grounds that a Special Prosecutor didn't believe he had sufficient evidence to convict Meese of felonies, even though they had probably been committed. (This tale goes back a long way; for summary, see the *Washington Post* 1/27/89). The other clause inserted in this paragraph of special note—"if we wish to lead meaningful lives"—also applies equally to Angus and myself: "'How shall I live' is the question from which philosophy starts and which eternally renews it" (p. 157).

10. See note 3.

11. While I argue below that Graham's position does in its own right require that the concept of choice be downgraded, if not abandoned, I must also confess to a not-so-subtle attempt to persuade him of the consonance of many of his views with those of the early Confucians, in whose ethics the

concept of choice plays no role. See my 'Why Take Rights Seriously? A Confucian Critique' in Leroy Rouner, ed., *Human Rights & the World's Religions*, Notre Dame, IN, 1988.

12. One might even go so far as to suggest that over-intellectualizing a relationship, or talking about it constantly with the other, will fairly well guarantee that the relationship will not long endure.

13. *Patterns, Thinking, and Cognition* (Chicago, 1987), p. 22. Italics added.

14. It is for this reason that I do not believe my statement that Graham must celebrate spontaneity conflicts with his statement that spontaneity is not in itself a virtue (p. 68).

15. Indeed, he says explicitly that questions about the goodness or "badness" of human nature are "pointless" (p. 29).

16. For further discussion on this topic, and citations, see my 'Against Relativism' in Gerald Larson and Eliot Deutsch, eds. *Interpreting Across Boundaries*, Princeton, NJ, 1988.

17. Graham does not give us a definition of 'good', but characterizes evil " . . . as the pure will to hurt others" (p. 176).

18. For fuller discussion, see 'Against Relativism', op. cit.

19. Blaise Pascal, *Pensées* (Harmondsworth, 1966) 423. Graham, I believe, would place Pascal in the anti-rationalist camp despite the latter's Christian devotion, for he stated succinctly what must be the anti-rationalist credo: "Two excesses: to exclude reason, to admit nothing but reason" (ibid., p. 183).

20. Not to mention all the topics not discussed herein, especially science, the sacred, and Graham's insights into texts as different as the Torah and *The Genealogy of Morals*, the *Chuang Tzu* and *Justine*.

21. References to Kierkegaard on this point are in my 'Kierkegaard & Confucius: On Finding the Way', in *Philosophy East & West*, vol. 36, no. 3. The quote from Paul Tillich is in his *Dynamics of Faith* (New York, 1958), p. 3.

22. Here I must confess forgetfulness or be liable to a charge of plagiarism, and opt for the former. I have long thought that something very like this quote came either from Yeats or Wilfred Owen, but have not been able to find it in either of their collected works, nor have I been able to locate it anywhere else; but I remain fairly certain that it is not original with myself.

23. Robert Frost, 'The Mending Wall'. Frost is, of course, equally well known for the line "Something there is that doesn't love a wall," which is not easy to square with "good fences make good neighbors"—at least in the realm of logic.

24. *A Theory of Justice*, op. cit., p. 12. Italics added.

25. Ibid., p. 18. Italics added.

26. Graham, I am confident, would rely on the *OED*; being even more old-fashioned, I take *Webster's Second International Dictionary* as gospel.

27. Thomas Nagel, *The View from Nowhere* (Oxford, 1986). Angus might object to my adopting Nagel's phraseology to his own, but the several descriptions of viewpoints in *R & S* countenances my interpretation. Awareness must be, variously, from "your viewpoint", (p. 16); the "sufferer's viewpoint", (p. 70); "another's viewpoint", (p. 25); "other viewpoints", (p. 45); "all other viewpoints", (p. 16); "independent of viewpoint", (ibid.); and more.

28. Paraphrased from the section 'Of Personal Identity' in Book I of *A Treatise of Human Nature* (Harmondsworth, 1985), p. 300, uniformly replacing "perception" with "role", and making suitable adjustments elsewhere. Accepting as I do the Socratic possibility—enunciated in the *Apology*—that I may have to confront Hume's shade in the next world, I draw sustenance from the belief that Confucius would be sufficiently amused by my altering of Hume's wording that he would intervene on my behalf, so that I might escape the good Scotsman's wrath. For fuller discussion of the significance of roles even within the modern Western moral tradition, see 'Role as a Complex Moral Concept', by Judith Andre of Old Dominion University (unpublished mss.).

29. To be sure, Graham does wonder about the reference of 'I' in *R & S*. He includes his 'Sun Beneath the Coral' poem as an Interlude in the book because it was the result of his experiments with "automatic writing", prompted by his reading of texts discussed in the section on "anti-rationalism" in *R & S*. And his wonder is reflected both before and after the Interlude. But a careful reading suggests strongly that the wonder never ceases, and the 'I' that Graham analyzes retains, in the end, essential features of the 'I' portrayed in the Cartesian/Humean picture of what it is to be a human being. Relatedly, while I believe Graham's critique of Nietzsche is important and incisive, his neglect of a Nietzschean theme allows a refutation of the critique, very different from, but nevertheless akin to, my own arguments against Graham in this section. In *The Will to Power*, Nietzsche maintains that

> . . . The assumption of one single subject is perhaps unnecessary; perhaps it is just so permissible to assume a multiplicity of subjects, whose interacton and struggle in the bases of our thought and our consciousness—in general? . . . My hypothesis: the subject as multiplicity.

Whether Nietzsche altogether rejects the conceptual framework of modern Western value theory, or is simply in reaction thereto, is irrelevant for present purposes. If Graham, after (correctly) criticizing the Swiss philologist's egoism, orders him to "Be aware", the latter may appropriately ask to whom the order is being given. As he says again in the *The Genealogy of Morals*:

> It is only the snare of language . . . presenting all activity as conditioned by an agent—the 'subject'—that blinds us to this fact . . . that no such agent exists; there is no 'being' behind the doing, acting, becoming; the 'doer' has simply been added to the deed by the imagination—the doing is everything.

Similarly, even though her own position is anti-Nietzschean, Hannah Arendt in *The Human Condition* stresses the question against Graham, "*Who* is aware (who is moved)?" Only through our deeds, Arendt argues, do

> . . . men show who they are, reveal actively their unique personal identities and thus make their appearance in the human world. But this can almost never be achieved as willful purpose as though one possessed and could dispose of his qualities. On the contrary, it is more than likely that the "who", which appears so clearly and unmistakeably to others, remains hidden from the person himself.

For a fuller discussion of these issues of the self in Nietzsche and Arendt, see 'Arendt, Identity, and Difference', by B. Honig in *Political Theory*, vol. 16, no. 1, from which all the quotations in this endnote were taken. I hope that my own criticisms of Graham's retention of the concept of the individual self—as a *self*, not merely that which can be individuated—are sufficiently clear that no one will assume that I am here merely invoking Nietzsche (or Arendt) in support for my basic case.

30. See note 11.

PART TWO

Reflections
and Replies
Angus C. Graham

When my friend Henry Rosemont first told me of this project my delight in being so honoured was not in the least sullied by my carefree promise to write reflections and replies. My alarm grew as it became clear that this particular *Festschrift* was not going to be delayed year after year, was *not* going to be posthumous. However, the papers have turned out to be very interesting, and in the words of *The Importance of Being Earnest*, replying to them has been more than a duty, it has been a pleasure.

Lau

We begin modestly with a case of the minute scholarly disagreement, with each of us hoping, by the addition of a few particles more to the tiny accumulation of evidence, to tip the scales in his own favour. The words *zai* 在 and *you* 宥 appear together at the head of *Zhuangzi* chapter 11, referring to a way of running the Empire which instead of ruling confines the people to a simple life in which they have no opportunity to corrupt their nature by sophisticated desires. This is the only generally acknowledged example of the two words in conjunction; but I claim to find another (graphically corrupted) in *Zhuangzi* chapter 2, Professor Lau another (with the words rather far apart) in *Lushi chunqiu*. We agree in taking *zai* as some sort of causative usage or derivative of *zai* 'be in', and *you* as *you* 囿 'pen, enclosure'. On my account, *zai* 'recognizing as there' and *you* 'enclosing by a line' in *Zhuangzi* chapter 2 are the first and least disruptive steps in organizing a cosmos, prior to dividing up and disputing over; similarly in chapter 11 *zai* 'keeping in place' and *you* 'keeping within bounds' are the first and least disruptive steps in organizing society, preceding social divisions and the apparatus of government. In terms of the Taoist rural Utopia where everyone hears the cocks and dogs of neighbouring villages without leaving his own, they amount to keeping each person content to stay where he was born with horizons too limited to allow further ambitions.

Lau gives an excellent account of *bie you* 別 宥, which he translates 'detach oneself from one's confinement', a concept of Song Xing which has attracted little attention. My only reservation is that although in later Chinese *bie* can of course be used transitively of parting *from*, in pre-Han language one expects it to mean 'distinguish *between*'. *Bie you* is perhaps 'separating pens', showing how different thinkers are confined by different limitations, as when Xunzi criticizes Mozi's vision as confined by utility, Hui Shi's by words, Zhuangzi's by Heaven (*Xunzi* HY 21/2f). The following would then be illustrations of *bie you*

Zhuangzi 24/33f 知士無思慮之變則不樂, 辯士無談說之序則不樂, 察士無淩誶之事則不樂, 皆囿於物者也.

"The man of knowledge is unhappy without something new to think about, the rhetorician without a case to organize, the investigator without a matter for interrogation; they are all men penned in by other things."

33/79f 能勝人之口, 不能服人之心, 辯者之囿也.

"Being able to make others submit from the mouth but not from the heart was the penning-in [the limitation] of the sophists."

It is in a criticism of narrow-minded vision that Lau finds his example of *zai* with *you*, although not in immediate conjunction with it

(Lau p. 17). Narrow minds "are penned in somewhere" 有 所 尢 (=囿) and this is because "their thoughts are on something" 意 有 所 在 . There are a couple of difficulties here. The ideal villager, like the narrow thinker, has limited horizons, but not surely because his mind is fixed in one direction. No doubt he concentrates on the affairs of his own village to the extent of seeing nothing outside, but this hardly fits the description "One who looks eastwards does not see the west wall and one who looks southwards does not see the north." Moreover, even if we grant that the Taoist ruler distracts people from looking outside the village and ensures that their minds "are on" (*zai*) their own affairs, that is a long way from establishing a usage by which *zai* itself can be translated 'distract'. Lau is claiming a technical use of *zai* which amounts to 'cause to keep the mind on something'.

In developing his case for this suspect usage, Lau offers actual examples of the phrase *zai tianxia* with *tianxia* 'empire' as object of *zai* as in the *locus classicus*. The first is not in doubt but is only partially relevant: 未 暇 在 天 下 也. "I have no time to attend to the empire". This is evidence that *zai tianxia* can mean 'have one's mind on the empire', not 'cause the empire to have its mind on something', which would assume a quite different syntax. Lau's crucial example is the second of two in *Laozi*; we must look at both.

Laozi 32 譬 道 之 在 天 下 猶 川 谷 之 於 江 海.

Lau (*Lau Tzu: Tao te ching* Penguin Classics 91): "The way *is to* the world as the River and the Sea are to rivulets and streams".

(Mawangdui text) 俾 道 之 在 天 下 也, 猷 小 浴 之 與 江 海 也.

Lau (*Chinese classics* 317): "The way in *distracting* the empire is similar to the case of a small valley in relation to the River and the Sea."

Here the comparison is with a spatial relation, so that the normal sense of *zai* ('be in') fits perfectly. Lau himself originally took it for granted, but in his new version has changed it to agree with his new interpretation of the next passage.

Laozi 49 聖 人 在 天 下, 歙 歙 為 天 下 渾 其 心. [5]
(Mawangdui text) 耴 人 之 在 天 下 也, 歙 歙 焉 為 天 下 渾 心.

Lau: "The sage in his attempt to distract the attention of the empire seeks urgently to muddle its mind".

But without a single other example of *zai* in the sense of 'distract' (as distinct from *zai* in contexts which are about distraction), we have no reason to depart from Wang Pi's understanding of the passage: "The sage in his position in the empire urgently for the sake of the empire muddles his own mind". The sage reduces himself to the perfect ignorance of the common man, as implied at the beginning of the stanza (Lau: "The sage has no constant mind of his own. He takes as his own the mind of the people"). It may be noticed that in order to make it the people who have their minds muddled, Lau in his translation has had to slide past the phrase *wei tianxia* "for the sake of the empire".

Lau leaves open the question whether we have another example of *zai you* corrupted in chapter 2, observing that "even if we choose to see a connection, not much light is thrown by the chapter 2 passage on the expression." This may be so, but the connection if accepted would certainly have a negative implication; the chapter 2 passage is about dividing up the cosmos, and a restored *zai you* could not refer to providing fixed objects of attention to distract the people. It would at least commit us to assuming the causative use of *zai* 'be in' implied by my translations, "recognize as there" in chapter 2 where the context is cosmic, "keep in place" in chapter 11 where it is social. But Lau has himself added to the evidence for taking chapter 2 into account. My original evidence was:

(1) In chapter 2, for *zuo you* 左 右 'left and right' the Cui version had 左 宥 , differing only slightly from 在 宥 .

(2) Among the words referred back to later in the passage, with slightly different graphs (we ignore the question of whether the differences are significant) we have 倫/論, 義/議 and 左 or 右/存, suggesting in the last case an emendation to 存 or to its graphic, phonetic and semantic cognate 在 .

(3) In the context *zuo you* 'left and right' makes no sense, while *zai you* makes good sense as 'recognize as there' and 'enclose by a line'.

To these Lau adds two more points.

(4) The original example of *zai you* in *Zhuangzi* chapter 11 itself has a variant *zuo you* in a *Huainanzi* parallel—a complete and pleasant surprise to me.

(5) The graph 宥 is attested for *you* 'right' (Lau n 25). This implies that a scribe seeing the unfamiliar 在 宥 would be likely to read it as the familiar 左 宥. Wherever we meet both readings the presumption must be that, as the *lectio difficilior*, *zai you* is preferable to *zuo you*. I would still insist therefore that whatever we make of *zai you* we cannot afford to ignore the evidence of chapter 2.

As for whether the Primitivist chapters are closer to *Laozi* or to *Zhuangzi*, this is an issue on which I have contradicted myself in print. In 'How Much of *Chuang-tzu* Did Chuang-tzu Write?' I described the Primitivist as "an exponent of Lao-tzu's ideal of government, only incidentally interested in Chuang-tzu".[1] The grounds were the apparent abundance of direct quotations from *Laozi* in the Primitivist chapters.

(1) There are no less than three introduced by *Gu yue* 故曰 'Therefore it is said' (10/21, 26, 11/28). But when I came to translate *Zhuangzi* in 1981 it turned out that these and another passage with the same introductory formula (10/14) fit their context so badly that I rejected them all as glosses.

(2) There is a considerable parallel between *Zhuangzi* 10/31f and *Laozi* 80. Such parallels however impose no presupposition as to which text is the borrower. In *Laozi*, chapters 80, 81 stand at the end of the standard text but between 66 and 67 in the two Mawangdui manuscripts, so may be later additions. There is some reason to suspect that for chapter 80 (the rural Utopia) both *Laozi* and the Primitivist could be borrowing from a common source, possibly the *Shennong* classic.[2]

There is no presumption therefore that it is more profitable to read the Primitivist in the light, such as it is, of *Laozi* 49, than of a passage in the 'Inner' Chapters which seems actually to use *zai you*. Thus the Primitivist's dismissal of "being suited by what suits others and not by

what suits oneself" (8/32 適 人 之 適 而 不 自 適 其 適 者 也.)
is a thought in the manner of Zhuangzi rather than Laozi, and in fact
comes word for word from the 'Inner' Chapters (6/14).

Pulleyblank

It is agreeable that our long and fruitful dispute over negative *fu*
seems to be ending with both of us settling somewhere near the middle,
and new prospects for pre-Classical and Classical syntax opening in all
directions. We now find ourselves with two sets of words which in
Classical behave as though they incorporated an anaphoric pronoun.

(1) Verbs or quasi-verbs with termination -*n*: *ru* 如 'like'/*ran* 然 'so',
yu 於 'in'/*yan* 焉 'in it', *yue* 曰 'say'/*yun* 云 'say it'. Ted Pulleyblank shows
that these have other syntactic features in common.

(2) Pre-verbal negatives with termination -*t*: *bu* 不 'not'/*fu* 弗 'not
. . . it', *wu* 毋 'don't'/*wu* 勿 'don't . . . it'.

There is another word, not introduced by Pulleyblank here, which
may be seen as bridging the two series: *wu* 無 'not have'/*wang* 亡 'not
have it' (cf. my *Studies* 254–256). This is negative but a full verb, and the
termination, although not identical, is close to -*n*. The semantic
distinctions between the pairs of negatives (including *wu*/*wang*) do not
hold for pre-Classical, which implies that the terminations did not
originally serve an anaphoric function. I suggested that the function of
pre-Classical -*t* was aspectual, marking a change of state, which would
make it comparable with final particle *yi* 矣 in Classical. Pulleyblank
takes the further step of treating both terminations as originally
aspectual and possibly identifiable in other Chinese words and in
Tibetan, where "very generally, one might suggest that, where there is a
contrast, -*d* is associated with punctual actions and concrete nouns,
while -*n* is associated with states and abstract nouns" (p. 30).

Exploring these new prospects, how do we relate the earlier
aspectual and later anaphoric functions? Pulleyblank suspects that in
the case of -*n* they are somehow related by descent (p. 33). There seems
indeed to be no other explanation of the puzzling fact to which he calls
attention, that *yan* although anaphoric excludes *ye* 也 and *yi* 矣, as

though it were a final particle. For the classical negatives however Pulleyblank returns to Boodberg's proposal of phonetic fusion with pronoun object *zhi* 之, which implies that the phonetic and graphic identity of the pre-classical and classical words is coincidental. Although this is conceivable, and has a parallel in the particles *yue* and *yun* in the *Songs* which we agree in dissociating from the classical verbs, I am reluctant to give different solutions to what looks like the same problem. There may be a relation between anaphora and the aspect of the verb harking back to a preceding state, whether as continuing or as changed. If formerly I played football, now 'I still play' or 'I again play', or else 'I no longer play', which imply 'I play *it*' or 'I don't play *it*' respectively.

	Change of State	*Continuation or Recurrence of State*
ru X 'like X'		*ran* 'as before like' . . . 'like it (= so)'
yu X 'in X'		*yan* 'as before in' . . . 'in it'
	yue X 'say X'	*yun* 'as before say' . . . 'say it'
wu X 'not have X'		*wang* 'as before not have' . . . 'not have it'
bu verb X 'not do-to X'	*fu* verb 'not as before do-to' . . . 'not do-to it'	
wu verb X 'don't do-to X'	*wu* verb 'don't as before do-to' . . . 'don't do-to it'	

Yue 'say' is the only *-t* form which is affirmative. This would explain why it is also the only one which does not become anaphoric; it is only when negative that the punctual harks back to a preceding positive state.

The pre-verbal particles in the *Songs* which we take as unrelated to the verbs of saying fit this scheme only for *-t*.

Inception and Continuation	*Change of State*	*Prospect*
yu 于 (event gets going)	*yue* 曰 (event occurs)	*yun* 云 (event impends)

Like Pulleyblank, I take all three particles to derive from a single word probably with the sense 'go' ("*yun* and *yue*", p. 56f.). In prospective *yun* I guessed that the final *-n* marks circular motion ('goes round and round'), appealing to a variety of words for circular shape or motion which have this final (Pulleyblank in the study to which he refers pointed out a partially overlapping set, but sharing not the final but the initial), and to the tendency throughout the history of the language for verbs of circular motion such as *huan* 還 to generate temporal particles (ut sup 59). This speculation carries little weight, but Pulleyblank's new evidence about *-n* would not require one to abandon it. It might be possible to treat its use for the circular as a special case of a more general tendency to use *-n* of continuous or repeated motion, in which case I would no longer have to assume its entire independence of anaphoric *-n* (as ut sup 56).

Harbsmeier

Christoph Harbsmeier's classification of count, mass, and generic nouns is the most interesting contribution to classical grammar since Cikoski's of ergative and neutral verbs,[3] and demands a full rethinking of the conclusions for Chinese philosophy which Hansen drew from the no longer tenable assumption that classical nouns in general approximate to mass rather than count nouns.[4] My only serious reservation is as to whether Harbsmeier has successfully established a formal distinction between count and generic nouns, or whether we have to be content with the semantic difference that a preceding number counts individuals in the former case and variously divisible and countable kinds in the latter. The test of the classifiers does formally distinguish both these types from mass nouns, with which a classifier commonly precedes the noun and is obligatory in counting. But granted that the optional classifiers which follow some count nouns are not found with generic, even the count nouns with which we find them are too few to establish a clear distinction from generic. Harbsmeier proposes certain quantifiers as a further criterion, but here his account is confused.

> It turns out that count nouns may not only be quantified by *duo* 'much/many' and *shao* 'little/few' but also by *shu* 'a number of', *ge* 'each', *jian* 'each of the objects', *mei* 'every'. Mass nouns are never quantified by *shu*, *ge*, *jian* or *mei* . . . (p. 52)

It appears then that these quantifiers are shared by count and generic but not by mass nouns. But the next sentence treats them as exclusive to count nouns.

> If we study the scope of quantifiers like *ge*, *jian*, *mei* and *shu* we can make an extensive list of count nouns in Classical Chinese.

Later, when dealing with generic nouns, he mentions only *shu* 'a number of', as distinctive of count nouns (p. 55). But even his examples of *shu* on page 52 included one with *wu* 物 'thing', which he later declares himself inclined to class as generic (p. 57). Granted that, as he says, its classification deserves further study, it seems difficult on the face of it to think of a more obvious example of a generic noun than *wu* (*wan wu* 萬 物 'the myriad (kinds of) thing' 百 物, *bai wu* 'the hundred (kinds of) thing'). It appeals to me especially because in *Later Mohist Logic* 196f., 210, I noted as an isolated fact that *wu* in the *Canons* is mostly general but *shi* 實 'object' is particular, a distinction which immediately makes sense when they are recognized as a generic and a count noun respectively. If, as Harbsmeier was at one point suggesting, *ge*, *jian*, and *mei* also go exclusively with count nouns, there is the further difficulty that generic nouns would require quantifiers of their own of the type of 'each', and Harbsmeier does not propose any. With *wu* at least we certainly find the usual ones: *Zhuangzi* 17/44 兼 懷 萬 物 "cherish each of the myriad (kinds of) thing", *Gongsun Longzi* chapter 3 生於 物之各有名 " . . . . is born from each (kind of) thing having a name". However, it seems reasonable to accept count and generic nouns as sufficiently differentiated by the test of whether a preceding number counts individuals or kinds.

The most interesting conclusion for Chinese philosophy drawn by Hansen from his mass noun hypothesis was that China tends to divide the world down into variously divisible and countable parts, the West tends to assemble it from individuals marked by singular and plural number. This still holds if we reclassify philosophical terms as generic rather than mass nouns (few would be count nouns). A number preceding *dao* 道 'way', *li* 理 'pattern', *wu* 物 'thing', *lei* 類 'kind', *qi* 氣 'breath', is counting variously divisible units. That horses or chariots will be counted in only one way goes without saying irrespective of one's language, but it does seem that Classical Chinese, because it does not assimilate other nouns to count nouns by number termination, escapes our tendency to assimilate things in general to the organisms and artifacts which stand out from their surroundings as discrete individuals. Here is an unhackneyed example from a text in which I happen to be interested at the moment and would date about 230–200 B.C.E., *Heguanzi* 鶡冠子. In expounding a philosophy of the One it puts trees and grains on the same level as divisions of land.

> *Heguanzi* (chapter 9), Taoist Patrology edition, B, 15A/7f, 16A/4–7 古者亦我而使之久. 衆者亦我而使之 衆耳(天)夫度數之而行, 在一不少, 在萬不衆同 如林木積如倉粟斗石以陳, 升委無失也. 列地 分民, 亦尚一也耳.
>
> "It's simply that what is from the past we ourselves cause to continue, what is multiple we ourselves cause to be multiple . . . However you proceed in measuring and counting them, in the One there are no less of them, in the myriad no more. They are the same like trees of a forest, a collection like grains in the granary; in what you lay out in pecks nothing is missing in the pints. Lands you distribute and populations you divide are after all still simply one."

I am too ignorant of logic to want to appeal to the mereological set, but Harbsmeier's critique of its use by Hansen is a non-starter. Nobody does or could "anachronistically" attribute to the ancient Chinese "the *notion* of a spatio-temporal fusion", "the *notion* of a mereological set". To say "I find nothing whatever in all of traditional Chinese literature that even remotely suggests that the ancient Chinese ever thought of anything like mereology" (p. 50) is as though one were to dismiss Harbsmeier's own discovery with a "I find no evidence that the ancient Chinese had ever heard of your mass, count, and generic nouns." The argument is about the channelling of thinking by different linguistic structures, pre-philosophical, pre-literate. When a modern Chinese says *yige ren* and *yizhong ren*, is he thinking of 'one specimen of man' as parallel with 'one sort of man', as though dividing up man in two different ways? An elusive and perhaps wrongheaded question, but if we do pursue it we have to ask: 'How in our differently structured language are we to conceive a mankind divisible into individuals only as it is into kinds?' As a mass with discontinuous but similar parts perhaps, or if we are logicians as a mereological set; or we may prefer just to say that a language which classifies in this way treats class/member as one type of whole/part. Whatever the advantages and disadvantages of such descriptions, they are not being projected on to Chinese philosophers; on the contrary, until comparison between the languages raises the issue, Westerners and Chinese are on this matter simply thinking differently without conceptualizing how they think.

At every level of interpretation we are using our own 'notions' to explain Chinese notions to ourselves; we could not say even such a simple thing as 'Chinese philosophical thinking is primarily ethical and political' if it were open to the objection that 'philosophy', 'ethics' and 'politics' are un-Chinese concepts. There is no reason in principle why a reclassification of class/member under whole/part being tried out in the West at the highest level of abstraction by the most advanced logicians should not correspond to the natural classification in the language of a culture which could as well be pre-literate as philosophically sophisticated.

As for the 'White Horse', Hansen's great contribution in my judgment was to break our habit of approaching it as a class/member problem and switch attention to whole/part. My own explanation of the essay, which descends directly from one strand in Hansen's, is that it infers that a white horse is not a horse by applying the principle that the whole is not one of its own parts; the combination of white and horse is not the horse which is only one constituent. When writing on the sophism it did not occur to me that this whole/part interpretation had already become detached from the mass noun hypothesis which originally suggested it; my references in introducing the analysis to *ma* as mass noun and horse as 'mass with discontinuous parts similar in shape' were extraneous to the argument, as Harbsmeier perceives. With the recognition of *ma* as on Harbsmeier's classification a count noun, I am happy to discard them, and have done so in the account of Kung-sun Lung in *Disputers of the Tao*.

Major

It has long been recognized that 'Five Elements' is a seriously misleading equivalent for *Wu xing* 五 行, and John Major's proposal 'Five Phases' is with good reason coming to be accepted as a substitute. The only difficulty, as we both agree, is that although adequate from the Han onwards it does not fit pre-Han usage, for which I proposed 'Five Processes'. Here I must begin by clearing up a minor misunderstanding by Major, of my statement in *Yin-Yang and the Nature of Correlative Thinking* 77 that the old question "Why would wood or metal be called a *xing* 'going'?" has turned out to be a pseudo-problem. My point was not that it is useless to speculate about the pre-Han meaning but that before the Han wood or metal were *not* called *xing*; that term was indeed used for their 'goings', how they behaved in the hands of the craftsman—wood bending, metal oozing into the shape of the mould—so that there is no problem. In pre-Han usage wood, metal and the rest are the *wu cai* 五 材 'Five Materials', the processes proper to them are the *Wu xing* 五 行 'Five Processes', and the specific potencies actualized as the processes are the *Wu de* 五 德 'Five Powers', distinctions preserved right down to *Huainanzi*.

From Major's very interesting account of the *Huainanzi* cosmology we may see why the distinctions would lose their significance. The crucial change is that all process is now seen as transformation of the *qi* 氣. In the older cosmology that we find in the *Zuozhuan* the *Wu xing* are not *qi* at all; the 'Six *Qi*' (shade and sunshine, wind and rain, dark and light) belong to Heaven while the *Wu xing* belong to Earth.[5] In the new cosmology the *Wu xing* become phases in the cyclic transformations of the universal *qi*. Since *qi* is at once matter and process, an energetic fluid called Yang when active and Yin when passive, it ceased to be necessary to distinguish between Five Materials and Five Processes, which would only be the *qi* in its five phases seen from different aspects. Here my only reservation is that Major seems not to have quite thrown off the assumption that *qi* is *either* material *or* process. He asks: "If substance is *qi*, what is the *process* by which undifferentiated *qi* becomes the myriad things?" (p. 69). His answer is that the Four Seasons "transform undifferentiated turbid *qi* into the myriad things" (p. 70). He adds that "the creation of the seasons transforms the universe from a timeless to a temporal world, spacetime". But this does not agree with the *Huainanzi* text, which puts the four seasons rather late in the evolution of the cosmos but introduces *yu zhou* 宇宙 "cosmos-as-it-extends and cosmos-as-it-endures" before the *qi* itself, in the passage which Major translates "The nebulous void produced spacetime: spacetime produced *qi*" (p. 68 虛霩生宇宙，宇宙生氣). This confirms that Major's question is unnecessary; the nebulous becomes process enduring through time simultaneously with becoming material extended in space, and is then the *qi*.

Such capacity as I have to visualize the Chinese cosmos derives largely from Major's earlier paper 'The Five Phases, Magic Squares and Schematic Cosmography',[6] and his analysis here of the *Huainanzi* account of the Five Planets, with the Four Seasons fitting neatly without the need of a fifth to correlate with the centre, makes a significant addition.

Roth

Hal Roth's paper should cure us of any lingering tendency to think in terms of a Taoist school originating with Laozi and Zhuangzi, and of religious Taoism as a degenerate descendant or an independent movement only accidentally passing under the same name. In *Xunzi* and in 'Below in the Empire' Laozi and Zhuangzi appear separately among the rival philosophers without any suggestion that they belong together in a school called Taoist competing with Confucians and Mohists. The Taoist school which appears among the Six Schools of Sima Tan is a retrospective classification; and Roth shows clearly that it represented for him the early Han syncretism expounded in the final stratum of *Zhuangzi* and in *Huainanzi*, centered on the nurture of the *qi* 氣 (which at its purest is the *jing* 精) in order to become *shen* 神 'daimonic, clairvoyant' and *ming* 明 'illumined', and directly ancestral to the religious Taoism of the Later Han. This newly emerging school recognized *Laozi* as its classic and Zhuangzi as a forebear; but it is only by a much later retrospection in the third century C.E. that readers of *Laozi* and *Zhuangzi* began to pair them as representatives of a purer philosophy, the 'Lao-Zhuang' which we now call 'philosophical Taoism'.

This paper, and earlier contacts with Roth, have done much to shift my own perspective on Taoism. There remain however a few points of disagreement. I am not persuaded that the early Han Taoism so well elucidated by Roth can be fully identified with the Huang-Lao, 'the doctrine of the Yellow Emperor and of Laozi', which Sima Qian mentions as prevalent in this period, and would prefer to think of it more generally as a '*Laozi*-centred syncretism' in contrast with the 'Confucius-centred syncretism' of the *Yi* appendices and Dong Zhongshu. Our clearest evidence for Huang-Lao is the Mawangdui manuscript combining *Laozi* with previously unknown documents which claim the authority of the Yellow Emperor. The Yellow Emperor documents teach a much narrower syncretism, based primarily on *Laozi* and Legalism, combined much as in chapters 5 and 8 of *Han Feizi*. Sima Qian mentions the Jixia thinkers as well as Shen Buhai and Han Fei as learning from Huang-Lao, which Guo Moruo took as evidence that there was an established Huang-Lao school going right back to Jixia in the fourth century B.C.E.[7] But if we are to treat Sima Tan's 'Taoist school' as a retrospective classification we must certainly do the same with the 'doctrine of the Yellow Emperor and Laozi'; neither the book *Laozi* nor the philosophical exploitation of the Yellow Emperor can be confidently traced further back than 250 B.C.E. Sima Qian's references are evidence only that in the books of Han Fei and the rest of them he found the doctrine which was called Huang-Lao in his own time. It is notable that of those he mentions the ones of whom we know anything came to be classed as Legalists; and the one of whom more than fragments survive, Han Fei, is very far from the kind of Taoism examined by Roth, but in chapters 5 and 8 does approach the *Laozi*-Legalist fusion of the Mawangdui manuscript. There is the further point that none of the documents on which Roth relies gives a special place to the Yellow Emperor. Throughout the literature of the third and second century B.C.E. the legends of Shennong and the Yellow Emperor develop in interaction as representatives of rival tendencies to political centralization and decentralization (cf. my *Studies* 94–100). The name of the Yellow Emperor, the inventor of the state and of war, may well have been chosen to represent the Legalist side of Huang-Lao; whether this was the case or not, we can hardly class a text as Huang-Lao if it shows a positive preference for Shennong. But the main political chapter of *Huainanzi*, the *Zhushu* (chapter 9), mentions only Shennong, in agreement with Roger Ames's claims in his *Art of Rulership*[8] for the anti-authoritarian tendency of this chapter.

A well substantiated, and exceedingly remarkable, conclusion of Roth's paper is that, if we look back from the perspective of the school first identifying itself as Taoist in the second century B.C.E., the direct ancestor of its special combination of cosmology, psychology, and politics and its constellation of key terms (*Dao, qi, jing, shen, ming*) is not *Laozi* but the long neglected *Neiye* 'Inward Training' in *Guanzi*, which I agree with him in dating not later than 300 B.C.E. It seems that the heart of the teaching first called 'Taoism' is not the thought of *Laozi* and *Zhuangzi* but a technique of meditation starting from breath control, which before the Han had not been associated with any particular philosophical school, but lay at the disposal of anyone for the care of health or longevity, for the cultivation of powers of mind, even for Confucian moral training. It left few traces in pre-Han literature because it belonged to that world of specialists—of astronomers, music masters, physicians, diviners, shamans—whose systems of cosmic correlations were ignored by the philosophical schools until the late third century B.C.E., but became dominant during the Qin and Han. It was never embodied in a text accepted as canonical by all, and the *Neiye* merely happens to be its first surviving document. Among pre-Han thinkers who occasionally mention the nurture of the *qi* we find

Zhuangzi of course, but also the Confucians Mencius and Xunzi. The Han bibliography enters under the Confucian school a *Neiye* in 15 *pian*, one of which could well be the extant *pian* with this title, which acknowledges the Confucian virtues. Why then did Han Taoism see Laozi as its ancestor? Because, I would suggest, the Way of *Laozi* was understood to be the unformulable path which opens when you return to the ultimate source of things in meditation. As the Taoist school emerges, its techniques and concepts demand a unifying philosophy, for which meditation is a means, not merely to health, immortality, magical powers or Confucian moral education, but to the discovery of the Way itself.

Guan Feng's proposal that *Zhuangzi* was compiled in the court of the Prince of Huainan remains very attractive but without clinching proof. There are two questions here: (1) Does the present text descend from a version annotated by the Huainan circle? (2) Were the Huainan circle themselves the compilers of the book? The first question can be answered with a confident Yes. According to Lu Deming, the fifty-two chapter *Zhuangzi* on which Sima Biao commented included, in addition to the Inner, Outer and Mixed Chapters, three chapters of 'Explanations' (*Jie shuo* 解 説). The *Zhuangzi* of the Han bibliography had fifty-two chapters, so included these explanations. Of the two Huainan writings on *Zhuangzi* known by the quotations which Roth translates, the *Hou jie* 后 解 has a suggestively similar title, and the *Lue yao* 略 要 is actually cited with Sima Biao's comment; moreover, as Roth observes, Guo Xiang is abridging the book mentioned that 'some comes from Huainan' (或 出 淮 南). The chances that the extant book has glosses from these lost explanations are high; Roth notes some possibilities, and another which might be worth inquiry is raised by the commentary on the 'Yangist miscellany' chapters 28–31. The notes are sparse and do not look like Guo Xiang's.

(1) Chapters 28 and 31 end with summaries of the thought of 'this chapter' (此 篇).

(2) Of the three episodes of chapter 29 ('Robber Zhi'), the first ends with a summary of 'this chapter', the others with summaries of 'this section' (此 章). Apparently the notes come from a version in which the 'Robber Zhi' chapter consisted only of the first episode.

(3) Other than the summaries there are only two notes, earlier in chapter 28.

The *Lue yao* ('Summarized Essentials') would have consisted of such summaries. Although I have made no detailed comparison with *Huainanzi* or with the rest of the Guo Xiang commentary, it is worthy of remark that this very limited material shares no less than three phrases with the tiny *Lue yao* quotation, 'knights of the river and the sea' (江 海 之 士), 'mountains and valleys' (山 谷) as retreats for hermits, and 'take the world lightly' (輕 天 下), the last a phrase not found anywhere in the text of *Zhuangzi*.

However, the annotator of a book is not usually under suspicion of having compiled the book himself. As for the compilation of *Zhuangzi*, Roth shows that the syncretism of the last stratum is very close to that of *Huainanzi*, and that the paired words in the 'Inner' Chapter titles are even commoner in the latter than in the former. Of early Han centres of learning in which *Zhuangzi* might be compiled, the Huainan is no doubt the most suitable that we know, and the date is about right. But it is part of Roth's case that this kind of syncretism is *not* specific to the Huainan circle, that it is the general early Han trend to which the name 'Taoist' was originally applied. I do not see that the Huainan ascription can be more than a very attractive conjecture.

Nivison

David Nivison's interesting account of the derivation of Xunzi's 'detachment' from Zhuangzi's and the difference between them left me with the uneasy feeling of assenting most of the time yet suspecting something elusive in his presuppositions with which I profoundly disagree, and which I think I have tracked down. After discussing at length the strand in their thought which he calls "detached", "disengaged", "unattached", he notes a respect in which " 'detachment'—our word, not Zhuangzi's—is misleading" (p. 132). Nivison resorts frequently to such phrases as " 'spectator' of the self" (p. 130) and "the cool, distanced analytical attitude" (p. 130), which suggest assimilation to a Western attitude of scientific objectivity, perhaps also to Indian models of non-attachment. My feeling of something wrong clarifies with his discussion of the episode of Zhuangzi poaching in the gamepark, which we both suspect represents a conversion experience. (I must confess, by the way, to not having noticed that this suggestion goes back to Maspero, to whom I should have paid more attention). Zhuangzi, we agree, is here abandoning the Yangist 'philosophy of withdrawal'; but according to Nivison what the incident discredited was not merely the possibility of escaping ties with other things, but "the philosopher's conceit that he can distance himself by simply observing" (p. 134). But is this a *Chinese* philosopher's conceit? Even if one claims to find it in the 'mystical' attitude of Taoism, is there anything to suggest that Yangists cultivated the attitude of pure observer? Yangists seem from the little we know of them to be quite unmystical, coolly weighing benefit against harm like Mohists, judging that the greatest external possession is not worth the slightest injury to the body, and consequently avoiding office for the sake of a moderate satisfaction of the desires which will not endanger health. Zhuangzi goes to the gamepark to poach, not to birdwatch; and granted that he forgets his purpose in the fascination of spectacle his insight that 'it is inherent in things that they are ties to each other' springs from observing as hunter a chain of hunter and hunted in which he himself turns out a moment later to be another of the hunted. Would Zhuangzi or any other Chinese thinker, pre-Buddhist at least, have to be told that "any philosophically saving 'spectator'-like quiescence must be concomitant with ongoing psychic and emotional 'activity' " (p. 135–36)?

Here I shall ride one of my hobby-horses, the place of awareness and spontaneity at the foundations of ancient Chinese thought. As modern Westerners our own paradigm is 'the rational Ego striving to control spontaneity', with spontaneous inclination located outside the Ego and subjected to its rational ends. We all perceive that this paradigm does not fit Chinese thought, but as Kuhn pointed out in philosophy of science, we do not escape one paradigm until we have another to put in its place.[9] When we meet the image of the mirror in Chinese thought, it remains natural for us to think of the mirroring as an objective knowledge detached from all subjective reactions, and of the 'True Men of old' who "did not know how to be pleased with life or to hate death" (*Zhuangzi* Harvard-Yenching 6/7f.) as pure observers detached from all emotion. I propose however as the Chinese paradigm 'the whole man guiding spontaneity by awareness', with his motivations never ceasing to be spontaneous however aware he becomes. In that case spontaneous reaction is modified by clarifying awareness without ever being suspended even in the mirror-like awareness of the sage. "The utmost man uses the heart like a mirror . . . he responds and does not store" (7/32f.). "If mere water clarifies when it is still, how much more the stillness of the quintessential-and-daimonic, the heart of the sage! It is the reflector of heaven and earth, the mirror of the myriad things. . . . At rest he empties, emptying he is filled, and what fills him sorts itself out. Emptying he is still, in stillness he is moved, and when he moves he succeeds." (13/4, 5f.) "Its stillness is like a mirror, it responds like an echo" (33/57). Then if Zhuangzi's sage mirroring things neither rejoices in life nor hates death, it is because his vision embraces both life and death without drawing a line between them; Xunzi's sage, also mirroring like clear water, does recognize the distinction, does rejoice and grieve, and so requires ritual to control joy and grief.

On this approach, one cannot take for granted that Xunzi's detachment is an advance on Zhuangzi's. They differ fundamentally in that the divisions marked by naming are subjective for Zhuangzi but objective for Xunzi. Zhuangzi soon escapes from grief at his wife's death, not into the impassivity of the detached observer, but into the exaltation of responding to the undivided, with the emotions specific to life and to death dissolving in the ecstatic acceptance of everything. For Xunzi on the contrary, although naming is conventional, the divisions they mark are inescapably *there*; and although instituted rituals are conventional, the emotions they guide are man's inevitable responses to the realities of life and death. For Zhuangzi (or his school, since the 'Inner' Chapters are not explicit on this point) the community of the idealized past was socially undifferentiated, and although (as Nivison points out) you do adapt to the social order in which you happen to find yourself, it is a matter of "roaming free inside its cage" (*Zhuangzi* 4/29); but for Xunzi divisions have the same unchanging validity between social superior and inferior as between Heaven above and earth below.

Nivison notes that Xunzi's viewpoint "is simply blind to the 'facts-values' dichotomy that is natural to most of us" (p. 140), "a way of

thinking that just seemed obvious to third and second century B.C.E.
China". I would add that, being myself a convert to what I take to be the
Chinese paradigm ("the whole man guiding spontaneity by awareness"), it also seems obvious to me. My justification would be from the
quasi-syllogism on which I debate with Fingarette and Rosemont below.
Granted the value of knowledge, the fully informed reaction—how you
do spontaneously react when mirroring the object as though in clear
water—is also the better reaction. For Zhuangzi, this is the unique
response, of one person at one moment, when conventional classifications fixed by names are no longer obscuring his vision of the scene.
Xunzi on the contrary accepts these classifications, and holds that you
mirror most accurately when you understand that things are related in
a series of proportional oppositions—Heaven : earth :: male : female ::
husband : wife :: father : son :: ruler : subject :: high : low. . . . (I follow
Nivison in taking the examples from the *Xu gua*). Throughout this
series of binary oppositions, Xunzi (and Chinese culture generally)
responds by valuing A above B. Then granted that the cosmos is so
ordered that Heaven *does* contrast with earth as man with woman and
ruler with subject, and Xunzi in comprehending this order *does* find
himself spontaneously preferring Heaven to earth, man to woman,
ruler to subject, then this is the right way for Xunzi to react; and for all
who with the same knowledge would react similarly (all mankind,
Xunzi supposes), this is the right Way to recommend to them. We
cannot object to Xunzi that he confuses fact and value, only that (1) the
cosmos isn't ordered like that, and (2) even if it is, Xunzi's Way will not
be valid for such as the author of *Laozi* who does not share his
spontaneous preference for A.

Ames

One of the most familiar generalizations about Chinese thought is
that it tends to treat opposites not as conflicting but as complementary,
as in Yin-Yang schematism. It is a thought which has been given new
life by the proposal of Derrida that at the back of the 'logocentric'
tradition of the West there is a chain of oppositions in which we strive to
abolish B in favour of A, signified/signifier, speech/writing, reality/

appearance, nature/culture, life/death, good/evil.[10] In *Thinking through Confucius*[11] Roger Ames and his collaborator David Hall developed the thesis that for the West A is 'transcendent' in the sense that you can have A without B but not B without A, while for China A and B are mutually dependent. In the Chinese cosmos all things are interdependent, without transcendent principles by which to explain them or a transcendent origin from which they derive; it does not however quite fit Needham's description of it as 'organic', since it is also without transcendent ends. A novelty in this position which greatly impresses me is that it exposes a preconception of Western interpreters that such concepts as *Tian* 'Heaven' and *Dao* 'Way' must have the transcendence of our own ultimate principles; it is hard for us to grasp that even the Way is interdependent with man. However, Confucius said that 'Man is able to enlarge the Way, it is not that the Way enlarges man' (*Analects* 15/29); and if I may quote again the neglected text from circa 230–200 B.C.E. in which I happen at the moment to be especially interested, *Heguanzi* treats the Way as interdependent with the active and passive kinds of intelligence in the spirits and in man, *shen* 'clairvoyance' and *ming* 'illumination'.

Heguanzi (chapter 14) C, 10A/2–7 道乎道乎與神明相保乎.龐子曰何如而相保.鶡冠子曰賢生聖聖生道道生法法生神神生明神明者正之末也.末受之本是故相保.

" 'The Way, the Way!
It protects and is protected by clairvoyance and illumination.' 'How do they protect each other?' said Pangzi. Heguanzi said,
'Worth generates sagehood, sagehood the Way, the Way law, law clairvoyance, clairvoyance illumination. Clairvoyance and illumination adjust it at the tips, the tips draw it from the root, therefore they protect each other.' "

Ames's paper persuades me that the translation of *xing* 性 by 'nature' predisposes us to mistake it for a transcendent origin, which in Mencian doctrine would also be a transcendent end. (Whether it is worth looking for a more adequate equivalent is another matter; since all translation equivalents of philosophical concepts are inadequate, my own view is that it is useless to tinker with them beyond a certain point.) *Xing* is conceived in terms of spontaneous development in a certain direction rather than of its origin or goal. Admittedly I have myself elsewhere referred to the *sheng* 生 'generation' and *cheng* 成 'completion' of each thing according to its *xing* 'nature' as recalling Aristotelian potentiality and actualization (*Studies* 55), and described Yangist and Mohist discussions of what action is 'for the sake of' (*wei* 為) in terms of ends versus means (*Studies* 404–407). However, as I acknowledged in the latter case, Chinese thinkers talk about desires and dislikes (*yu wu* 欲 惡) and about intent (*zhi* 志) without having a term for the goal of desire or intent other than *so wei* 所為 'what it is for the sake of', which is used more often of the beneficiary (oneself, family, state, the world) than of the goal. The *cheng* 成 'completion' of a thing's development, which in man is his *cheng* 誠 'integrity', is the interdependent becoming integral rather than the realization of an end.

Although I am convinced by much of Ames's paper, and of *Thinking through Confucius*, both seem to me the worse for a confusion between translation and exposition which undermines his own argument. Thus Ames says that the opening of the *Zhongyong* (天命之謂性) "is often conceptualized and translated with strongly essentialistic assumptions to assert that 'What is decreed by Heaven is called the *xing*' ", and decides that this phrase "might be more appropriately rendered 'the relationships that obtain between man and his world (*tian ming*) are what is meant by *xing*'." (p. 154) To me, the second version is not a translation at all. Granted that there can be different opinions about what counts as legitimate translation, it is reasonable to insist that a philosophical translator does his best to approximate to the key concepts of the original and to their logical relations, to follow the structure of the thought rather than reprocess it; full success is unattainable of course, so to the extent that translation fails one supplements it by exposition. The key terms here are *tian* 'Heaven' and *ming* 'decree', linked in *tian ming* 'decree of Heaven' to make a metaphor from the edicts of human rulers; why is this crucial metaphor missing in the second version? Instead we have a completely Westernized reconceptualization, with 'relationships' between man and '*his* world', the last a startlingly un-Chinese concept. As for 'relationships', relation is no doubt an indispensable concept in *exposition* of Chinese thought, which generally impresses a Westerner as more concerned with the relations between things than with their qualities; but the concern is with concrete patterns rather than relations abstracted from them, as Ames knows well. There are few if any terms in Chinese philosophical discourse sufficiently close for one to risk 'relation' or 'relationship' as English equivalent in a context where it will carry philosophical weight. Ames's English would do as exposition, but presented as translation it conveys the false information that the Chinese *says* that *xing* consists of relationships. One must insist that there is no latitude for more than trivial variations on 'It is the decreed by Heaven which is called "*xing*" '.

This may look like nit-picking, but the point is that here Ames professes to test his thesis against a concrete example. He has to show that it fits a Chinese definition, *not* as the relationship between man and his world, but as the decreed by Heaven. The metaphor of the decree is in the Chinese and cannot be conjured away by manipulating the English. If it does imply 'essentialism', then so be it; this will have to be acknowledged by Ames as a serious counter-example. But all Ames does is substitute for *tian ming* a summary of what, assuming his thesis, the text should have said. The consequence is that the *Zhongyong* definition will no longer serve as a test case; and if all examples are to be handled in this way, the thesis will be irrefutable in principle, so meaningless. The odd thing is that this undermining of his own case is quite unnecessary. Why does Ames suppose that a translation faithful to the metaphor of the decree has 'strong essentialistic assumptions'? The decree of the ruler is not a transcendent A; on the contrary it suggests just that interdependence of A (changing commands and prohibitions) and B (changing behavior and conditions of subjects) on which Ames insists. *Mencius* 7A/2 is explicit that, although "There is nothing which is not the Decree" (莫 非 命 也), what is decreed for me changes with how I behave: 'Therefore someone who knows the Decree does not go on standing under a toppling wall' (是 故 知 命 者 不 立 乎 巖 牆 之 下). Similarly, *xing* will be spontaneous process with a direction continually modified by the effects on it of deliberate action. For this to be fully intelligible, however, we have to break out of the paradigm of an Ego utilizing the spontaneous in the service of rational ends; for one still thinking inside it, any change which his actions effect in his own character is most easily conceived as not spontaneous but deliberate, not decreed by Heaven but chosen by himself. Chinese philosophy however, according to my own favourite Grand Generalization, has a different paradigm for man, with deliberate action starting from inclinations which not by choice but spontaneously shift with shifts of awareness. This would explain how personal development can be affected by choice without itself being chosen. Not only in childhood or adolescence, but at every stage in the lives even of the most intellectual, changes in valuation have little to do with deduction from rational principles, indeed are largely unconscious; the shifts in a person's tastes and aspirations with developing knowledge and experience, or in what we call his 'character' or even his 'nature', are more clearly apparent to others than to himself. For many, to acknowledge this is to impugn the rationality of man; but I would appeal to the logic of the quasi-syllogism which I defend against Fingarette below, by which preferring the inclination which matures with increasing awareness is on the contrary supremely rational.

Still riding my own hobby-horse, might one distinguish *xin* 'heart' and *xing* 'nature' as the centres of awareness and spontaneity respectively? This would agree with the account of the heart in *Mencius* 6A/15.

耳目之官不思,而蔽於物。物交物,則引之而已矣。心之官則思,思則得之,不思則不得也。

"The organs eye and ear do not think, and are deluded by other things; it is simply that, as things in touch with things, the others attract them. As for that organ the heart, it does think; and if you do think you get it [the right course of action], if you don't think you don't."

With the exercise of the heart for thinking, spontaneous inclination shifts away from the direction in which it is pulled by the mere action of the perceived thing on the senses. Mencius had no need to specify what the thinking is about—facts of the case, maxims, exemplars; it is enough that, since by thinking one becomes more aware, spontaneous change will be for the better. This would account for the passage which Ames cites (p. 000) as having misled readers into confusing *xing* with *xin* 'heart':

Mencius 7A/1 盡 其 心 者 知 其 性 也。知 其 性 則 知 天 矣。

"To exhaust your heart is to know your nature, and if you know your nature you know Heaven."

In unawareness you know only present inclination; it is by full exertion of the heart to understand the things which act on you that you come to know what Heaven has ordained as the spontaneous preference of your nature in full awareness of them.

Hansen

Chad Hansen, with whom I share the combination of a respect for Chinese thought with a distaste for the assumption of some of its admirers that it is a compliment to it to call it irrationalist, sets out to clarify the conceptual differences between Chinese rationality and Western. I like this kind of try at the Grand Generalisation establishing some fundamental distinction between Western and Chinese thought; and although my own happens to be different—so that I shall be on the offensive throughout—Hansen's has certainly progressed since its first statement in *Language and Logic in Ancient China*.[12] He starts with a detailed account of the system of concepts—truth, logic, meaning, sentence, centred on Reason—which he takes to be characteristically Western. Arriving at an objective view of one's own preconceptions is the biggest difficulty in comparing one's own scheme with another, so that Hansen deserves our gratitude for putting the comparison on such a firm basis. Since the whole group of concepts is missing in China, he infers that Chinese thinkers cannot be classed either as defenders of the *concept* of Reason ('contrastive rationalists') or as opponents of it ('contrastive irrationalists' or 'contrastive anti-rationalists'). Since however they do give reasons for their claims, he calls them 'non-contrastive rationalists'. This classification has no point of contact with my own (in

which, for example, a contrast between 'anti-rationalism' and 'irrationalism' is the theme of part 3 of *R & S*), so that I have no quarrel with
it if it suits him. Hansen however assumes that I do credit the Chinese
with the concept of Reason, which would make the issue real. Here we
find ourselves divided by fundamentally different attitudes, mine being
that of an empiricist-bred Brit suspicious of abstractions, whose study
of Chinese language and thought has tended to reinforce for him some
of the elsewhere fading influence of the English school of what used to
be called Linguistic Philosophy. For me, to think of a Western concept
such as Reason as hovering somewhere up in the air, and to ask whether
it ever came down in China, is Platonism, of which neither of us would
wish to be accused; the point is, on the one hand to decide how much of
Chinese thinking is what *we* would call rational, on the other to look for
the Chinese words which can profitably be compared and contrasted
with 'Reason', as one compares and contrasts the philosophical terms
with multiple and shifting meanings in different periods or schools in
the West. I find it convenient to call the Mohists and Sophists
'rationalistic' in tendency because they rely on analytic thinking, and
Taoists 'anti-rationalistic' because they deride it. However described,
this is an important difference which disappears if all Chinese thought
is reduced to 'non-contrastive rationalism', including presumably even
that of texts such as the *Analects*, *Laozi*, and the *Yi* which hardly ever
offer us what a Westerner would acknowledge as a reason. There is a
point in asking how far the Chinese concept of *bian* resembles and
differs from ours of rational discourse, but none to my mind in
stressing that China lacks the concept of Reason, or of Philosophy,
Ethics, Politics, Freedom, Justice, Civilization, Art. . . . If a culture so
remote from ours did turn out to have a word with the same complex
ramifications of meaning as one of these, indeed had any perfect
synonym of a term outside logic and mathematics, what could it be but a
freak of chance without significance?

   In recent years, partly under the influence of Hansen's *Language
and Logic in Ancient China*, I have become increasingly interested in the
place of distinguishing, classifying and regulative naming in Chinese
thought. But by asking "Do they have the concept of Reason (or Truth,
or Meaning), yes or no?", Hansen manoeuvres himself into a position of
making the Chinese preoccupation with dividing and naming the

Chinese *alternative* to the Western with establishing truths by reason. It seems to me crucial to maintain the distinction between the structures of thinking, which may be presumed to be transcultural (2 and 2 make 4 wherever you are), and its varying conceptualizations in different cultures. In *Yin-Yang and the Nature of Correlative Thinking* I contrasted 'correlative' with 'analytic' thinking, using for the former Roman Jakobson's terminology of similarity/contiguity, paradigm/syntagm, metaphor/metonym. You are thinking correlatively if you justify grading ruler above subject by their places in a scheme of things dividing along a chain of superior A contrasting with inferior B by the proportional oppositions 'Heaven : earth :: above : below.....::ruler : subject', which is *lun* 論 'sorting, grading'; you are thinking analytically when like Mozi or Xunzi you argue that only unification under a ruler saves mankind from anarchy, or like Mencius that some men ruling and others obeying belongs to a division of labour to the advantage of all, which is *bian* 'argumentation'. The former kind of thinking tends in Chinese to short parallel phrases, the latter to long sentences syntactically organized by particles. I argued (against the assumption of the Western tradition that Reason equated with analyis can be fully independent) that the analytic depends on the correlative, which however is untestable without it. In our ordinary common-sense thinking (which is also that of Xunzi or Han Fei), correlation is guided and corrected by analysis; on the other hand even the purest analysis never, outside logic and mathematics, escapes the formation of its initial concepts by correlation. Correlative thinking fits Hansen's account of Chinese thinking in general, in operating with names not sentences, in order to establish the appropriate, not the true. But there is nothing specifically Chinese about it; even the excesses of correlative system-building in cosmology are common to China (Yin-Yang, Five Processes) and the West up to the Renaissance (Four Elements, Four Humours). Why then, in the analytic thinking also common to both, should there be anything specifically Western about using sentences to judge whether this thing exists as well as names to distinguish this thing from that?

   With growing controversy between the Hundred Schools, attention shifts from distinguishing and grading by names to defending or criticizing what is said with them. In the *bian* introduced by the early

Mohists, the logical structure of arguments composed of sentences is the same as in the West, just as correlation is the same whether of Five Colours with Five Processes in China or Four Humours with Four Elements in the pre-modern West. The logical relations in Hui Shi's demonstration to Zhuangzi that he does not know the fish are happy, or the proof in *Canon* B 73 that the number of men being infinite is compatible with loving them all, are transcultural. The validity, for him and for us, of the accidental syllogism in Wang Chong's *Dao xu* 道 虛 chapter 夫 人 物 也。雖 貴 為 王 侯，性 不 異 於 物。物 無 不 死, 人 安 能 仙。"Man is a thing; though honoured as king or noble, by nature he is no different from other things. No thing does not die, how can man be immortal?") has nothing to do with whether he has a concept of Reason, or knows that he is using sentences or that the form is syllogistic.

Hansen and I agree that this is what the West calls rational discourse, exhibiting 'non-contrastive rationalism' according to Hansen, although apparently no more than the thinking of Confucius. But it is radically different from the correlative thinking which Hansen's account more obviously fits, and there can be no presumption that his generalization that the focus of Chinese thought is on "how we project distinctions on things, not on our proofs and presuppositions" (p. 193) is any longer relevant. Any inquiry into *bian* will be crippled in advance if one starts with preconceptions about how far or whether it is still bound up with the marking of distinctions and regulative naming. The danger of drawing a general contrast between Western and Chinese thought, as with system-building in general, is of being pulled oneself into a Yin-Yang type of scheme in which one tries to fill the logical gaps, 'China : West :: Tao : Truth :: *bian* : logic : name : sentence . . . .', tempting one to cretinise the Chinese by excluding anything which looks too like 'Euclidean reason', or recognition of the sentence, or concern for objective fact. Once the Sophists and Later Mohists learn to tighten arguments to make them irrefutable, there can be nothing to decide for us in advance that they are not going to notice the difference between the sentences they are using and mere sequences of names, or discover logical forms such as the syllogism, or conceive the possibility of a priori proofs; one simply has to find out from the texts whether they did or not. In fact, assuming the results of my *Later Mohist Logic*, they did finally notice the sentence in the last of the documents, *Names and Objects*; they did *not* isolate any logical forms; they did design interlocking definitions leading from similarity up to the circle to show that the circle is 'known beforehand' (*xian zhi* 先 知) and from desire to the moral concepts to show that morality embodies "what the sage desires and dislikes beforehand on behalf of men" (*Expounding the Canons* 2, 聖 人 所 為 人 欲 惡).

Hansen clings to the assumption that even *bian*, its primary meaning being 'distinguishing' (of the admissible alternative from the inadmissible) is still concerned with the marking of distinctions by naming. But in *bian*, as described in *Canons* A 74 and B 35, the line between ox and non-ox has already been drawn by the agreed-on name 'ox', and the issue is whether some object fits the name, whether it is an ox or not. To say that the issue is on which side of the object to draw the line would be meaningless, since any Western issue could similarly be described as the placing of the line between real and unreal, true and false, good and bad, on one side or other of some thing, proposition or act. When *bian* deals with factual questions Hansen's efforts to force it into his Yin-Yang scheme become desperate; since it is the West which has the concept of Truth, it becomes for him unacknowledgeable that Chinese could concern themselves with a fact. Of the three Mohist tests of doctrine, which Hansen wishes to interpret as 'standards for the correctness of distinctions and the application of terms which make them up' (p. 199), the second is formulated in *Mozi* chapter 35 as 'to scrutinize what is real for the ears and eyes of the common people below'; it is applied only to and to both the two factual questions raised by Mohist doctrine, the existence of Destiny (disproved by the absence of witnesses who have seen Destiny or heard its voice) and of the spirits (proved by many indubitable cases of people who have seen and heard ghosts). Hansen's summary of this second test, which in *Language and Logic* 87 was 'the reporting practices of the people', is now quite unrecognizable: 'social conformity and ease in application' (p. 199). Why would seeing a ghost confirm, not the existence of spirits which is the point at issue, but the correctness of a distinction and application of a term?

In *Later Mohist Logic* I argued that the *Canons* and *Expounding the Canons* are organized to deal in turn with the four branches of knowledge classified in *Canon* A 80.

1. Knowledge of names, illustrated by logical demonstrations.
2. Knowledge of objects, with examples of causal explanation from optics and mechanics.
3. Knowledge of how to join names to objects, with tests for the similarities and differences on which naming is based.
4. Knowledge of how to act, established by the weighing of benefit and harm.

Whether one accepts these results or not, a commitment to them has nothing to do with supposing that the Mohists have noticed that Idea of Truth which has already descended to the earth in Greece. One would not expect another culture, with a language unrelated to the Indo-European family, to have a word with the same range of ambiguities as our 'true'; the Mohists say that a white horse in being a horse 'is-this' (*shi* 是) and that it is 'so' (*ran* 然) that one rides it, they say of logical conclusions *ke* 可 'admissible' and of name or description fitting object *dang* 當 'fits, is plumb with'. The West on the other hand tends to stretch the single word 'true' from the factual to knowledge in general, so that the themes of numbers 1, 2, and 4 of the Mohist disciplines might be described by us as logical, factual and moral truths respectively. For us philosophy transcends the factual but its goal is called by the same word 'Truth'; for the Mohist, facts belong to the second of four branches of knowledge, and the goal of all of them is social order. (*Names and Objects* 6 夫辯者, 將以明是非之介, 審治亂之紀 .... "The purpose of *bian* is by clarifying the shares of 'is-this' and 'is-not' to explore the skein of order and disorder. . . . ").

Can we still make a generalization about Chinese thought which covers both the correlative and the analytic? Certainly we do not have to discard the old commonplace that China pursues the Way (primarily the proper course of government) while the West pursues Truth. But I would agree that there is a deeper difference between Chinese and Western philosophical discourse, on which Hansen touches at times without making it central to his case. He notes that the extending from like to like in *Mencius* is not analogical reasoning but 'an emotive transfer' (p. 195), also that Mozi's utilitarianism 'doesn't have a moral axiom—a fundamental moral truth—that we ought to maximize utility. His appeal is to a basic *bian* ('distinction') between *li-hai* ('benefit-harm') that serves as a natural motivational split'. Here Hansen approaches my own Grand Generalization, that for Chinese thought the purpose of knowledge is the maturing of valuations which spontaneously follows advances in awareness. This assumption is no doubt less obvious in the *Canons* than in *Zhuangzi*, where the sage has only to trust to spontaneity while mirroring things with perfect clarity. But we can discern it right at the bottom of Later Mohist thought. The starting-point of its chain of ethical definitions is not what men do desire (which would involve the illegitimate leap from fact to value of which Western utilitarianism is accused) but 'what the sage desires beforehand on behalf of men', what the *most aware* do desire, a starting-point which would be legitimated by the quasi-syllogism. The paradigm for the sage even in Later Mohism is that 'whole man guiding spontaneity by awareness' which I have been preaching as alternative to the characteristically Western 'rational Ego striving to control spontaneity'. I am seriously suggesting that Chinese philosophy avoids a conceptual confusion at the foundations of Western moral philosophy, which we can now correct without abandoning those achievements in logic and science which distinguish our own tradition. This meeting of Chinese philosophy with my own pet idea is of course no coincidence; as perhaps is the case with all of us contributing to the philosophical side of this volume, my personal philosophizing has always for better or for worse influenced and been influenced by my reading of Chinese texts. We all seem to have some post-modernist vision of shaking up and realigning the conceptual scheme of the West.

Fingarette

It was a great pleasure to read Professor Fingarette's thoughtful critique of the quasi-syllogism applicable to particular situations with which I propose to undermine the fact/value dichotomy:

> In awareness of everything relevant to the issue (= everything which would spontaneously move me one way or the other), I find myself moved towards X, overlooking something relevant I find myself moved towards Y.
> *In which direction shall I let myself be moved?*
> Be aware.
> Therefore let yourself be moved towards X (= choose X as end).

(The minor premise may also be a generalization about the reactions of more than one person; then the formula will generate a standard applicable to all within the scope of the generalization, but with only the provisional authority of the generalization itself.)

Fingarette's approach is to start from 'Be aware' as a demand for ideal awareness, and show step by step how I am forced into concessions which empty it of most of its significance. But ideal awareness has no place in the argument. It is true that the major premise 'Be aware' amounts to 'Be aware of everything relevant to the issue'. (In *Disputers of the Tao* I have taken to filling in the missing words.) But this universalizes like the 'All men are mortal' of the classical syllogism, and whether one is aware of everything would be similarly judged, by induction if you like or by Popper's sustained failure to refute. We do in making decisions commit ourselves to having overlooked nothing important, indeed every firm decision assumes such a commitment; in a complicated and urgent situation this may be made on very little evidence, but once made however hazardously it submits one to the logic of the quasi-syllogism. Moreover, my 'Be aware' is not offered as in itself a new and controversial proposal, but as a digest of imperatives which everyone, whatever his theory of morals, takes for granted in practice. In choices of means it is no more than a banal 'Be aware of what you want and the facts of the case'; it is only in the choice of the ends they serve that it becomes interesting. If the quasi-syllogism is logically valid (which Fingarette seems not to question), the choice of ends requires *nothing but* 'Be aware' and spontaneous inclinations interacting causally with the objects of increasing or fading awareness. This may come as a surprise, since we are in the habit of assuming that we need moral and prudential principles as well. We do however apply 'Be aware' in addition whenever we apply the others in practice, and without bothering about the difficulties which Fingarette raises. Taking as example a choice of means—the sort which for the present issue I hope is uncontroversial—suppose that someone is pondering whether to sign a cheque for a charity, in obedience to some such moral imperative as 'Help the needy', which he accepts on the authority of religion, the categorical imperative, the quasi-syllogism itself with generalized minor premise, the *li*, or what you will. To decide he has also to listen to obvious and trivial imperatives to be aware: 'Make sure you have the money in the bank, that it is likely to be put to good use. . . .' In opening up this potentially infinite series of relevant factors he no doubt recognizes that, as Fingarette reminds us, 'awareness must be limited, and too obsessive a concern with *full* awareness may be self-defeating', that 'criteria for assessing the appropriateness of the limited selection attainable' cannot be reduced to a formula, that 'a fuller but incomplete awareness may lead one astray from where ideal awareness would have led one'. (p. 215) But he would not see these as concessions and retreats from ideal awareness which make it useless to look for factors which might be relevant, and which forbid him to commit himself to a final 'I think I've taken everything into account'. If these considerations discredit 'Be aware', then 'Help the needy' or any other moral imperative is discredited with it, as without practical application. Elevation of 'Be aware' to sole principle in the choice of ends, by which all standards are ultimately to be tested, leaves all these practical difficulties, and their irrelevance to its validity, precisely as before.

What Fingarette, unnecessarily climbing up to and then working down from ideal awareness, sees as the most damaging concession, is my acknowledgement that I may have to act on what is at present the weaker spontaneous tendency if that was the stronger when I was more aware, so that I should do what I *would* want to do if I *were* still more aware. This introduces "elements of reason, deliberateness and 'will' into the choice process rather than allowing 'mere' causality to operate"; by this retreat I have "frankly abandoned spontaneity itself" (p. 216). But although Fingarette is duly on guard against exaggerating the Taoist side of me, he seems to overlook that the whole discussion of choices of means and of ends assumes that there is nothing spontaneous about them except the impulses themselves and their relative strength at the height of awareness. I do hold that one can act spontaneously in sufficient awareness, and therefore rightly (the rightness being judged by the quasi-syllogism retrospectively or by another person), but then there is no considered choice. In choice of ends I struggle to attend to all factors and reason clearly about them, and when my responses (interacting by 'mere causality' with everything of which I become aware) spontaneously settle on a fixed goal, I adopt it as an end to which means may be chosen. This is the kind of choice, 'existential' if you like, for which standards are inadequate and from which on the present account they derive, the *discovery* of what I do spontaneously prefer in an episode of widened and intensified awareness (with rigorously logical thinking perhaps and ruthless self-examination), a preference which may even come as a surprise to me, contrary to my acknowledged standards and my self-image. Afterwards, such a concentration of attention being only temporary, or with distractions, disappointments, the fading of memory, I may no longer spontaneously prefer it, and have to hold on to it by an effort of 'will' (a concept I accept without having any very clear ideas about it). Fingarette understands that I sometimes take this position, but sees me as vacillating between deliberate and "actually spontaneous decisions", his evidence for the latter being only that "the key formula strongly suggests this" (p. 224). But there is always the danger that what one takes as the other man's inconsistency may be merely the contradiction between what one knows he must mean and what he actually says. Another look at the key formula will confirm that to "*let* myself be moved. . . . " after considering the two premises is a deliberate act, and that if I am at present "overlooking something relevant" the imperative still requires me to decide for a past reaction "in awareness of everything relevant."

I must admit however that an argument in *R & S* (p. 17) criticized by Fingarette (p. 211ff.) does lay me open to his objections. It starts from the quasi-syllogism with the "In awareness. . . . " of the first premise expanded to "In awareness from all spatial, temporal and personal viewpoints", with all viewpoints allowed equal status. It acknowledges that I cannot in practice be as aware from a future as from a present viewpoint, and from yours as from mine, yet know that if I could I would respond as strongly as from my own present viewpoint. I inferred fallaciously that I ought to choose *as though I were* as aware and responding as strongly. "How strongly one feels has nothing to do with the argument". That this is clearly a mistake is testimony of a sort to the clarity of my model of decision-making. I would be choosing to act on a response which may never have been the stronger, which however aware in practice I may become might still be the weaker. It is significant that the infidelity to my decision-making model also introduces the ideal awareness with which I should have no truck. The proper inference would seem to be that I should strive for as equal an awareness as possible but choose my actual response in the awareness available to me. Indeed, this does not seem to me inadequate for private morality, entitling a Confucian not Mohist preference for my own kin and friends. For public justice on the other hand there is no problem about being equally aware from all viewpoints. I would be designing law from the viewpoint of *anyone*, as in Rawls's *Theory of Justice*, and would be tempted to confuse this impersonal creature with myself only if I were the dictator of the state.[13]

There is another place at which Fingarette sees me as wavering towards another position than the one I have just been trying to clarify.

> On pages 8 and 9 (especially page 9) of *R & S*, Graham seems to be talking about what he labels 'ultimate' goals, where 'ultimate' seems at least to mean *logically* ultimate. In the end, as he argues, there is no logical way to pass from 'is' to 'ought'. At some point—'ultimately'—we *must* simply move, spontaneously, from awareness to the choice of the end, i.e., we *must* be moved by inclination inasmuch as reason will not provide the final link between 'is' and 'ought', between awareness and choice. . . . (p. 216).

But I think that on a closer reading Fingarette will see that, far from slipping back into anything so commonplace, I am saying the same as before: " . . . once he takes fully into account that his ultimate goals are spontaneous (*are*, not ought to be; what they ought to be is intelligent as well as spontaneous) he will require no first principle other than 'Be aware' for choosing between them." I do hold that a logical process of justifying ends by ends stops at ultimate goals which are spontaneous. But at this point one has to discard that secondary method of justifying goals and, not *start* to move spontaneously, but turn back to the spontaneous process which has been moving all the time in shifting and conflicting directions, to ask whether there are more fundamental grounds for choosing between its goals. Far from abandoning logic for a spontaneous leap, because "reason will not provide the final link between 'is' and 'ought'", it turns out that reason now compels me to choose the direction in fullest awareness, by the logic of the quasi-syllogism. Ethical thinking starts from spontaneous tendency as factual thinking from perception; one no more resorts to spontaneity after failing to deduce 'ought' from 'is' than one resorts to looking at the kettle after failing to deduce a priori that it is boiling. That Fingarette turns my thesis inside out interests me because I perceive him as reading me inside what I think of as the old paradigm (the rational Ego striving to control the spontaneous which is outside it), which I am trying to replace by the one I noticed in Zhuangzi and now find myself seeing everywhere in Chinese philosophy (the whole man guiding his always continuing spontaneity by his awareness, with—for me although not for Zuangzi—reason as its test). It confirms for me that until one breaks out of the old paradigm the gap between 'is' and 'ought' always reopens. This may seem unjust to a philosopher who to my enrichment seems to share my equal appreciation of reason and spontaneity. But when it comes to the question of the *li*, Fingarette does seem to me still to assume that to value the spontaneous is to put it beyond the reach of reason.

Fingarette's position is that the Confucian bedding of conduct in *li* takes us nearer to the heart of moral philosophy than does 'Be aware'. Although there was some discussion of ritual in *R & S* chapter 2/3 I had not at the time of writing it yet appreciated the importance of Fingarette's argument. However, I already held that the spontaneous preferences shaping social custom have the same status as the individual's, which are his personal variation on them; there was no question for me of recovering the impulses of one's biological constitution in their original purity. I was concerned only with the spontaneous in custom, not with it as an object of awareness; I fully agree that "we are not in general *aware* of the *li* by which we act, but rather we have learned to act that way without having to be *aware* of it at all—we do so spontaneously." (p. 219). Least of all did I want to include within the scope of 'Be aware' being aware that one *ought* to do the done thing; that would reduce my whole case to nonsense, and was therefore carefully excluded on the introduction of 'aware' on page 6 of the book. If Fingarette could catch me out in that particular confusion I think I would stick from then on to Chinese textual criticism. If I were writing the book now after assimilating Fingarette I dare say it would be with a less individualistic slant, attending to the spontaneous rather more in the tendencies of social interaction which shape custom and less in the isolated person. But I would still see the spontaneous in social formation as sometimes wiser than the individual intelligence which wants to reform it but also sometimes stupider, leaving it to oneself to judge whether a custom is alive or dead, fertile or sterile, enriching or constricting, civilized or barbarous, by the same imperative by which one judges the spontaneous in oneself, good old 'Be aware'. We need to listen to both Confucius and Zhuangzi, and the biases of Fingarette and myself towards one of them or the other are merely personal.

In my considerable measure of agreement with Fingarette on the *li* (much more I think than he has noticed) the point at which I stick is his declaration that they "*define* for me what I am to find good and worthy, and thus preclude the need for further awareness, for they have their own autonomous authority independently of consequences." (p. 219). "Independently of consequences", yes, since I too distinguish ritual as socially valued for its own sake from conventions chosen for their social utility; I am not clear why Fingarette describes me as treating social rules as merely "prudential" (p. 219). "Autonomous authority", no. Let us suppose that it is laid down in the *li* that our village must annually toss a virgin into the river at the spring festival in order to encourage the growth of the crops. The authority of this picturesque custom "precludes the need for further awareness", for example of whether the sacrifice does make a difference to the crops, or whether there is good evidence that the gods sacrificed to actually exist, or how it feels to be the victim or her family. Indeed, the awakening of such awareness would probably sooner or later lead to the abandonment of the sacrifice, and to some such modification of the *li* as the replacement of the girl by a doll. But would not we outsiders with our sophisticated awareness be bound to judge this a change for the better? Fingarette himself chooses a less loaded example, a case where there is some "incentive for me to betray the trust of my wife or a friend, but I simply ('spontaneously') don't do it" (p. 219). Here "the principles, maxims, character dispositions and habits which constitute the internalization of the *li* suffice without any inclination or need to become more fully 'aware'". No doubt, but is it enough for us critical spirits to judge betrayal wrong simply on the autonomous authority of the *li*, which might oblige us to accept human sacrifice? The point is surely that 'Be aware' has no immediate relevance because a deeper awareness of how wife or friend feels would only intensify the revulsion against betraying them. Certainly 'Be aware' as the most general imperative is no substitute for more specific rules in the routines of ordinary life. But the habitual preferences shaping customary rules require critical judgment like our personal appetites; both belong to the spontaneous inclinations from which we choose our ends, spontaneously alter in causal interaction with expanding or contracting awareness, and can be judged by 'Be aware' to be changing for the better or the worse. Granted that there is fortunately a wide range of standards reflecting habitual preferences, social and personal, which it is reasonable to trust without bothering about 'Be aware', it is because past experience has correctly or incorrectly assured us that they are unlikely to be shifted by further awareness.

That the individual's valuations are generated by his society and nourished by communion within it may indeed be said to give social norms a limited authority, in that they set the lines of his growth and he may wither if uprooted from them. But this authority, which might be acknowledged equally for the personal tastes and enthusiasms the starving of which would restrict his potentialities, falls far short of the "autonomous authority" which Fingarette claims for them. Fingarette writes that "the *li* help determine how we will become aware, and of what. . . . the *li* are in this respect the shapers, not the content, of awareness" (p. 219). If Fingarette were to go so far as to assert that the *li* allow us to become aware only of what fits in with the *li*, he would be offering a radical objection to my claim that they can be criticized by 'Be aware'. But his position seems merely to be that the facts of which a society becomes aware have significance for it only in relation to its *li*. Certainly I am not pretending that a simple appeal to fact would be enough to persuade our villagers to give up human sacrifice. We may suppose that they have satisfactory institutionalized explanations of why the crops sometimes fail after a meticulously performed sacrifice, and accept dreams as irrefutable evidence of the existence and wishes of the gods, also that a vivid empathy into the feelings of the victim and her family might overwhelm us with a sacred exaltation which outweighs all their fears and regrets. But we are not talking about a detached recognition of objective fact but of experiences which attract or repel, which consolidate one's conceptual scheme or disrupt it. That changing awareness interacting with spontaneity can and does alter valuations is surely not in question. Granted that Reality bursting in on us whether we like it or not has significance for us only in relation to our valuations, it is as likely to shake them as to be accommodated to them. For some, AIDS is the vengeance of God against homosexuals and careless addicts who do not clean their needles, and only confirms one's categorization of them as sinners; for others, it is a disaster which transforms the most life-enhancing of joys into a suicidal indulgence and discredits the ideals of the Sexual Revolution. Fingarette thinks it self-evident that no one could question a norm except in terms of "a larger context of norms, unquestioned within this context" (p. 222). But this familiar assumpton, which would imprison each of us in the code in which he was reared, is one of those undermined by the quasi-syllogism, which allows new valuations to spring from new reactions which satisfy the test of awareness. Do we really have to say that the sexual libertarian revises his standards only because in a wider context his social code requires him to put self-preservation before pleasure? That preference is pre-social, animal; and for his revision to be rational it is enough that it is in awareness of the consequences of the disease that he is moved by his terror of death.

My point may be illustrated from a very fine account of the breakdown of a traditional code, like that which Westerners remember in their own background, in the Nigerian Chinua Achebe's *Things Fall Apart*.[14] Achebe presents an impressive picture of the dignity of the old way of life in a pre-colonial African village. Moral issues twice arise in the story. The wife of a man in Okonkwo's village is killed in another village, which compensates for the killing with another wife and a boy whom the village may deal with as it pleases. Okonkwo brings up the boy in his own family, but the village oracle finally pronounces that he must be killed. As the boy Ikemefuna is attacked he cries out "My father, they have killed me!", but Okonkwo joins in striking him down. Afterwards he "did not taste any food for two days", and "drank palm-wine from morning till night". He is proud of his victory over womanish feelings, but a friend reproaches him.

> "If I were you I would have stayed at home. What you have done will not please the Earth. It is the kind of action for which the goddess wipes out whole families. . . . If the Oracle said that my son should be killed I would neither dispute it nor be the one to do it."

The other issue is the exposure of twins, who as monstrosities are left to die in the forest. When passers-by hear the infants wailing they fall silent and hurry away. Okonkwo's son is deeply moved by both experiences; "something seemed to give way inside him, like the snapping of a tightened bow". When the first missionaries arrive the son is quickly converted, to the disgust of his father; "the poetry of the new religion, something felt in the marrow . . . seemed to answer a vague and persistent question that haunted his young soul—the question of the twins crying in the bush and the question of Ikemefuna who was killed". The novel shows how "things fall apart" when an alien religion disrupts a traditional code, in particular by the catastrophic discrediting of factual assumptions; the Christians do not, as confidently expected, die within twenty-eight days when they ignorantly build their church in the Evil Forest. In spite of Achebe's respect for the old order one is not in doubt that on the two points at issue he thinks that Christian morality is superior; and Fingarette seems not to be the sort of relativist who would disallow such a judgment. But is it compatible with Fingarette's analysis, which leaves no room for allowing that the son could be morally more sensitive than his society? It is not clear what criteria could give meaning to a claim that the village has "a larger context of norms" with implications which the son is ahead of others in perceiving. Within its code, the father is criticizable for joining in the execution, but to let personal emotion interfere with the duties to allow the boy's execution by others or to expose twins could only be sentimentality; there would be nothing to give such emotions any moral authority. On my approach however reactions stirred in awareness from another's viewpoint may reasonably be preferred to the code because they have the authority of the imperative to be aware. To resist the impulse of sympathy with exposed twins the passers-by have to hurry on closing themselves to awareness. Obeying the logic of the quasi-syllogism would be reconcilable with retreat from a local awareness only if the emotion is blinding one to awareness of further consequences or from wider viewpoints, as would be the case if for example allowing twins to live does have the dreadful consequences the villagers expect. But aren't we entitled to say that on this point they are simply mistaken, and could discover their mistake, as in the case of dwelling in the Evil Forest?

The common ground between Fingarette and myself is that we both accept the failure to ground values in pure reason, both divine prospects of an alternative somewhere in spontaneous behaviour, both reject the irrationalism of a full trust in individual spontaneity. Fingarette as I understand him finds the way out in trusting to the spontaneous shaping of norms by social process; I find it in a critical test of all spontaneity social or personal, by which the unaware reaction is rejected for the aware. While for my part I hold myself guiltless of assuming an ideal awareness, it is not clear to me how Fingarette's ethic works outside an ideal community with unequivocal messages to its members. When community breaks up, as it has for Achebe and for us, how does one convert one's spontaneous preferences into a code with autonomous authority? Granted that these preferences are social in origin, with the norms by which one was brought up visible somewhere at the back of them, they carry no authority other than their subjective weight for oneself. Any code that they generate can only be a personal code, which at best will contribute to sowing the seeds of true community in the future. *R & S* part 3 classed approaches which put the relative stress on reason and on an aware spontaneity as "rationalism" and "anti-rationalism" respectively, allowing places for both, but repudiated an elevation of spontaneity without awareness as "irrationalism". To insist that one's code develops from one's own spontaneous preferences, with nothing but its own internal logic to shape it, would be individualistic irrationalism, however far from individualism it might be in intention. Would Fingarette deny that in the absence of firm social guidelines one needs something else to guide spontaneity? My analysis of the young man's decision to go to Bali in chapter 1/4, whatever it may be worth, did offer an account of how the choice between conflicting standards may *both* start from spontaneity *and* be critically testable by the principle of awareness.

Rosemont

I was delighted to read Henry Rosemont's long exposition of the argument of *R & S*, based on a very close reading, and especially appreciated his remark that "we must be prepared to break with the regnant paradigms in modern Western philosophy if we are to understand him aright", and his willingness to look again when the temptation might arise to dismiss at first sight. As always, it was interesting to notice places where one's own terminology is translated into someone else's. Thus my break with the mind/body dichotomy is consistently described as a linking of mind and body, although I am among those who, at some risk of seeming to have turned into automata, have dropped out of the habit of using the word 'mind'. There is only one theme on which I felt that important steps in the argument were missing, the "capacity, weak or strong, to be genuinely empathetic, sympathetic, compassionate and so on" (p. 236). The account suggests that in grounding an ethic in these feelings I simply accept their existence as a psychological fact, so evident that it is unnecessary to deal with such difficulties as that 'I cannot feel *your* pain, because it is in *your* body'. There is also no explanation of why the quasi-syllogism requires me to act on these feelings however weak they may be, rather than on the destructive passions which are given just as much space in the book.

A crucial argument of *R & S* chapter 1/2 is that our escape from being trapped in the viewpoint of 'I' and 'Now' is by simulation of the experience of other times (memory, anticipation) and of other persons. Imagination is simulation of perception; but it is commonly supposed that in assuming another personal or temporal viewpoint I imagine, not only what is perceived from it, but what is thought and felt. This overlooks an essential difference from imagination; to simulate thought or feeling is myself to think or feel similarly. Since this is especially clear in the case of thought, a passage which Rosemont quotes (p. 237) is considerably weakened by the omission of the first clause, the relevance of which he evidently overlooks.

> When trying to guess where someone went when I missed him at the airport I do not imagine his thoughts, I try to imagine his situation as someone like him would see it, and think; if he tells me he has just learned he has cancer I may hear in imagination the doctor's grave voice, but I do not imagine the fear, I feel the chill of it; if I see him cut his finger I do not imagine the pain as something before my "mind's eye", either I look on as though the knife were cutting through cheese or I incipiently wince. (R & S 17)

Seeing from another's viewpoint is therefore in this respect strictly analogous with seeing from a future viewpoint of my own; 'If I explore in imagination a coming danger, I cannot simulate the future fear without already being afraid, and moved to avert the danger'. 'I cannot feel *your* pain', but in awareness from your viewpoint I do feel similarly, and am moved to relieve your pain. The chapter examines many ways in which we shrink from or welcome awareness from the viewpoints of others, or respond to it with hatred, envy or cruelty rather than with sympathy, so that unless guided by 'Be aware' the awareness is disproportionate and impulses irrational. They may be either in others' favour or in one's own: "I feel myself spontaneously pulled towards admiration as well as pride, submission as well as power, masochism as well as sadism, judging myself from others' viewpoints as well as judging others from mine" (R & S 21). The reason why the quasi-syllogism may require me to act on very weak impulses of sympathy is because it enjoins the inclination which is stronger at the very height of awareness. "Even if it is only for one moment that a spasm in your face draws my attention to the intensity of your pain, a glimpse from which I shrink back into insensibility, it is during that moment that a choice between my conflicting pulls to help and to ignore will be made in fullest awareness" (R & S 18).

Until reading Rosemont's critique I had not appreciated how far R & S had moved from the conception of choice still current in moral philosophy. The quasi-syllogism is framed in terms of choice, and 'aware of X' defined as "prepared to take X into account in choices" (R &

S 6). An early stimulus had been the work of R. M. Hare, for whom choice is fundamental (as also is the imperative mood I adopt for the principle of awareness, and still find appropriate, not that I am a natural deontologist, but as sharpening the contrast with factual statements and as stressing the implacability with which the real forces itself on us whether we like it or not). However, the fluctuations of spontaneous drives with changing awareness, with one finally emerging as the stronger when 'I think I've taken everything into account', is *not* what philosophers are in the habit of calling a choice. But it is what, according to me, common usage refers to by 'choice', and I continue to use the word in the vernacular sense. The quasi-syllogism entitles one to judge an action whether or not there was any pondering of alternatives, and allows for such commonly shared appreciations as that it is better for a person to keep his word unthinkingly than to have to decide not to lie after an agonising crisis of choice. Since the project of moral philosophy is to help us to decide *whether or not* something is good or right, which is a choice (and makes the quasi-syllogism a suitably designed formula for the decision), it has a natural bias to conceive all initiation of the morally appraisable after its own image, whether or not there was any weighing of alternatives. Rosemont is, however, more radical than myself in denying that there is choice, in the broad sense of the word, even in his prisoner's dilemma, which will be discussed below.

Rawls, whose approach is indeed at the opposite extreme from mine, was never mentioned in *R & S*. A dissatisfaction with systems such as his which deduce from unsupported first principles has been one of my strongest incentives. But I did begin to see him as relevant quite recently, after thinking about a bad argument of mine exposed by Fingarette in this volume (p. 211ff.). The reference in my reply to Fingarette is so brief that it invited misunderstanding, and I am glad of the chance to say more about it.

In a particular situation, say deciding whether to report a theft, 'Be aware of all relevant factors' will of course cover a mass of facts about and insights into the thief, the victim, and their circumstances. But how would legislators apply the quasi-syllogism in designing a law against theft?

'In full awareness from all personal, spatial, and temporal view-points of everything relevant to the issue, we find ourselves moved to support a law against theft in this state. . . '

Plainly it would be more practical to base the law on some such generalisation as that insecurity of property will, much more often than not, interfere with the goals of citizens whatever and whoever they may be. But that remains only a factual statement; something more is required to make it a *good* law. On the present approach, this will be that in awareness from the viewpoints of potential and actual victims of theft, ourselves and others, we do find ourselves moved to forbid it. However few the viewpoints within our experience, the generalisation, if we accept it, assures us, without knowing anything particular about more than a tiny minority of people, that adding more to the examples will not alter the reaction. But in that case it might be more economical to assume the single viewpoint of a person of whom we know nothing except that he would be harmed by theft. A thought experiment behind 'the veil of ignorance' would be the reverse image of the impossibly complicated operation in fullest awareness, leading to the same result. To what extent the convergence approaches coincidence with Rawls's position need not concern us; the thought experiment remains entirely detached from Rawls's philosophy and re-grounded in my own. But there may be interesting possibilities in the thought that the procedure which Rawls, starting from the Social Contract, adopted to elucidate a presupposed concept of Justice, may in the light of the quasi-syllogism abolish the need merely to presuppose it.

It is notable that both Fingarette and Rosemont, with their Confucian respect for custom, are critical of the individualistic temper of *R & S*. For a couple of reasons I take this objection very seriously. Whatever my personal bias I do not want individualism or any other mode of life to be implicit in the central argument. The quasi-syllogism is supposed to be a logical form without content until applied to the inclinations of persons in awareness of their situations. It does not, for example, oblige us to side with spontaneity against reason, anti-rationalism against rationalism—to illustrate by two famous natural enemies briefly drawn together, both of whom I admire, with D. H.

Lawrence against Bertrand Russell. I want someone on the latter side to acknowledge that his ends are not rationally grounded but can be rationally chosen from spontaneous inclinations, but how much of his life is entrusted to reason or to spontaneity is not my business. As for individualism, the 'I' of the quasi-syllogism does make the individual the final judge of what he himself is to do. This position is no doubt especially, and increasingly clearly, articulate in our own individualistic tradition, but seems to me not to be culture-bound; it is implicit in simply being surer that one acts rightly when persuaded than when forced.

Secondly there is Rosemont's point that my individualism looks like an anomalous survival from the Cartesian/Humean paradigm the rest of which I have discarded. This disturbs me because I would prefer to suppose that like Nietzsche, also an individualist although of another sort, I have broken radically with the conception of the self-contained Ego. According to *R & S*, within as much of the person as is spontaneous there is no clear line between what he acknowledges as himself by "I" and what he distances by "it". It also treats the person, not as emerging only with difficulty from his own viewpoint, but as constantly pulled between multiple viewpoints by compulsions which are neither moral nor rational; even his pride, self-centred as it is, may lead him to risk his life rather than see himself with scorn through others' eyes. My position is not at all that "becoming aware from another's viewpoint must require a good deal of effort, for we are essentially alone" (p. 250); for me the self is fluid and never ceases to be drawn to other viewpoints, as much by conformism, power-lust or cruelty as by sympathy; it is the maintenance of a balanced awareness from multiple viewpoints which I think of as requiring effort. My remark that "birth, orgasm and death are breaches of the fence between self and other" (which was about nothing less than the loss of personal identity) was followed shortly by "The stability of selfhood depends on an *almost.voluntary* (present italics) closure of memory and imagination against the beginning and end of life" (*R & S* 144).

Rosemont's rejection of the self-contained Ego is on quite different grounds. He sees as the flaw in the quasi-syllogism that it assumes an 'individual self' which does not exist; one acts always from the viewpoint of friend or frightened man, sister of Polyneices or niece and subject of Kreon. Here I would object at the start that the validity of the formula has nothing to do with how we conceive the agent. If someone invited to come mountain-climbing wavers between enthusiasm when he forgets his recent illness and disappointment when he remembers, and at last reluctantly faces facts and decides not to go, one would hardly object: 'Your decision depended on the false idea that you are an individual self. There's no reason why you shouldn't go'. Moreover the 'relevant' for the quasi-syllogism is by definition ($R \& S$ 6f.) everything awareness of which would spontaneously move the agent in one direction or the other, which here will be whatever is relevant to a climber and a sick man. The formula is addressed not to an individual self in Rosemont's sense, nor to a friend or a sister, but to a person who is friend or sister, or is a climber *and* a sick man, and who does not shrink to being only one thing at a time whenever he prepares to act.

For $R \& S$ viewpoints are of persons in space and time, like the points from which eyes view in the literal sense of the word; my usage avoids the further metaphorical extension by which the husband, father, lawyer, clubman, and golfer which the person is, are distributed over different viewpoints, not to mention the "viewpoint from nowhere" which I am accused of assuming (p. 257). Rosemont does offer a quotation claimed to be a free confession that I go in for viewing from nowhere, but I am glad to say that reading it in context you will not find that I 'keep my distance' from myself, and that when 'lifted above myself' I remain all of one piece. The further examples in note 27 ('your viewpoint', the 'sufferer's viewpoint' . . .) are normal cases of multiple viewpoints involved in a situation, and at first puzzled me by their apparent irrelevance. But examination of page 257 uncovered one of those unnoticed differences in underlying assumptions which so often leave debaters talking at cross-purposes. Rosemont takes it as obvious that to imagine from another viewpoint I have to "abandon my own viewpoint, at least for the nonce"; the claim throughout $R \& S$ is the opposite, that I am always looking from multiple viewpoints except when attention contracts completely to what is present to myself here and now (if indeed that limiting case is ever actualised in nature). For Rosemont, then, a viewer from multiple viewpoints would be a viewer from nowhere, so cannot exist. "Who or where is the supra-aware 'I', and which shoes is the 'I' wearing?" The shoes of the person who is imagining and feeling from a sufferer's viewpoint, most vividly and intensely *only while* seeing through his own eyes a spasm of pain in his face. There is no contradiction here. Granted that organisms have distinct bounds (when not Siamese twins), what 'I' refers to does not; it is continually expanding towards the whole organism or contracting towards its centre of control, and in the latter case simulations of other persons are outside its scope, as simulations of other times (memory, anticipation) are outside what is experienced as 'now'. We operate the first person pronoun unthinkingly and confidently even when its range is shrinking within a single sentence: 'I am not considering this issue only from my own point of view' (wider 'I', narrower 'my'). We may conceive, if we want to be scientific, a sub-system in the brain at the centre of control, interacting with other sub-systems which simulate the external systems which are other organisms, with the interactions causing the motions of the body. There is then no reason to suppose that the sub-system to which 'I' contracts is ever wholly disengaged from interaction with the rest. It seems to me that it is Rosemont who has not taken his final leave of the self-contained Ego. He replaces it by analogues of it; he splits the person into a variety of subjects still imprisoned behind the same old pair of eyes, all of them clearly bounded entities taking turns to do appearing and vanishing acts inside the body.

Rosemont's presentation of his case for abolishing the individual self hinges on my own word 'overlook', which he is careful to elucidate. Here I confirm that I understand by it 'not take into account', whether by accident or design. These alternatives do not for me make the word ambiguous; one can apply the quasi-syllogism in either case, treating a wrong choice as bad luck if the agent could not have known, and as culpable if he could. In the prisoner's dilemma Rosemont seems to confuse several possible criteria for distinguishing the non-existent individual self from the close friend or frightened man.

(1) The prisoner is a friend if spontaneously moved to overlook the document, a frightened man if moved to overlook the possibility of forgery; if *per impossible* he were quite unmoved he would be "an isolated

individual self into which awareness flows neutrally" (p. 254). But then the agent of the quasi-syllogism is *not* an individual self; he is conceived as a person in whom awareness from his own and his friend's viewpoints waxes and wanes with his fear, faith, and suspicion, but who is commanded by 'Be aware' to resist these fluctuations. Shunning awareness is indeed the one spontaneous reaction expressly forbidden by the imperative, and the most urgent occasion for reminding oneself of it, as 'Face facts' or 'You're not thinking straight' or 'Keep your mind on the job'.

(2) He is friend or frightened man if he is not only moved to but does refuse awareness. But then the two become in effect rival souls of which only one can occupy the body. Even the most loyal person will on unimpugnable evidence decide that his friend had betrayed him and terminate the friendship. The friend committed to permanent unawareness could never have occasion to abolish himself.

(3) He is a friend if although taking the document into account, for example as evidence of how far his persecutors will go (forging, torturing), dismisses it as irrelevant to his behaviour as a friend. The objection to (2) still holds. Moreover there is no longer symmetry with being a frightened man, who is not taking into account the possibility of forgery while dismissing it as irrelevant to the behaviour *demanded* of him as a frightened man.

The line between the individual self and the various beings who are more real to Rosemont seems then impossible to draw. The prisoner is a frightened close friend who may well be wavering between fear and loyalty until one prevails decisively. Let us suppose that he is strongly tempted to believe the document genuine because it frees him from the responsibility which is endangering him. Then his reflections might be on these lines:

> In awareness, on the one hand of the threat to me if I do not betray him, and of the document in which he appears to betray me, on the other of our friendship and of the possibility that the document is a forgery, I still find myself moved to remain loyal to him.

> Overlooking the possibility that it is a forgery, I find myself moved to betray him.

Be aware.

Therefore remain loyal.

Why would friendship matter more to him than the danger to himself? A recurring theme of *R & S*, not among the more original, is that the function of means being to serve ends, a life reduced, as it tends to be nowadays, to an infinite regress of means to means, is mechanical, self-alienated, meaningless. For a philosophy in which ends are the goals to which we are spontaneously moved in awareness from each other's viewpoints, intercourse will be good in itself, not as means but as end, when we do not merely consent to but spontaneously welcome seeing things through each others' eyes, when intimacy is effortless, talk and play are informal and co-operation in work is unforced, when we help and trust each other without appeal to rules—love, friendship. To betray a friend is therefore to degrade life for both of us, in the sense that it destroys an instance of the relationship most valuable for itself, and wounds the general capacity for it. Only if the other has already betrayed the prisoner is the damage now done and friendship no longer a factor. Consequently, even if we simplify the situation by leaving out the document and its doubtful genuineness, the choice is not a straightforward matter of taking account of both the friendship and the danger to himself, and betraying if fear prevails over loyalty. Resisting the fear will strengthen the friendship, and in the same sense as before elevate life for them instead of degrading it. In awareness of both factors the prisoner is moved to resist, not that this will necessarily prevent him later failing to live up to the choice, and yielding to the fear in shame and regret.

The quasi-syllogism does not however provide an orthodox solution to a prisoner's dilemma, since people may react differently in the same situation. Thus trust or suspicion in estimating the probabilities of betrayal by another depends very much on the company one keeps. To assume too easily that he is betrayed would be a sign of cowardice if the prisoner is normally a trusting person; but for someone in whose experience it takes very little to induce a friend to let you down, it could be a realistic estimate of the chances. In the latter's milieu there are presumably no *close* friends. However, even if in Rosemont's example there turns out to be only one legitimate choice, as I am inclined to concede, there is no guarantee of a unique solution in the form of the quasi-syllogism itself. A more usual approach to a problem set up like this does expect a clear solution, so you try to sort out a pile of facts and principles which distressingly often turn out to be logically disparate, and finding yourself confronted by an unbridged gap between argument and choice you have to make an irrational jump. But there is no such gap if one is using the quasi-syllogism to approach from the opposite direction. Then choice is rational to the extent that it is not mere surrender to the impulse strongest at the moment, and is fully rational when it is of whichever is the strongest (whether permanently or temporarily) in the episode of fullest awareness after reasoning out all available factors.

Late in the discussion Rosemont introduces a new point of great interest. As a friend, who will overlook "a great deal of evidence" against the other, "my *reason* (my italics) will tell me that the document is a clever forgery, or that my friend must have undergone extreme torture. . . . If the other person relevant to the issue was a relative stranger, my reason would undoubtedly operate differently" (p. 256). It is not simply that I am prejudiced in his favour (a bias which 'Be aware' would command me to resist), nor that I know him better than I do a stranger (a consideration not brought into the argument), but that I owe it to a friend not to believe the worst about him on evidence which would satisfy me in the case of a stranger. This interests me as a case where the obligation to be aware weakens, to be added to those discussed in *R & S* (for example that of a local awareness interfering with a wider one). Plainly failure to apply the same standards of evidence to friend as to stranger does increase the chances of choosing wrong, for example when trusting him with money in spite of stories of his dishonesty. However, meticulousness over a relatively minor choice could conflict with a major one. In the quasi-syllogism, as in any logical form, it is unnecessary to include the qualification 'If you insist on getting the answer right'. However in a personal situation that may not always be the first priority. One may prefer the risk of choosing wrong to the violation of friendship in acting on a suspicion which might turn out later to be unjust.

But does this imply that the issue is presenting itself not to an individual self but to a friend? Suppose that there is reason to suspect that someone travelling to New York has a miniaturized nuclear bomb in his suitcase. Then I cannot risk a wrong choice; whether he is stranger, friend, brother, I have to apply 'Be aware' with the same rigour. I choose as a person who, even if among other things a friend (and perhaps ready to remain one, knowing the pressures which have driven him to desperate solutions, concerned that he is mentally sick), must for the present act otherwise. In the less dramatic case of trusting money to a possibly unreliable friend, I judge that a wrong choice is a less serious matter; but to judge it *less* serious I must still be choosing from the viewpoint not of a friend but of a person who is a friend.

Does Rosemont's own position amount to an alternative solution of the fact/value problem? It is only briefly sketched, but let us try out a series of questions. If the prisoner *is* either a friend or a frightened man, why is he committed to *being* the former rather than the latter? Presumably because applying the concept of friend to yourself commits you to acting as such, while acknowledging yourself to be a frightened man does not. What commits him to being loyal if he calls himself a friend? Language being social, you use 'friend' as your society does, with loyalty implicit. What commits him to calling himself a friend if he wants to behave otherwise? This is the crucial question, to which the answer I take it would be that within the society to which an ethical concept belongs, 'sister' as understood by Antigone in ancient Greece, 'friend' perhaps universally, you cannot understand the concept without being motivated to live up to it. Even a Westerner could hardly claim to know the full meaning of *Tianzi* 'Son of Heaven' without some flicker of awe from the viewpoint of the subject. The habitual users of a term will be spontaneously inclined to courses of action by having accepted the term into their language; otherwise they "clearly do not understand the concept", and "have cognitive and emotional defects" (p. 256). But what is it about failure to understand a concept which entitles us to judge it a 'defect', the first clearly evaluative word introduced? It is a defect because understanding is *better* than misunderstanding, knowledge than ignorance . . . awareness than unawareness. The last step could be rephrased in my terms as 'You cannot be aware of what friendship is without being spontaneously moved to resist betraying a friend', and supported by the analysis of friendship offered above. Our two arguments are unexpectedly converging. But understanding concepts is only one sort of awareness; Rosemont's thesis seems to be a special case of mine.

Now Rosemont is advocating a noun-centred ethic rooted like the Confucian in custom, which is clearly relative to a particular society. He can escape relativism, as he hopes to do, only by centring his ethic on concepts acceptable as universal constants of human nature. An obvious if suspect example would be 'mother'. It is in some sense 'natural' for mothers of our own and cognate species to be strongly impelled to care for their children; of a human mother who does not, it might be claimed that in remaining unconscious of the impulse or of its importance to her the incomprehension of the full meaning of 'mother' is also misunderstanding of herself. Rosemont, who would not need to be reminded of the pitfalls in biologically based examples, prefers 'friend', and uses 'sister' only in the context of Greek custom. Universal constants will be needed, not only to escape relativism, but to complete the closure of the fact/value gap. As long as a concept is merely local, one can understand it without being moved except incipiently, as a Westerner is by 'Son of Heaven'. Granted that a speaker cannot disown the whole web of his language, the whole value system of his society, he can disengage himself at any point. There is always the option of refusing to call oneself by the name; and since societies and their norms change, a philosophy of value has to explain when it will be right to do so. I am not myself optimistic—or as defender of a rival position should I say pessimistic?—about finding universal concepts founded in human nature by which the local may be evaluated, and would prefer to take a line here similar to that I took in answering Fingarette. If incomprehension of a concept is a defect only as one kind of unawareness, we can appeal to 'Be aware' itself for the appraisal of socially imposed concepts. A subject of the Son of Heaven some time before 1911 is right in acting on the motivations incipient in understanding the title, as long as he is so inclined in the fullest awareness available to him; but after travelling to the West and becoming aware of alternative forms of government, he is right to start resisting those motivations if in awareness of more factors he finds himself inclined to republicanism. The same applies to an individual life when, for example, one ceases to be a friend. When nursing suspicions of what his friend has in his suitcase on the journey to New York, Henry would perhaps say that he must now act not as a friend but as a human being. I would object that he was always a human being, and if he was always a human being who became friend, teacher, philosopher, we may as well switch to my usage and speak of the viewpoints of persons who are friends, teachers, and philosophers. But the point more immediately relevant here is that it becomes right for him to stop being a friend because he has become aware of the possibility of a plot to blow up New York.

Noun-centred ethics may well have a natural fit with a philosophy based on awareness and spontaneity; chapter 1/1 of *Disputers of the Tao* argues that the thinking of Confucius himself starts from the value of wisdom and the spontaneity of motivations. But Rosemont's crowning example, Antigone, does not add to the evidence that a noun-centred system can stand alone without the support of a principle of awareness. Antigone, as Rosemont says, does not choose, she simply acts as in ancient Greece a sister does and a frightened woman does not. But we have seen that for judging an act by the quasi-syllogism it does not matter whether there has been a balancing of alternatives. That Antigone acts according to Greek custom is no more than a neutral fact without some such consideration as that custom reflects a fuller awareness of life than does a ruler's decree (putting it in my terms) or is more human (in Rosemont's), vague descriptions over which it would be pointless to argue. Antigone has no occasion to remind herself that she must be aware of the consequences of her act; but what matters for my argument is that, not only is she fully aware of the danger of defying Kreon, without that awareness her act would lose its value. For judging the act right for her as an individual even if for no one else—not of course a Greek concern—we have the assurance that no possible addition to awareness of uncle and lord can be conceived as lessening her impulsion to act as sister; you might say she is an ideal example of acting on a spontaneous drive in awareness of everything relevant.

It is interesting that Fingarette, Rosemont, and myself have so much in common. All of us find in ancient China something which helps us to break away from the current problematic of Western moral philosophy, undermining the concepts of the self-contained Ego and of the choice in terms of principles, and such dichotomies as fact/value, morals/ aesthetics, rationality/spontaneity, absolutism/relativism. The last area of agreement is especially interesting, since evidence from other cultures has so often encouraged moral relativism. We all combine this search for new directions with an old-fashioned distaste for relativistic chaos and faith that reason is still some protection against it. The main line of division has Fingarette and Rosemont on the other side as supporters of Confucius against Zhuangzi, of custom against the individual who sets himself above it. Finally each of us especially treasures his own approach to the fact/value problem, so that debate is most lively when it centres on the quasi-syllogism.

My thanks again for honouring me with a book in which so many fine intellects dispute over such a wide selection of the topics which fascinate me.

NOTES

1. *Studies*, p. 307.

2. *Studies*, p. 82.

3. John S. Cikoski, 'An Outline Sketch of Sentence Structure and Word Classes in Classical Chinese', *Computational Analysis of Asian and African Languages* No. 8, Tokyo, 1978, pp. 128–144. There is a full classification of verbs in the *Zuozhuan* in his *Classical Chinese Word-classes* Yale University thesis, 1970.

4. Chad Hansen, *Language and Logic in Ancient China*, Ann Arbor, 1983, pp. 30–54.

5. Cf. *Yin-Yang*, pp. 70–81.

6. *Explorations in Early Chinese Cosmology*, ed. Henry Rosemont, Jr., *Journal of the American Academy of Religion Studies* 50/2 (1984), 133–166.

7. Guo Moruo 郭沫若, *Shi pipan shu*, 十批判書 Peking, 1962.

8. Roger T. Ames, *The Art of Rulership*, Honolulu, 1983.

9. Thomas S. Kuhn, *The Structure of Scientific Revolutions*. Chicago, 1970, p. 77.

10. Jacques Derrida, *Of Grammatology*, tr. G.C. Spivak, Baltimore, 1976.

11. David L. Hall and Roger T. Ames, *Thinking through Confucius*, Albany, NY, 1987, pp. 17–21 and passim.

12. As note 4 above.

13. For this point about Rawls, cf. p. 251 below.

14. Chinua Achebe, *Things Fall Apart*, London, 1958.

BIBLIOGRAPHY OF THE WRITINGS OF ANGUS C. GRAHAM

(I) Books

1. *Two Chinese Philosophers: Ch'eng Ming-tao and Ch'eng Yi-ch'uan*, Lund Humphries, London, 1958.

2. *The Book of Lieh-tzu*, John Murray, London, 1960 (UNESCO Chinese translation series).

3. *The Problem of Value*, Hutchinson's University Library, London, 1961.

4. *Poems of the Late T'ang*, Penguin Classics, London, 1965 (UNESCO Chinese translation series).

5. *Later Mohist Logic, Ethics and Science*, Chinese University Press, Hong Kong, 1978.

6. *Chuang-tzu: The Seven Inner Chapters and Other Writings from the Book Chuang-tzu*, Allen and Unwin, London, 1981.

7. *Chuang-tzu: Textual Notes to a Partial Translation*, School of Oriental and African Studies, London, 1982.

8. *Reason and Spontaneity*, Curzon Press, London, and Barnes and Noble, New York, 1985.

9. *Studies in Chinese Philosophy and Philosophical Literature*, IEAP, Singapore, 1986. State University of New York Press, Albany, 1990.

10. *Disputers of the Tao; Philosophical Argument in Ancient China*, Open Court, La Salle, IL, 1989.

11. *Poems of the West Lake*, Wellsweep Press, London, 1990.

12. *Unreason within Reason*, Open Court, La Salle, IL, forthcoming.

(II) Articles

1. A probable fusion word: WUH (勿) = WU (毋) + JY (之), *BSOAS* 14/1 (1952).

2. Kung-sun Lung's essay on meanings and things, *Journal of Oriental Studies* 2/2 (1955).

3. The final particle FU (夫), *BSOAS* 17/1 (1955).

4. The composition of the Gongsuen Long tzyy (公 孫 龍 子), *AM* 5/2 (1957), reprinted *Studies*.

5. The relation between the final particles YU (與) and YEE (也), *BSOAS* 19/1 (1957).

6. Confucianism, in *Concise Encyclopedia of Living Faiths*, edited by R. C. Zaehner, Hutchinson, London, 1959.

7. Being in Western philosophy compared with SHIH/FEI (是 非) and YU/WU (有 無) in Chinese philosophy, *AM* 7/1,2 (1959), reprinted *Studies*.

8. Observations on a new Classical Chinese grammar, *BSOAS* 22/3 (1959).

9. The dialogue between Yang Ju (楊 朱) and Chyntzzy (禽 子), *BSOAS* 22/2 (1959).

10. The date and composition of Liehtzyy (列 子), *AM* 8/2 (1961), reprinted *Studies*.

11. The prosody of the SAO (騷) poems in the Ch'u tz'u (楚 辭), *AM* 10/2 (1963).

12. Tone patterns in Chinese poetry (with G. B. Downer), *BSOAS* 26/1 (1963).

13. Natural goodness and original sin, *Rationalist Annual* (1963).

14. Reason in the Chinese philosophical tradition, in *The Legacy of China*, edited by Raymond Dawson, Clarendon Press, Oxford, 1964.

15. The logic of the Mohist Hsiao-ch'ü (小 取), *T'oung Pao* 51/1 (1964).

16. Liberty and equality, *Mind* 74/293 (1965).

17. Two dialogues in the *Kung-sun Lung tzu* (公 孫 龍 子), *AM* 11/2 (1965), reprinted *Studies*.

18. Translations of poems and *fu* (賦) in *Anthology of Chinese Literature*, edited by Cyril Birch, Grove Press, New York, v. 1 (1965), v. 2 (1972).

19. 'Being' in philosophy and linguistics, *Foundations of Language* 1/3 (1965), reprinted in *The Verb 'Be' and its Synonyms,* edited by John W. M. Verhaar, Part 5 (1972), Dordrecht-Holland.

20. The 'Hard and White' (堅白) disputations of the Chinese sophists, *BSOAS* 30/2 (1967).

21. Chinese logic, in *Encyclopedia of Philosophy*, New York, 1967.

22. The background of the Mencian theory of human nature, *Tsing Hua Journal of Chinese Studies*, 6/1,2 (1967), reprinted *Studies*.

23. 'Being' in Classical Chinese, in *The Verb 'Be' and its Synonyms*, edited by John W. M. Verhaar, Part 1 (1967).

24. The archaic Chinese pronouns, *AM* 15/1 (1969).

25. Chuang-tzu's 'Essay on seeing things as equal' (齊物論) *History of Religions*, 9 (1969/70).

26. Some basic problems of Chinese syntax, *AM* 14/2 (1969).

27. Ch'eng Hao (程顥) and Ch'eng Yi (程頤), *Encyclopedia Britannica*, Chicago, 1970.

28. The grammar of the Mohist dialectical chapters, in *A Symposium on Chinese Grammar*, edited by Inga-Lill Hansson, Lund, 1971.

29. China, Europe and the origins of modern science, AM 16/1,2 (1971), reprinted *Chinese Science*, edited by Shigeru Nakayama and Nathan Sivin, Cambridge, Mass., 1973.

30. A new translation of a Chinese poet: Li Ho (李賀), *BSOAS* 34/3 (1971).

31. Later Mohist treaties on ethics and logic reconstructed from the *Ta ch'ü* (大取) chapter of *Mo-tzu* (墨子), *AM* 17/2 (1972).

32. The Classical Chinese topic-marker FU (夫), *BSOAS* 35/1 (1973).

33. A systematic approach to the Mohist optics (with Nathan Sivin), *Chinese Science*, edited by Shigeru Nakayama and Nathan Sivin, Cambridge, Mass., 1973.

34. The terminations of the Archaic Chinese pronouns, *BSOAS* 36/2

(1973).

35. The concepts of necessity and the 'a priori' in Later Mohist disputation, *AM* 19/2 (1975).

36. Chuang-tzu and the Rambling Mode, in *The Art and Profession of Translation*, edited by T. C. Lai, Hong Kong, N.D. (1976).

37. The Chinese particle TZENG (曾), *Early China*, No. 3 (1977).

38. The organization of the Mohist Canons, in *Ancient China: Studies in Early Civilization*, edited by David T. Roy and Tsuen-hsuin Tsien, Hong Kong, 1978.

39. Entries for the Ch'eng brothers (二程) in *A Sung Bibliography*, edited by Yves Hervouet, Hong Kong, 1978.

40. A post-verbal aspectual particle in Classical Chinese: the supposed preposition HU (乎), *BSOAS* 41/2 (1978).

41. The Nung-chia (農家) 'School of the Tillers' and the origins of peasant Utopianism in China, *BSOAS* 42/1 (1978), reprinted *Studies*.

42. How much of *Chuang-tzu* did Chuang-tzu write? In *Studies in Early Chinese Thought*, edited by Henry Rosemont, Jr. and Benjamin I. Schwartz, Thematic Studies Series of the JAAR, 1979, reprinted *Studies*.

43. Structure and license in Chinese regulated verse, *Journal of Chinese Linguistics*, v. 8 (1980).

44. The origins of the Legend of Lao Tan (老聃), *Kuo-chi Han-hsueh, hui-yi lun-wen chi* (國際漢學會議論文集) Taipei, 1981, reprinted *Studies*.

45. Other schools of philosophy, in *Encyclopedia of China*, London, 1983.

46. Taoist spontaneity and the dichotomy of 'is' and 'ought' in *Experimental essays on Chuang-tzu*, edited by Victor H. Mair, Honolulu, 1983.

47. YÜN (云) and YÜEH (曰) as verbs and as particles, *Acta Orientalia*, (Copenhagen), 1984.

48. Value, fact and facing fact, *Journal of Value Inquiry*, v. 19 (1985).

49. Divisions in early Mohism reflected in the core chapters of Mo-tzu, IEAP Occasional paper and monograph series No. 1, Singapore, 1985.

50. The right to selfishness: Yangism, Later Mohism, Chuang Tzu, in *Individualism and Holism*, edited by Donald Munro, Ann Arbor, 1985.

51. Translation of Li Po, 'The hard road to Shu', in *A Brotherhood of Song*, edited by Stephen C. Soong, Hong Kong, 1985.

52. What was new in the Ch'eng-Chu (程朱) theory of human nature? in *Chu Hsi and Neo-Confucianism*, edited by Wing-tsit Chan, Honolulu, 1986, reprinted *Studies*.

53. The disputation of Kung-sun Lung as argument about whole and part, *Philosophy East and West*, v. 36/2 (1986), reprinted *Studies*.

54. Yin-Yang and the nature of correlative thinking, *ut sup.* No. 6, 1986.

55. Vampiri in un solo morso, *Il Manifesto*, Rome, Sept. 1, 1986.

56. Poems of the West Lake, *Renditions*, No. 25, Hong Kong, 1987.

57. Hsien-Ch'in Ju-chia tui jen-hsing wen-t'i ti t'an-t'ao (先秦儒家對人性問題的探討) in *Ju-chia lun-li, yen-t'ao-hui lun-wen chi* (儒家論理研討會論文集) edited by Liu Shu-hsien, IEAP, Singapore, 1987.

58. A neglected pre-Han philosophical text: *Ho-kuan-tzu,* (鶡冠子), *BSOAS* 52/3 (1989).

59. Conceptual schemes and linguistic relativism in relation to Chinese, *Synthesis Philosophica* (Zagreb, Yugoslavia) 4/2 (1989), also forthcoming *Culture and Modernity*, edited by Eliot Deutsch, University of Hawaii Press, and *Epistemological Questions in Classical Chinese Philosophy*, edited by Hans Lenk and Gregor Paul, State University of New York Press.

60. Rationalism & Anti-rationalism in Pre-Buddhist China, in *Rationality in Question*, edited by S. Biderman and Ben-Ami Scharfstein, Brill, Leiden, 1990.

61. Reflections and Replies, in *Chinese Texts and Philosophical Contexts*, edited by Henry Rosemont, Jr., Open Court, La Salle, IL, 1991.

62. Chinese philosophy of language, *Handbuch Sprachphilosophie*, edited by K. Lorenz et al., De Gruyter, Berlin, forthcoming.

63. Mysticism and the question of private access, *Rules, Rituals, and Responsibility: Essays Dedicated to Herbert Fingarette*, edited by Mary I. Bockover, forthcoming Open Court, La Salle, IL.

INDEX